CAMBRIDGE TEXTS IN THE
HISTORY OF PHILOSOPHY

BENEDICT DE SPINOZA
Theological–Political Treatise

CAMBRIDGE TEXTS IN THE HISTORY OF PHILOSOPHY

Series editors
KARL AMERIKS
Professor of Philosophy at the University of Notre Dame

DESMOND M. CLARKE
Professor of Philosophy at University College Cork

The main objective of Cambridge Texts in the History of Philosophy is to expand the range, variety and quality of texts in the history of philosophy which are available in English. The series includes texts by familiar names (such as Descartes and Kant) and also by less well-known authors. Wherever possible, texts are published in complete and unabridged form, and translations are specially commissioned for the series. Each volume contains a critical introduction together with a guide to further reading and any necessary glossaries and textual apparatus. The volumes are designed for student use at undergraduate and postgraduate level and will be of interest not only to students of philosophy, but also to wider audience of readers in the history of science, the history of theology and the history of ideas.

For a list of titles published in the series, please see end of book.

BENEDICT DE SPINOZA

Theological–Political Treatise

EDITED BY
JONATHAN ISRAEL
Institute for Advanced Study, Princeton

TRANSLATED BY
MICHAEL SILVERTHORNE
AND
JONATHAN ISRAEL

CAMBRIDGE
UNIVERSITY PRESS

CAMBRIDGE UNIVERSITY PRESS
Cambridge, New York, Melbourne, Madrid, Cape Town, Singapore, São Paulo,
Delhi, Mexico City

Cambridge University Press
The Edinburgh Building, Cambridge CB2 8RU, UK

Published in the United States of America by Cambridge University Press, New York

www.cambridge.org
Information on this title: www.cambridge.org/9780521530972

First published 2007
6th printing 2012

Printed in the United Kingdom at the University Press, Cambridge

A catalogue record for this publication is available from the British Library

Library of Congress Cataloging-in-Publication Data
Spinoza, Benedictus de, 1632-1677.
[Tractatus theologico-politicus. English]
Theological-political treatise / Bendedict de Spinoza; edited by
Jonathan Israel; translated by Michael Silverthorne and Jonathan Israel.
p. cm. – (Cambridge texts in the history of philosophy)
Includes bibliographical references and index.

ISBN-13: 978-0-521-82411-8 (hardback : alk. paper)
ISBN-10: 0-521-82411-7 (hardback : alk. paper)
ISBN-13: 978-0-521-53097-2 (pbk. : alk. paper)
ISBN-10: 0-521-53097-0 (pdk. : alk. paper)

1. Philosophy and religion – Early works to 1800.
2. Free thought – Early works to 1800.
3. Political science–Early works to 1800.
I. Israel, Jonathan, 1946- II. Title. III. Series.
B3985. E5S55 2007
199'.492–dc22
2006036798

ISBN 978-0-521-82411-8 Hardback
ISBN 978-0-521-53097-2 Paperback

Contents

Contents

Introduction

Spinoza's aims

The *Theological-Political Treatise* (1670) of Spinoza is not a work of philosophy in the usual sense of the term. Rather it is a rare and interesting example of what we might call applied or 'practical' philosophy. That is, it is a work based throughout on a philosophical system which, however, mostly avoids employing philosophical arguments and which has a practical social and political more than strictly philosophical purpose, though it was also intended in part as a device for subtly defending and promoting Spinoza's own theories. Relatively neglected in recent times, and banned and actively suppressed in its own time, it is also one of the most profoundly influential philosophical texts in the history of western thought, having exerted an immense impact on thinkers and writers from the late seventeenth century throughout the age of the Enlightenment down to the late nineteenth century.

Spinoza's most immediate aim in writing this text was to strengthen individual freedom and widen liberty of thought in Dutch society, in particular by weakening ecclesiastical authority and lowering the status of theology. In his opinion, it was these forces which were chiefly responsible for fomenting religious tensions and hatred, inciting political sedition among the common people, and enforcing damaging intellectual censorship on unconventional thinkers like himself. He tried to lessen ecclesiastical power and the prestige of theology as he himself encountered these in the Dutch Republic – or, as it was then more commonly known, the United Provinces – partly as a way of opening a path for himself and those who sympathized with his ideas, or thought in similar ways, to

viii

propagate their views among contemporaries freely both verbally and in writing. But still more he did so in the hope, and even expectation, of helping by this means to build a freer and more stable society.

His strategy for establishing and reinforcing toleration and freedom of thought, as he himself explains in his preface, relies in the first place on exposing what he judges to be the basic causes of theological prejudice, confessional rivalry, intolerance, and intellectual censorship as they plagued the Europe (and America) of his time. He sought to show that conventional – and officially approved – religious teaching and dogmas are based mostly on mistaken notions, indeed profound misconceptions about the character of Scripture itself. In this way, he attempted to expose what he saw as a near universal and dangerous ignorance about such matters as prophecy, miracles, piety and the true nature of divine commandments and revelation. Especially useful for undermining the power of theology and lessening respect for theologically based structures of authority and tradition, he thought, was his method of demonstrating that 'prophecy' is not divine inspiration in the way that most people then believed, and is not the work of divine wisdom in action, but is rather a consequence of certain individuals being endowed with a particularly powerful 'imagination'.

The *Theological-Political Treatise* offers a comprehensive theory of what religion is and how ecclesiastical authority and theological concepts exercise their power over men while, at the same time, providing a new method of Bible exegesis. But Spinoza's challenge in this anonymously published book was not only to contemporary views about Scripture, faith, piety, priestly authority and text criticism. In the second place, but no less importantly, he also strove to reinforce individual liberty and freedom of expression by introducing, or rather further systematizing, a new type of political theory (albeit one strongly influenced by Machiavelli and Hobbes). This was a distinctively urban, egalitarian and commercial type of republicanism which Spinoza mobilized as a vehicle for challenging then accepted ideas about the nature of society and what the state is for.

To Spinoza, a thinker who grew up in the closing stages of the Thirty Years War – a ruthless and vastly destructive struggle between the European states only ostensibly about religion – changing prevailing ideas about politics and statecraft seemed no less essential than combating religious prejudice, intolerance and authoritarianism. What he regarded as fundamentally false notions about government, public policy, education and morality appeared to him to threaten and damage not only the lives of individuals but the also fabric of society more generally. It is owing to these defective but strongly prevailing ideas about politics as well as religion, he argues, that 'superstition' is built up (often by ambitious clergy), into a force sufficiently potent to overshadow if not direct all aspects of men's lives, including intellectual debate and the administration of ordinary justice. Religious dogma comes to be enforced on everyone by force of law because the common people are persuaded by religious teachers that they should insist on doctrinal uniformity in the interests of their own and everyone else's salvation and relationship to God. Religion is concocted into a powerful force in human affairs, he argues, chiefly by means of dogmatic appeals to Scripture, though also 'with pomp and ceremony, so that everyone would find it more impressive than anything else and observe it zealously with the highest degree of fidelity'.[1] A correct understanding of the mechanics by which all this happens, based on a realistic analysis of human drives and needs, he contends, will not just help ground a solid toleration and reduce inter-confessional strife but also diminish internal ideological threats to legitimate government and generally render the individual happier and society more peaceful and stable.

Spinoza's method

Although a particular system of philosophy inspired and underpins the whole of the *Theological-Political Treatise*, it does so in most of the chapters unobtrusively and frequently in a hidden fashion. While his revolutionary metaphysics, epistemology and moral philosophy subtly infuse every part and aspect of his argumentation, the tools which Spinoza more conspicuously brings to his task are exegetical, philological and historical. In fact, it is the latter features rather than the underlying philosophy to which scholars chiefly call attention when discussing this particular text. Spinoza's hermeneutical methodology constitutes a historically rather decisive step forward in the evolution not just of Bible criticism as such but of hermeneutics more generally, for he contends that reconstructing the historical context and especially the belief system of a given era is always the essential first and most important step to a correct understanding of any text. In this respect his approach was starkly different from that of traditional exegetes of Scripture and from Renaissance text criticism as a whole (as well as from that of our contemporary postmodernist criticism).

[1] Spinoza, *Theological-Political Treatise, Preface*, para. 6.

But while Spinoza's technique in the *Theological-Political Treatise* is predominantly hermeneutical, philological and historical, at certain points, notably in chapter 6 'On Miracles', he adopts a very different and more explicitly philosophical procedure. Mostly, when discussing biblical phraseology and expressions, Spinoza claims purposely to have 'asserted nothing concerning prophecy which I could not infer from principles revealed in Scripture' itself.[2] For especially when dealing with issues like prophecy which 'is beyond human understanding and is a purely theological issue', no one can specify what it actually is, in itself, other than 'on the basis of revealed principles'. Hence, comprehending such a phenomenon must involve constructing 'a history of prophecy' from the text of Scripture itself as well as the derivation of 'certain dogmas from it which would show me its nature and characteristics, so far as that can be done'.[3] When discussing miracles, on the other hand, the position was entirely different. There, he had no alternative, he claims, but to elucidate this question only from principles known by the natural light of reason, for with 'miracles', the question we are investigating (namely, whether we may concede that something happens in nature which contradicts its laws or which does not conform to them) is wholly philosophical.[4]

The *Theological-Political Treatise* has been called, with some justification, 'the most important seventeenth-century work to advance the study of the Bible and religion generally', being the book which 'disarmed the religious interpreters who would enforce conformity'.[5] The novelty of Spinoza's approach does not lie in his affirming that Moses was not the author of the Pentateuch, as Hobbes and La Peyrère (and others) had said before, nor in pointing out that its texts must have been composed and redacted long after the events they describe, nor in emphasizing the special characteristics, peculiarities and limitations of the Hebrew language. Rather, Spinoza revolutionized Bible criticism by insisting on the need to approach the subject free of all prejudgments about its meaning and significance, eyeing every chain of tradition and authority whether Jewish, Catholic, Protestant or Muslim with equal suspicion and, above all, by stressing the importance of the distinction – never previously systematized in the history of criticism – between the intended or 'true' meaning of a passage of text and 'truth of fact'.

---

[2] Ibid., ch. 6, para. 21. [3] Ibid. [4] See below.
[5] J. Samuel Preus, *Spinoza and the Irrelevance of Biblical Authority* (Cambridge, 2001), p. x.

The 'true meaning' of a text, for Spinoza, consists of a correct account of the thought processes, assumptions and intended meanings of its author or authors, something which can be done only by carefully reconstructing both the historical and linguistic circumstances in which it was written and analysing the concepts used in terms of a strictly naturalistic interpretation of human nature, that is one that itself makes no appeal to supernatural forces or authority. Given the facts of human nature and the complex ways such belief systems develop, this 'true meaning' of the text may not have much, or even anything, to do with truth of fact. For Spinoza, truth of fact is an absolute and purely physical reality grounded on the laws of 'true' philosophy and science, an explanation devoid of all supernatural agents and forces, and all spirits and qualities separate from bodies, being expressed solely in terms of mechanistic cause and effect.

A cogent investigation of the significance of a text therefore requires that one carefully avoid mixing the intended meanings of the narrative one is studying with one's own views (or those of anyone else other than the authors of that particular text) about what is true generally. 'In order not to confuse the genuine sense of a passage with the truth of things, we must investigate a passage's sense only from its use of the language or from reasoning which accepts no other foundation than Scripture itself.'[6] Hence, a consistent, coherent historical-critical method of exegesis cannot be either combined with, or used alongside, the dogmas and received opinions of believers as to what that text (or any other text) truly signifies, or mixed with the dictates of sound commonsense or cogent philosophy.[7] The true meaning of a text (including Scripture) and truth of fact are simply two quite distinct and largely unconnected things. Spinoza was certainly right here at any rate in so far as the 'true' meaning of biblical or other texts, and 'truth of fact', had in his own day, and previously, invariably been merged and broadly at least identified as one, or as he would say 'confused'.

Hence, for Spinoza, understanding a text is not a matter of ascertaining what is 'true' in it or searching for what is authoritative or divinely inspired, but strictly an historical-critical as well as linguistic exercise anchored in a wider naturalistic philosophical standpoint. What was both quintessentially 'modern' and revolutionary in Spinoza's text criticism and

---

[6] Spinoza, *Theological-Political Treatise*, ch. 7, para. 2.
[7] Preus, *Spinoza and the Irrelevance*, 161, 163–4.

what chiefly sets it at odds with the text criticism of all varieties of contemporary Postmodernism, is precisely its insistence that there can be no understanding of any text which is not in the first place a 'historical' interpretation setting writings in their intellectual context, 'historical' now being defined in a highly innovative and naturalistic sense. The 'historical' in Spinoza's sense (which is also the characteristic 'modern' meaning) was in fact conceptually impossible until, philosophically, all supernatural agency had been consciously stripped out of all forms of historical explanation, a development that was remote from the thoughts of most early modern thinkers and writers.

It is hence insufficient, according to Spinoza's rules of criticism, to know the language in which a text is composed, and be familiar with its characteristic idioms, usages and grammar. Of course, one must first determine the grammatical signification of a given passage as accurately as possible; but one must then be able to locate this *sensus literalis* [literal sense] as a fragment of a wider complex of beliefs and notions, a self-defining and contained, if rarely coherent, human system of ideas and assumptions about the world. One must also take account of specific political circumstances at the time, as well as of motives, ambitions and preoccupations typical of that context. All of this then in turn needs to be explained, philosophically, as a product of nature and natural forces. Here was an idea which depended on a prior theory of culture and religion such as that embodied, since the mid 1660s, in Spinoza's not yet completed *Ethics* – his principal work but one which was not published until late 1677, some months after his death and more than seven years after the appearance of the *Theological-Political Treatise*. It was a 'revolutionary' theory in the most fundamental sense of the term.

For Spinoza, all religions and human dogmas are forms of belief concerned with imagined transcendental realities answering to men's deepest psychological and emotional needs and concerns. The life of primitive man, he surmises, much like Hobbes, was highly insecure, fearful and uncomprehending. Religion in his terms is thus a purely natural phenomenon especially in the sense that human emotions, as he argues in the appendix to Part One of the *Ethics*, are so structured as to lead us to attribute anthropomorphic and teleological explanations to natural phenomena. This applies particularly to all occurrences that we do not understand, especially those that fill men with dread. It is natural, he believes, for men to become deeply fearful in the face of natural occurrences they cannot explain in ordinary terms and assume that there really is a transcendental order existing on high outside our imaginations which governs those forces, and that some exceptionally chosen or inspired men, blessed with divine favour, enjoy special access to these invisible higher beings and values which the great majority of humans utterly lack. This access then confers on them a power and status far above that of ordinary men.

To reconstruct the meaning of a text successfully, holds Spinoza, every relevant historical detail about those who wrote it, its circumstances of composition, revision, reception and subsequent preservation and copying, as well as changes in linguistic usage and concepts, must be meticulously examined. Likewise, one must consider the fact that language is employed differently not only from period to period but also by the learned and unlearned; and while it is the former who conserve and propagate texts, it is not chiefly they who fix the meaning of words or how they are used. If it often happens, by intention or error, that scribes and scholars afterwards alter wording or even subvert the meaning of whole passages of written text, or construe them in new ways, no one can change the way current words and phrases are understood in a given society, at a particular place and time, so that by correlating everything relevant to a given usage within a specific historical period, a methodology can be devised for detecting subsequent corruptions of wording, misinterpretation, interpolation and falsification. Even so, we often lack sufficient historical data, he warns, to justify even the most tentative efforts to clarify obscure passages.

While his emphatic rejection of all *a priori* assumptions about its revealed status and his rigorous linguistic and historical empiricism are undoubtedly key features of Spinoza's Bible criticism, it is nevertheless incorrect to infer from this that his method was, as has been claimed, basically a 'bottom-up, inductive approach – more British-looking than Continental' – or maintain that 'Spinoza wants to start not with general presuppositions, whether theological or philosophical dogma, but with particulars and facts – with history – and then work his way up to broader generalizations'.[8] Far from dramatically contrasting his approach with that of the many Cartesians of his time, or likening it to that of the 'other great propagator of a new philosophy and patron of the new sciences, Sir Francis Bacon, whose works

[8] Ibid., 160–1.

Spinoza knew in detail', the systematic differentiation between the natural and supernatural on which Spinoza's philosophical naturalism insists rests intellectually on a reworking of the Cartesian conception of nature and a drastic reformulation of Descartes' idea of substance. In other words, he begins with lots of prejudgments about the real meaning of texts. Had Spinoza really admired and emulated Bacon (of whom in fact he was rather disdainful), and had the 'contours of Bacon's thought' and the more narrowly experimental empiricism of the Royal Society really been closely akin to Spinoza's approach, the result would certainly have been a complete inability either to envisage and treat history as a purely natural process devoid of supernatural forces or to treat all texts wholly alike. Had Spinoza's austere empiricism genuinely been akin to that of Boyle or Locke (in fact it was very different), it would certainly have led him to a much more reverential and literalist conception of the Bible, and willingness to endorse the reality of miracles and prophesy, of the sort Bacon, Boyle, Locke, Newton and their followers actually evinced.

Far from strictly eschewing 'general presuppositions', Spinoza's text criticism, then, was firmly anchored in his post-Cartesian metaphysics without which his novel conception of history as something shaped exclusively by natural forces would certainly have been inconceivable. Spinoza's philosophical system and his austerely empirical conception of text criticism and experimental science are, in fact, wholly inseparable. His particular brand of empiricism, important though it is to the structure of his thought, in no way detracts from the fact that his metaphysical premises, rooted in one-substance doctrine, result from conflating extension (body) and mind (soul) in such a way as to lead him – quite unlike the members of the Royal Society, or followers of Boyle, Locke or Newton – to reduce all reality including the entirety of human experience, the world of tradition, spirit and belief no less than the physical, to the level of the purely empirical. This was Spinoza's principal innovation and strength as a text critic. But at the same time it is an inherent feature of his system (and his clash with Boyle) and more generally, part of the radical current which evolved in late seventeenth-century Dutch thought, in the work of writers such as Franciscus van den Enden (1602–74), Lodewijk Meyer (1629–81), Adriaen Koerbagh (1632–69), and Abraham Johannes Cuffeler (*c.* 1637–94) and the late works of Pierre Bayle (1647–1706), at Rotterdam. It was a current of Early Enlightenment thought altogether distinct from both the Lockean and Newtonian strands of the British Enlightenment, to which indeed it was often consciously antagonistic, albeit no less important in shaping the subsequent course of Enlightenment thought.

When we study natural phenomena of whatever sort, contends Spinoza in the seventh chapter of his *Treatise*, we must first try to discover those features which are most universal, such as the laws governing motion and rest, laws which are eternally true, and then descend by degrees from the most general to the more specific. When studying texts, including Scripture, he urges us to do the same, seeking out first what is most universal and fundamental in the narrative. What is most universally proclaimed (whether by prophets, scribes, or Christ) in Scripture is 'that there is a God, one and omnipotent, who alone is to be adored and cares for all men, loving most those who worship Him and love their neighbour as themselves, etc.'[9] Although such universals are historically determined and are therefore poetic concepts, inexact, limited and vague, and while it is totally impossible to infer from the biblical text 'what God is' or how he 'provides for all things', nevertheless such universals are not just wholly fictitious or arbitrary intended meanings. To his mind, they are inadequate but still significant perceptions, that is, vague but natural approximations to the 'truth of things'.

In short, progress in understanding the history of human thought and belief, and Man's ancient texts, depends on combining a particular set of naturalistic philosophical criteria with new rules of text criticism which supplement the philology of the past with the strict elimination of all supernatural agency and miracles and a constant stress on reconstructing historical context. The general principles guiding Spinoza's text criticism are identical to those he applies to the study of nature. Both are rooted in the same type of empiricism, so that, at least in his terms, correctly undertaken Bible criticism is 'scientific' in a wholly novel sense which, however, was not one of which Boyle, Locke or Newton could approve. With Spinoza, as with Bayle, it is a fundamental principle that natural processes are exclusively determined by mechanistic cause and effect, that mind and human belief is part of this determined chain of natural cause and effect. Consequently, history, study of religion and generally what in German are called the *Soziale und Geisteswissenschaften* [social and intellectual sciences] are methodologically no different in principle from the other sciences: 'I say that the method of interpreting Scripture', as Spinoza expresses it in one of his most famous formulations, 'does not

---

[9] Spinoza, *Theological-Political Treatise*, ch. 7, para. 6.

differ from the [correct] method of interpreting nature, but rather is wholly consonant with it'.[10]

Detaching Christ from the churches

Spinoza creates a whole new 'science' of contextual Bible criticism, analysing usage and intended meanings, and extrapolating from context, using reason as an analytical tool but, except in the case of the rudiments of moral theory, never trying to uncover elements of philosophical truth embedded in Scripture. What one finds in Scripture is truth generally very obscurely and vaguely expressed, albeit in one very important case, namely its basic moral precepts, truth which is propagated more or less adequately. It is in teaching the rudiments of true morality that Spinoza, like his Dutch ally, the radical Cartesian and controversial Bible exegete Lodewijk Meyer, fully accepts that religious teaching based on the Bible plays not just a positive but also, given that most people cannot become philosophers, an indispensable role in underpinning society.

This positive dimension to what most contemporaries (and many since) regarded as Spinoza's 'anti-Scripturalism' merged in a remarkable and characteristic manner with his attack on ecclesiastical authority and what soon came to be called, in those Early Enlightenment circles influenced by Spinoza, 'priestcraft'. This campaign made extensive use of the circuitous tactic, introduced by Spinoza in the *Theological-Political Treatise* and later elaborated by a long line of other radical, Deist and sceptical writers,[11] of sharply differentiating between the high-minded, idealistic visions of those great founders of religions, like Jesus (and, in later radical authors such as Radicati and Boulainvilliers, also Muhammed), and the sordid perversion and corruption of their ideals by self-seeking 'priests' motivated chiefly by ambition and greed. In this way, radicals could argue that 'true' Christianity, or 'true' Muhammedanism, that is the genuine teaching of Christ and Muhammed, in no way corresponds to the actual doctrines and pretensions of the theologians, priests and mullahs who build and exploit socially and politically powerful organizations while falsely claiming to be their followers.

[10] Ibid., ch. 7, para. 2.
[11] Such as John Toland (1670–1722), Anthony Collins (1676–1729), Bayle, Henri de Boulainvilliers (1659–1722), Count Alberto Radicati di Passerano (1698–1737) and the Huguenot author and publisher, Jean-Fréderic Bernard (1683–1744).

Spinoza claims that Christ was not a 'prophet', a term which has a rather pejorative resonance in his terminology, but rather someone whose mind was adapted 'to the universal beliefs and doctrines held by all mankind, that is to those concepts which are universal and true'. Christ, in other words, was a moral teacher and hence a philosopher whose thought had little or nothing to do with what ecclesiastics and theologians subsequently turned it into. Jesus' message, held Spinoza, belonged by definition not to the realm of theology which, in his scheme, is solely directed at inculcating 'obedience' rather than 'truth' but, insofar as what he taught was true and clearly expressed, belongs rather to the sphere of philosophy. While Spinoza stopped short of explicitly identifying Jesus with his own philosophy, in the way that John Toland afterwards subversively identified Moses with primitive 'Spinozism', he did expressly claim, as his German friend and disciple, Ehrenfried Walther von Tschirnhaus (1651–1708), reported to Leibniz, that in so far as Christ was a universal moral teacher who proclaimed true religion to consist in 'justice and charity', he was no 'prophet' speaking from 'imagination' rather than on the basis of reason, but rather 'the supreme philosopher'. The Piedmontese *Spinosiste* Radicati later added to this the idea that Jesus was really a great social reformer and egalitarian, the wisest and most just of legislators, someone who desired men to live in 'perfect democracy', his legacy being then wholly subverted by the first bishops, patriarchs and popes, who outrageously abused his teaching to erect their own authority and pretensions to pre-eminence and were, in effect, responsible for destroying the 'democratical government settled by Christ'.[12]

Spinoza's emphatic if idiosyncratic eulogy of Christ as a uniquely inspired moral teacher who was not, however, a superhuman individual has long puzzled commentators of both Christian and Jewish background. Evidently, Christ, for Spinoza, was someone who was in no way divine. Equally clearly, as he admitted in letters to Henry Oldenburg, secretary of the Royal Society in London, in December 1675 and January 1676, in Spinoza's eyes, the Resurrection never took place.[13] Doubtless, one should infer from both his remarks about Jesus in the *Theological-Political Treatise* and his letters, and from his philosophical system as such, that to his mind Christ neither performed any miracles nor could do so. In the

---

[12] Alberto Radicati di Passerano, *Twelve Discourses concerning Religion and Government, inscribed to all Lovers of Truth and Liberty* (2nd edn. London, 1734) pp. 46, 49, 75.

[13] Baruch de Spinoza, *The Letters*, trans. Samuel Shirley (Indianapolis, IN, 1995), pp. 338–9, 348.

Theological-Political Treatise, Spinoza declares as an absolute principle that 'no event can occur to contravene nature which preserves an eternal, fixed and immutable order'. During the Enlightenment, this was generally and rightly taken to mean that Spinoza flatly denied that there have ever been, or ever could be, any miracles. However, for reasons of prudence, and so as not to contravene the laws of his country at the time, he preferred not to say this in so many words. He was accused of holding this very doctrine in a letter written by the Cartesian regent Lambert van Velthuysen (1622–85), in Utrecht, in January 1671. The letter charged him with putting the Koran on the same 'level with the Word of God', and a copy of the letter was sent on by the recipient, the Mennonite preacher, Jacob Ostens, to the 'Political Theologian' [i.e Spinoza] at The Hague. Spinoza defended himself by saying that what he had 'proved' concerning miracles was that miracles, which he defines as something that goes outside the bounds of the normal laws of nature, 'afford no knowledge of God. God is far better comprehended from the unchanging order of Nature'.[14]

It was clear even to those who remained unaware that Spinoza's philosophical system actually precludes all possibility of miracles *a priori* that, for him, we can learn nothing of importance about, and nothing from, 'miracles', which means that Christ's miracles could have had no particular significance even if they really occurred. The value of Christ's mission among men, in Spinoza's eyes, lay not in any reported signs, wonders, or mysteries, but entirely in his moral teaching. But this he considered to be of surpassing value. He clearly looked forward to the day when, as he puts it in chapter 11, 'religion is finally separated from philosophical theories and reduced to the extremely few, very simple dogmas that Christ taught to his own',[15] which would result in a new golden age free from all superstition. This remark clearly shows that in Spinoza's system *religio* is by no means the same thing as *superstitio*, despite its relatively lowly status compared with philosophy.[16] In fact, true 'religion' and true 'piety' are completely redefined by Spinoza in the *Theological-Political Treatise* to mean simply devotion and obedience to worldly good conduct, especially justice and charity.

Perhaps the best way to explain Spinoza's special emphasis on the significance of Christ for all humankind is to link it to his deeply felt need

[14] Ibid., p. 229.   [15] Spinoza, *Theological-Political Treatise*, ch. 11, last para.
[16] Preus, *Spinoza*, 178.

to form a tactical and strategic alliance with those fringe Christians, especially Collegiants[17] and Socinians,[18] willing to assist him in promoting the sort of campaign that could eventually help to strengthen toleration and individual liberty, reform society and politics, and institute true 'freedom to philosophize'. Several such men, including Pieter Balling (d. 1669) who translated much of his early work from Latin into Dutch, Jarig Jelles (*c.* 1620–83) who wrote the preface to his *Posthumous Works*, and his publisher Jan Rieuwertsz (*c.* 1616–87), figured among his closest allies and friends. During the course of his own personal development it had long been of great concern to him, especially during the years after his expulsion from the synagogue in 1656, to form ties with this exceptionally tolerant Christian fringe milieu which professed to accept the overriding status of reason in explicating both Scripture and Christ's spiritual significance. They too denied Christ's divinity, the Trinity, and Resurrection along with most other conventional Christian 'mysteries' and sacraments on the ground that these are incompatible with 'reason'.

As for the major churches, Orthodox, Catholic and Protestant, these, like rabbinic tradition and the Talmud, had little status in Spinoza's eyes. The Early Church may originally have been inspired by the authentic teaching of Christ and may therefore have genuinely been a 'religion of love, joy, peace, temperance and honest dealing with all men', based on wisdom. But it had soon become debased in his opinion, losing its authenticity immediately after Christ's death even during the time of the Apostles. The Early Church, he argues, everywhere degenerated into warring factions which ceaselessly vied with each other for supremacy, forging theological doctrines as their weapons and deploying dogma and ceremonies as the building-blocks of their power.[19]

This 'rise of ecclesiastic superiority and dominion', as Radicati calls it, went hand-in-hand, moreover, with a constant further elaboration of

---

[17] 'Collegiants' is a name given to a movement which developed in the Netherlands in the seventeenth century, especially in Amsterdam, Rotterdam and at Rijnsburg of mostly highly literate townspeople who sought to base their lives on the Bible and Christ's example but dispensed with formal doctrines and clergy and prized toleration, equality and freedom of speech; on this subject see Andrew Fix, *Prophecy and Reason. The Dutch Collegiants in the Early Enlightenment* (Princeton, 1991).

[18] A radical Reformation Christian tendency, originally an organized sect, which became established in Poland in the sixteenth century but later diffused to parts of Germany, the Netherlands, Britain and North America; they rejected the divinity of Christ, the Trinity, and other traditional Christian doctrines.

[19] Spinoza, *Theological-Political Treatise*, preface para. 9.

doctrine. 'As soon as this abuse began in the church', explains Spinoza in the preface of the *Theological-Political Treatise*, 'the worst kind of people came forward to fill the sacred offices and the impulse to spread God's religion degenerated into sordid greed and ambition.'[20] To make their 'mysteries' appear more impressive intellectually, theologians also utilized the 'the speculations of the Aristotelians or Platonists'; and as 'they did not wish to appear to be following pagans, they adapted the scriptures to them'.[21] In this way, faith has become identical, holds Spinoza, 'with credulity and prejudices' and 'piety and religion are reduced to ridiculous mysteries and those who totally condemn reason and reject and revile the understanding as corrupt by nature, are believed without a doubt to possess the divine light, which is the most iniquitous aspect of all.'[22] In their subsequent debased condition, lacking moral and intellectual status, the religions of the Christians, Jews, Muslims and pagans, he argues, have long really all been equivalent, that is all equally adulterated and lacking in genuine authority.

Far from being, as some maintained at the time, a confused idea of deities or the Deity, 'superstition', contends Spinoza, proceeds from emotional frenzy, especially dread and foreboding, and like other forms of emotional disturbance assumes very varied and unstable forms. But no matter how unstable (and destabilizing) 'superstition' can be, wherever the multitude is ruled by it more than by anything else, it remains a constant means of accumulating power for the crafty and ambitious, especially those who know how to channel it effectively by dressing it up in pompous and impressive ceremonies, dogmas and great mysteries (as well as impenetrable Platonic philosophy), all of which serve to extend and reinforce its reach, rendering popular 'superstition' the overriding danger to those who are independent-minded or who dissent from theological dogmas and what the majority thinks.

Spinoza's theory of toleration

One of the key features of the *Theological-Political Treatise* is the theory of toleration that it so powerfully formulates and its general defence of freedom of expression and publication. Spinoza, Bayle and Locke are undoubtedly the three pre-eminent philosophical champions of toleration

---

[20] Ibid., para. 9.   [21] Ibid., para. 9.   [22] Ibid., para. 9.

of the Early Enlightenment era. But of these three great and distinct toleration theories, Spinoza's is unquestionably not just the earliest but also the most sweeping, and is arguably also historically the most important – especially from the perspective of 'modernity' conceived as a package of egalitarian and democratic values – even though in the Anglo-American intellectual tradition it is customary to stress the role of Locke much more than that of Spinoza. Radical Enlightenment thinkers such as Diderot, d'Alembert, d'Holbach and Helvétius, in any case, were plainly much closer to Spinoza's conception of toleration than they were to Locke's, whose theory depends in large part on theological premises and which emphatically excludes 'atheists' and therefore also materialists and to a lesser degree agnostics, Catholics, Muslims, Jews and the Confucians whom Bayle, Malebranche and many other Early Enlightenment authors classified as the 'Spinozists' of the East.

It was one of Spinoza's chief aims in the *Theological-Political Treatise* to demonstrate that 'not only may this liberty be granted without risk to the peace of the republic and to piety as well as the authority of the sovereign power, but also that to conserve all of this such freedom must be granted'.[23] At the same time, liberty of worship, conceived as an ingredient separate from freedom of thought, always remained marginal in Spinoza's theory of toleration, so much so that in contrast to Locke, for whom religious freedom remained always the foremost aspect of toleration, Spinoza scarcely discusses it in the *Theological-Political Treatise* at all, despite this being the work where he chiefly expounds his theory of individual freedom and toleration. He does, though, say more about religious freedom, later, in his unfinished *Tractatus Politicus* [Political Treatise] (1677). This unusual and at first sight surprising emphasis derives from Spinoza's tendency to conceive liberty of conscience and worship as something strictly subordinate in importance to freedom of thought and not as something of itself fundamental to the making of a good society and establishing the good life. He therefore treats religious freedom as an element necessarily comprised within, but yet strictly subsidiary to, toleration conceived in terms of liberty of thought and expression.[24]

But while encompassing freedom of worship in his toleration, Spinoza in both the *Theological-Political Treatise* and the later *Tractatus Politicus* shows

---

[23] Ibid., ch. 20, para. 16.
[24] Benedict de Spinoza, *The Political Works* (ed.) A. G. Wernham (Oxford, 1958), pp. 410–11.

a marked reluctance to encourage organised ecclesiastical structures to expand their influence, compete for followers, assert their spiritual authority over individuals, or engage in politics, in the way that Locke's theory actively encourages churches to do. For Spinoza was acutely aware that such latitude can have deeply ambivalent results with regard to individual freedom and liberty of expression. In fact, he carefully distinguishes between toleration of individual worship, which he sees as one thing, and empowering churches to organize, expand and extend their authority freely, just as they wish, which he sees as something rather different. While entirely granting that everyone must possess the freedom to express their beliefs no matter what faith or ideas they profess, he simultaneously urges the need for certain restrictions on the pretensions and activities of churches, a line subsequently carried further by Diderot. While dissenters should enjoy the right to build as many churches as they want and individuals should freely fulfil the duties of their faith as they understand them, Spinoza does not agree that minority religions should, therefore, be given a wholly free hand to acquire large and impressive ecclesiastical buildings and still less to exercise a near unrestricted sway over their members, as the Amsterdam Portuguese synagogue had once sought to dictate to him.

Still more urgent, in his view, was the need to keep the majority or state church under firm secular control: 'in a free republic (*respublica*)', he argues, 'nothing that can be devised or attempted will be less successful' than to render the official religion powerful enough to regulate, and consider itself justified in seeking to control, the views and expressions of opinion of individuals. 'For it is completely contrary to the common liberty to shackle the free judgment of the individual with prejudices or constraints of any kind.'[25] Officially condoned persecution justified by the alleged need to enforce religious truth is an oppressive intrusion of the law into the private sphere and arises only because 'laws are enacted about doctrinal matters, and beliefs are subjected to prosecution and condemnation as if they were crimes, and those who support and subscribe to these condemned beliefs are sacrificed not for the common welfare but to the hatred and cruelty of their enemies'.[26]

Consequently, holds Spinoza, the state should only punish men for deeds and never for their utterances or opinions. The publicly established

---

[25] Spinoza, *Theological-Political Treatise*, preface, para. 7.   [26] Ibid., para. 7.

churches in his view are not upright, praiseworthy and justified religious institutions but rather debased and corrupt bodies in which what he considers to be the church's true function, namely to instruct the people in 'justice and charity', is being continually adulterated and thwarted, not just by 'base avarice and ambition' and use of doctrine to defeat rivals, but also by exploiting popular ignorance and credulity to intimidate, marginalize and condemn freethinking individuals. Hence, 'faith amounts to nothing more than credulity and prejudices', something which degrades human reason completely inhibiting men's free judgment and capacity to distinguish true from false, a system of theological doctrines apparently 'designed altogether to extinguish the light of the intellect'.[27]

Where a republic, whether democratic or aristocratic, or any monarchy permits an organized clergy to evolve distinct from the ruling elite, from the office-holders of the state, and preside over the publicly proclaimed religion, the 'multitude', admonishes Spinoza, will always consider the clergy and its leaders an alternative, and higher, source of authority than the secular government, believing, as they do, that ecclesiastics are closest to God. Churchmen, as is only to be expected, will then devise more and more dogmas and rulings further to enhance their power and subordinate secular authority to their judgment and approval. Hence, a vital safeguard for preserving liberty in any republic, argues Spinoza, is to prevent the factions that form among the ruling oligarchy, and the office-holders, from dividing into competing sects or churches supporting rival priesthoods and schools of doctrine. The more office-holders seek the approval and support of ecclesiastics in their battles with other political factions, the more they must defer to theologians, and hence the more they will become helpless prey to 'superstition', Spinoza's shorthand for subservience to theology and ecclesiastical control. In such cases, he maintains, adherents of religious congregations and doctrines condemned by the dominant priesthood are ruthlessly sacrificed not, he insists, for the public good but solely 'to the hatred and cruelty of their enemies'.[28]

Freedom of religion, then, as distinct from freedom to expand ecclesiastical authority, wealth and influence, is accommodated within Spinoza's scheme but remains secondary to freedom of thought and tied to restrictions on priestly independence and the authority of churches over their members. Freedom to embrace a particular faith, practise the

---

[27] Ibid., para. 9. [28] Ibid., para. 7.

observances it prescribes, and profess its doctrines, not only should be respected but is politically useful where well managed, albeit only when accompanied by robust safeguards against religious zeal and intolerance. Preventing the growth of a separate and powerful public priesthood is a prerequisite, in Spinoza's opinion, for a free republic because the outward forms of religion and religious authority fundamentally affect the cohesion, stability and orderliness of the state as well as individual liberty and freedom of thought. Where ecclesiastical authority is permitted to follow an independent line, the masses will inexorably become estranged from their government the moment it tries to uphold freedom of thought, expression and the press against the church hierarchy, the ignorant inevitably rushing to assist those who thirst for power over others 'so that slavery may return once more', as Spinoza characteristically puts it, and 'superstition' again reign supreme. Having himself witnessed the street riots, and the murder of the Brothers De Witt, in The Hague, in 1672,[29] he knew at first hand the disastrous consequences of enabling ministers of religion to denounce office-holders of the state with a view to inflaming the ignorant and credulous against government policies by proclaiming these ungodly and heretical.

It is not then religious toleration, for Spinoza, but freedom of thought and expression which principally safeguard individual liberty under the state, constituting the most precious possession not just of the wise but of those who are genuinely 'religious'. Unfortunately, he argues, this essential point is very rarely grasped in society. To regulate men's thoughts, beliefs and judgments may be impossible, but in his time, as subsequently, it was generally not deemed appropriate for individuals to form their own views, freely and independently, as to what is true and what is not, what is morally right and what is not, and what is just. Rather governments, churches and educational institutions took it for granted that individuals have no right to decide the most fundamental questions of conviction for themselves and that what is proper for them to believe should be enforced and what is incompatible therewith suppressed. Among the various censorship laws, anti-heresy statutes and decrees of religious uniformity applying in Europe in his day, those with which Spinoza himself had most directly to

---

[29] Johan de Witt (1625–72) was 'Pensionary' or chief minister of the States of Holland and the presiding figure in Dutch politics between 1653 and 1672; he and his brother Cornelis, also a high office-holder of the state, incurred the hostility of the strict Calvinist clergy through their policy of religious toleration and general opposition to hard-line Calvinist attitudes.

deal were the Dutch anti-Socinian laws of 1653, a code designed not just to curb Socinianism but to serve as a tool of theological censorship more generally. It was under these decrees, for instance, that the books of Spinoza's friends and allies, Lodewijk Meyer and Adriaan Koerbagh (1632–69) as well as the Dutch version of Hobbes' *Leviathan* were all suppressed.

For Spinoza, book censorship posed a formidable problem. Indeed, the question of whether, when, and how to publish his own writings dogged him in his later years on an almost daily basis. There was also a wider pall of disapproval and condemnation hanging over him (he was formally placed under surveillance by the Reformed Church council of The Hague, in 1675), so that, by the early and mid 1670s, he had some reason to feel anxious and insecure. The famous reference in the preface of his *Theological-Political Treatise* to his co-citizens and himself enjoying the 'rare happiness of living in a republic where everyone's judgment is free and unshackled, where each may worship God as his conscience dictates and where freedom is esteemed above all things dear and precious' was undoubtedly tactful but it was also more than a touch sarcastic and was probably also designed to prod his readers in a particular direction by hinting that, with its current laws, the Dutch Republic was not living up to the true ideals of its founders.

A key aim of Spinoza's toleration doctrine, in any case, was to establish the desirability of freedom to publish one's views no matter how decried they might be by theologians and by the majority. No other Early Enlightenment theory of toleration, certainly not those of Locke or Le Clerc, or even that of Bayle, seeks to clear a comparably broad path for liberty of the press. For Spinoza, the principle that society may rightly demand of the individual submission with respect to actions but not with regard to his or her desires, thoughts, opinions and conversation, meant that men should also be free to express their views in print. All efforts to curb expression of opinion, and freedom to write and publish, he insists, not only subvert the sphere of legitimate freedom but spell constant danger of instability for the state. The bitter strife between Remonstrants and Counter-Remonstrants in the United Provinces and the overthrow of the Advocate of Holland, Johan van Oldenbarnevelt (1547–1619),[30] in

---

[30] The Remonstrants were the more tolerant and liberal, and the Counter-Remonstrants the strict Calvinist, faction of the Dutch Reformed Church during the early seventeenth century; the regime of Oldenbarnevelt strongly supported the former against the latter but was overthrown, in 1618, by

1618, he contends, sufficiently proves that in times of spiritual turmoil the 'real schismatics are those who condemn other men's books and subversively instigate the insolent mob against their authors, rather than the authors themselves, who for the most part write only for the learned and consider reason alone as their ally. Hence, the real agitaters are those who attempt to do away with freedom of judgement in a free republic – a freedom which cannot be suppressed.'[31]

Spinoza and the rise of modern democratic republicanism

Another crucially important aspect of the *Theological-Political Treatise* is its advocacy of democracy. By thoroughly subordinating freedom of conscience and worship to individual freedom of thought and expression, Spinoza, like Bayle, placed his toleration entirely beyond the then pale of respectability. Aside from a few Collegiants and Socinians, few contemporaries considered such a concept of individual liberty of thought and conviction to be in any way compatible with a proper Christian outlook or fitting for a well-ordered society. His doctrine was widely condemned in the United Provinces as well as elsewhere. Generally, during the eighteenth century Locke's toleration was vastly preferred to Spinoza's and, in this slightly pejorative sense, it is doubtless true that 'Locke provided the theoretical defence of the toleration which would rule the outlook of the coming age'.[32] However, Locke's 'Christian argument' was decidedly not that of Bayle, Diderot, Helvétius, d'Holbach and the radical wing of the Enlightenment which was the source of our own 'modernity', although until recently this has seldom been acknowledged. By prioritizing freedom of the individual, and of expression, in preference to freedom of worship and religious observance, Spinoza in fact cleared a much wider space for liberty, and human rights, than did Locke, and cut a historically more direct, and ultimately more important, path towards modern western individualism.

Spinoza's highly unHobbesian rule that the 'less freedom of judgement is conceded to men the further their distance from the most natural state,

---

a *coup-d'état* led by the Prince of Orange, Maurice of Nassau (1567–1625) and backed by the Counter-Remonstrants; for further details, see Jonathan Israel, *The Dutch Republic. Its Rise, Greatness and Fall. 1477–1806* (Oxford, 1995), pp. 426–57.

[31] Spinoza, *Theological-Political Treatise*, ch. 20, para. 15.

[32] J. R. Cragg, *Church and the Age of Reason, 1648–1789* (1960; Harmondsworth, 1970), p. 80.

and consequently the more oppressive the regime',[33] besides firmly anchoring everyone's unrestricted right of access to information and ideas in a free republic, also afforded a readily available method for evaluating any given state. No doubt this highly original perspective arose partly out of personal needs and preferences, especially Spinoza's inclination to judge the worth of any state in terms of whether or not it encourages the free thinking man's rational love and understanding of Nature – and of society where the latter is deemed a part of Nature. Nevertheless, as the twentieth-century British philosopher Stuart Hampshire pointed out, such an approach, with its stress on promoting learning, freedom of expression and encouragement to debate, clearly results in practice in a much wider criterion for judging societies on a purely secular basis than does the political theory of Hobbes, whose criteria for judging the worth of states were essentially confined to issues of security and stability.[34]

According to Spinoza's deterministic philosophy, human beings have the power, and hence the natural right, to do whatever their circumstances, abilities and environment enable them to do. But of all the different things individuals could conceivably do, they will actually do only what they consider to be 'best' for them. The fact that in all spheres of activity people behave in markedly different ways despite our all being determined in the same way is due to the fact that their mostly 'inadequate' notions give people very different ideas as to what *is* best for them. It is because the desires and ideas of each individual, whatever they may want or believe, serve the same purpose and are determined in the same way, that Spinoza is able to argue that everyone's primal desire to be happy in their own way must be treated as strictly equal in any realistic discussion of society and politics. On this ground and because of the indispensable role of this principle of equality in erecting his strictly non-theological moral theory, Spinoza's system was from the outset intrinsically linked to the idea that the democratic form is always the most natural, freest and best kind of state. Historically, this is something of huge importance, for Spinoza was actually the first great philosopher since the rise of philosophy itself, in ancient Greece, to argue unequivocally, forcefully, and as an intrinsic and central part of his system that democracy is and must always be the best form of human organization.

---

[33] Ibid.   [34] Stuart Hampshire, *Spinoza and Spinozism* (Oxford, 2005), p. 138.

In Spinoza, consequently, unlike in Bayle or Locke, freedom of thought is not just broadly couched but also expressly tied, through freedom of expression, to an anti-monarchical, anti-ecclesiastical and anti-aristocratic politics. Spinoza's political thought endeavours to maximize individual liberty under the state by demonstrating, and emphasizing, the positive interaction between Man's individual and collective interests and the power of the sovereign. In his view, the state's true strength and stability depends on the willingness of citizens to identify with, participate in, and support it. Hence, in Spinoza, toleration and freedom of thought and expression are grounded on a particular conception of political power and of the role and functions of the state. Since the 'right' of the state is identical to the power of the state, according to his conception, and since no one can control the thoughts or desires of someone else, it follows that it lies entirely outside the proper scope of the state even to try to control men's thoughts and discussions. When setting up the state, holds Spinoza, each individual surrendered, for the sake of added security, co-operation and also freedom, his or her natural right to act unrestrictedly, as he or she pleases – but not his or her right to reason, judge and express opinions. And since everybody retains the right to think and judge independently, it follows that it remains everyone's right to express whatever views one wishes about religion, politics, law and everything else pertaining to the 'common interest' and the state, provided such freedom is exercised without undermining the law or prejudice to the state. Expressing views about this or that decree, event, political decision, or office-holder only becomes seditious and hence liable for punishment, he maintains, if it directly obstructs implementation of laws and decrees.

Whether the sharp divide this theory presupposes between action, on one side, and thought and expression, on the other, is likely to be clearly apparent in practice may well strike us as doubtful. When exactly, by Spinoza's criterion, is political or religious propaganda seditious and when not? But however he proposed to substantiate it in particular instances, this divide between action, on the one hand, and thought and expression, on the other, remained fundamental to Spinoza's (and the Spinozists') conception of individual liberty. Where Hobbes, preferring monarchs to democracy, suppresses the 'natural right' of individuals under society and the state, postulating a 'contract' which cancels it, Spinoza always preserves the 'natural right' intact as far as he can. Whatever thoughts, utterances, speeches and publications can safely be allowed in society should be permitted, he concludes early in the twentieth chapter of the *Theological-Political Treatise*, since 'the true purpose of the state is in fact freedom'.[35]

Ultimately, the close connection between individual liberty and politics in Spinoza's philosophy revolves around the idea that personal freedom, and satisfaction of individual desires, is greater or less, and the individual more or less secure, depending on the degree to which the state strives to maintain 'the common good', something which Spinoza argues is inherently more likely to happen the more the state is broad-based and democratic in character. Conversely, the more autocratic the state – though he regards pure monarchy along the lines eulogized by Hobbes as an impossible fantasy – the weaker it is. This means that the rational individual will learn to see that his or her private personal aspirations and interests are more likely to prosper the more individual liberty in general is buttressed, something which can only happen where the free republic receives the support of individuals like him or herself. Eventually, this will lead the more rational part of the population to grasp that true individual self-interest directly depends on the prosperity or otherwise of the 'common good' as furthered, defended and presided over by the state.

The urban, commercial, egalitarian 'democratic republicanism' Spinoza expounds in the *Theological-Political Treatise* and his later *Tractatus Politicus* is of great importance but was no isolated phenomenon. Historians of political thought in recent decades have devoted a great deal of attention to the development of republican theories in early modern times. However, attention has focused primarily on the Anglo-American 'classical republican' tradition, which, with its agrarian country gentry background, tended to be aristocratic in orientation, anti-commercial and 'soft' on monarchy. Curiously enough, there has been much less interest in the historical origins of the kind of full-blooded 'democratic republicanism' that developed not in the gentry-dominated but rather in the urban, mercantile context especially of the Dutch Republic, where pro-burgher, aggressively anti-monarchist and anti-aristocratic writers like Franciscus van den Enden (1602–74), Johan (1622–60) and Pieter de la Court (1618–85), Spinoza, Ericus Walten (1663–97) and Frederik van Leenhof (1647–1713), and later Bernard Mandeville developed a body of political theory of which Spinoza's contribution is only part. Anglo-American 'classical republicanism' may be a

---

[35] Spinoza, *Theological-Political Treatise*, ch. 20, para. 6.

much more familiar story to historians of political thought, but there must be some question as to whether it is really as important historically as the tradition of urban democratic republicanism, which obviously stood much closer to the more robustly egalitarian, anti-ecclesiastical, and anti-monarchical republican tendencies based on the 'general will' developed in mid-eighteenth century France by Diderot, Mably, Boulanger, La Beaumelle and Rousseau.

Impact and legacy

Spinoza never expected to have any impact on the common people and frankly explains, in a letter to Henry Oldenburg at the time he began work on this text in 1665, that he sought only to address the most independent-minded and literate section of society.[36] But he believed that if he could persuade some of these this could be enough, under certain circumstances, to steer everything in the right direction; and to an extent he succeeded, for the *Theological-Political Treatise* was very widely distributed, discussed, and reacted to, both immediately after its publication in 1669–70 and over subsequent decades. Even though it appeared without Spinoza's name on its title-page and with the place of publication falsely given as 'Hamburg' (it was actually published in Amsterdam), it became a book in demand in certain quarters, although it was never freely sold in the Netherlands and was formally banned by the States of Holland, and the States General, in 1674 – along with Meyer's *Philosophia S. Scripturae Interpres* (1666) and Hobbes' *Leviathan* – chiefly owing to its denial of miracles, prophecy and the divine character of Scripture. Subsequently, it was prohibited also by many other governmental and ecclesiastical authorities, including the French crown and the Papacy; and most of the intellectual reaction, predictably, was also intensely hostile. Nevertheless, despite the huge outcry and its being a clandestine book, not a few Christian and deist scholars later admitted to being influenced in significant ways by Spinoza's conception of Bible criticism and a few fringe Protestants with Socinian tendencies openly embraced his doctrine, while secular-minded libertine, republican and irreligious dissidents, the evidence suggests, were in some cases more than a little enthusiastic.

---

[36] Spinoza, *The Letters*, 185–6; Steven B. Smith, *Spinoza's Book of Life. Freedom and Redemption in the Ethics* (New Haven, CT, 2003), pp. 5–6.

The first of many published refutations appeared in May 1670 in Leipzig, under the title *Adversus anonymum, de liberate philosophandi*, written by Leibniz's teacher Jakob Thomasius (1622–84), an important figure in the history of text criticism in his own right and one of the founders of Enlightenment study of 'history of philosophy'. In England, the first response came mainly in the wake of the 1674 octavo edition. By late 1674, Boyle was among those who were reported to have adamantly condemned the work. In June 1675, Bishop Stillingfleet alluded to the writer of the *Theoligical-Political Treatise* as being 'mightily in vogue among many'. At Cambridge, Henry More read the *Theological-Political Treatise* in 1676 and his close ally, Ralph Cudworth (1617–88), darkly refers to Spinoza in his *True Intellectual System of the Universe* (1678) as 'that late *Theological Politician* who [wrote] against miracles [. . .] contending that a miracle is nothing but a name, which the ignorant vulgar gives to *Opus Naturae insolitum*, any unwonted work of Nature, or to what themselves can assign no cause of; as also that if there were any such thing done, contrary to nature or above it, it would rather weaken than confirm, our belief of the divine existence'.[37]

The post-1678 penetration of the *Theological-Political Treatise* in France was even faster and deeper. We know from his letters that Bayle, who read it in its French version in 1679, was one among many who read the book in France in the late 1670s. It is noteworthy that he was acutely aware that the anonymous text (which he says in a letter he considered the most impious work he had ever seen) was written by 'the famous Spinoza'. Furthermore, we know that he acquired his personal copy of Spinoza's *Ethics* and his exposition of Descartes' philosophy, of 1663, in France, a mere few months later, suggesting that he was already then intensely preoccupied, as he remained until his death in 1706, with Spinoza's philosophy as an entire system. In subsequent decades, Spinoza's thought continued to exert a strong influence in France. Only very much later, in the nineteenth century, was there a strong tendency towards marginalizing both Spinoza and Bayle as key influences on modern thought.

The prevailing lack of interest in the origins of modern democratic republicanism today is thus by no means the only reason for Spinoza's distinctly odd posthumous career since his death in 1677. For in both the history of philosophy and the wider historiography of modern thought not

---

[37] Ralph Cudworth, *The True Intellectual System of the Universe* (1678; 2 vols. repr. New York, 1978), ii, 707.

only Spinoza's democratic republicanism, but the importance of his toleration theory and impact of his system as a whole, have continually been played down, indeed masked by the persistence of a number of (after 1850) curiously durable and interlocking presumptions about the relationship of Spinoza to modern thought and 'modernity' as such. First, there is what might be called a deeply rooted tradition, still very much alive today, of idealizing Renaissance humanism and text scholarship and representing it as much more 'modern' and closer to the spirit of the Enlightenment than it actually was. This had the effect of obscuring the importance of the revolution in text criticism at the end of the seventeenth century, something to which Richard Simon, Jean le Clerc, Fontenelle, and Pierre Bayle, no less than Spinoza, all made major contributions. Secondly, there is the long-standing tendency to underestimate the general significance of pre-1720 Dutch democratic republican, anti-clerical and scientific thought in shaping the early stages of the Western Enlightenment as a whole, something which has served to mask the importance of Spinoza's immediate local intellectual background in shaping the characteristic values of 'modernity'.

Thirdly, and perhaps hardest of all to explain, there has been, almost everywhere since the mid-nineteenth century, a pervasive misconception that Spinoza was a thinker whom practically no one read, understood or was influenced by. This post-1850 view of him as a thoroughly isolated thinker, exemplary and lofty no doubt but very little read and exerting no influence, came completely to obscure the reality that he was actually a socially and politically highly *engaged* thinker. This remains today an entrenched and widely accepted view despite its being wholly unhistorical and at odds with how Spinoza was actually received in the late seventeenth and eighteenth centuries. For during the Enlightenment every important thinker and commentator centrally engaged with Spinoza, even if only silently, as in the case of Locke (who had several copies of his works, including the *Theological-Political Treatise* in his personal library). Bayle, indeed, became nothing less than obsessed with Spinoza and was far more preoccupied with him than with either Hobbes, Locke, or Newton. Likewise, it was entirely representative and typical of the Enlightenment that Condillac in his *Traité des systèmes* (1749) should have devoted more space to Spinoza than to any other thinker.

As a historical phenomenon, the almost universal tendency since the nineteenth century to marginalize, if not Spinoza the lofty philosopher, then certainly the historical, politically engaged Spinoza (and by the Dutch to write him out of Dutch history) may perhaps best be explained by the expansion of reading and education and the view that children, students and the general public should be shielded as far as possible from such 'atheistic', anti-Scriptural, democratic and libertarian concepts, ideas which down to the 1940s continued to be generally regarded in the world as deeply subversive, licentious and shocking. How far Spinoza's thought is sufficiently relevant today to merit widespread revival and study in universities is something about which I leave readers, in the true tradition of his subversive critical-historical-empirical philosophy, to make up their own minds.

Chronology

1618   Calvinist-inspired *coup d'état* in the Dutch Republic, led by the Prince of Orange, leading to the execution of Oldenbarnevelt and imprisonment of Grotius.

1632   November 24; birth of Spinoza in Amsterdam to a Portuguese Jewish immigrant family; his father Michael d'Espinoza was a merchant trading with Portugal, Morocco, the Canaries and Brazil.

1648   Treaty of Westphalia ends the Thirty Years War and simultaneously the Eighty Years War between the Spanish and the Dutch.

1652–4   First Anglo-Dutch War; capture of several cargoes belonging to Spinoza's father, and near ruin of the Spinoza family firm.

1653   States of Holland and States General pass edicts introducing new procedures of book censorship and outlawing anti-Trinitarianism and Socinianism.

1654   The Dutch West India Company loses its last outposts in Brazil.

1654   Death of Michael d'Espinoza; Spinoza briefly becomes head of what remains of the family business.

1655–6   Spinoza involved in heated exchanges, at the week-day evening *Keter Torah yeshivah* discussion group with the Amsterdam Sephardic rabbis.

1656	July 27, the twenty-four-year-old Spinoza expelled from the Synagogue and placed under a general ban in the Jewish world by the Amsterdam Sephardic rabbis.
1656	Spinoza writes his *Apologia* against the rabbis in Spanish, a work later lost.
1655–7	Probable timing of Spinoza's attendance at philosophy lectures in Leiden.
1660	The end of the Cromwellian Commonwealth in England and Restoration of the English Monarchy.
1660	Publication of the first work of Dutch 'democratic republicanism', Johan de la Court's *Considerations of State*.
1661–2	Spinoza's encounter, via cross-Channel correspondence, with Robert Boyle.
1663	Spinoza moves house from Rijnsburg (near Leiden) to Voorburg (near The Hague).
1663	Publication of Spinoza's geometric exposition of the principles of Descartes' philosophy, the only work to be published under his own name during his life-time, together with his own *Cogitata metaphysica* inserted as an appendix.
1664–7	The English seize New Amsterdam (New York); the Second Anglo-Dutch War.
1665	Van den Enden's *Free Political Institutions* anonymously published in Amsterdam.
1666	Lodewijk Meyer's *Philosophia* published by Rieuwertsz in Amsterdam.
1668	The trial and imprisonment in Amsterdam of the Dutch free-thinker Adriaen Koerbagh.
1669	Spinoza moves house from Voorburg to the centre of The Hague (Pavilioensgracht).
1669–70	*Tractatus Theologico-Politicus* clandestinely published in Amsterdam.
1672–4	Third Anglo-Dutch War.

1672	French Invasion of the Dutch Republic; overthrow of the anti-Orangist regime in Holland; Spinoza close to the scene of the mob murder of the Brothers de Witt, in The Hague.
1674	States of Holland and States General formally ban the *TTP* together with Meyer's *Philosophia* and Hobbes' *Leviathan*.
1676	Leibniz visits Spinoza in The Hague and confers with him 'several times and at great length'.
1677	February 21, death of Spinoza at The Hague.
1677	Alerted by the Catholic leadership in Holland, the Holy Office in Rome takes steps to try to prevent publication of Spinoza's *Ethics*.
1677	Posthumous publication in Amsterdam under the soon legendary initials *B.D.S.*, of the *Opera Posthuma* including Spinoza's *Ethics*, correspondence, and unfinished treatises.
1678	The States of Holland and States General formally ban Spinoza's philosophy, *in toto* together with all re-workings and restatements of his ideas, threatening authors, publishers and printers who violate the ban with heavy fines and long terms of imprisonment.
1678	Appearance of the *TTP* in French translation under three different clandestine titles.
1679–80	in France, Bayle acquires copies of and reads all the works of 'le fameux Spinosa'.
1683	Publication in London of Charles Blount's *Miracles, no Violations of the Laws of Nature*, much of which consists of an English rendering of the sixth chapter of the *TTP*.
1689	*TTP* becomes the first work of Spinoza to be published in English, appearing in London (without his name on the title-page) under the title *A Treatise Partly Theological and Partly Political, Containing some few Discourses to Prove that the Liberty of Philosophizing (that is, Making Use of Natural Reason) may be allow'd without any Prejudice to Piety, or to the Peace of any Commonwealth*.

Further reading

The best recent account of Spinoza's life and circle of friends is undoubtedly Steven Nadler, *Spinoza. A Life* (Cambridge, 1999). A useful additional recent summary of his intellectual development is Richard H. Popkin, *Spinoza* (Oxford, 2004).

For a general bibliography of Spinoza in English from the seventeenth century to the present see Wayne I. Boucher, *Spinoza in English* (Leiden, 1991).

For a general survey of Spinoza's philosophy in context, see *The Cambridge Companion to Spinoza*, ed. Don Garrett (Cambridge, 1996). Further introductory and general outlines of Spinoza's philosophy as an integrated system are Theo Verbeek, 'Baruch de Spinoza' in Alan Kors (ed.), *The Encyclopedia of the Enlightenment* (4 vols. Oxford, New York, 2003), iv, pp. 117–20; Edwin Curley, *Behind the Geometric Method. A Reading of Spinoza's* Ethics (Princeton, NJ, 1988); G. H. R. Parkinson, 'Editor's Introduction' to B. Spinoza, *Ethics* (Oxford, 2000), pp. 5–54; Steven B. Smith, *Spinoza's Book of Life. Freedom and Redemption in Ethics* (New Haven, CT, 2003) and Stuart Hampshire, *Spinoza and Spinozism* (Oxford, 2005). For an excellent English translation of the *Ethics* by a major expert on Spinoza's philosophy, see Edwin Curley (ed.), *The Collected Works of Spinoza* volume 1 (Princeton, NJ, 1988).

On the Dutch intellectual and philosophical context of Spinoza's time, and the other Dutch radical republicans and philosophical dissidents of the age, see the essays in Wiep van Bunge (ed.), *The Early Dutch Enlightenment in the Dutch Republic, 1650–1750* (Leiden, 2003), and in Wiep van Bunge and Wim Klever (eds.), *Disguised and Overt Spinozism around 1700* (Leiden, 1996). Further helpful contributions are Wiep van Bunge,

From Stevin to Spinoza, An Essay on Philosophy in the Seventeenth-Century Dutch Republic (Leiden, 2001); Steven B. Nadler, 'Spinoza and the Downfall of Cartesianism' in Th. M. Lennon, *Cartesian Views. Papers Presented to Richard A. Watson* (Leiden, 2003), pp. 13–30; Wim Klever, *The Sphinx. Spinoza Reconsidered in Three Essays* ('Vrijstad', 2000); and Michiel Wielema, *The March of the Libertines* (Hilversum, 2004). On the Dutch Collegiants and Socinians in the late seventeenth century, see Andrew C. Fix, *Prophecy and Reason. The Dutch Collegiants in the Early Enlightenment* (Princeton, NJ, 1991). For a general overview of the Spinozist impact on late seventeenth and early eighteenth-century intellectual life, see Jonathan Israel, *Radical Enlightenment. Philosophy and the Making of Modernity, 1650–1750* (Oxford, 2001) and its sequel, *Enlightenment Contested* (Oxford, 2006).

On the Jewish dimension of Spinoza's life and philosophy, see Manfred Walther, 'Was Spinoza a Jewish Philosopher? Spinoza in the Struggle for a Modern Jewish Cultural Identity in Germany', *Studia Spinozana* xiii (1997), pp. 207–37; Heide M. Ravven and Lenn E. Goodman, *Jewish Themes in Spinoza's Philosophy* (Albany, NY, 2002); Steven Nadler, *Spinoza's Heresy. Immortality and the Jewish Mind* (Oxford, 2001) and Jonathan Israel, 'Philosophy, Commerce and the Synagogue: Spinoza's Expulsion from the Amsterdam Portuguese Jewish Community in 1656' in J. Israel and R. Salverda (eds.), *Dutch Jewry. Its History and Secular Culture (1500–2000)* (Leiden, 2002), pp. 125–39. A searching and interesting but curiously unhistorical reconsideration of Spinoza's conception of God is to be found in Richard Mason's *The God of Spinoza. A Philosophical Study* (Cambridge, 1997).

On Spinoza's 'democratic republicanism' there is now a good choice of works available, with lively recent discussions, including Etienne Balibar, *Spinoza and Politics* (1985); (New York, 1998); E. H. Kossmann, *Political Thought in the Dutch Republic. Three Studies* (Amsterdam, 2000); Ed Curley, 'Kissinger, Spinoza and Genghis Khan', in Garrett (ed.), *The Cambridge Companion*, pp. 315–42; Steven B. Smith, *Spinoza, Liberalism and the Question of Jewish Identity* (New Haven, CT, 1997); Raia Prokhovnik, *Spinoza and Republicanism* (Basingstoke, 2004) and Jonathan Israel, 'The Intellectual Origins of Modern Democratic Republicanism (1660–1720)', *European Journal of Political Theory*, 3 (2004), pp. 7–36.

Specifically on the question of Spinoza's relation to Hobbes, see E. Curley, "I Durst Not Write so Boldly", in D. Bostrenghi (ed.), *Hobbes e Spinoza. Scienza e politica* (Naples, 1992), pp. 497–593 and Noel Malcolm,

'Hobbes and Spinoza' in *The Cambridge History of Political Thought, 1450–1700*, (ed.) J. H. Burns and M. Goldie (Cambridge, 1991), pp. 530–57. For Spinoza's relation to Leibniz, see the lively volume by Matthew Stuart, *The Courtier and the Heretic. Leibniz, Spinoza and the Fate of God in the Modern World* (New Haven, CT, 2005).

On Spinoza's separation of theology from philosophy, see Theo Verbeek, *Spinoza's Theologico-Political Treatise. Exploring the Will of God* (Aldershot, 2003). On Spinoza's Toleration theory, see Michael A. Rosenthal, 'Tolerance as a Virtue in Spinoza's Ethics', *Journal of the History of Philosophy*, 39 (2001), pp. 535–57; Michael Rosenthal, 'Spinoza's Republican Argument for Toleration', *The Journal of Political Philosophy*, 11 (2003), pp. 320–37; Jonathan Israel, 'Spinoza, Locke and the Enlightenment Battle for Toleration', in O. P. Grell and Roy Porter (eds.), *Toleration in Enlightenment Europe* (Cambridge, 2000), pp. 102–13.

On Spinoza's Bible criticism, see J. Samuel Preus, *Spinoza and the Irrelevance of Biblical Authority* (Cambridge, 2001); J. Samuel Preus, 'A Hidden Opponent in Spinoza's *Tractatus*', *Harvard Theological Review*, 88 (1995), pp. 361–88; Edwin Curley, 'Notes on a Neglected Masterpiece: Spinoza and the Science of Hermeneutics' in G. Hunter (ed.), *Spinoza: the Enduring Questions* (Toronto, 1994), pp. 64–97; Pierre-François Moreau, 'Louis Meyer et l'*Interpres*', *Revue des Sciences Philosophiques et Théologiques* (Paris), 76 (1992), pp. 73–84; Wim Klever, 'In Defence of Spinoza: Four Critical Notes on Modern Scholarship', *Studia Spinozana*, 7 (1991), pp. 205–23; and Richard H. Popkin, 'Spinoza and Bible Scholarship' in Garret, *Cambridge Companion*, pp. 383–407. Specifically on the question of the doctrine of the election of Israel, see David Novak, 'Spinoza and the Doctrine of the Election of Israel', *Studia Spinozana*, 13 (1997), pp. 81–99.

On Spinoza's ethics and theory of the passions and psychology, see Don Garrett, 'Spinoza's Ethical Theory' in Garrett (ed.), *The Cambridge Companion*, pp. 267–314; Antonio Damasio, *Looking for Spinoza. Joy, Sorrow and the Feeling Brain* (Orlando, FL, 2003); and J. Thomas Cook, 'Spinoza and the Plasticity of the Mind', *Studia Spinozana* 14 (1998), pp. 111–34. For a discussion of Spinoza's redefinition of the term 'piety', see Wim Klever, 'Spinoza's Concept of Christian Piety', in North American Spinoza Society Monograph no. ix (2000), pp. 17–27.

On Spinoza's general intellectual legacy, see Pierre-François Moreau, 'Spinoza's Reception and Influence' in Garrett (ed.), *Cambridge Companion to Spinoza*, pp. 408–33; Willi Goetschel, *Spinoza's Modernity. Mendelssohn,*

Lessing and Heine (Madison, WI, 2004); David Bell, *Spinoza in Germany from 1670 to the Age of Goethe* (London, 1984); Rosalie L. Colie, 'Spinoza in England, 1665–1730', *Proceedings of the American Philosophical Society*, 107 (1963), pp. 183–219; Luisa Simonutti, 'Premières réactions anglaises au *Traité théologico-politique*' in Paolo Cristofolini (ed.), *L'Heresie Spinoziste* (Amsterdam, 1995), pp. 123–37; on the erasure of Spinoza from the Dutch historical consciousness, see Wijnand Mijnhardt, 'The Construction of Silence: Religious and Political Radicalism in Dutch History', in Van Bunge (ed.), *Early Enlightenment*, pp. 231–62.

Finally on Spinoza's Latinity and terminology, see the collection of essays in Fokke Akkerman and Piet Steenbakkers (eds.), *Spinoza to the Letter. Studies in Words, Texts and Books* (Leiden, 2005) and Fokke Akkerman, *Studies in the Posthumous Works of Spinoza* (Meppel, 1980).

Note on the text and translation

The present translation was first made by Michael Silverthorne and scrutinized by Desmond Clarke, then extensively revised by Jonathan Israel in close collaboration with the translator.

Spinoza wrote his *Tractatus Theologico-Politicus* in Latin, and although some scholars regard it as quite likely that he also had some hand in the subsequent French (1678) translation, it is not certain that he did. Hence the Latin version, anonymously and clandestinely published and distributed in Amsterdam by Jan Rieuwertsz, ostensibly in 1670 (but in fact in 1669), is the original and only definitely authentic version of the text. Despite its clandestine nature and the fact that it was widely banned, copies of the book surviving in libraries today are surprisingly numerous. This seems to have been mainly due to the brisk demand for copies all over Europe during the late seventeenth century and Rieuwertsz's ruse of issuing several unnoticed new editions through the 1670s, retaining what looked like the original title-page bearing the original false date and place of publication 'Hamburg, 1670'.

Until quite recently the best modern critical edition of the original text was that prepared by Carl Gebhardt and published at Heidelberg in 1925, in the third volume of his complete edition of Spinoza's works.[1] An improved critical edition prepared by the expert Dutch Latinist, Fokke Akkerman, was published in a bilingual Latin–French version by the Presses Universitaires de France, in Paris, in 1999. It was this excellent and very scholarly edition of the Latin, correcting Gebhardt's version (albeit

[1] Benedict de Spinoza, *Opera*, ed. Carl Gebhardt (4 vols., Heidelberg, 1925).

mostly in small details), which we have used as the basis for this present translation. In breaking up Spinoza's mostly immensely long paragraphs into smaller, more easily negotiable blocks, something all translators of this text have agreed is really unavoidable, we have followed the order and numbering of the paragraphs as given in the Akkerman edition rather than simply divide the paragraphs anew at our own discretion.[2] This should make cross-referencing easier in cases where any reader wishes to consult the Latin original. We have added the Gebhardt page numbers in the margins.

Although Spinoza's Latin style is superficially relatively straightforward and his choice of words and constructions limited, given the highly original and transforming purposes to which he devotes his Bible criticism and political theory, it is scarcely surprising that many of his terms and phrases have been rendered in significantly different and sometimes highly questionable ways in different translations. At the same time, owing doubtless to the general tendency, noted in the introduction, to discourage reading of Spinoza during the nineteenth and much of the twentieth centuries, until the last few years there have been remarkably few modern translations from Spinoza's Latin into most major languages, including English. English in fact seems to have been particularly poorly served, since until the publication of Samuel Shirley's translation in 1989, the only available rendering of the full text was that of R. H. M. Elwes, which was first published in 1883 (reprinted in 1951); this was long regarded by Spinoza scholars as seriously inadequate owing especially to what one scholar called its 'misleading renderings of the Latin', though it also has other shortcomings, such as its astounding omission of Spinoza's subtitle and of some of his notes.[3]

At the same time, Spinoza, whose classical education began later, and was less elaborate, than was the case with most other great thinkers of the seventeenth century, developed a Latin written style which was distinctly less 'classical' in both vocabulary and syntax than, for instance, that of Descartes.[4] Like the 'scholastics' whom he tends to deride, Spinoza used a number of late Latin terms and also some non-classical forms of syntax.

---

[2] See the 'Introduction' to Benedict de Spinoza, *Oeuvres*, ed. Pierre-François Moreau vol. III. *Tractatus Theologico-Politicus* texte établi par Fokke Akkerman, traduction et notes par Jacqueline Lagrée et Pierre-François Moreau (Paris, 1999), p. 26.

[3] B. S. Gregory, 'Introduction' to Baruch Spinoza, *Tractatus Theologico-Politicus* (translated by Samuel Shirley) (Leiden, 1989), p. 1.

[4] Michelle Beyssade, 'Deux latinistes: Descartes et Spinoza', in F. Akkerman and P. Steenbakkers (eds.), *Spinoza to the Letter. Studies in Words, Texts, Books* (Leiden, 2005), pp. 57–8.

But what chiefly distinguishes his style is his reliance on a relatively restricted vocabulary, unsophisticated and straightforward syntax, tight argumentation and a relentless reiteration of key terms. The general effect, is of a spare, lucid and incisive argument with little rhetorical embellishment, although the 'prefaces' which open some chapters (eg. ch. 7) and introduce the book itself, and occasional other passages, reveal a Spinoza who commands a different register which he mostly chose not to use. While he makes no display of his classical reading, Spinoza does sometimes weave well-known phrases from Latin writers into his own text generally without acknowledging their derivation. These phrases, not infrequently, are from Terence – a favourite teaching tool of his Latin master, Van den Enden – but he also draws on Horace, Tacitus and a few others. Rather remarkably he allows Tacitus (again without acknowledging the fact) to provide a key phrase of the book which figures in the title of chapter 20: 'et sentire quae velit et quae sentiat dicere licet" (cf. Tacitus, *Histories* 1.1) [(that everyone) be allowed to think what they wish and to say what they think].

The most striking feature of Spinoza's Latinity, though, and the most problematic for any translator, is certainly his distinctive terminology and in particular his subtle and sometimes not so subtle altering of the usual meaning of words to fit the requirements of his philosophical system. In the introduction, mention is made of how he redefines the meaning of 'prophecy', 'religious', 'superstition', and 'piety' to make these words signify something quite distinct from what was then, or previously, generally meant by them. But there are also many other examples of this procedure, some of which involve frequent repetition of terms which would be highly misleading if translated in the usual manner and which therefore raise all sorts of complications for the translator. As has previously been remarked, it is invariably difficult or impossible adequately to translate Spinoza's term *philosophia* as 'philosophy' as it is usually understood, because Spinoza means by it the whole of science together with all other soundly based knowledge.[5] This rules out, for instance, our always rendering the term *libertas philosophandi*, which occurs in the subtitle and which is the main objective fought for in the concluding chapter, as 'liberty to philosophize', since the phrase as used by Spinoza clearly signifies freedom of (particularly intellectual) thought in general.

---

[5] Wim Klever, *Definitie van het Christendom. Spinozas* Tractatus Theologico-Politicus *op nieuw vertaald en toegelicht* (Delft, 1999), p. 9.

Another notable example of the difficulty of translating Spinoza's Latin adequately is the idea of 'divine law' which he discusses at some length in the fourth chapter of the TTP, a place where again he is being openly philosophical rather than philological. For Spinoza, 'divine law' is not, and has never been, something possessing supernatural status and is therefore not delivered to men by means of Revelation. Nor are there any religious leaders who have special access to it. *Lex divina*, as one scholar has aptly put it recently, 'is simply Spinoza's term for the power of nature as a whole'. Spinoza's 'divine law' expects no ceremonies; its reward is simply that of knowing the 'law' itself, and its highest precept 'is to love God as the supreme good', that is, 'not from fear of punishment or penalty, nor from the love of some other thing by which we desire to be pleased', but from a mature awareness that 'knowledge and love of God is the ultimate end to which all our actions are to be directed'.

Furthermore, Spinoza frequently employs his redefined terms in close interaction with each other, in this way developing a closely textured, new and highly idiosyncratic form of philosophical discourse in which, for instance, the only genuine measure of who is 'religious' and who is not is that of how far any individual practises 'piety', which turns out to be always outside the bounds of 'theology' and to consist solely of charity and justice. His chief aim in the *Theological-Political Treatise*, using terms as he does, is thus to bring 'religion' as much as possible into politics and society while simultaneously shutting 'theology' and dogma as much as possible out. Since his 'divine law' is the basis of the 'universal law', 'common to all men', something which Spinoza claims to have deduced from 'universal human nature' and which most men are incapable of understanding, it requires, by its very nature, other structures of authority and direction, surrogate kinds of law, with which to shape the lives of the common people. Such a lower, or less philosophical, code of law, like the Law of Moses, is therefore not just remote from but in some sense actually opposed to 'divine law' in Spinoza's parlance, despite the fact that it is the latter which is called 'divine law' by nearly all other writers. Spinoza is perfectly aware of how subversive his use of words is but at the same time he strives to be clear: hence, what is commonly called 'divine law', he insists, differs from what is truly 'divine law' in not being 'universal' and being 'adapted solely to the temperament and preservation of one people', as well as built around ceremonies and observances which subsequently became superfluous. One consequence of such idiosyncratic use of terminology is that Spinoza's 'divine law' is highly unlikely ever to converge with the pronouncements of the biblical prophets: 'it must be said of all the prophets who gave laws in the name of God', he remarks loftily, 'that they did not perceive the decrees of God adequately as eternal truths.'

Finally, Spinoza supplied all the original Old and New Testament quotations in Hebrew, Aramaic and Greek, as well as some citations from Maimonides and Ibn Ezra in Hebrew, providing his own translations into Latin. We have not reproduced his original Hebrew, Aramaic and Greek quotations here. While Spinoza's Hebrew texts are not always identical in every word, or in punctuation, with the text in the Hebrew Bible and while we are very conscious that even where his wording is identical his interpretation of these passages often radically diverges from those adopted in the Vulgate and in the ecclesiastically approved Protestant Latin and vernacular translations of Scripture, it seemed clear that in translating Spinoza's text what really matters is to convey accurately the way he renders these biblical and other citations into Latin. Hence, following the procedure adopted by nearly all the vernacular translations, early modern and modern, we have simply translated Spinoza's Latin rendering of the Hebrew originals as these are (almost identically) reproduced in the Gebhardt and Akkerman editions.

Spinoza

Theological-Political Treatise

Containing
several discourses
which demonstrate that
freedom to philosophize may not only be
allowed without danger to piety and the stability of the
republic but cannot be refused without destroying the
peace of the republic and piety itself

The First Epistle of John, chapter 4, verse 13:

*'By this we know that we remain in God, and God remains in us,
because he has given us of his spirit.'*

HAMBURG
Published by Heinrich Kuhnraht
1670[1]

[1] The *Tractatus* was actually published, we know, in Amsterdam and not in Hamburg. The false place of publication, 'Hamburg', was doubtless inserted by Spinoza's publisher Jan Rieuwertsz (*c.* 1616–87) as a precaution, as the work was illegally and clandestinely published in violation of the Dutch Republic's censorship laws and without the name of any author or (true) name of the publisher. The choice of the false publisher's name, Heinrich Kuhnraht, was probably intended by Rieuwertsz as an arcane joke, this being the name of a well-known early seventeenth-century German mystical writer, Heinrich Kuhnraht (1560–1605).

Preface

[1] If men were always able to regulate their affairs with sure judgment, or if fortune always smiled upon them, they would not get caught up in any superstition. But since people are often reduced to such desperate straits that they cannot arrive at any solid judgment and as the good things of fortune for which they have a boundless desire are quite uncertain, they fluctuate wretchedly between hope and fear. This is why most people are quite ready to believe anything. When the mind is in a state of doubt, the slightest impulse can easily steer it in any direction, and all the more readily when it is hovering between hope and fear, though it may be confident, pompous and proud enough at other times.

[2] I think that everyone is aware of this, even though I also believe that most people have no self-knowledge. For no one can have lived long among men without noticing that when things are going well, most people, however ignorant they may be, are full of their own cleverness and are insulted to be offered advice. But when things go wrong, they do not know where to turn and they will seek guidance from anyone. No suggestion they hear is too unwise, ridiculous or absurd to follow. Moreover, for the flimsiest of reasons they are conditioned one moment to expect everything to go better and the next to fear the worst. For when they are afraid, anything they see that reminds them of some good or bad thing in the past seems to prognosticate a happy or unhappy outcome, and so they call it a good or a bad omen, even though they have been disappointed a hundred times in the past. Again, if they see anything out of the ordinary that causes them great astonishment, they believe it to be a prodigy which indicates the anger of the gods or of the supreme deity, and they think it would be sinful not to

expiate it by offering sacrifice and prayers, because they are addicted to superstition and adverse to [true] religion. They develop an infinite number of such practices, and invent extraordinary interpretations of nature, as if the whole of nature were as senseless as they are.

[3]   This being the case, we see at once that it is especially those who have a boundless desire for things that are uncertain who are the most prone to superstition of every kind and especially that all humans when they find themselves in danger and are unable to support themselves implore divine assistance with pleas and womanish tears. They swear that reason is blind and human wisdom fruitless because it cannot show them a sure way of acquiring the empty things they want. On the other hand, they believe that the delirious wanderings of the imagination, dreams and all sorts of childish nonsense are divine replies, that God is adverse to the wise and that rather than inscribe his laws in the mind, he writes them in the intestines of animals, and that fools, madmen and birds reveal them by divine inspiration and impulse. It is dread that makes men so irrational.

6   [4]   Hence, fear is the root from which superstition is born, maintained and nourished. If anyone wants to go further into this matter and consider particular examples, let him contemplate Alexander the Great. Although superstitious by nature, he did not begin to consult prophets until he first learned to fear fortune at the Gates of Susa (see Curtius, 5.4).[2] However, after he succeeded in defeating Darius, he ceased using soothsayers and seers, until he was once again caught up in a frighteningly difficult situation with the Bactrians in revolt and the Scythians provoking conflict while he himself was laid up with a wound. As Curtius himself says at 7.7: 'turning again to superstition, that mockery of human minds, he commanded Aristander, to whom he entrusted his credulous fear, to make sacrifices to predict how things would turn out'. Many similar examples could be given which show with complete clarity that people are swayed by credulity only so long as they are afraid; that all the things they have ever worshipped under the influence of false religion are nothing but the fancies and fantasies of despondent and fearful minds; and that prophets have

---

[2] Quintus Curtius, *History of Alexander*, 5.4.

been most influential with the common people and most formidable to their kings when their kingdoms were in the greatest distress. But I think this is all well enough known to everyone, and I will not go further into it here.

[5]   Since dread is the cause of superstition, it plainly follows that everyone is naturally prone to it (despite the theory that some people hold that it arises from men's having a confused idea of God). It also follows that superstition must be just as variable and unstable as all absurd leaps of the mind and powerful emotions are, and can only be sustained by hope and hatred, anger and deception. This is because such instability does not spring from reason but from passion alone, in fact from the most powerful of the passions. Therefore it is easy for people to be captivated by a superstition, but difficult to ensure that they remain loyal to it. In fact, because the common people everywhere live in the same wretched state, they never adhere to the same superstition for very long. It is only a new form of credulity that really pleases them, one that has not yet let them down. Such instability of mind has been the cause of many riots and ferocious wars. For, as is clear from what we have just said, and as Curtius quite rightly notes at 4.10, 'nothing governs the multitude as effectively as superstition'.[3] Hence people are easily led, under pretence of religion, sometimes to adore their kings as gods and at other times to curse them and detest them as the universal scourge of mankind.

[6]   To cope with this difficulty, a great deal of effort has been devoted to adorning religion, whether true or false, with pomp and ceremony, so that everyone would find it more impressive than anything else and observe it zealously with the highest degree of fidelity. The Turks [i.e., the Muslims] have organized this very effectively.[4] Believing as they do that it is wicked even to argue about religion, they fill the minds of every individual with so many prejudices that they leave no room for sound reason, let alone for doubt.

7

---

[3] Ibid., 4.10.

[4] Spinoza's father, Michael d'Espinoza, a substantial merchant in Amsterdam, had traded, using Dutch ships, with Morocco as well as Portugal, the Canaries and Brazil, while a cousin, Jacob d'Espinoza, spent many years in the Middle East. Spinoza, consequently, probably knew rather more about Islamic lands than would most educated people in western Europe at the time but was still not particularly sympathetic.

[7] It may indeed be the highest secret of monarchical government and utterly essential to it, to keep men deceived, and to disguise the fear that sways them with the specious name of religion, so that they will fight for their servitude as if they were fighting for their own deliverance, and will not think it humiliating but supremely glorious to spill their blood and sacrifice their lives for the glorification of a single man. But in a free republic (*respublica*),[5] on the other hand, nothing that can be devised or attempted will be less successful. For it is completely contrary to the common liberty to shackle the free judgment of the individual with prejudices or constraints of any kind. Alleged subversion for ostensibly religious reasons undoubtedly arises only because laws are enacted about doctrinal matters, and beliefs are subjected to prosecution and condemnation as if they were crimes, and those who support and subscribe to these condemned beliefs are sacrificed not for the common welfare but to the hatred and cruelty of their enemies. However, if the laws of the state 'proscribed only wrongful deeds and left words free',[6] such subversion could not be made to proclaim itself lawful, and intellectual disputes could not be turned into sedition.

[8] We are fortunate to enjoy the rare happiness[7] of living in a republic where every person's liberty to judge for himself is respected, everyone is permitted to worship God according to his own mind, and nothing is thought dearer or sweeter than freedom.[8] I thought therefore that I would be doing something which was neither offensive nor useless were I to show that this freedom may not only be allowed without danger to piety and the stability of the republic but cannot be refused without destroying the peace of the republic and piety itself.[9] This is the core thesis that I have set out to demonstrate in this treatise.

In order to do so, it is chiefly necessary for me to describe our most powerful prejudices about religion, which are vestiges of our ancient

---

[5] In late seventeenth-century Holland it came to be widely asserted, not only by Spinoza but also by other republican writers such as Johan de la Court and Franciscus van den Enden, that the 'free' or democratic republic is the highest form of state.

[6] Compare Tacitus, *Annals*, 1.72.

[7] An allusion to the famous phrase ('rara temporum felicitate ubi sentire quae velis et quae sentias dicere licet') at Tacitus, *Histories*, 1.1. Tacitus is speaking of the reign of Trajan.

[8] Although Spinoza was actually highly critical of some aspects of the Dutch Republic and its laws, it is part of his rhetorical tactics in the *Theological-Political Treatise* to put as optimistic a gloss as he can on the libertarian aspects of the Dutch constitution.

[9] Almost the same words are used in the sub-title of the *Treatise*.

servitude, as well as our assumptions about the authority of sovereigns. For there are many men who take the outrageous liberty of trying to appropriate the greater part of this authority and utilize religion to win the allegiance of the common people, who are still in thrall to pagan superstition with the aim of bringing us all back into servitude again. I plan to give a brief outline of the order in which I shall demonstrate these things, but first I want to explain why I was impelled to write.

[9]   I have often been amazed to find that people who are proud to profess 8
the Christian religion, that is [a religion of] love, joy, peace, moderation and good will to all men, opposing each other with extraordinary animosity and giving daily expression to the bitterest mutual hatred. So much so that it has become easier to recognize an individual's faith by the latter features than the former. It has been the case for a long time that one can hardly know whether anyone is a Christian, Turk, Jew or gentile, other than that he has a certain appearance and dresses in a certain way or attends one or another church and upholds a certain belief or pays allegiance to one magistrate rather than another. Otherwise their lives are identical in each case.

In searching out the reason for this deplorable situation, I never doubted that it arose because, in the religion of the common people, serving the church has been regarded as a worldly career, what should be its unpretentious offices being seen as lucrative positions and its pastors considered great dignitaries. As soon as this abuse began in the church, the worst kind of people came forward to fill the sacred offices and the impulse to spread God's religion degenerated into sordid greed and ambition. Churches became theatres where people went to hear ecclesiastical orators rather than to learn from teachers. Pastors no longer sought to teach, but strove to win a reputation for themselves while denigrating those who disagreed with them, by teaching new and controversial doctrines designed to seize the attention of the common people. This was bound to generate a great deal of conflict, rivalry and resentment, which no passage of time could heal.

Unsurprisingly, then, nothing remains of the religion of the early church except its external ritual (by which the common people seem to adulate rather than venerate God), and faith amounts to nothing more than credulity and prejudices. And what prejudices they are! They turn rational men into brutes since they completely prevent each person from using his own free judgment and distinguishing truth from falsehood. They seem purposely designed altogether to extinguish the light of the intellect. Dear God! Piety and religion are reduced to ridiculous mysteries and those who totally condemn reason and reject and revile the understanding as corrupt by nature, are believed without question to possess the divine light, which is the most iniquitous aspect of all. Clearly, if these men had even a spark of divine light, they would not rave so arrogantly. They would learn to revere God with more good sense, and surpass other men in love as they now surpass them in hatred. Nor would they persecute so fiercely those who disagree with them, but would have compassion for them (if they really do fear for those people's salvation more than for their own advancement).

9   Furthermore, if they had any godly insight, that at least would emerge clearly from their teaching. But while I admit that they could not express greater veneration for the deepest mysteries of Scripture, what I see in their actual teaching is nothing more than the speculations of the Aristotelians or Platonists. Since they did not wish to appear to be following pagans, they adapted the scriptures to them. It was insufficient for them to be mouthing nonsense themselves, they also desired, together with the Greeks, to render the prophets equally nonsensical. This proves clearly that they cannot even imagine what is really divine in Scripture. The more vehemently such men express admiration for its mysteries, the more they show they do not really believe Scripture but merely assent to it. This is also clear from the fact that most of them take it as a fundamental principle (for the purpose of understanding Scripture and bringing out its true meaning) that Scripture is true and divine throughout. But of course this is the very thing that should emerge from a critical examination and understanding of Scripture. It would be much better to derive it from Scripture itself, which has no need of human fabrications, but they assume it at the very beginning as a rule of interpretation.

[10]   As I reflected on all this – that the natural light of reason is not only despised but condemned by many as a source of impiety, that human fabrications are taken as divine teaching, that credulity is deemed to be faith, and that doctrinal conflicts are fought out in Church and Court with intense passion and generate the most bitter antipathies and struggles, which quickly bring men to sedition, as well as a whole host of other things that it would take too long to explain here – I resolved in all seriousness to

make a fresh examination of Scripture with a free and unprejudiced mind, and to assert nothing about it, and to accept nothing as its teaching, which I did not quite clearly derive from it. With this proviso in mind, I devised a method for interpreting the sacred volumes.

In accordance with this method, I began by inquiring first of all: What is prophecy? In what manner did God reveal himself to the prophets?[10] Why were they acceptable to God? Was it because they had elevated conceptions of God and nature, or was it simply due to their piety? Once I knew this, I was easily able to conclude that the authority of the prophets carries weight only in moral questions and with regard to true virtue, and that for the rest their opinions matter very little to us.[11]

Once I had understood this, I sought to know why it was that the Hebrews were called the chosen of God. When I saw that this was simply because God had chosen a certain part of the earth for them where they could dwell in safety and prosperity, I realized that the Laws revealed by God to Moses were nothing but the decrees of the historical Hebrew state alone, and accordingly that no one needed to adopt them but the Hebrews, and even they were only bound by them so long as their state survived.[12]

Next I set myself to discover whether we should really conclude from Scripture that human understanding is corrupt by nature. To find this out, I began to consider first whether universal religion, or the divine law revealed to the whole human race through the prophets and Apostles, was really anything other than the law which the natural light of reason also teaches.[13] Secondly, I inquired whether miracles have occurred contrary to the order of nature and whether they show the existence and providence of God more surely and clearly than things which we understand clearly and distinctly through their own first causes.[14]

I found nothing in what Scripture expressly teaches that does not concur with our understanding and nothing that is in conflict with it. I also perceived that the prophets taught only very simple things which could be easily understood by everyone, and had elaborated them with the kind of style, and supported them with the sort of reasons that might most effectively sway the people's mind towards God. In this way, I became completely convinced that Scripture leaves reason absolutely free and has nothing at all in common with philosophy, but that each of them stands on its own separate footing. In order to demonstrate these things conclusively

[10] Ch. 1.   [11] Ch. 2.   [12] Ch. 3.   [13] Ch. 4.   [14] Ch. 6.

and settle the whole issue, I demonstrate how Scripture should be interpreted, proving that we must derive all our knowledge of it and of spiritual matters from Scripture alone and not from what we discover by the natural light of reason.[15]

After this I pass on to show the prejudices which have arisen because the common people (who are addicted to superstition and cherish the relics of time rather than eternity itself) adore the books of Scripture rather than the word of God as such. Then I prove that the revealed word of God is not a certain number of books but a pure conception of the divine mind which was revealed to the prophets, namely, to obey God with all one's mind by practising justice and charity. I show that this is taught in Scripture according to the understanding and beliefs of those to whom the prophets and the Apostles normally preached this word of God. This they did in order that people might embrace it without any reluctance and with their whole minds.[16]

[11] Having thus demonstrated the fundamentals of faith, I conclude finally that the object of revealed knowledge is simply obedience. It is therefore entirely distinct from natural knowledge both in its object and in its principles and methods, and has nothing whatever in common with it. Each of them [i.e. faith and natural knowledge] has its own province; they do not conflict with each other; and neither should be subordinate to the other.[17]

[12] Furthermore, human beings have very different minds, and find themselves comfortable with very different beliefs; what moves one person to devotion provokes another to laughter. Taking this together with what I said above, I conclude that everyone should be allowed the liberty of their own judgment and authority to interpret the fundamentals of faith according to their own minds; and that the piety or impiety of each person's faith should be judged by their works alone. In this way everyone will be able to obey God in a spirit of sincerity and freedom, and only justice and charity will be esteemed by everyone.[18]

[13] Having in this way demonstrated the freedom the revealed divine law accords to every person, I proceed to the second part of my thesis,

---

[15] Chs. 7–11.   [16] Chs. 12 and 13.   [17] Ch. 14.   [18] Ch. 15.

which is that this liberty can be granted without endangering the stability of the state or the right of the sovereign authorities, and even that it must be granted, and cannot be suppressed without great danger to peace and immense harm to the whole republic.

To demonstrate this, I begin with the natural right of the individual person. This extends as far as his desire and power extend, and no one is obliged by the right of nature to live according to the views of another person: rather each is the defender of his own liberty. Furthermore, I establish that no one truly cedes this right without transferring to someone else his power to defend himself. Moreover the man to whom each person has transferred their right to live according to their own views together with their power of defending themselves, would then necessarily hold this right absolutely. Those who hold sovereign authority, I show, have the right to do all things that they have the power to do, and are the sole defenders of right and liberty, and everyone else must do everything [over which the sovereign exerts authority] by their decree alone.

But no one can deprive himself of his power of defending himself in such a way that he ceases to be a human being. Hence, I conclude that no one can be absolutely deprived of their natural right, but that subjects retain certain things, by right of nature as it were, that cannot be [decreed to be] taken from them without grave danger to the state. Either therefore these things are tacitly granted or else they are expressly contracted with those who hold sovereign authority.[19]

[14]   After establishing these points, I move on to the commonwealth of the Hebrews, describing it at some length to show by what means and by whose decision religion acquired the force of law, and 'in passing' pointing out also some other things that I thought deserved to be known.[20] Next I prove that those who hold sovereign power are the defenders and interpreters of sacred as well as civil law, and that they alone have the authority to decide what is just and what is unjust, what is pious and what is impious.[21] Finally, I conclude that they can best retain their authority and   12 fully conserve the state only by conceding that each individual is entitled both to think what he wishes and to say what he thinks.[22]

---

[19] Ch. 16.   [20] Chs. 17 and 18.   [21] Ch. 19.
[22] Ch. 20. The final phrase again reflects Tacitus, *Histories*, 1.1; cf. n. 7.

[15]   These are the topics, philosophical reader, that I here offer for your examination. I trust they will not be unwelcome given the importance and usefulness of the subject matter both of the work as a whole and of each chapter. I could say more, but I do not want this Preface to swell into a volume, especially as I believe the main points are well enough known to philosophers [i.e. those capable of rational reasoning]. As for others, I am not particularly eager to recommend this treatise to them, for I have no reason to expect that it could please them in any way. I know how obstinately those prejudices stick in the mind that the heart has embraced in the form of piety. I know that it is as impossible to rid the common people of superstition as it is to rid them of fear. I know that the constancy of the common people is obstinacy, and that they are not governed by reason but swayed by impulse in approving or finding fault. I do not therefore invite the common people and those who are afflicted with the same feelings as they are [i.e. who think theologically], to read these things. I would wish them to ignore the book altogether rather than make a nuisance of themselves by interpreting it perversely, as they do with everything, and while doing no good to themselves, harming others who would philosophize more freely were they able to surmount the obstacle of believing that reason should be subordinate to theology. I am confident that for this latter group of people this work will prove extremely useful.

[16]   For the rest, as many people will have neither the leisure nor the energy to read it right through to the end, I must give notice here, as I do again at the end of the treatise, that I maintain nothing that I would not very willingly submit to the examination and judgment of the sovereign authorities of my country. If they judge anything I say to be in conflict with the laws of my country or prejudicial to the common good, I wish it unsaid. I know that I am human and may have erred.[23] I have however taken great pains not to err, and to ensure above all that everything I write entirely accords with the laws of my country, with piety, and with morality.

---

[23] Compare Terence, *Adelphi*, 579.

On prophecy

[1] Prophecy or revelation is certain knowledge about something revealed to men by God. A prophet is someone who interprets things revealed by God to those who cannot themselves achieve certain knowledge of them and can therefore only grasp by simple faith what has been revealed. The Hebrew for 'prophet' is *nabi*,[1] which means 'orator' or 'interpreter', but is always used in Scripture to mean an interpreter of God. We may infer this from Exodus 7.1, where God says to Moses, 'Behold, I make you Pharaoh's God, and your brother Aaron shall be your prophet'. It is as if God were saying that, since Aaron acts as a prophet by interpreting your words to Pharaoh, you will be like Pharaoh's God, i.e., someone who performs the role of God.

[2] We will discuss prophets in the next chapter; here we will discuss prophecy. From the definition of prophecy just given, it follows that the word 'prophecy' could be applied to natural knowledge. For what we know by the natural light of reason depends on knowledge of God and his eternal decrees alone. But the common people do not place a high value on natural knowledge, because it is available to everyone, resting as it does on foundations that are available to all. For they are always eager to discover uncommon things, things that are strange and alien to their own nature, and they despise their natural gifts. Hence when they speak of prophetic knowledge, they mean to exclude natural knowledge.

And yet, natural knowledge has as much right to be called divine as any other kind of knowledge, since it is the nature of God, so far as we share in

---

[1] Spinoza's footnote: see Annotation 1.

it, and God's decrees, that may be said to dictate it to us. It does not differ from the knowledge which all men call divine, except that divine knowledge extends beyond its limits, and the laws of human nature considered in themselves cannot be the cause of it. But with respect to the certainty which natural knowledge involves and the source from which it derives (namely God), it is in no way inferior to prophetic knowledge – unless perhaps one is willing to accept the nonsensical suggestion that the prophets did not have human minds though they had human bodies, and that their sensations and consciousness therefore were of a quite different nature from ours!

[3]   But despite the fact that natural knowledge is divine, its practitioners cannot be called prophets.[2] For other men may discern and embrace what they teach with as much certainty and entitlement as they do themselves. They do not just accept it on faith.

[4]   Since therefore our mind possesses the power to form such notions from this alone – that it objectively contains within itself the nature of God and participates in it – as explain the nature of things and teach us how to live, we may rightly affirm that it is the nature of the mind, in so far as it is thus conceived, that is the primary source of divine revelation. For everything that we understand clearly and distinctly is dictated to us (as we have just pointed out) by the idea of God and by nature, not in words, but in a much more excellent manner which agrees very well with the nature of the mind, as every man who has experienced intellectual certainty has undoubtedly felt within himself.

[5]   But as my principal purpose is to discuss things which concern only Scripture, these few words about the natural light of reason will suffice. I now move on to the other causes and the other means by which God reveals to men things that exceed the limits of natural knowledge (as well as things that do not exceed those limits, since nothing prevents God from communicating to men by other means knowledge which we learn by the light of nature). I will discuss these other means at some length.

---

[2] Spinoza's footnote: see Annotation 2.

[6]   Truly, however, whatever we are able to say about them must be derived from Scripture alone. For what can we say of things that exceed the limits of our understanding apart from what comes to us from the very lips of a prophet or his writings? Since we have no prophets in our day so far as I know, our only recourse is to peruse the sacred scrolls the prophets have left us. But we must take great care not to say anything about such matters, or to attribute anything to the prophets, which they have not clearly stated themselves. And here at the outset we must note that the Jews never specify intermediate or particular causes and take no notice of them, but owing to religion and piety, or (in the common phrase) 'for devotion's sake', refer   17 everything back to God. For example, if they have made some money by a business transaction, they say that it has been given to them by God; if they happen to want something, they say that God has stirred their heart; and if they think of something, they say that God has said it to them. Therefore we should not consider as prophecy or supernatural knowledge everything that Scripture claims God says to someone but only what Scripture expressly designates as prophecy or revelation or which, from the circumstances of the narrative, clearly is such.

[7]   If therefore we peruse the sacred books, we shall see that everything that God revealed to the prophets was revealed to them either in words or in images, or by both these means together, i.e. in words and images. But the words, and the images too, were either true and independent of the imagination of the prophet who heard or saw them, or else imaginary, that is the prophet's imagination, even when he was awake, was so disposed that it seemed to him that he was clearly hearing words or seeing something.

[8]   It was with a real voice that God revealed to Moses the Laws which he wished to be given to the Hebrews, as is apparent from Exodus 25.22, where he says, 'and I will be ready for you there, and I will speak with you from that part of the covering of the ark, which is between the two cherubim'. This plainly shows that God used a real voice, since Moses found God ready to speak to him there whenever he wished. But it was only this voice with which the Law was proclaimed that was a real voice, as I shall show directly.

[9]   I might perhaps be inclined to think that the voice in which God called Samuel was also a real one since at 1 Samuel 3.21 it is stated: 'And

God appeared again to Samuel in Shiloh, because God was manifested to Samuel in Shiloh by the word of God.' This might mean that the appearance of God to Samuel was nothing other than God manifesting himself to Samuel by a word or Samuel hearing God speak. Yet because we are compelled to distinguish between the prophecy of Moses and that of the other prophets, we must conclude that the voice Samuel heard was imaginary. This can also be inferred from its resemblance to the voice of Eli, which Samuel was very used to hearing, and thus could even more easily be imagined: when he was called by God three times, he thought he was being called by Eli.

18

[10]   The voice Abimelech heard was imaginary; for it is said at Genesis 20.6, 'and God said to him in sleep', etc. Therefore it was not when he was awake but only in his sleep (a time when the imagination is naturally most inclined to imagine things which do not exist) that he was able to imagine the will of God.

[11]   Some Jews are of the opinion that the words of the Ten Commandments or Decalogue were not spoken by God. They think that the Israelites merely heard an inarticulate noise without words, and whilst this continued, they conceived the laws of the Decalogue in their own minds alone. I too thought this at one time, because I saw that the words of the Ten Commandments in Exodus differ from those of the Ten Commandments in Deuteronomy. It seems to follow from this that the Decalogue does not intend to give us God's actual words but only the meaning of what he said. However, unless we are willing to do violence to Scripture, we must concede without reservation that the Israelites heard a real voice. For Scripture expressly says (Deuteronomy 5.4), 'God spoke to you face to face', etc., that is, in the manner in which two men normally communicate their thoughts to each other by means of their two bodies. It seems therefore more in accord with Scripture to acknowledge that God really created a voice by which he revealed the Ten Commandments. (For the reason why the words and justifications of the one passage differ from the words and justifications of the other, see chapter 8.)

[12]   Admittedly, though, this does not altogether remove the difficulty. For it seems quite contrary to reason to assert that a created thing depending upon God in the same way as other created things, could

express or explain in its own person the essence or existence of God in fact or words, that is, by declaring in the first person, 'I am Jehovah your God', etc. It is true that when someone uses his mouth to say, 'I have understood', no one supposes it was the speaker's mouth that understood; we know rather it was his mind. But consider the reason for this: the mouth is part of the nature of the man who spoke, and he to whom the remark was uttered also knows what an intellect is and easily understands what is the speaker's mind by making a comparison with himself. However, in the case of a people who previously knew nothing of God but his name, and desired to speak with him so as to be assured of his existence, I do not see how their desire was met by means of a created thing (which no more relates to God than do other created things, and does not belong to God's nature) proclaiming, 'I am God.' What if God had manipulated Moses' lips (but why Moses and not some animal?) to pronounce the same words and say, 'I am God', would they have understood the existence of God from that?

[13]   Also, Scripture unequivocally states that God himself spoke (and descended from heaven to Mount Sinai for this purpose), and not only did the Jews hear him speaking, but the elders also saw him (see Exodus, ch. 24). Nor did the Law revealed to Moses, to which nothing could be added or subtracted and which became the law of the land, ever prescribe the belief that God is incorporeal or even that he has no image or shape, but only that he is God and that they must believe in him and adore him alone. The reason why it enjoined them not to assign any image to him or to make any image was so that they would not cease worshipping him. For given they had not seen an image of God, they could not have made one which would represent him, but only one which would necessarily represent some other created thing that they had seen. Therefore when they adored God through that image, they would not be thinking of God but of the thing which that image reflected, and thus in the end they would be giving to that thing the honour and worship due to God. Moreover, Scripture clearly affirms that God does have a shape, and that when Moses was listening to God talking, he actually caught a glimpse of him, but saw nothing but God's back.[3] For this reason I do not doubt that some mystery lies hidden here, of which we shall speak at greater length below. Here I will

---

[3] Exodus 33.17–23.

go through the passages of Scripture that point to the means by which God has revealed his decrees to men.

[14] That revelation occurred through images alone is evident from 1 Chronicles 21, where God manifested his anger toward David by means of an angel holding a sword in his hand. So also toward Balaam.[4] And although Maimonides and others maintain that this story happened in sleep (and likewise all the narratives which tell of the appearance of angels, like the one to Abraham at Minoah, when he was thinking of sacrificing his son, etc.) and refuse to accept that anyone could have seen an angel with his eyes open, they are surely talking nonsense. They were only concerned to derive Aristotelian trifles and some figments of their own from Scripture, than which, to my mind, nothing could be more ridiculous.

[15] It was also by means of visions that were not real but derived from the imagination of the prophet alone that God revealed to Joseph his future pre-eminence.[5]

20 [16] By visions and words God revealed to Joshua that he would fight for them [i.e. the Hebrews]. For he showed him an angel with a sword, like the leader of an army, and also revealed it to him in words and Joshua heard it from the angel.[6] Visions were also the means by which it was represented to Isaiah (as we are told in ch. 6) that the providence of God would desert his people, namely by his imagining the thrice holy God on his lofty throne and the Israelites stained with the filth of their sins and immersed so to speak in a pile of manure and thus very distant from God. By this he understood the miserable state of his people in the present, and their future calamities were revealed to him in words as if pronounced by God. I could give many more examples of this sort from the holy Scriptures, if I did not think that everybody knows them well enough.

[17] But it is all most plainly confirmed by the text of Numbers 12.6–7 which reads as follows: 'If one of you shall be a prophet of God, I will reveal myself to him in a vision' (that is, through images and holy signs, whereas the prophecy of Moses is said to be a vision without holy signs); 'I will speak to him in dreams' (that is, not in real words and a real voice).

[4] Numbers 22–4.   [5] Genesis 37.5–11.   [6] Joshua 5.13–15.

'But that is not how' (I reveal myself) 'to Moses; I speak with him face to face and not in riddles, and he sees the image of God'. That is, in seeing me he speaks with me as a friend, not as one who is terrified, as is the case at Exodus 33.11.[7] Thus there is no doubt that the rest of the prophets did not hear a real voice, and this is still more clearly confirmed by Deuteronomy 34.10, where it is said, 'and there has not been' (literally, 'arisen') 'a prophet in Israel like Moses, whom God knew face to face', which has to mean, 'by voice alone', for not even Moses ever saw the face of God (Exodus, ch. 33).

[18]   These are the only means I find in the holy Scriptures by which God communicated with men, and therefore, as we showed above, we should not invent or admit any other method. Although we clearly understand that God can communicate with men directly (for he communicates his essence to our minds without the use of any physical means), nevertheless, for a person to know things which are not contained in the first foundations of our knowledge and cannot be deduced from them, his mind would necessarily have to be vastly superior, far surpassing the human mind. I do not believe that anyone has reached such a degree of perfection above others except Christ, to whom the decrees of God which guide men to salvation were revealed not by words or visions but directly; and that is why God revealed himself to the Apostles through the mind of Christ, as he did, formerly, to Moses by means of a heavenly voice. Therefore the voice of Christ may be called the voice of God, like the voice which Moses heard. In this sense we may also say that the wisdom of God, that is, the wisdom which is above human wisdom, took on human nature in Christ, and that Christ was the way of salvation.

[19]   Here I must point out that I am not speaking at all of the things that certain churches affirm of Christ nor do I deny them; for I freely admit that I do not understand them. What I have just said, I infer from Scripture. Nowhere have I read that God appeared to Christ or spoke with him, but that God was revealed to the Apostles through Christ, and that he is the way of salvation, and finally that the old Law was given through an angel and not directly by God, etc. Therefore if Moses spoke with God face to face as a man with his friend (that is, through the mediation of two bodies), Christ communicated with God from mind to mind.

21

---

[7] This may refer to 33.11 or 33.17.

[20] We assert therefore that, apart from Christ, no one has received revelations from God except by means of the imagination, namely by means of words or visions, and therefore prophecy does not require a more perfect mind but a more vivid imagination, as I shall show more clearly in the next chapter.

[21] But now we must ask what the holy Scriptures mean by the spirit of God that inspired the prophets and what they mean when they say that the prophets spoke by the spirit of God. In order to investigate this, we must first ask what is intended by the Hebrew word *ruagh*, which is usually translated as 'spirit'.

[22] The word *ruagh* in its literal sense means 'wind', as noted, but it is very often used to refer to many other things, all of them, however, derived from 'wind'. It is used:

(1) to signify 'breath', as in Psalm 135.17, 'also there is no spirit in their mouth';

(2) 'life' or 'breathing', as in 1 Samuel 30.12, 'and spirit returned to him', i.e., 'he breathed'.

(3) Hence it is taken for 'courage' and 'strength', as at Joshua 2.11, 'and there was afterwards no spirit in any man'. Likewise Ezekiel 2.2, 'and spirit' (or power) 'came into me, which made me stand on my feet'.

(4) Hence it is taken for 'ability' and 'capacity', as at Job 32.8, 'surely it is the spirit in a man', that is, knowledge is not to be sought only in old men, for I now find that it depends upon the individual's particular ability and capacity. Similarly Numbers 27.18, 'a man in whom there is spirit'.

(5) It can also denote a 'sentiment' of the mind, as at Numbers 14.24, 'since there was another spirit in him', i.e., a different 'sentiment', or another 'mind'. Likewise Proverbs 1.23, 'I will tell you my spirit' (i.e., 'my mind'). In this sense it is used to signify 'will' or 'decision', 'desire' and 'movement of the mind', as at Ezekiel 1.12 'they went wherever there was a spirit' (or 'will') 'to go'. Likewise Isaiah 30.1, 'and make a league but not of my spirit', and 29.10, 'because God poured over them the spirit' (i.e., 'desire') 'to sleep'. And Judges 8.3, 'then their spirit' (or 'passion') 'was moderated'. Likewise Proverbs 18.33, 'he who masters his spirit (or 'appetite') surpasses him who captures a city'. Proverbs 25.28, 'the man who does not restrain his spirit'. And Isaiah 33.11, 'Your spirit is a fire which consumes you'. Further, this word *ruagh*, in so far as it signifies 'mind', serves to express all the passions of the mind and even its talents; for example, 'a lofty spirit' serves to denote pride, 'a lowly spirit' humility, 'an evil

spirit' hatred and melancholy, 'a good spirit' kindness; we also find 'a spirit of jealousy', 'a spirit' (or appetite) 'of fornication', and 'a spirit of wisdom' (or 'counsel' or 'courage'), which signifies (for in Hebrew we employ nouns more frequently than adjectives) a wise, prudent or brave mind, or the virtue of wisdom, counsel or courage; also, 'a spirit of benevolence', etc.

(6) It denotes the mind or soul itself, as at Ecclesiastes 3.19, 'The spirit' (or soul) 'is the same in all men', 'and the spirit returns to God'.   23

(7) Finally it can refer to the quarters of the world (because of the winds that blow from them), and also the sides of any thing which look toward those quarters: see Ezekiel 37.9, 42.16–19, etc.

[23]   We must also note that something is referred to God and is said to be of God,

(1) because it belongs to the nature of God and is, so to speak, a part of God, as in the expressions, 'the power of God' and 'the eyes of God'.

(2) because it is in the power of God and acts at his command; thus in the Scriptures the heavens are called 'the heavens of God', because they are the chariot and the home of God; Assyria is called the scourge of God, and Nebuchadnezzar the servant of God, etc.

(3) because it is dedicated to God, as 'the temple of God', 'a Nazarene of God', 'bread of God', etc.

(4) because it is taught by the prophets and not revealed by the natural light of reason; this is why the Law of Moses is called the law of God.

(5) to express a thing to a superlative degree, as 'mountains of God', i.e., very high mountains, 'a sleep of God', i.e., a very deep sleep. This is the sense in which Amos 4.11 is to be interpreted, when God himself says, 'I overthrew you just as God's overthrowing came upon Sodom and Gomorrah', i.e., just like that noteworthy overthrow: this is the only possible correct explanation, since it is God himself who is speaking. Even the natural knowledge of Solomon is called God's knowledge, i.e., divine knowledge, or a knowledge that is above ordinary knowledge. In the Psalms we even find 'cedars of God', to express their extraordinary height. And at 1 Samuel 11.7 to signify a very great fear, it is said, 'and the fear of God fell upon the people'. In this sense everything that surpassed the Jews' understanding and whose natural causes were unknown at that time, tended to be attributed to God. Thus a storm was called, 'a rebuke from God', and thunder and lightning the arrows of God; for they thought that God kept the winds shut up in caverns which they called the treasuries of God, differing in this belief from the gentiles in that they believed God, not Aeolus, was their governor. For the same reason miracles are called works of God, that is, astounding works. For all natural things are undoubtedly works of God and exist   24

and act by divine power. In this sense therefore the Psalmist calls the miracles of Egypt powers of God, because they opened up a path to safety for the Hebrews in their extreme danger when they were not expecting any exit to appear, and so they were totally amazed.

[24] Since therefore unusual works of nature are termed works of God and trees of unusual height called trees of God, it is not surprising that in Genesis the strongest men, men of great stature, are referred to as sons of God even though they ravish women and consort with prostitutes. The ancients, gentiles and Jews alike, referred everything to God where one man excelled others. When Pharaoh heard Joseph's interpretation of a dream, he said there was a mind of the gods in him, and Nebuchadnezzar said to Daniel that he had the mind of the holy gods. It was likewise just as common among the Romans, who say that things that are skilfully created have been made by a divine hand; if one wanted to turn this into Hebrew, one would need to say 'made by the hand of God', as is well known to students of Hebrew.

[25] These then are the ways in which biblical passages mentioning the spirit of God may readily be understood and explained. For example, 'spirit of God' and 'spirit of Jehovah', signify nothing more in some places than an extremely violent, very dry and fatal wind, as in Isaiah 40.7, 'a wind of God blew upon him', i.e., a very dry, lethal wind; also Genesis 1.2: 'and a wind of God' (or, a very powerful wind) 'moved over the water'.

It can also mean a great heart; for both the heart of Gideon and Samson is called in Scripture, 'a spirit of God', that is, a very bold heart, ready for anything. For in this way any virtue or force out of the ordinary is designated a 'spirit' or 'virtue' of God, as in Exodus 31.3 'and I shall fill him' (Bezalel) 'with the spirit of God', that is (as Scripture itself explains), with talent and skill above the common lot. So Isaiah 11.2: 'and the spirit of God shall rest upon him', that is, as the prophet himself specifies when he explains this later in the normal manner of the Bible, the virtue of wisdom, counsel, courage etc. Likewise, the melancholy of Saul is called 'an evil spirit from God', i.e., a most profound melancholy; for the servants of Saul who called his melancholy a 'melancholy of God', suggested to him that he should summon a musician to ease his spirits by singing to him, which shows that by a 'melancholy of God' they meant a natural melancholy.

Further, 'spirit of God' may mean the human mind itself, as in Job 27.3, 'and the spirit of God in my nose', which alludes to the passage in Genesis in which God blew the breath of life into the nose of man. Thus Ezekiel, prophesying to the dead, says at 37.14, 'and I will give my spirit to you, and you will live', i.e., 'I will restore life to you'. And in this sense it is said at Job 34.14, 'if he' (i.e., God) 'so wills, he will take back to himself his spirit (that is, the mind which he has given us) and his breath'. This is how Genesis 6.3 is to be understood, 'my spirit will not ever reason' (or, will not decide) 'in man, because he is flesh'; that is, henceforth man will act according to the decisions of the flesh and not of the mind which I gave him to discern the good. So also Psalm 51.12–13, 'create in me a clean heart, O God, and renew in me a proper' (or, modest) 'spirit' (i.e., desire). 'Do not cast me away from your sight, nor take the mind of your holiness from me'. Because sins were believed to arise from the flesh alone, and the mind was believed to urge nothing but good, he invokes the help of God against the desires of the flesh, but for the mind which the holy God gave him, he only prays God to preserve it.

Now since Scripture, deferring to the limitations of the common people, is accustomed to depict God like a man, and to ascribe to God a mind and a heart and the passions of the heart, as well as body and breath, 'the spirit of God' is often used in the Bible for mind, i.e., heart, passion, force and the breath of the mouth of God. Thus Isaiah 40.13 says: 'who has directed the spirit' (or mind) 'of God?' that is, who set the mind of God to willing anything except God himself? and 63.10: 'and they afflicted the spirit of his sanctity with bitterness and woe'. And hence it often comes to be used to designate the Law of Moses because it explains, as it were, God's mind, as Isaiah himself states in the same 26 chapter, verse 11, 'where is' (he) 'who has put in the midst of them the spirit of his sanctity?' that is, the Law of Moses, as is clearly implied by the whole context of the speech; and Nehemiah 9.20, 'you gave them your spirit or good mind, so that you might make them understand', for he means the occasion of the giving of the Law; Deut. 4.6 also alludes to it when Moses says, 'since it' (namely the Law) 'is your knowledge and prudence', etc. So also in Psalm 143.10, 'your good mind will lead me into a smooth place', that is, your mind revealed to us will lead me into the right way.

The spirit of God, as we have said, also signifies the breath of God, which, like mind, heart and body, is also improperly attributed to God in Scripture, as in Psalm 33.6.

It can also denote the power, force or virtue of God, as at Job 33.4, 'the spirit of God made me', i.e., the virtue or power of God, or if you prefer, the decree of God; for the Psalmist, speaking poetically, even says, 'by the command of God the heavens were made, and all their host by the spirit' or breath 'of his mouth' (i.e. by his decree, as if it were expressed as a breath). Likewise at Psalm 139.7, 'whither shall I go' (that I may be) 'beyond your spirit, or whither shall I flee' (that I may be) 'beyond your sight?', that is (as is clear from the way the Psalmist continues here), 'whither can I go that I may be beyond your power and presence?'

Finally, 'the spirit of God' is used in Scripture to express the sentiments of God's heart, namely, his kindness and mercy, as in Micah 2.7: 'surely the spirit of God' (i.e. the mercy of God) 'has not been straitened? Are these' (dreadful) 'things his works?' Likewise Zechariah 4.6, 'not by an army, not by force, but by my spirit alone', that is, by my mercy alone. In this sense, too, I think, we must understand 7.12 of the same prophet: 'and they made their hearts hard as rock,[8] so that they would not obey the Law and the commands which God sent from his spirit' (i.e., from his mercy) 'by means of the first prophets'. In this sense too Haggai says at 2.5, 'and my spirit' (or my grace) 'remains among you; do not be afraid'.

27   The phrase of Isaiah at 48.16, 'but now the Lord God and his spirit have sent me', can also be understood of God's kindness and mercy, though it *might* refer rather to God's mind as revealed in the Law. For Isaiah says: 'From the beginning' (that is, as soon as I came to you, that I might preach the wrath of God and the judgment he has pronounced against you) 'I have not spoken secretly; from the time that the sentence was' (pronounced), 'I have been with you' (as Isaiah himself had testified in ch. 7); 'but now', he continues, 'I am a glad messenger, sent by the mercy of God, that I may sing of your restoration.' This passage may indeed, as I said, be understood of the mind of God as revealed in the Law: on this interpretation, Isaiah has come to warn them (in obedience to the command of the Law at Leviticus 19.17), and does so in the same conditions and in the same manner as Moses had done, and ends, like Moses, by predicting their restoration. However the former interpretation [that it refers to God's mercy] seems to me the more probable.

[26]   To return, after all this, to our main point: scriptural expressions such as 'the spirit of God was in the prophet', 'God poured his spirit into

---

[8] Reading *cautem* as suggested by Fokke Akkerman.

men', 'men were filled with the spirit of God and with holy spirit', etc., become perfectly clear. These merely mean that the prophets had a unique and extraordinary virtue,[9] and cultivated piety with a unique constancy of purpose. Such expressions also denote that they perceived the mind or thought of God; for 'spirit' in Hebrew, as we showed, signifies both a mind and the thought of a mind, and for this reason the Law itself was called the spirit or mind of God because it disclosed God's mind; and in as much as the decrees of God were revealed through the imagination of the prophets, their imagination could with equal right also be designated the mind of God. God's mind and his eternal thoughts are indeed inscribed on our minds also, and consequently we too perceive the mind of God (to speak in biblical terms), but natural knowledge, as we have already noted, is not highly regarded by men because it is common to all, and in particular was not prized by the Hebrews, who thought very highly of themselves, and were even prone to despise other peoples and consequently to disdain such knowledge as is common to everyone. Finally the prophets were said to have the spirit of God because men were ignorant of the causes of prophetic knowledge, though they also admired it, and therefore, as with other extraordinary things, they tended to ascribe it to God and to call it God's knowledge.   28

[27] We can therefore now assert, without reservation, that the prophets perceived things revealed by God by way of their imagination, that is via words or visions which may have been either real or imaginary. These are the only means that we find in Scripture and we are not permitted to invent others, as we have already shown. But I confess that I do not know by what natural laws prophetic insight occurred. I might, like others, have said that it occurred by the power of God, but then I would be saying nothing meaningful. For this would be the same as explaining the shape of some individual thing by means of a transcendental term. For everything is done by the power of God. Indeed, because the power of nature is nothing other than the power of God itself, it is certain that we fail to understand the power of God to the extent that we are ignorant of natural causes. Therefore it is foolish to have recourse to this same power of God when we are ignorant of the natural cause of some thing, which is, precisely, the power of God. In any case, there is no need for us

[9] Spinoza's footnote: see Annotation 3.

at this point to know the cause of prophetic knowledge. For as I have already pointed out, here we are only trying to examine the teachings of Scripture in order to draw our conclusions from them, as we would from facts of nature; we are not concerned with the causes of these teachings.

[28] Since therefore the prophets perceived the things revealed by God through their imaginations, there is no doubt that they may have grasped much beyond the limits of the intellect. For far more ideas can be formed from words and images than from the principles and concepts alone on which all our natural knowledge is built.

[29] It also becomes clear why the prophets understood and taught almost everything in parables and allegorically, expressing all spiritual matters in corporeal language; for the latter are well suited to the nature of our imagination. Neither shall we any longer be surprised that Scripture or the prophets speak so inappropriately and obscurely about the spirit or mind of God, as at Numbers 11.17, 1 Kings 22.2, etc., or that Micah saw God seated, Daniel saw him as an old man dressed in white clothes, and Ezekiel as a fire, while those who were with Christ saw him as a dove descending, the Apostles saw him as tongues of fire, while Paul, when he was first converted, saw him as a great light. For all this is clearly well suited to the imaginings of ordinary men about God and spirits.

[30] Finally it is because imagination is capricious and changeable that prophecy did not remain long with the prophets, and was not at all common but very rare, occurring in just a handful of men, and in them only very occasionally.

[31] Since this is so, we are now compelled to ask what could be the source of the prophets' assuredness or certainty about things which they perceived only via the imagination and not from clear reasoning of the mind. Whatever can be ascertained about this must also be derived from Scripture, since we do not have true knowledge of the matter (as we have said), that is, we cannot explain it by its first causes. What the Bible teaches about the prophets' assuredness, I shall explain in the next chapter, where I propose to discuss the prophets.

CHAPTER 2

On the prophets

[1]   It follows from the previous chapter, as we have pointed out, that the prophets were not endowed with more perfect minds than others but only a more vivid power of imagination, as the scriptural narratives also abundantly show. It is clear from the case of Solomon, for instance, that he excelled others in wisdom but not in the gift of prophecy. Heman, Darda and Calcol[1] were also very discerning men but they were not prophets. On the other hand, rustic fellows without any education, and insignificant women like Hagar, the serving girl of Abraham, were endowed with the prophetic gift.[2] This also accords with experience and reason. Those who are most powerful in imagination are less good at merely understanding things; those who have trained and powerful intellects have a more modest power of imagination and have it under better control, reining it in, so to speak, and not confusing it with understanding. Consequently those who look in the books of the prophets for wisdom and a knowledge of natural and spiritual things are completely on the wrong track. I propose to explain this here at some length, since the times in which we live, philosophy, and the subject itself require me to do so without worrying about the outcry from credulous people who detest none more than those who cultivate real 30 knowledge and true life. Distressingly, it has now come to the point that people who freely admit that they do not possess the idea of God and know him only through created things (whose causes they are ignorant of), do not hesitate to accuse philosophers of atheism.

---

[1] 1 Kings 4:29–31 extols the wisdom of Solomon and adds that it surpassed the wisdom of Heman, Darda and Calcol among others.
[2] Genesis 16.7–13.

27

[2] In order to treat this subject in proper order, I will show that prophecies have varied not only in accordance with the imagination and temperament of each individual prophet, but also according to the beliefs in which he was brought up. That is why prophecy has never made prophets more learned, as I shall explain presently at greater length. But we must first discuss their certainty or assuredness both because it concerns the argument of this chapter, and because it also goes some way towards demonstrating what we intend to demonstrate.

[3] Plain imagination does not of its own nature provide certainty, as every clear and distinct idea does. In order that we may be certain of what we imagine, imagination must necessarily be assisted by something, and that something is reason. It follows from this that prophecy by itself cannot provide certainty, because as we have already shown, prophecy depends upon imagination alone. It was not because of the revelation itself therefore that the prophets were assured that they had received a revelation from God but because of some sign. This is clear from the case of Abraham (see Genesis 15.8): when he heard God's promise, he asked for a sign. He believed God, and asked for a sign not in order to have faith in God but so as to know that it was a promise from God. The same thing is even plainer in the case of Gideon: this is what he says to God, 'and make me a sign' (so that I may know) 'that you are speaking with me' (see Judges 6.17). God also tells Moses, 'and let this be a sign to you that I have sent you'.[3] Hezekiah, who had long known that Isaiah was a prophet, asked for a sign confirming Isaiah's prophecy predicting that he would be healed. This shows that the prophets always received a sign assuring them of what they had prophetically imagined, and for that reason Moses admonishes the Hebrews (Deuteronomy 18, final verse) to seek a sign from prophets, such as the outcome of some future event.

In this respect, consequently, prophecy is inferior to natural knowledge since it has no need of any sign but provides certainty by its very nature. For this prophetic certainty was not mathematical certainty but only moral certainty. This is also made plain by Scripture; for in Deuteronomy 13, Moses admonishes that, should any prophet attempt to teach of new gods, he is to be condemned to death, even if he confirms his teaching by signs and miracles, for, as Moses himself goes on to say, God [also] offers signs

---

[3] Exodus 3.12.

and miracles to test the people. Christ too warned his disciples of this, as is clear from Matthew 24.24. Ezekiel 14.9 plainly teaches that God sometimes deceives men by false revelations: he says, 'and when a prophet' (that is, a false prophet) 'is deceived and has spoken a word, it is I God that has deceived that prophet'. Micaiah says the same thing about the prophets of Ahab (see 1 Kings 22.21).

[4]   Although this might seem to show that prophecy and revelation are something altogether dubious, yet, as we have said, it did have a good deal of certainty. For God never deceives the pious and the elect, but as the ancient proverb says (see 1 Samuel 24.14), and as the narrative of Abigail and her prayer makes clear, God uses the pious as the instruments of his own piety, and the impious as the agents and executors of his wrath. This is abundantly clear from the case of Micaiah, just cited; for though God had determined to deceive Ahab by means of prophets, he made use only of false prophets, and revealed the truth of the matter to a pious man and did not forbid him to tell the truth. However, as I said, the certainty of a prophet was only a moral certainty, since nobody can justify himself before God or claim to be an instrument of divine piety, as Scripture itself teaches and is evident from the thing itself: thus the wrath of God misled David into counting the people, yet Scripture abundantly testifies to his piety.

[5]   All prophetic certainty therefore was grounded upon three things:

(1) that the matters revealed were very vividly imagined, as we are affected by objects when we are awake;
(2) upon a sign; and
(3) most importantly, that the minds of the prophets were directed exclusively to what is right and good.

Scripture does not always actually mention a sign, but we must nevertheless suppose that the prophets always had one. The Bible does not always mention every condition and circumstance (as many have already noted) but assumes some things as known. We may further grant that the 32 prophets who prophesied nothing new beyond what is contained in the Law of Moses, had no need of a sign, because they were corroborated by the Law. For example the prophecy of Jeremiah about the destruction of Jerusalem was confirmed by the prophecies of the other prophets and by the admonitions of the Law, and therefore did not need a sign. But

Hananiah who prophesied, contrary to all the other prophets, a swift restoration of the city, necessarily required a sign; otherwise he would have to be in doubt about his own prophecy, until the outcome of his prediction confirmed it: see Jeremiah 28.9.

[6]   As therefore the certainty the prophets derived from signs was not mathematical certainty (that is, a certainty which follows from the necessity of the perception of the thing that is perceived or seen) but only moral certainty, and the signs were given for nothing other than to convince the prophet, it follows that the signs were given according to the prophet's beliefs and understanding. Hence a sign that reassured one prophet as to his prophecy might not convince another imbued with different beliefs; and hence these signs varied from prophet to prophet.

[7]   The revelation itself also varied from one prophet to another, as we have already said: it depended upon the disposition of his bodily temperament, his imagination and the beliefs he had previously adopted. As regards temperament, it differed in this way: if the prophet was cheerful, his revelations were of victories and peace and other things that conduce to happiness, for such men are apt to imagine such things quite often; if on the other hand he was gloomy, his revelations concerned wars, torments and everything bad. The prophet would be more inclined towards one or the other kind of revelation depending on whether he was merciful and kindly or wrathful and harsh, and so on. Revelation also varied according to the cast of his imagination: if the prophet was a discerning man, he perceived God's mind with clarity, but if he was muddled, he did so in a confused manner. So too with revelations made through visions: if the prophet was a country fellow, it was oxen and cows and so on that were what was represented to him; if he was a soldier, generals and armies; and if he was a courtier, a royal throne and such like. Finally, the prophecy varied according to the different beliefs of the prophets: for example, the nativity of Christ was revealed to the Magi (see Matthew 2), who believed in the nonsense of astrology, through their imagining a star risen in the east; the destruction of Jerusalem was revealed to the augurs of Nebuchadnezzar in entrails (see Ezekiel 21.26), and the king also divined it through oracles and from the direction of the arrows which he shot into the air. Then again, those prophets who supposed that men act of their own free choice and power, received revelations representing God as indifferent to and

33

ignorant of future human actions. We will now demonstrate each of these points one by one from Scripture itself.

[8]　The first point is evident from the case of Elisha (see 2 Kings 3.15), who, in order to prophesy to Jehoram, requested a musical instrument. Nor could he perceive God's mind other than when charmed by its music. Only then did he predict joyful things to Jehoram and those around him. This he could not do before, because he was angry with the king, and those who are angry with someone are inclined to imagine bad and not good things about them. As for those who insist that God is not revealed to those who are angry and gloomy, they are wide of the mark. God revealed to Moses, who was angry with Pharaoh at the time, the terrible massacre of the first-born (see Exodus 11.8), and without using any musical instrument. God was also revealed to Cain when he was furiously angry. The future misery and disobedience of the Jews was revealed to Ezekiel when he was seething with fury (see Ezekiel 3.14). Jeremiah prophesied the calamities of the Jews when he was thoroughly morbid and experiencing great disgust for life, so much so that Josiah was unwilling to consult him, and consulted a female colleague of Jeremiah's, supposing that with her woman's mind she would be more likely to receive a revelation of God's mercy (see 2 Chronicles 34).[4] Micaiah also never prophesied anything good to Ahab, though other true prophets did (as is clear from 1 Kings 20); throughout his life he prophesied bad things to him (see 1 Kings 22.8, and more clearly 2 Chronicles 18.7). Thus the prophets were more inclined toward one or another kind of revelation depending upon their differing bodily temperaments.

[9]　The style of prophecy also varied according to the eloquence of the individual prophet. The prophecies of Ezekiel and of Amos are not elegantly expressed like those of Isaiah and Nahum but written in a rougher style. If anyone with a good knowledge of Hebrew cares to study this question more carefully, he may compare certain chapters of the prophets with each other and will find a great deal of stylistic difference. Let him compare for instance chapter 1 of the courtier Isaiah, verses 11–20, with chapter 5 of the rustic Amos, verses 21–24. Then let him compare the order 34 and arguments of the prophecy that Jeremiah wrote to Edom (chapter 49)

---

[4]　2 Chronicles 34.19–28. The name of the prophetess was Huldah.

with the order and arguments of Obadiah. Let him also compare Isaiah 40.19–20 and 44.8 ff. with Hosea 8.6 and 13.2. And so for the rest; and if all these passages are duly examined, they will readily show that God has no particular speaking style, but that he is elegant, concise, severe, rough, prolix or obscure according to the learning and capability of the prophet.

[10] Prophetic visions and images, even when referring to the same thing, varied markedly: the glory of God departing the Temple was made apparent to Isaiah differently from how it was represented to Ezekiel. The Rabbis insist that both revelations are exactly the same except that Ezekiel, as a country fellow, was completely overwhelmed by it and therefore narrated it fully in all its circumstantial detail, but they are obviously making this up – unless they had a reliable tradition for it, which I do not believe. For Isaiah saw seraphim with seven wings each, while Ezekiel saw beasts with four wings each; Isaiah saw God clothed and seated on a royal throne, while Ezekiel saw him as a fire. Each undoubtedly saw God as he was accustomed to imagine him.

[11] Revelations differed, moreover, not only in form but also in clarity. What was revealed to Zechariah was too obscure for him to be able to understand it himself without explanation, as is clear from his account of it, and what was revealed to Daniel could not be understood by the prophet himself even when it was explained to him. This was not because of the difficulty of what had to be revealed (for these were only human matters, not beyond the limits of human understanding except in being in the future), but merely because Daniel's imagination was not as able to prophesy when he was awake as when he was asleep. This emerges from the fact that when his visions began, he was so terrified that he almost despaired of his capacities. Owing to the debility of his imagination and his incapacity, things were revealed to him which seemed very obscure to him, and he could not grasp them even when they were explained to him. Here
35 we should note that the words that Daniel heard (as we showed above) were only imaginary; hence it is not surprising that, in his disturbed state at that time, he imagined all these words in such a confused and obscure manner that he could make nothing of them afterwards. Those who say that God did not want to give Daniel a clear revelation seem not to have read the words of the angel, who explicitly said (see 10.14) that 'he had come to make Daniel understand what would happen to his people in the latter days'. It

all remained obscure, because there was no one at that time who had such a powerful imagination that it could be revealed to him more clearly. Finally, the prophets to whom it was revealed that God would take Elijah away attempted to persuade Elisha that he had been taken to some other place where they might still find him; this plainly shows that they had not properly understood God's revelation.[5]

[12] I need not press this point further, for nothing is clearer in Scripture than that God granted some prophets a far greater gift of prophecy than others. But I will demonstrate more precisely and more fully that prophecies or revelations also varied according to the beliefs which the prophets had embraced, and that prophets held different, or even incompatible, beliefs from one another and had different preconceptions. (I am speaking about purely philosophical questions here; we must take a very different view of anything relating to uprightness and good conduct.) I think this question is of major importance, for I ultimately conclude from it that prophecy never made the prophets more learned, but left them with their preconceived beliefs and that, for this reason, we are in no way obliged to believe them in purely philosophical matters.

[13] It is astounding how readily all the commentators have embraced the notion that the prophets knew everything that human understanding can attain. Even though certain passages of the Bible tell us in the plainest terms that there were some things the prophets did not know, the [commentators] prefer either to say that they do not understand the sense of Scripture in these passages or attempt to twist the words to make it say what it plainly does not, rather than admit that the prophets were ignorant of anything. Obviously if we take either course, Scripture has no more meaning for us; if we may regard the clearest passages as obscure and impenetrable or interpret them in any way we please, it will be pointless to try to prove anything from it at all.

For example, nothing in the Bible is clearer than that Joshua, and perhaps the author who wrote his history, thought that the sun moves round the earth and the earth is at rest and the sun stood still for a period of time. Some are unwilling to allow that there can be any change in the heavens and hence interpret this passage in such a way that it will not seem to say

---

[5] 2 Kings 2.15–18.

anything like that. Others who have learnt to philosophize more accurately and recognize that the earth moves and the sun is at rest, or does not move around the earth, make great efforts to derive this from this passage even though it obviously will not permit such a reading. I am really astonished at them. Are we obliged, I ask, to believe that Joshua, a soldier, was an expert in astronomy and that a miracle could not be revealed to him, or that the light of the sun could not be above the horizon longer than usual, without Joshua understanding the cause of it? Both explanations seem utterly ridiculous to me. I prefer to say frankly that Joshua was ignorant of the true cause of that longer-lasting light. He and all the people with him believed both that the sun moves in a daily motion around the earth and that on this day it stood still for some time, and they believed that this was the cause of the longer-lasting light. They had no idea that as a result of the large amount of ice which was in the air there at that time (see Joshua 10.11),[6] there was a greater refraction than normal, or something of that kind. But we will not go into this at the moment.

For Isaiah too[7] the sign of the shadow moving backwards was revealed to him in a manner suited to his understanding, namely as a backward movement of the sun, since he too thought that the sun moves and the earth is at rest. Of parhelia he probably had not even the faintest notion.[8] We may assert this unreservedly. For the sign really might have occurred and Isaiah might have predicted it to the king, even though he did not know its true cause.

The same must also be said for Solomon's building of the Temple, if indeed that was revealed by God, i.e., that all its measurements were revealed to Solomon according to his understanding and assumptions. For as we have no reason to believe Solomon was a mathematician, we are entitled to assert that he did not know the true ratio between the circumference of a circle and its diameter, and supposed like most craftsmen that it was 3 to 1. For if it is permissible to say that we do not understand the text of 1 Kings 7.23, I simply do not know what we can understand from Scripture, since the edifice is merely reported in that passage in a purely descriptive manner. If one is permitted to claim that Scripture meant something else here, but for some reason unknown to us it was decided to

---

[6] 'And as they fled before Israel, while they were going down the ascent of Beth-Horon, the Lord threw down great stones from heaven upon them as far as Azekah, and they died; there were more who died because of the hailstones than the men of Israel killed with the sword.' (Joshua 10.11).
[7] Isaiah 38.7–8.   [8] i.e., sundogs or mock suns.

put it this way, the consequence is the complete and utter subversion of the 37
whole of the Bible. Everyone will be able to say the same with equal justification about every single passage. It will be possible to perpetrate and
justify every absurd or malicious thing that human perversity can dream
up, without impugning the authority of Scripture. Nor does our position
involve any impiety: for Solomon, Isaiah, Joshua, etc., though prophets,
were still men, and nothing human is to be thought alien to them.[9] Likewise, the revelation that God was going to destroy the human race was
accommodated to the limited understanding of Noah, since he thought
that the world was uninhabited outside of Palestine.

The prophets could be ignorant of things such as these without piety
being put at risk, and not only of these but also of more important matters,
of which indeed they were truly ignorant. For they taught nothing out of
the ordinary about the divine attributes, but rather had thoroughly commonplace conceptions of God and their revelations were accommodated
to these notions, as I will now show by many citations from Scripture. You
will readily see from this that the reason why they are so highly praised and
commended was not for the sublimity and excellence of their intellects but
for their piety and constancy.

[14]   Adam, the first man to whom God was revealed, did not know that
God is present everywhere and is all-knowing: he hid himself from God
and attempted to excuse his offence before God, as if he were dealing with a
man. Hence God was revealed to him to the extent of his understanding,
namely, as one who is not present everywhere and was ignorant of Adam's
location and of his sin. He heard, or seemed to hear, God walking through
the garden, and calling him, and asking where he was, and then asking, as a
result of Adam's embarrassment, whether he had eaten of the forbidden
tree.[10] Adam therefore knew only one attribute of God, that he was the
maker of all things. God was also revealed to Cain to the extent of his
understanding, namely as [seeming to be] ignorant of human affairs; he did
not need a more elevated conception of God to repent of his sin.[11] God
revealed himself to Laban as the God of Abraham, because Laban believed
that every nation has its own particular god: see Genesis 31.29. Abraham
too was ignorant that God is everywhere and foreknows all things. When

[9] Compare Terence, *Heautontimoroumenos* (*The Self-Tormentor*) 77.
[10] Genesis 3.7–13.   [11] Genesis 4.9.

35

38 he heard the sentence against the men of Sodom, he prayed that God would not carry it out until he knew whether all of them deserved that punishment; for he says (see Genesis 18.24), 'perhaps there are fifty just men in that city'. Nor was God revealed to him as any other than this [i.e. a being of limited knowledge who has descended to Sodom to see how many just men there are there]; for this is how God speaks in Abraham's imagining: 'now I will go down, so that I may see whether they have indeed acted as reported by the great outcry which has come to me, and if it is not so, I will know it'.[12] Equally, the divine testimony concerning Abraham (on which see Genesis 18.19) contains only the requirement that he should obey and instruct his servants regarding what is just and good, saying nothing about higher conceptions of God.

Nor did Moses adequately grasp that God is omniscient and directs all human actions by his decree alone. For although God had said (see Exodus 3.18) that the Israelites would obey him, he nevertheless doubted this and replied (see Exodus 4.1): 'what if they do not believe me or obey me?' Thus to him also God was revealed as uninvolved and ignorant of future human actions. For God gave him two signs and said (Exodus 4.8), 'should it happen that they do not believe the first, they should believe the latter; but should they not believe this one either, (then) take a little water from the river', etc.

In fact, anyone who reflects on Moses' opinions without prejudice, will plainly see that he believed God to be a being that has always existed, exists and will always exist, and for this reason he calls him 'Jehovah' by name, which in Hebrew expresses these three tenses of existence. But Moses taught nothing else about his nature except that he is merciful, kind, etc., and in the highest degree jealous, as is clear from several passages in the Pentateuch. He also believed and taught that this being is so different from all other beings that he cannot be represented by the image of any visible thing nor even be seen himself, owing less to the impossibility of the thing in itself than to human limitations; as regards his power, furthermore, he deemed him a singular or unique being. Moses did indeed concede that there are beings who (doubtless by the order and command of God) acted in God's name, that is, beings to whom God gave authority, right and power to govern nations and to provide and care for them. But he taught

39 that the being whom they were obliged to worship is the highest and

---

[12] Genesis 18.21.

supreme God, or (to use the Hebrew phrase) 'the God of gods', and therefore in the book of Exodus (15.11) he said, 'who among gods is like you, Jehovah?' and Jethro says (18.11), 'now I know that Jehovah is greater than all gods', that is, I am finally compelled to admit to Moses that Jehovah is greater than all other gods and unequalled in power. But one may doubt whether Moses believed that these beings acting in God's name were created by God; he said nothing, so far as we know, about their creation and origin.

He also taught that this being reduced the visible world from chaos to order (see Genesis 1.2), and sowed the seeds of nature, and therefore has supreme jurisdiction and supreme power over all things. Hence he (see Deuteronomy 10.14–15) chose the Hebrew nation for himself alone by this his supreme right and supreme power, together with a certain region of the earth (see Deuteronomy 4.19, 32.8–9), and left the other nations and territories to the care of other gods who had been put there by himself. That is why he was called the God of Israel and the God of Jerusalem (see 2 Chronicles 32.19), and the other gods were called the gods of other nations. This is also the reason why the Jews believed that the territory God had chosen for them required the exclusive worship of God, and one which was very different from the cults of other lands, and which could not in fact permit the worship of other gods proper to other parts. The peoples that the Assyrian king brought into the land of the Jews were believed to have been torn apart by lions because they were ignorant of the [correct] form of divine worship of that country (see 2 Kings 17.25, 26, etc.). According to Ibn Ezra,[13] Jacob told his children when setting out to find his native land, that they should prepare themselves for a new form of worship and lay aside alien gods, that is the worship of the gods of the land in which they then were (see Genesis 35.2, 3). Also when David informed Saul that he had been forced, by the latter's persecution of him, to live in exile from his native land, he said that he had been driven from God's inheritance and obliged to serve other gods (see 1 Samuel 26.19). Finally, Moses believed that this being, or God, had his home in the heavens (see Deuteronomy 33.27), a belief which was then very current among the gentiles.

[15]   If we now consider the revelations of Moses, we shall see that they were adapted to these beliefs. He believed that the nature of God was   40

---

[13] Abraham Ibn Ezra (1089–1164) of Tudela (northern Spain) was one of the major medieval Jewish Bible commentators.

subject to the emotions we have spoken of – mercy, kindness, etc. – and therefore God was revealed to him in conformity with this belief of his and under these attributes: see Exodus 34.6–7, which tells how God appeared to Moses, and verses 4 and 5 of the Ten Commandments. Again at 33.18 we are told how Moses beseeched God to allow him to see him; but as Moses, as already said, had formed no image of God in his mind, and God (as I have already shown) is only revealed to the prophets according to the tenor of their own imagination, God did not appear to him in an image. The reason for this, I say, is that it conflicted with Moses' own imagination; for other prophets – Isaiah, Ezekiel, Daniel, etc. – testify that they have seen God. It was also for this reason that God replied to Moses, 'you will not be able to see my face'. Because Moses believed that God was visible, i.e., that this implies no contradiction on the part of the divine nature – for otherwise he would not have made any such request – God adds, 'since no one shall see me and live', thus giving a reason which fits in with Moses' own belief. He does not say that it implies a contradiction on the part of the divine nature, as in fact it does, but rather that it cannot be done because of human incapacity. Afterwards, when God revealed to Moses that in worshipping a calf the Israelites had become like other nations, He says at 33.2–3 that He will send an angel (i.e. a being that would take care of the Israelites in place of the supreme being) and does not wish to be with them Himself. Consequently, Moses had nothing left to prove that the Israelites were dearer to God than other nations, since God also entrusted them to the care of other beings, or angels, as is clear from verse 16 of the same chapter. Finally, because He was believed to reside in the heavens, God was revealed as descending from heaven on to a mountain, and Moses even ascended the mountain to speak with God, which he would have had no need to do had he been able to imagine God readily everywhere.

The Hebrews knew almost nothing of God, despite His having been revealed to them, as they made very plain a few days later when they transferred to a calf the honour and worship due to Him, and identified this with the gods they believed had brought them out of Egypt. In fact it is hardly likely that people accustomed to Egyptian superstition, who were primitive and reduced to the most abject slavery, should have any sound conception of God, or that Moses taught them anything other than a way of life, and that not as a philosopher, so that they might eventually live well, from liberty of mind, but as a legislator obliging them to live well by

41

command of the law. For this reason the right way of living or the true life and worship and love of God was more servitude to them than true liberty and the grace and gift of God. For Moses commanded them to love God and observe his Law in order to show their gratitude for God's past blessings (liberation from Egyptian servitude, etc.); he also thoroughly frightens them with menaces should they would transgress these laws while at the same time promising many rewards if they would observe them. Thus he taught them in the same way as parents teach their children prior to the age of reason. That is why it is certain that they were ignorant of the excellence of virtue and true happiness. Jonah considered fleeing from the sight of God, which seems to show that he too believed that God had given the care of other lands, beyond Judea, to other powers which he had however established himself.

[16] No one in the Old Testament is regarded as speaking about God more rationally than Solomon, who surpassed all the men of his age in natural light [i.e. intellectual capacity], and for that reason he also thought himself to be above the Law (for the Law was delivered only to those who lack reason and the lessons of natural understanding). He therefore paid little regard to any of the laws concerning the king which consist principally of three (see Deut. 17.16–17), and openly violated them. In this, however, he did wrong and behaved unworthily of a philosopher (that is, by indulging in luxury). He taught that all the goods of fortune are vain for mortals (see Ecclesiastes), that men possess nothing which is superior to their intellect, and can suffer no greater punishment than stupidity (see Proverbs 16.22).

[17] But let us return to the prophets, whose differing opinions we have also undertaken to examine. The rabbis who handed down to us the books of the prophets (the only ones now extant) found the opinions of Ezekiel to be so much in conflict with those of Moses (as we are told in the treatise *Shabbat* chapter 1, folio 13, page 2)[14] that they almost decided not to admit that book among the canonical books, and would have completely suppressed it if a certain Hananiah had not taken it upon himself to explain it. They say he did this with great industry and zeal (as our source tells us), but how he proceeded is not altogether clear. Did he 42 write a commentary which happens to have perished, or had he the

---

[14] In the Babylonian Talmud.

audacity to change the actual words and statements of Ezekiel and embellish them at his own discretion? Whatever the case, chapter 16 does not seem to agree with Exodus 34.7 or Jeremiah 32.18, etc.

[18] Samuel believed that God never repented of any decree he had once made (see 1 Samuel 15.29), for even when Saul regretted his offence and was willing to adore God and seek forgiveness from him, Samuel said that God would not change his decree against him. The opposite was revealed to Jeremiah (see 18. 8–10), that God does repent of his decree, whether he has decreed something good or something bad for a people, if, after giving his sentence, they also change for better or for worse. Joel however taught that God repents only of something bad (see 2.13.). Finally, from Genesis 4.7 it plainly emerges that a man can overcome temptations to do wrong and can behave well; for Cain is told so, though it is evident, from Scripture itself and from Josephus, that Cain himself never overcame them. The same thing is also clearly indicated by the chapter of Jeremiah just cited; for he said that God repents of any decree he has made for men's good or ill, if they are willing to change their behaviour and way of life. Paul on the other hand teaches nothing more plainly than that men have no power over the temptations of the flesh except by the calling and grace of God alone. See the Epistle to the Romans 9.10ff., and note that in 3.5 and 6.19, where he attributes justice to God, he corrects himself by saying that he is speaking there in human fashion and through the weakness of the flesh.

[19] Thus what we set out to prove is more than adequately established, namely that God adapted his revelations to the understanding and opinions of the prophets, and that the prophets could be ignorant of matters of purely philosophical reasoning that are not concerned with charity and how to live; and indeed they really were ignorant in this respect and held contradictory views. Hence knowledge about natural and spiritual matters is by no means to be sought from them. We therefore conclude that we are not required to believe the prophets in anything beyond what constitutes the end and substance of revelation; for the rest, everyone is free to believe as he pleases. For example, the revelation of Cain only teaches us that God admonished Cain to lead a true life; that is the only aim and substance of the revelation; it is not intended to teach freedom of the will or other philosophical matters. Hence,

43

although the words and reasonings of that admonition very clearly entail freedom of the will, we are nevertheless permitted to adopt a contrary opinion, since those words and reasons were merely adapted to Cain's understanding. Similarly, the revelation of Micaiah merely teaches that God revealed to Micaiah the true outcome of the struggle between Ahab and Aram, and therefore this is all we are obliged to believe; whatever else is contained in this revelation we need take no notice of – whether concerning the true and false spirit of God and the army of heaven standing on either side of God, or the other details of the revelation; and thus everyone is free to make his own judgment of them as seems most acceptable to his own reason. The same should be said about the reasoning by which God reveals to Job his power over all things (if indeed it is true that they were revealed to Job, and that the author is intending to narrate a history, and not, as some think, to elaborate his own ideas). Being accommodated to Job's understanding and meant merely to convince him, these reasons are not universal ones intended to convince everybody.

Nor should we think any differently about the reasons with which Christ convicts the Pharisees of obstinacy and ignorance and exhorts his disciples to the true life: for clearly, he adapted his arguments to the beliefs and principles of those individuals. For instance, when he said to the Pharisees (see Matthew 12.26), 'and if Satan casts out Satan, he is divided against himself; how then *will* his kingdom stand', he meant only to sway the Pharisees on the basis of their own notions and not to teach men that demons exist or that there is some sort of realm of demons. Equally, when he said to his disciples (Matthew 18.10), 'See that you do not despise one of these little ones, for I say to you that their angels in heaven', etc., the only thing he intends to teach is that they should not be proud and should not despise anyone, but not the other things contained in his arguments, which he only makes use of to better convince his disciples of the main point. Precisely the same, finally, should be said about the arguments and signs of the Apostles about which I need not speak any further. If I had to enumerate all the passages in Scripture that are adapted to [the notions of] particular persons or to the level of their understanding, and which cannot be defended as divine doctrine without 44 great prejudice to philosophy, I would stray far from the brevity I aim at. It suffices therefore to cite just a few, general instances, and leave the curious reader to ponder other instances for himself.

[20]   This discussion of prophets and prophecy is highly relevant to the purpose which I have in view, namely to separate philosophy from theology. But now that I have entered in a general way on the subject, it is best to inquire at this point whether the prophetic gift was peculiar only to the Hebrews or common to all nations, and what we are to think of the 'vocation' of the Hebrews. About all this, see the following chapter.

CHAPTER 3

On the vocation of the Hebrews, and whether the prophetic gift was peculiar to them

[1] True joy and happiness lie in the simple enjoyment of what is good and not in the kind of false pride that enjoys happiness because others are excluded from it. Anyone who thinks that he is happy because his situation is better than other people's or because he is happier and more fortunate than they, knows nothing of true happiness and joy, and the pleasure he derives from his attitude is either plain silly or spiteful and malicious. For example, a person's true joy and felicity lie solely in his wisdom and knowledge of truth, not in being wiser than others or in others' being without knowledge of truth, since this does not increase his own wisdom which is his true felicity. Anyone therefore who takes pleasure in that way is enjoying another's misfortune, and to that extent is envious and malign, and does not know true wisdom or the peace of the true life.

When therefore Scripture states that God chose the Hebrews for himself above other nations (see Deuteronomy 10.15) so as to encourage them to obey the law, and is near to them and not to others (Deuteronomy 4.4–7), and has laid down good laws solely for them and not for others (Deuteronomy 4.2), and has made himself known to them alone, in preference to others (see Deuteronomy 4.32), and so on, Scripture is merely speaking according to their understanding. As we showed in the last chapter, and as Moses also testifies (see Deuteronomy 9.6–7), they did 45 not know true happiness. They would certainly have been no less felicitous if God had called all men equally to salvation; and God would not be less gracious to them for being equally good to others. Their laws would not have been less just, nor they themselves less wise, even if those laws

43

had been prescribed to all men. Their miracles would not display the power of God any less, if they had also been performed for other nations; nor would the Hebrews be less obliged to worship God, had he equally bestowed these gifts on all men. God's remark to Solomon (see 1 Kings 3.12) that no one who came after him would be as wise as he is, seems to be merely an expression with which to stress his outstanding wisdom. In any case, one cannot believe that God promised him that he would not give as much happiness to anyone else after him, in order to make Solomon happier. For this would not in any way enhance Solomon's understanding, and had God said he would give the same wisdom to everybody, that wise king would not have shown less gratitude to God for so great a gift.

[2]   Even so, though we say that Moses in the passages just cited from the Pentateuch spoke according to the understanding of the Hebrews, we do not mean to deny that God prescribed the laws of the Pentateuch to them alone or that he spoke only to them or that the Hebrews saw wonders that occurred to no other nation. We mean rather that Moses desired to teach the Hebrews in such a manner and inculcate into them such principles as would attach them more closely to the worship of God on the basis of their childish understanding. We also wanted to show that the Hebrews excelled other nations neither in knowledge nor piety but in something quite different, or (to speak in terms of Scripture, according to their understanding) that the Hebrews were chosen above others by God not, despite their being frequently admonished, with a view to the true life and elevated conceptions but rather for something completely different. What this was, I will show here directly.

[3]   But before I begin, I want to explain in a few words what I mean in what follows by 'God's direction', by 'God's external and internal help', by 'divine election', and finally what I mean by 'fortune'. By 'God's direction', I mean the fixed and unalterable order of nature or the interconnectedness of [all] natural things. We have shown above, and have previously demonstrated elsewhere,[1] that the universal laws of nature according to which all things happen and are determined, are nothing other than the eternal

---

[1] I.e., in the *Cogitata metaphysica*, the 47-page text published by Spinoza, under his own name, as a supplement to his geometrical exposition of the principles of Descartes' philosophy, entitled *Renati Des Cartes, Principiorum philosophiae pars I & II, more geometrico demonstrata* (Amsterdam, 1663).

decrees of God and always involve truth and necessity. Whether therefore we say that all things happen according to the laws of nature, or are ordained by the edict and direction of God, we are saying the same thing. Likewise, as the power of all natural things together is nothing other than the very power of God by which alone all things happen, it follows that whatever a man, who is also part of nature, does for himself in order to preserve his being, or whatever nature offers him without any action on his part, is all given to him by divine power alone, acting either through human nature or through things external to human nature. Whatever therefore human nature can supply from its own resources to preserve man's own being, we may rightly call the 'internal assistance of God', and whatever proves useful to man from the power of external causes, that we may properly term the 'external assistance of God'.

We can readily conclude from this what we are to understand by 'God's election'. For given that nobody does anything except by the pre-determined order of nature, that is, by the eternal decree and direction of God, it follows that no one chooses any way of life for himself nor brings anything about, except via the particular summons of God, who chose this man in preference to others for this task or that way of life. Finally, by 'fortune' I understand nothing other than the direction of God inasmuch as he governs human affairs through external and unforeseen causes.

[4]   After these preliminaries let us return to our theme in order to see why it was that the Hebrew nation was said to be chosen by God above others. To show this, I proceed as follows.

[5]   All things which we honestly desire may be reduced to three principal categories:

(i)   to understand things through their primary causes
(ii)   to control the passions, that is to acquire the habit of virtue
(iii) and, lastly, to live securely and in good health.

The means which lead directly to the attainment of the first and second goals and which may be considered as their immediate and efficient causes, are to be found in human nature itself, so that their attainment depends chiefly on our own capabilities, that is, on the laws of human nature alone. Accordingly, it may be categorically asserted that these gifts

47 were never peculiar to any one nation but were always common to the entire human race, unless we want to delude ourselves that once upon a time nature created different species of men. The factors conducing to safe living and conserving the body, on the other hand, lie chiefly in external things and are consequently called gifts of fortune because they depend mostly upon the direction of external causes of which we are ignorant. Hence, in this respect, a foolish person is almost as happy or unhappy as a wise person.

Even so, human intervention and vigilance can do much to help us live in safety and to avoid injury from other people and from animals. For this purpose, reason and experience have taught us no surer means than to establish a society with fixed laws, to occupy a determinate region of our earth and to bring everyone's resources into one body, if we may call it that, the body of a society. But to establish and conserve a society, much intelligence and vigilance is required. Therefore that society will be safer, more stable and less vulnerable to fortune, which is for the most part founded and directed by wise and vigilant men. On the other hand, a society that consists of men of limited intelligence depends for the most part on fortune and is less stable. If in spite of this it has proved to be lasting, this will be due, not to its own policies, but to someone else's. Indeed, if it has overcome great dangers and its affairs have prospered, it can do no other than admire and adore God's government (that is, in so far as God acts through hidden external causes and not as He acts through human nature and the human mind). For everything that happened to that society was beyond expectation and beyond belief and this can truly be considered a miracle.

[6]   Hence, nations are distinguished one from another only by the [form of] society and laws in which they live and under which they are governed. The Hebrew people, accordingly, was chosen by God above others not for its understanding or for its qualities of mind, but owing to the form of its society and the good fortune, over so many years, with which it shaped and preserved its state. This is also fully evident from the Bible itself. Anyone who peruses it even superficially will clearly see that the Hebrews excelled other peoples in merely one thing: they conducted the affairs that affected their security of life successfully and overcame great dangers, and did so, on the whole, solely through God's external assistance. In other respects,

48 they were on the same footing as the rest of the nations, and God favoured all equally.

For as regards comprehending reality, it is clear (as we showed in the last chapter) that they had entirely commonplace notions of God and nature, and thus they were not chosen by God, above others, for their understanding. Nor was it for their virtue or [attainment of] the true life; for in this respect too they were on the same footing as other nations and very few were chosen. Their election and vocation therefore lay only in the success and the prosperity at that time of their commonwealth. Nor do we see that God promised anything other than this to the patriarchs[3] or their successors. In fact nothing else is promised in the Bible in return for their obedience but the continued prosperity of their state and the other good things of this life; while, conversely, for disobedience and the breaking of the covenant, they are threatened with the ruin of their polity and severe hardship. And no wonder; for the aim of all society and every state (as is clear from what we have just said and will show more fully later) is [for men] to live securely and satisfyingly, and a state cannot survive except by means of laws that bind every individual. If all the members of a society disregard the laws, they will, by that very action, dissolve society and destroy the state. Therefore nothing more could be promised to the society of the Hebrews in return for their constant observance of the laws than security of life and its advantages. On the other hand no surer retribution could be threatened for their disobedience than the destruction of the state and the bad consequences that generally follow, besides the special sufferings they would undergo resulting from the ruin of their own commonwealth, though there is no need to discuss this at greater length here. I would add merely that the laws of the Old Testament too were revealed and prescribed only to the Jews; for since God chose them alone to form a particular commonwealth and state, they had necessarily to have unique laws as well.

[7] In my opinion, it is not entirely clear whether God also gave specific laws to other nations and revealed himself to their legislators in a prophetic manner (i.e., under the attributes in which they were accustomed to imagine God). But it is evident from Scripture, at least, that other nations also acquired their own particular laws and government via God's external direction. To demonstrate this, I will cite just two passages. At Genesis 14.18–20 we are told that Melchizedek was king of Jerusalem and priest of

---

[2] Spinoza's footnote: see Annotation 4.   [3] Spinoza's footnote: see Annotation 5.

49   the most high God, and that he blessed Abraham, as was the right of a priest (see Numbers 6.23), and that Abraham, the beloved of God, gave a tenth part of all his booty to this priest of God. All this sufficiently shows that, before God founded the Israelite nation, he had appointed kings and priests in Jerusalem and given them rites and laws; although as I said, it is not wholly clear whether he did so by means of prophecy. In any case, I am convinced that while Abraham lived there he lived religiously, according to those laws: for he received no rites specifically from God, but nevertheless it is stated in Genesis 26.5 that Abraham observed the cult, precepts, practices and laws of God, and this must certainly be construed as meaning the cult, precepts, practices and laws of king Melchizedeck. Malachi 1.10–11 reproaches the Jews in these terms: 'Who is there among you to close the doors' (i.e. of the Temple) 'lest the fire be placed in vain on my altar? I take no delight in you, etc. . . . for from the rising of the sun even to its setting, my name is great among the nations, and everywhere incense is brought to me, and a pure offering; for my name is great among the nations, says the God of hosts'. If we do not want to do violence to these words, which can only refer to Malachi's own time, we must surely grant that Malachi provides very clear evidence that the Jews in his time were no more beloved of God than other peoples; indeed, that God had made himself more conspicuous by miracles to other nations than to the Jews who, without [the aid of] miracles, had at that time partly recovered their state; and that the other peoples had rites and ceremonies which made them acceptable to God.

But I leave all this aside, for it suffices for my purposes to show that the election of the Jews concerned only their material welfare at that time and their freedom, or independent state, and the manner and means by which they acquired it. It therefore also concerned their laws, in so far as these were essential to stabilizing that particular polity; and finally the way in which these laws were revealed. But as regards everything else, including those things in which the true happiness of man consists, they were on the same footing as other men.

When therefore it is said in the Bible (see Deuteronomy 4.7) that no 50   people has their gods 'so near to them' as the Jews have God, this is to be understood only with regard to their state and only in that period in which so many miracles took place among them, etc. For as regards intellect and virtue, i.e., as regards happiness, as we have already said and proven by reason itself, God is equally favourable to all, as is indeed evident from

Scripture itself. For the Psalmist says (Psalm 145.8), 'God is near to all those who call upon him, to all who call upon him in truth'. Likewise at 145.9, 'God is kind to all men, and his mercy is to all things that he has made'. At Psalm 33.15 it is plainly stated that God gave the same intellect to all men, in these words, 'who forms their heart in the same manner'. For the heart was believed by the Hebrews to be the seat of the soul and of the intellect, as I suppose is well enough known to everyone. Again it is clear from Job 29.28.[4] that God prescribed this law to the whole human race, to fear God and abstain from wrongdoing, that is, to do good, and that is why Job, though a gentile, was the most acceptable of all men to God, since he surpassed all others in piety and religion.[5] Finally from Jonah 4.2 it is abundantly evident that it is not only to the Jews but to all men that God is well-disposed, merciful, long-suffering, full of kindness and unwilling to inflict suffering;[6] for Jonah says: 'That was precisely why I decided to flee to Tarshish before, because I knew' (i.e., from the words of Moses contained in Exodus 34.6) 'that you were a propitious God, merciful', etc., and therefore would forgive the gentiles of Nineveh.

[8]   We conclude therefore (since God is well-disposed to all men and the Hebrews were chosen only by reason of their society and state) that no individual Jew considered apart from his society and state possesses any gift from God beyond what other men have, nor is there any difference between him and a gentile.

Since therefore it is true that God is equally kind, merciful, etc., to all men and that the duty of the prophet was not so much to prescribe the particular laws of his country as to teach true virtue and to admonish men concerning it, there is no doubt that all nations have had prophets, and that the prophetic gift was not peculiar to the Jews. Profane as well as sacred histories likewise provide evidence of this; and while from the sacred narratives of the Old Testament it is not evident that other nations had as many prophets as the Hebrews, or that any gentile prophet was expressly sent by God to the nations, this is of no consequence, for the 51

---

[4] Job 28.28 in RSV.
[5] Note that here as in many other places Spinoza redefines 'religion' to mean obedience to the universal moral law and not adherence to any particular confession, faith or doctrine.
[6] 'Deum ... paenitentem mali': see Jonah 3.10 'When God saw what they did, how they turned from their evil way, *God repented of the evil which he had said he would do to them*; and he did not do it' (RSV). Spinoza explains this characteristic of God from scripture at ch. 2, para 18 (see p.40).

Hebrews only cared to write about their own affairs and not those of other nations. Hence it suffices to find in the Old Testament that gentile and uncircumcised men like Noah, Enoch, Abimelech, Balaam, and so on, prophesied, and that Hebrew prophets were sent by God to many other peoples besides their own. For Ezekiel prophesied to all the then known nations, Jonah prophesied especially to the Ninevites, and Obadiah, so far as we know, prophesied only to the Idumeans. Isaiah predicts and bewails not only the calamities of the Jews but also those of other peoples, and celebrates their restoration. For he says at 16.9, 'therefore will I lament Jazer with weeping', and at chapter 19 he predicts first the disasters of the Egyptians and then their restoration (see 19, 20, 21, 25 of the same chapter). He says that God will send a saviour to them who will liberate them; God will become known to them; the Egyptians will worship the Lord with sacrifices and offerings; and he ends by calling this nation 'the blessed Egyptian people of God': all this is surely well worth noting. Finally Jeremiah is called the prophet not of the Hebrew people alone but also of the nations and without any reservation (see 1.5). He weeps copiously in predicting disasters among the peoples and foretells their restoration. He says of the Moabites (48.31), 'therefore I will wail for Moab and cry for the whole of Moab', etc., and at verse 36 he says, 'therefore my heart beats like a drum for Moab', and finally he predicts their restoration, as well as the restoration of the Egyptians, the Ammonites and the Elamites. Thus, there is no doubt that other peoples also had their prophets, as the Jews had, and that they prophesied both to them and to the Jews.

[9]   Although the Bible cites only Balaam as someone to whom the future affairs of the Jews and other nations were revealed, one must not suppose that Balaam prophesied merely on that sole occasion. Rather it is quite clear from the narrative itself that he had become famous for prophecy and other divine gifts long before. For when Balak commands that he be summoned, 52   he says (Numbers 22.6), 'since I know that he whom you bless is blessed and he whom you curse is cursed'; thus he had the same gift that God had bestowed upon Abraham (see Genesis 12.3). Then Balaam, as a man who is accustomed to prophesy, tells the envoys to wait for him until the will of God is revealed to him. When he was prophesying, i.e. when he was revealing the true mind of God, he was accustomed to say of himself: 'the speech of one who hears the words of God and who knows the knowledge' (or mind and foreknowledge) 'of the Most High, who sees a vision of the Almighty, falling

down but having his eyes uncovered'.[7] Finally, after he blessed the Hebrews by the command of God (evidently as he was accustomed to do), he begins to prophesy to other nations and to predict their future affairs.

All this more than adequately shows that he had always been a prophet, and that he prophesied quite frequently, and (a further point) possessed the thing that particularly rendered prophets certain of the truth of prophecy which is a mind disposed to what is right and good alone. For he did not bless whomever he chose to bless or curse whomever he chose to curse, as Balak thought, but only those whom God wished should be blessed or cursed. That is why he said to Balak: 'Even though Balak should give me as much silver and gold as would fill his house, I shall not be able to transgress the command of God, to do good or evil of my own will; what God will speak, I will speak'. As for the fact that God was angry with him while he was on his journey, that happened also to Moses when he was setting out for Egypt at the command of God (see Exodus 4.24). As regards his acceptance of money for prophesying, Samuel did the same (see 1 Samuel 9.7–8), and if he sinned in anything (on which see the Second Epistle of Peter, 2.15–16 and Jude, verse 11), 'no one is so good that he always behaves well and never sins' (see Ecclesiastes 7.20). Surely his prayers must always have had much influence with God, and his power to curse was certainly very great, since we find so often in Scripture as a testimony to God's great mercy towards the Israelites, that He refused to heed Balaam and converted his curse to a blessing (see Deuteronomy 23.6, Joshua 24.10, Nehemiah 13.2).

Without a doubt, therefore, he was most agreeable to God; for the prayers and curses of the impious move God not at all. Thus he was a true prophet, yet he is called by Joshua (13.22) a *diviner* or *augur*. Hence it is certain that this term too can have a positive meaning, and those whom the gentiles called diviners and soothsayers were true prophets, and it is only false diviners whom the Bible denounces and condemns in so many passages. For these deceived the gentiles in the same way as false prophets deceived the Jews, as is clear enough from other passages of Scripture. Thus we conclude that the prophetic gift was not peculiar to the Jews but was common to all peoples.

[10]   The Pharisees however vehemently insist that this divine gift was peculiar to their own nation, and that other peoples (what will superstition

---

[7] Numbers 24.4.

not concoct?) predicted the future via some kind of diabolic power. The passage which they chiefly cite from the Old Testament to lend authority to their opinion is the text at Exodus 33.16, where Moses says to God: 'how shall it be known that I and your people have found favour in your eyes? It will surely be when you go with us, and I and your people are separated from every people which is on the face of the earth'. From this passage, I say, they want to infer that Moses was asking God to be with the Jews and to reveal himself prophetically to them and, further, not to grant this favour to any other nation.

It is of course ridiculous that Moses would begrudge the presence of God to the nations, or that he would dare request such a thing of God. The reality is that after Moses got to know the obstinate temper and spirit of his people, he saw clearly that they were not able do what they had undertaken to do, without great miracles, and special external from help God, and would inevitably perish without such assistance. He therefore sought this particular external help from God, so that it might be clear that God wished them to be preserved. This is what he says (34.9): 'if I have found favour in your eyes, Lord, let the Lord, I pray, go among us since this people is obstinate', etc. Thus the reason why he sought special external help from God, was because his people was obstinate, and what makes it still plainer that Moses sought nothing other than this particular external aid from God is God's own answer. God immediately replies (verse 10 of the same chapter): 'Behold, I make a covenant that I will do before your whole people marvels which have not been done in all the earth nor in all the nations', etc. Hence what Moses is discussing here is simply the election of the Hebrews, as I have explained it, and he was not requesting anything else of God.

However, I find another text, in the Epistle of Paul to the Romans, which weighs still more with me, namely 3.1–2, where Paul appears to teach something different from what we are asserting here. He asks: 'What therefore is the preeminence of the Jew? Or what is the advantage of circumcision? Much in every way; for it is of the first importance that the pronouncements of God were entrusted to them.' But if we consider the principal doctrine Paul is trying to teach here, we shall find that it does not conflict with our view at all; on the contrary, he is saying the same thing. For at verse 29 of this chapter he affirms that God is the God of the Jews and of the gentiles, and at 2.25–6 he says: 'if the circumcised break the law, their circumcision will become uncircumcision, and on the other hand if the uncircumcised obey the command of the law, their uncircumcision is regarded as circumcision'. Again 3.9 and 4.15 state that all men equally, that is, both Jews and gentiles, were under sin, but that there is no sin without commandment and law. It is entirely evident from this that the law has been revealed to everyone without exception (as we also proved above from Job 28.28), that all men have lived under it, and that this law is the law which aims at true virtue alone, and is not the law which is shaped by the form and constitution of one particular state and adapted to the character of a single people. Finally, Paul concludes that God is the God of all nations, that is, God is equally well-disposed to all, and all men are equally under law and sin, and that is why God sent his Christ to all nations, to free all men equally from the servitude of the law, so that they would no longer live good lives because the law so commanded, but from a fixed conviction of the mind.

Hence Paul teaches exactly what we want to affirm. When he says that 'the pronouncements of God were entrusted only to the Jews', he must mean one of two things. He may mean that the laws were entrusted in writing only to the Jews and given to the rest of the nations by revelation and intuition alone. Or he may be adapting his reply to the understanding and beliefs of the Jews at that point in time (since he is striving to refute an objection that could only have come from Jews). For in order to proclaim what he had partly seen for himself and partly heard from others, he was prepared to be a Greek with the Greeks and a Jew with the Jews.[8]

[11]   It remains only to respond to some arguments by which certain people seek to persuade themselves that the election of the Jews was not 55 temporal and applicable only to their commonwealth, but eternal. We see (they say) that, after the loss of their state, the Jews were scattered everywhere for so many years and separated from all nations, and yet they still survived, as no other nation has. The sacred books, we see also, seem to teach in many places that God has chosen the Jews for himself for ever, and therefore although they have lost their state, they still remain the chosen of God. The passages which they think show this eternal election most clearly are: (1) Jeremiah 31.36, where the prophet testifies that the seed of Israel will remain the people of God for ever and goes so far as to compare them with the fixed order of the heavens and of nature; (2) Ezekiel 20.32ff.,

---

[8] See 1 Corinthians 9.19–23.

which apparently means that although the Jews give every sign of abandoning the worship of God, he nevertheless will gather them together again from the many regions to which they have been scattered, and lead them to a place which is empty of peoples, just as he had led their parents to the empty places of Egypt, and in the end, after separating them from the rebels and the backsliders, he will bring them from there to his holy mountain, where the whole household of Israel will worship him.

Other passages besides these are frequently cited, especially by the Pharisees [i.e. the rabbis], but I think that responding to these two will adequately cover them all. I shall do it without much difficulty by demonstrating from the Bible itself that God did not choose the Hebrews for ever, but only on the same condition on which he chose the Canaanites before them. They too, as we showed above, had priests who worshipped God zealously yet God rejected them because of their luxury and idleness and bad behaviour. Moses warns the Israelites (Leviticus 18.27–8) not to be polluted with incest like the Canaanites, lest the land spit them out as it had spat out the nations that inhabited those places before them. And at Deuteronomy 8.19–20 he threatens destruction in very explicit words saying, 'I attest today that you will utterly perish; like the nations which the Lord caused to perish before you, so will you perish'. Other things to this effect are found in the Law, which expressly indicate that God did not elect the Hebrew nation absolutely and for ever.

If therefore the prophets announced to them a new and eternal covenant of God, a covenant of knowledge, love and grace, it is easy to show that it was promised only to the pious. For in the same chapter of Ezekiel which we have just cited, it is expressly stated that God will separate from them the rebels and backsliders, and at Zephaniah 3.12–13 that God will take the arrogant from their midst and conserve the poor. Since this election is made solely on the basis of true virtue, it is unthinkable that it has been promised only to pious Jews, to the exclusion of other pious people. Rather we must accept that the true gentile prophets, who, as we have shown, existed in all nations, also promised the same election to the faithful of their peoples and offered them its consolation. That this eternal covenant of God, the covenant of knowledge and of love, is universal, is entirely evident also from Zephaniah 3.10–11. On this issue then we can accept no difference between Jews and gentiles; and therefore there is no election which is peculiar to the Jews except the one which we have already explained.

54

As for the fact that when the prophets speak of election on the basis of virtue alone, they also say a good deal about sacrifices and other Temple ceremonies and about rebuilding the city, they were attempting, in the manner and nature of prophecy, to explain spiritual things under such figures, so that they might at the same time indicate to the Jews, whose prophets they were, the restoration of the commonwealth and the Temple, to be expected in the time of Cyrus.

[12] Thus the Jews today have absolutely nothing that they can attribute to themselves but not to other peoples. As for their being dispersed and stateless for so many years, it is not at all surprising that, after separating themselves from all the nations in this way, they brought the resentment of all men upon themselves, not only because of their external rites which are contrary to the rites of other nations, but also by the sign of circumcision which they zealously maintain. But experience has shown that it is the resentment of the gentiles to a large extent that preserves them. When the king of Spain at one time compelled the Jews to accept the religion of his kingdom or go into exile, a large number of Jews converted to the Catholic faith. All those who accepted it were granted the privileges of native Spaniards and were considered worthy of all positions of dignity. Hence they immediately integrated with the Spanish, so that in a short time there were no remnants of them left and no memory of them. But quite the opposite happened to those whom the king of Portugal compelled to convert to the religion of his kingdom.[9] For though they submitted to this faith, they continued to live apart from all men, doubtless because he declared them unworthy of all higher positions.

Furthermore, I think that the sign of circumcision has such great importance as almost to persuade me that this thing alone will preserve their nation for ever, and in fact, were it not that the principles of their religion weaken their courage, I would believe unreservedly that at some time, given an opportunity, since all things are changeable, they might re-establish their state, and God will choose them again. We also have an excellent example of this among the Chinese, who likewise zealously retain a kind of topknot on their heads, by which they distinguish themselves from all other men, and have preserved themselves in this distinctive

57

---

[9] A large proportion of the Jews expelled from Spain in 1492, estimated at around 40,000, migrated to Portugal where, however, in 1497 they were forcibly baptized, en masse, on the orders of the Portuguese king.

manner for many thousands of years, so that they far surpass all nations in antiquity. Nor have they always had their own state. They have lost it and then recovered it, and without doubt will recover it again, when the Tartars become demoralized through luxury and idleness.

[13]   A last point: if anyone wants to insist that the Jews have been chosen for this or any other reason by God for ever, I will not argue with him, if he will accept that this election, whether temporal or eternal, in so far as it is merely peculiar to the Jews, regards only their polity and their material interests (since this is all that can distinguish one nation from another), and that no people is distinguished from another with regard to understanding and true virtue, and hence in these spheres God does not choose one nation above any other.

CHAPTER 4

On the divine law

[1] The word law (*lex*) in an absolute sense signifies that, in accordance with which, each individual thing, or all things, or all things of the same kind, behave in one and the same fixed and determined way, depending upon either natural necessity or a human decision. A law that depends upon natural necessity is one that necessarily follows from the very nature or definition of a thing. A law that depends upon a human decision, which is more properly called a decree (*jus*), is one that men prescribe to themselves and to others in order to achieve a better and safer life, or for other reasons. For example, the fact that when one body strikes a smaller body, it only loses as much of its own motion as it communicates to the other, is a universal law of all bodies which follows from natural necessity. So too the fact that when a man recalls one thing he immediately remembers another which is similar or which he had seen along with the first thing, is a law which necessarily follows from human nature. 58

But the fact that men give up their right which they receive from nature, or are compelled to give it up, and commit themselves to a particular rule of life depends on human decision. And while I entirely agree that all things are determined by the universal laws of nature to exist and act in a fixed and determined manner, I insist that these decrees depend on willed human decision, and I do so for two reasons. Firstly, in so far as man is a part of nature, he is also a part of nature's power. Hence whatever follows from the necessity of human nature (that is, from nature itself in so far as we understand it to be expressly determined by human nature) results also, albeit necessarily, from the capacity of men. Hence the decreeing of these laws may quite correctly be said to follow from human will, because this depends especially on the power of the human mind in the sense that our mind, so far as it perceives what is true or false, can very clearly be conceived without these decrees, but not without the necessary law of nature as we have just defined it. Secondly, I have said that these laws depend upon human decisions because we ought to define and explain things by their proximate causes, and a general consideration of necessity and the connectedness of causes cannot help us at all in the formation and ordering of particular things. We are also ignorant of the actual coordination and connectedness of things, that is, of how things are really ordered and connected, and therefore it is better and indeed necessary for the conduct of life, to regard things as possible. So much about law considered in an absolute sense.

[2]   It seems to be only by a metaphor that the word law (*lex*) is applied to natural things. What is commonly meant by a law is a command which men may or may not follow, since a law constrains human powers within certain limits which they naturally exceed, and does not command anything beyond their scope. Law therefore seems to have to be defined more precisely as 'a rule for living which a man prescribes to himself or others for some purpose'. But the real purpose of laws is normally evident only to a few; most people are more or less incapable of grasping it, and hardly live by reason at all. Hence legislators have wisely contrived (in order to constrain all men equally) another purpose very different from the one which necessarily follows from the nature of laws. They promise to those who keep the laws things that the common people most desire, and threaten those who violate them with what they most fear. In this way they have tried to restrain the common people like a horse with a bridle, so far as it can be done. This is why the essence of law is taken to be a rule of life prescribed to men by the command of another; and consequently those who obey the laws are said to live under law and are regarded as subjects of it.

Truly he who gives other men what is due to them because he fears the gallows, is acting at the behest of another man and under a threat of suffering harm, and cannot be called just; but he who gives other men what is due to them because he knows the true rationale of laws and understands their necessity, is acting steadfastly and at his own and not another's command, and therefore is deservedly called just. I think this is what Paul meant to point out when he said that those who lived under the law could not be justified by the law.[1] For justice as it is commonly defined, is

---

[1] Epistle to the Romans 3.20.

'a constant and perpetual will to assign to each man his due',[2] and this is why the Proverbs of Solomon 21.15 says that the righteous man is happy when judgment comes but the unjust are afraid.

[3]   Since law, accordingly, is nothing other than a rule for living which men prescribe to themselves or to others for a purpose, it seems it has to be divided into human and divine. By human law I mean a rule for living whose only purpose is to protect life and preserve the country. By divine law I mean the law which looks only to the supreme good, that is, to the true knowledge and love of God. The reason why I call this law divine is because of the nature of the supreme good, which I will now explain here as briefly and clearly as I can.

[4]   Since the best part of us is our understanding, it is certain that, if we truly want to seek our own interest, we should try above all things to perfect it as much as possible; for our highest good should consist in its perfection. Furthermore, since all our knowledge and the certainty which truly takes away all doubt depends on a knowledge of God alone, and since without God nothing can exist or be conceived, and since we are in doubt about everything as long as we have no clear and distinct idea of God, it 60 follows that our highest good and perfection depends on a knowledge of God alone, etc. Again, since nothing can exist or be conceived without God, it is certain that every single thing in nature involves and expresses the conception of God as far as its essence and perfection allows, and accordingly the more we come to understand natural things, the greater and more perfect the knowledge of God we acquire. Further (since knowledge of an effect through a cause is simply to know some property of the cause) the more we learn about natural things, the more perfectly we come to know the essence of God (which is the cause of all things); and thus all our knowledge, that is, our highest good, not only depends on a knowledge of God but consists in it altogether. This also follows from the fact that a man is more perfect (and the opposite) according to the nature and perfection of what he loves above all other things; and therefore that man is necessarily most perfect and most participates in the highest happiness who most loves and most enjoys, above all other things, the intellectual knowledge of God, who is the most perfect being.

---

[2] Justinian, *Institutes* 1.1.

This then is what our highest good and happiness is, the knowledge and love of God. Therefore the means required by this end of all human actions, which is God himself so far as his idea is in us, may be called the commands of God, because they are prescribed to us, as it were, by God himself so far as he exists in our minds, and therefore the rule of life which looks to this end is best called the divine law. It is for universal ethics to inquire what these means are and what is the rule of life which this goal requires, and how the foundations of the best state and the rules for living among men follow from it. Here I propose only to speak of the divine law in general.

[5] Since love of God is the highest felicity and happiness of man, his final end and the aim of all his actions, it follows that he alone observes the divine law who is concerned to love God not from fear of punishment nor love of something else, such as pleasure, fame etc., but from the single fact that he knows God, or that he knows that the knowledge and love of God is the highest good. The sum of the divine law therefore and its highest precept is to love God as the highest good, that is, as we have already said, not to love Him from fear of punishment or penalty, nor for love of some other thing by which we desire to be pleased. For the idea of God requires that God should be our highest good: i.e., that the knowledge and love of God is the ultimate end to which all our actions are to be directed. The carnal man however cannot understand this; it seems foolish to him because he has too meagre a knowledge of God, and he finds nothing in this highest good that he can touch or eat or that makes any impression on the flesh in which he takes so much pleasure, for knowledge of God consists in philosophical reasoning alone and pure thought. But those who know that they possess nothing more excellent than understanding and a sound mind, will certainly judge that thought and reasoning are the most solid realities.

We have now explained what the divine law chiefly consists in and what human laws are; for human laws are all those edicts that have a different goal, unless they have been sanctioned by divine revelation. For this too is a ground on which things are attributed to God (as we have shown above), and in this sense the Law of Moses, even though it is not universal but adapted solely to the temperament and preservation of one people, may nevertheless be called a law of God or divine law, since we believe that it was confirmed by prophetic light.

[6] If we now consider the character of the natural divine law, as we have just explained it, we shall see:

(1) that it is universal or common to all men, for we have deduced it from universal human nature, and

(2) that it does not require belief in any kind of historical narrative. Since the natural divine law is inferred from the consideration of human nature alone, it is certain that we can conceive it in Adam as much as in any other man, as much in a man who lives among his fellow human beings as in a man who leads a solitary life. Belief in a historical narrative, however reliable it may be, can give us no knowledge of God nor consequently love of God either. For love of God arises from knowledge of him; and knowledge of him has to be drawn from universal notions which are certain in themselves and well-known, and so it is by no means the case that belief in a historical narrative is a necessary requirement for us to reach our highest good. But although belief in such histories cannot give us a knowledge and love of God, we do not deny that reading them is very useful for the purposes of civil life. The more we observe and the better we understand the manners and conditions of men, which can best be learned from their actions, the more wisely shall we be able to dwell among them, and the better we shall be able to adapt our actions and our lives to their ways. 62

(3) We shall also see that the natural divine law does not require ceremonies. Ceremonies are actions which are indifferent in themselves and are called good only by convention or which represent some good as necessary to salvation, or actions (if you prefer) whose rationale is beyond human understanding. For the natural light of reason requires nothing that this light itself does not reach; it requires only what carries the clearest evidence of being a good or a means to our happiness. Things that are good only by command or tradition or because they are symbolic representations of some good, cannot improve our understanding; they are no more than shadows and cannot be counted among actions that are the product or fruit, so to speak, of mind and sound understanding. We need not demonstrate all this here at greater length.

(4) Finally, we see that the supreme reward of the divine law is to know the law itself, that is, to know God and to love him in true liberty with whole and constant minds; the penalty is lack of these things and enslavement to the flesh, or an inconstant and wavering mind.

[7] Having made these points, we must now ask: (1) whether by the natural light of reason we can conceive of God as a legislator or a prince who prescribes laws to men; (2) what holy Scripture teaches about the natural light of

reason and this natural law; (3) for what purpose ceremonies were originally instituted; and (4) what is the point of knowing the holy Scriptures and believing them? I shall discuss the first two questions in this chapter and the latter two in the next.

[8]   What we should think regarding the first question is readily deduced from the will of God, which is distinct from God's intellect only in relation to our reason; that is, God's will and God's understanding are in reality one and the same thing in themselves, and are only distinguished in relation to the thoughts which we form about God's intellect. For example, when we focus simply on the point that the nature of the triangle is contained in the divine nature from all eternity as an eternal truth, we say that God has the idea of a triangle or understands the nature of a triangle. But we may also focus on the point that the nature of the triangle is thus contained in the divine nature by the necessity of the divine nature alone and not from the necessity and essence of the triangle, and that since the essence and properties of the triangle too are conceived as eternal truths, their necessity depends only upon the necessity of the divine nature and understanding and not on the nature of the triangle; and in this case what we have called the understanding of God, we are now calling the will or decree of God. Therefore with respect to God, we are affirming one and the same thing when we say that God has decreed and willed from eternity that the three angles of a triangle be equal to two right angles, or that God understood this. From which it follows that God's affirmations or negations always contain an eternal necessity or truth.

[9]   If, for example, God said to Adam that he did not wish him to eat of 'the tree of the knowledge of good and evil',[3] it would entail a contradiction for Adam to be able to eat of it, and therefore it was impossible that Adam should eat of it; for that eternal decree must have contained an eternal necessity and truth. However since Scripture narrates that God gave this command to Adam and in spite of this Adam did eat of the tree, we must necessarily infer that God only revealed to Adam the bad effects that would necessarily befall him if he ate of that tree, but not the necessity whereby that bad consequence would follow. This is how it was that Adam perceived that revelation not as an eternal and necessary truth but rather

---

[3] Genesis 2:17.

as a ruling, that is, as a convention that gain or loss follows, not from the necessity and nature of the action done, but only from the pleasure and absolute command of the prince. Therefore that revelation was a law and God was a kind of legislator or prince exclusively with respect to Adam, and only because of the deficiency of his knowledge.

It is for the same reason too, namely deficiency of knowledge, that the Ten Commandments were law only for the Hebrews. Since they did not know the existence of God as an eternal truth, i.e., that God exists and that God alone is to be adored, they had to understand it as a decree. If God had spoken to them directly without the use of any physical means, they would have perceived this same thing not as an edict but as an eternal truth. What we say about the Israelites and about Adam, must also be said of all the prophets who issued laws in the name of God: they did not perceive the decrees of God adequately as eternal truths. 64

For example, it has even to be said of Moses himself that he grasped, either through revelation or from principles revealed to him, how the people of Israel could best be united in a certain part of the world and form an integrated society and establish a state, and he also saw how that people might best be compelled to obey. But he did not grasp, nor was it revealed to him, that this was the best way, nor that the desired aim would necessarily follow from the common obedience of the people in such a part of the world. Thus he perceived all these things not as eternal truths but as precepts and teachings, and prescribed them as decrees of God. That is why he imagined God as ruler, legislator, king, merciful, just, etc., despite the fact that all the latter are merely attributes of human nature and far removed from the divine nature.

[10]   I emphasize that these things must be said only about the prophets who gave laws in the name of God, but not about Christ. For concerning Christ, although he too appeared to issue laws in the name of God, one must see, that he [on the contrary] understood things truly and adequately. Christ was not so much a prophet as the mouth-piece of God. For, as we showed in chapter 1, God revealed certain things to the human race through the mind of Christ, as he had done previously by means of angels, i.e., by means of a created voice, visions, etc. So it would be equally irrational to think that God adapted his revelations to Christ's beliefs as that he had previously adapted his revelations to the beliefs of angels (i.e. to the beliefs of a created voice and of visions) in order to communicate his

revelations to the prophets. No thought could be more absurd, especially as Christ was not sent to teach the Jews alone but the whole of humanity. It was not enough therefore that his mind should be adapted to the beliefs of the Jews alone; it was necessary rather that his mind should be adapted to the views and general doctrines of the human race, that is, to principles that are universal and true. Undoubtedly, since God revealed himself to Christ or his soul directly and not, as with the prophets, via words and visions, we can draw no other conclusion than that Christ perceived or understood real things truly; for something is understood when it is grasped by the mind alone without words or visions.

65

Christ therefore understood revealed things truly and adequately. Hence if he sometimes prescribed them as laws, he did so because of the ignorance and obstinacy of the people. In this matter therefore he took God's place and adapted himself to the character of the people; consequently, although he spoke altogether more clearly than the rest of the prophets, he nevertheless still taught revealed things obscurely and in many cases by means of parables, especially when speaking to those to whom it had not yet been given to understand the kingdom of heaven (see Matthew 13:10, etc.). To those who *were* capable of learning about the heavenly mysteries, he undoubtedly did teach things as eternal truths and not as commandments. Hence he freed them from servitude to the law and yet in this way also confirmed and stabilized the law, inscribing it deeply in their hearts.

Paul too seems to indicate as much in certain passages, such as the Epistle to the Romans, 7.6 and 3.28, although he too prefers not to speak openly. Rather, as he puts it (3.5 and 6.19 of the same Epistle), he spoke 'in human terms', expressly admitting this when he calls God 'just'. Likewise, it is undoubtedly due to this 'weakness of the flesh' that he attributes pity, grace, anger etc. to God, adapting his words to the character of the common people or (as he himself puts it at 1 Corinthians 3.1–2) 'carnal men'. For at Romans 9.18 he absolutely teaches that God's anger and mercy depend not upon men's works but upon God's vocation alone, i.e., upon his will. He also says that no one is justified by the works of the law but by faith alone (see Romans 3.28), by which he certainly means nothing other than full mental assent. Finally he says that no one is blessed unless he has the mind of Christ in him (see Romans 8.9) whereby, undoubtedly, one may understand God's laws as eternal truths.

We conclude therefore that God is described as a legislator or a prince, and as just, merciful etc., only because of the limited understanding of the common people and their lack of knowledge, and that in reality God acts and governs all things from the necessity of his own nature and perfection alone, and his decrees and volitions are eternal truths and always involve necessity. This is the first point that I proposed to explain and prove.

[11] Now let us pass to the second point, running through Scripture, to see what it teaches about the natural light of reason and this divine 66 law. The first thing that strikes us is the history of the first man where it is narrated that God forbade Adam to eat of the fruit of 'the tree of the knowledge of good and evil',[4] which seems to mean that God instructed Adam to do good, and to seek it under the aspect of good and not as the opposite of what is bad, that is, to seek good for the love of good rather than from the fear of harm. For as we have already shown, he who does good from a true love and knowledge of good, acts freely and with a constant purpose, but he who does good from fear of suffering injury, is simply driven to avoid what is bad, like a slave, and lives at the command of another. Hence, this one prohibition laid by God on Adam entails the whole divine law and agrees fully with the dictate of the natural light of reason. It would not be difficult to explain the whole history, or parable, of the first man on this basis, but I prefer to let it go. I cannot be absolutely sure whether my explanation agrees with the intention of the writer, and many people do not concede that this history is a parable, but insist it is a straightforward narrative.

[12] It will be better therefore to adduce other passages of Scripture and especially passages written by one who speaks according to the natural light of reason in which he surpassed all the wise men of his time, and whose opinions the people regarded with as much veneration as those of the prophets. I mean Solomon, who is more highly commended in the sacred writings for his prudence and wisdom than for his prophecy and piety. In his 'Proverbs' he calls human understanding the fountain of true life and locates misfortune in stupidity alone. This is what he says at 16.22: 'understanding is the fountain of life to him who is lord of it,[5] and the punishment of the stupid is their stupidity', where we should

---

[4] Genesis 2.17.
[5] Spinoza's footnote: a Hebrew idiom. He who has something or possesses it in his nature is said to be a lord of that thing. Thus a bird is called, in Hebrew, a 'lord of wings', because it has wings. An intelligent man is called a 'lord of intellect', because he has intellect.

note that 'life' in the Hebrew certainly means true life, as is evident from Deuteronomy 30.19. He therefore located the fruit of the understanding in true life alone and punishment exclusively in the lack of it, and this agrees completely with our fourth point above about the natural divine law. The same wise man also plainly taught that this fountain of life, or the understanding alone, prescribes laws to the wise, as we have often shown. He says
67 (13.14): 'The law of the wise man' (is) 'the fount of life', i.e., the understanding, as is clear from the text just quoted. Furthermore, 3.13 expressly teaches that understanding gives a person happiness and joy and confers true peace of mind. For he says, 'blessed is the man who finds knowledge, and the son of man who acquires understanding'. The reason is (as verses 16 and 17 go on to say) because it 'directly gives length of days[6] and indirectly riches and honour; its ways' (which are presumably revealed by knowledge) 'are pleasant, and all its paths are peace'. The wise alone therefore in Solomon's view live with a peaceful and stable purpose, not like the impious whose minds fluctuate between different passions, and therefore (as Isaiah 57.20 also says) possess neither peace nor calm.

Finally, in these 'Proverbs' of Solomon we should take special notice of the second chapter, because its contents confirm our position as clearly as can be. Verse 3 of this chapter begins: 'For if you cry out for wisdom, and raise your voice for understanding, etc., then you will understand the fear of God, and you will find the knowledge of God' (or rather 'love'; for the word *Jadah* signifies both these things); 'for' (note this well) 'God gives wisdom; from his mouth' (flow) 'knowledge and prudence'. In these words he very clearly indicates, firstly, that wisdom or understanding alone teaches us to fear God wisely, i.e., to worship him with a true worship. Secondly, he teaches that wisdom and knowledge flow from the mouth of God and that God provides them; this is what we too showed above – that our intellect and our knowledge depend upon the idea or knowledge of God alone and take their origin from it and are perfected by it.

He then goes on, in verse 9, to teach in the most explicit words that this knowledge contains true morality and politics and that these are derived from it: 'then will you understand justice and judgment and righteousness' (and) 'every good way'. Not content with this, he con-
68 tinues: 'when knowledge shall enter into your heart, and wisdom shall

---

[6] Spinoza's footnote: a Hebrew idiom, which merely signifies life.

be sweet to you, then will your foresight[7] watch over you, and your prudence protect you'. All this is plainly consistent with natural knowledge; for it teaches ethics and true virtue, after we have acquired a knowledge of things and have tasted the excellence of learning. Thus, in Solomon's view also, the happiness and peace of the person who cultivates natural understanding chiefly depend, not upon the realm of fortune (i.e., the external assistance of God), but upon their own internal power (or the internal assistance of God), because they preserve themselves best by alertness, action and good counsel.

Finally we must not forget this passage of Paul, found at Romans 1.20, where (as Tremellius translates it from the Syriac text)[8] Paul says, 'for the hidden things of God, from the creation of the world, are seen through the understanding in his creatures, as well as his power and divinity which is for ever, so that they are without a way of escape'. With this he indicates plainly enough that each man fully understands by the natural light of reason the power of God, and His eternal divinity, by which men can know and deduce what they should seek and what they should avoid. Hence Paul concludes that all are without a way of escape and can not be excused by ignorance, though assuredly they could have been excused were he talking about supernatural inspiration, the suffering of Christ in the flesh, the resurrection, etc. This is why, immediately below, at verse 24, he continues: 'for this reason God gave them over to the filthy lusts of their heart', and so on, down to the end of the chapter, where he is describing the vices of ignorance. This also agrees with the passage from the Proverbs of Solomon, 16.22 quoted above: 'the punishment of the stupid is their stupidity'. So it is not surprising that Paul says that wrongdoers have no excuse. As each man sows, so he reaps; from bad things, bad things necessarily follow, unless wisely corrected; from good things, good things necessarily follow, if allied with constancy of purpose. Thus the Bible fully endorses the natural light of reason and the natural divine law. And thus I have done what I proposed to do in this chapter.

---

[7] Spinoza's note: *mezima* properly signifies thought, deliberation, and vigilance.
[8] Tremellius and Junius published a Latin translation of the Old Testament and Apocrypha in 1575–9 which was in common use among Protestants. Some later editions added Tremellius' translation of the Syriac version of the New Testament.

CHAPTER 5

On the reason why ceremonies were instituted, and on belief in the historical narratives, i.e. for what reason and for whom such belief is necessary

[1] We showed in the previous chapter that the divine law which makes men truly happy and teaches the true life, is universal to all men. We also deduced that law from human nature in such a way that it must itself be deemed innate to the human mind and, so to speak, inscribed upon it. As for ceremonies, or those at least which are narrated in the Old Testament, these were instituted for the Hebrews alone and were so closely accommodated to their state that in the main they could be practised not by individuals but only by the community as a whole. It is certain, therefore, that they do not belong to the divine law and hence contribute nothing to happiness and virtue. They are relevant only to the election of the Hebrews, that is (as we showed in chapter 3), to the temporal and material prosperity and peace of their state, and therefore could have relevance only so long as that state survived. If in the Old Testament they are ascribed to the law of God, that is only because they were instituted as the result of a revelation or on revealed foundations. But since reasoning, no matter how sound, carries little weight with ordinary theologians, I propose now to adduce the authority of the Bible to confirm what I have just proved. Then, for yet greater clarity, I will show why and how these ceremonies served to establish and preserve the Jewish state.

[2] Isaiah teaches nothing more clearly than that the divine law in an absolute sense signifies, not ceremonies, but that universal law that consists in the true conception of living. At 1.10 the prophet summons his

people to hear the divine law from him. First he excludes all kinds of sacrifices and feast-days, and then proclaims the law itself (verses 16 and 17), summing it up in these few points: purity of mind, a disposition or habit of virtue or good actions, and giving help to the poor. Equally lucid is the testimony of verses 7–9 of Psalm 40, where the Psalmist says to God: 'Sacrifice and offering you did not wish, you have opened[1] your ears to me, you have not sought a holocaust and an offering for sin; I have sought to carry out your will, O God; for your law is in my entrails'. Thus he applies the term 'law of God' only to what is inscribed in the entrails or heart, and excludes ceremonies from it; for ceremonies are good only by convention and not by nature, and therefore are not inscribed in the heart. Other passages in Scripture testify to the same thing, but it is enough to refer to these two.

[3] It is also evident from Scripture itself that ceremonies contribute nothing to happiness, but are only relevant to the temporal prosperity of the state. Scripture promises nothing but material pleasures and advantages in return for ceremonies, whereas it promises happiness only for obedience to the universal divine law. In the Five Books which are commonly called the books of Moses, nothing is promised, as we noted above, other than this worldly well-being which is honour or fame, victory, wealth, pleasure and health. Although these Five Books contain much about morality as well as ceremonies, morality is not to be found there as moral teachings universal to all men, but only as instructions uniquely adjusted to the understanding and character of the Hebrew nation, and therefore relevant to the prosperity of their state alone. For example, it is not as a teacher or a prophet that Moses requires the Jews not to kill or steal; he decrees it as a legislator and prince. For he does not ground his teachings on reason, but rather attaches a penalty to his commands, and punishment can and should vary according to the character of each nation, as experience has taught well enough.

Equally, the commandment not to commit adultery relates only to the interest of the commonwealth and the state. If he had wanted to give moral instruction that would relate not only to the needs of the state but also the peace of mind and true happiness of each individual, then he would condemn not only the external act but also the consent of the mind itself, as

[1] Spinoza's footnote: This is an expression that signifies perception.

Christ did, who taught only universal truths (see Matthew 5.28). This is the reason why Christ promises a spiritual reward, not like Moses a physical one; for Christ, as I said, was sent not to conserve a commonwealth and institute laws, but to teach the universal law alone. Hence, we readily understand that Christ did not abolish the Law of Moses at all, since he did not intend to introduce any new laws into the state. His overriding concern was to offer moral teaching, and to distinguish it from the laws of the state, and this he did chiefly due to the ignorance of the Pharisees who supposed that man lived well by defending the laws of the state, or the Law of Moses, despite the fact that this Law, as we have said, related only to the state and sought to compel rather than instruct the Hebrews.

[4]   But let us return to our subject, and offer other passages of Scripture affording nothing but material advantages in reward for ceremonies while promising happiness for adherence to the divine universal law alone. None of the prophets has taught this more clearly than Isaiah. In chapter 58,[2] after condemning hypocrisy, Isaiah commends liberation [of the oppressed] and charity towards oneself and one's neighbour and, in return, makes this promise: 'Then shall your light break forth as the dawn, and your healing shall speedily flower, and your justice shall go before you, and the glory of God shall gather you',[3] etc. After this he also commends the sabbath, and as a reward for diligent observance promises this: 'Then you shall have joy with God,[4] and I will make you ride[5] upon the heights of the earth, so that you may feed upon the heritage of Jacob your father, as the mouth of Jehovah has spoken'.[6]

Thus we see that the prophet promises as the reward for liberating [the oppressed] and practising charity, a healthy mind in a healthy body[7] and the glory of God after death, but the reward for ceremonies is merely the security of the state, prosperity, and worldly success. In Psalms 15 and 24 no mention is made of ceremonies, but only of moral teaching, evidently because in these psalms only happiness is proposed and offered, albeit in figurative language. For it is certain that in these psalms the 'mountain of

---

[2] See Isaiah 58:1–9.
[3] Spinoza's footnote: A Hebrew idiom, by which the time of death is signified; 'to be gathered to one's people' means 'to die': see Genesis 49.29, 33.
[4] Spinoza's footnote: This means to enjoy honestly, just as also in Dutch, 'met Godt en met eere' ['with God and with honour'].
[5] Spinoza's footnote: This signifies governance, as in restraining a horse by the bridle.
[6] Isaiah 58.14.   [7] Juvenal, *Satires*, 10.356.

God' and 'God's tents' and living in them signifies happiness and peace of mind, not the mountain of Jerusalem or the tabernacle of Moses; for no one lived in these places, and they were served by men from the tribe of Levi alone. Further, all those opinions of Solomon's which I cited in the previous chapter hold out the promise of true happiness in return for cultivating understanding and wisdom alone, namely, that by wisdom in the end one will understand the fear of God and find knowledge of Him. 72

[5] On the other hand, it is clear from Jeremiah that after the destruction of their commonwealth the Hebrews were not obliged to keep up the ceremonies. When he saw that the destruction of the city was imminent, he prophesied it and said: 'God loves only those who know and understand that He himself practises loving-kindness, good judgment and justice in the world, and hence, from now on, only those who know this are to be esteemed worthy of praise' (see 9.23). It is as if he were saying that after the destruction of the city God asked for nothing particular from the Jews requiring of them only [that they uphold] the natural law by which all men are bound. The New Testament fully confirms the same thing, for as we said, it offers only moral teaching, and promises as a reward the kingdom of heaven, and the Apostles abolished the ceremonies as soon as the Gospel began to be preached to other nations which were subject to the laws of a different state.

As for the Pharisees retaining the [ceremonies] or at least a great part of them after the loss of their state, they did this more in a spirit of opposition to the Christians than to please God. For when they were led away into captivity in Babylon after the first destruction of the city, they immediately neglected the ceremonies, since at that time, so far as I know, they were not yet divided into sects. In fact they completely abandoned the Law of Moses, and let the ordinances of their country fall into oblivion as obviously superfluous, and began to mingle with other nations, as is abundantly clear from Ezra and Nehemiah.

Thus, now that their state is dissolved, there is no doubt that the Jews are no more bound by the Law of Moses than they were before the commencement of their community and state. For while they dwelt among other peoples before the exodus from Egypt, they had no special laws, and were bound only by the natural law and, indubitably, the law of the state in which they were living, so far as it did not conflict with the natural divine law. As for the fact that the patriarchs sacrificed to God, I think that they did so in order to rouse their hearts to greater devotion, for they had been accustomed to sacrifices from childhood. Everyone had been thoroughly familiar with sacrifice from the time of Enoch, which hence stimulated their devotion more than anything else. Thus the patriarchs sacrificed to God, not because of a divine law commanding them to do so, nor because they were schooled in the universal foundations of the divine law, but merely from the custom of the time. If they did it at anyone's command, that command was merely the law of the state in which they were living, which also applied to them (as we have already noted here and in chapter 3 in relation to Melchizedek).

[6] These passages, I think, support my position with the authority of the Bible. It remains now to show how and why ceremonies served to preserve and maintain the state of the Hebrews. I shall demonstrate this from universal principles in as few words as I can.

[7] Society is extremely useful, indeed wholly essential, not only for living safe from enemies but also for acquiring many other advantages. For unless human beings were willing to give each other mutual assistance, each one's own personal skill and time would be inadequate to sustain and preserve him as much as would otherwise be possible. For people are not equally able to do everything, nor would each individual on his own be able to get what he does not have. He would have neither the capacity nor the time to plough, sow, reap, grind, cook, weave and sew for himself as well as doing the many other things that are needed to sustain life – not to mention at this point the arts and sciences, which are also supremely necessary to the perfection of human nature and its happiness. For we see that those who lead primitive lives, without any political organization, lead wretched and brutish lives; yet, even so, they only manage to obtain the few crude and miserable things that they do have by means of mutual assistance.

[8] Now if human beings were so constituted by nature that they desired nothing but what true reason points them to, society would surely need no laws; men would only need to learn true moral doctrine, in order to do what is truly useful of their own accord with upright and free mind. But they are not so constituted, far from it. All men do indeed seek their own interest, but it is not from the dictate of sound reason; for the most part they pursue things and judge them to be in their interest merely because

they are carried away by sensual desire and by their passions (which have no regard for the future and for other things). This is why no society can 74 subsist without government and compulsion, and hence laws, which moderate and restrain desires. However human nature does not allow itself to be absolutely compelled, and as the tragedian Seneca says,[8] no one has maintained a violent régime for long; it is moderate régimes that endure. For while men are acting from fear alone, they are doing what they do not at all want to do; they have no reason of interest or necessity for doing what they do; they seek merely to avoid punishment or even execution. Indeed, they cannot help but rejoice when their ruler suffers pain or loss, even if this involves them in great suffering themselves; they cannot help but wish him every calamity and inflict it themselves when they can. Moreover there is nothing that people find less tolerable than to be ruled by their equals and serve them; and nothing is more difficult than to deprive people of liberty once it has been granted.

[9] It follows from all this, first, that either the whole of society (if this is possible) should hold power together, collegially, so that all are subject to themselves and nobody must serve their equal, or else a few men [hold power], or if one man alone holds power, he will need to have something above ordinary human nature – or at least strive with all his resources to convince the common people that he has. Secondly, in any form of state the laws should be so drawn up that people are restrained less by fear than hope of something good which they very much desire; for in this way everybody will do his duty willingly. Finally, since obedience consists in carrying out commands on the sole authority of a ruler, it follows that [such subordination] has no place in a society whose government is in the hands of all and where laws are made by common consent. In such a society, whether the number of laws is increased or reduced, the people still remain just as free, since they are not acting under the authority of another but by their own proper consent. The opposite is the case when one man alone holds power absolutely, for all are carrying out the commands of government on the sole authority of a single person. Hence, unless people have been raised from the outset to be subservient to the ruler's every word, he will find it difficult to institute new laws when they are needed and to take away the people's liberty once it has been granted.

[8] Seneca, *Trojan Women*, 258–9.

[10]   In the light of these general reflections, let us now consider the Hebrew commonwealth. As soon as they departed from Egypt, they were no longer under the jurisdiction of any other nation, and thus had the freedom to enact new laws or make new rules as they pleased and to establish a state wherever they might wish and occupy whatever lands they wanted. However, they were not in any way fit to make laws wisely or organize a government in a collegial manner among themselves; for they were all of rude intelligence and down-trodden by the miseries of slavery. Government therefore had to remain in the hands of one man alone who would rule the others, compel them by force, and make laws for them, and interpret those laws subsequently. Moses was well equipped to hold power since he far excelled the rest with a divine virtue and convinced the people of this by offering them many examples of it (see Exodus 14, last verse, and 19:9). On the basis of this divine virtue, which was the source of his power, he made laws and prescribed them to the people. But in all this he took great care to ensure that the people would do its duty willingly and not through fear. Two factors most influenced him to take this approach: the obstinate character of the people (which does not allow itself to be coerced by force alone), and the threat of war. For in war it is vital to success to encourage the soldiers rather than to cow them with threats and punishments, for each soldier is more eager to win distinction by gallantry and courage than merely to avoid punishment.

[11]   This is why Moses, with his virtue and by divine command, introduced religion into the commonwealth, so that the people would do its duty more from devotion than from fear. Then he bound them to him with benefits, and by divine inspiration made many promises to them for the future. He did not make the laws too severe, as anyone who has studied them will readily concede, particularly if he looks at the circumstances required for the condemnation of a defendant.[9] And finally, in order that a people which could not run its own affairs should depend upon the words of its ruler, he did not permit them, accustomed as they were to slavery, to do anything at their own pleasure. They could do nothing without being obliged at the same time to bring to mind a law and follow commands that depended upon the will of the ruler alone. They were not permitted to plough or sow or reap as they pleased, nor

---

[9] Deuteronomy 17.6, 19.15.

could they eat or dress or shave their heads or beards as they pleased, but all in accordance with a fixed and specific ordinance of the law. They could not rejoice or do anything at all except in obedience to orders and commands prescribed by the law. Not only that, but they were obliged to have certain symbols on their doorposts, in their hands and between their eyes, to remind them continually of their obedience.

76

[12]   This then was the purpose of the ceremonies, that they [i.e. the people] should do nothing at their own discretion and everything at the command of another, and should confess by their every action and thought that they did not exist in their own right at all but were entirely subject to someone else. From all of this it is clearer than daylight that ceremonies have no connection with happiness, and that the ceremonies of the Old Testament, and indeed the entire Law of Moses, related to nothing but the Hebrew state and consequently nothing other than material benefits.

[13]   Concerning Christian ceremonies, namely baptism, the Lord's supper, feast-days, public prayers, and any others that are and always have been common to the whole of Christianity – if they actually were instituted by Christ or the Apostles (which is still not clear to me), they were instituted only as external signs of a universal church and not as things that contribute to happiness or have any sanctity in them. Hence, although these ceremonies were not instituted for the purpose of [upholding] a state, they were instituted only for a community as a whole. Consequently, a man living alone is not bound by them, and anyone who lives under a government where the Christian religion is forbidden is obliged to do without them and yet will be able to live a good life notwithstanding. We have an example of this in the empire of Japan, where the Christian religion is forbidden and the Dutch who live there, must abstain from all external worship by command of the [Dutch] East India Company.[10] I do not think at the moment I can confirm this by another instance; yet it would not be hard to deduce the point itself also from the principles of the New Testament, and perhaps provide further evidence

---

[10] The Japanese Shogunate forced the English to leave Japan in 1623, the Spaniards in 1624 and the Portuguese in 1638, leaving the Dutch as the only Europeans permitted to maintain a trading 'factory' in Japan (at Nagasaki). This was on condition that they did not promote, or try to convert any Japanese to, Christianity, an understanding decried in Europe as shamefully base subservience on the part of the Dutch.

with clear testimonies, but I am willing to let this go, as I am anxious to get on to other things. I move on then to the second topic that I proposed to deal with in this chapter, namely, for whom, and why, belief in the narratives contained in the Bible is necessary. To investigate this question by the light of natural reason, it seems one should proceed as follows.

[14] Anyone seeking to persuade or dissuade people of something which is not known by itself, must, to gain their acquiescence, deduce it from things already accepted, convincing them by means of experience or reason. That is, one must convince them either by things which they know through their senses happen in nature or from clear intellectual concepts evident in themselves. However, unless the experience is such as to be plainly and distinctly understood, it will, even though it may convince a person, still not suffice to sway the understanding and dissipate its doubts as effectively as when the conclusion is deduced from intellectual axioms alone, that is, solely by the power of the understanding and in the order in which it comprehends things. This is especially so where it is a spiritual matter that is in question with no connection with the senses.

Often though, a long chain of linked inferences is required, to come to firm conclusions from basic ideas alone. Furthermore, this requires great caution and perspicacity and supreme mental discipline, qualities only seldom met with among human beings. People prefer to be taught by experience than to deduce all their ideas from a few premises and connect these together. Consequently, where someone seeks to teach a whole nation, not to speak of the entire human race, and wants to be understood by everybody, he must substantiate his points by experience alone and thoroughly adapt his arguments and the definitions of his teaching to the capacity of the common people (the majority of mankind), and not make a chain of inferences or advance definitions linking his arguments together. Otherwise he will be writing only for the learned, that is, he will be intelligible only to what is, in comparison with the rest of mankind, a very small handful of people.

[15] Therefore since all of Scripture was revealed for the benefit of a whole people in the first place and, ultimately, for the entire human race, its contents had necessarily to be entirely adjusted to the capacity of the common people and substantiated by experience alone.

[16]   Let us explain this more clearly. Among the questions the Bible seeks to teach that require purely philosophical reasoning, the most important are that there is a God, or being, that made all things and directs and sustains all things with the highest wisdom, and who takes the greatest care of men, or rather of those who live piously and honestly, while inflicting many punishments on the rest and segregating them from the good. These things Scripture proves by experience alone, by means of the histories which it narrates. It provides no definitions of these things but accommodates all its words and reasons to the understanding of the common people. But experience can neither yield nor teach any clear knowledge of these matters, nor tell us what God is or how he sustains and directs all things and cares for human beings, though it can still teach and illumine men sufficiently to instil obedience and devotion in their minds.   78

From this I think it is clear for whom and for what reason belief in the biblical narratives is necessary. From what we have just shown it very plainly follows that knowing them and believing them is supremely necessary to ordinary people whose minds are not competent to perceive things clearly and distinctly.[11] It also follows that anyone who rejects these histories because he does not believe there is a God or that He provides for men and things, is impious. But in the case of someone who is ignorant of them but who does know, by the natural light of reason, that there is a God and so forth, as we have expressed it above, and who also possesses a true code for living, he is entirely happy, and happier than the common people, because, besides true opinions, he possesses a clear and distinct understanding of them. It follows finally that anyone who neither knows the biblical histories nor knows anything by the natural light of reason, though not actually impious or obstinate, is however inhuman and almost brutish, and has no gift from God.

[17]   We should add, though, that when we say an awareness of the biblical narratives is most necessary for the common people, we do not mean awareness of literally all the histories in the sacred writings, but only the ones that are most important and which most clearly demonstrate, on their own, apart from the others, the doctrine just mentioned, and which have the most influence on people's minds. For if all the biblical histories were

---

[11] 'Clearly and distinctly' was almost a technical term in the late seventeenth century, being frequently used by Cartesians to denote rigorous philosophical deduction that is (supposedly) beyond challenge.

required to prove its doctrine, and it were impossible to draw a conclusion without a thorough consideration of absolutely all the narratives, then obviously the demonstration and derivation of the Bible's doctrine would surpass the capacity and abilities not just of the common people but all mankind. Who could simultaneously attend to such a large number of accounts, and all the circumstances and doctrinal aspects that should be derived from so many histories of such different types? I at least remain unpersuaded that those who left Scripture to us, as we have it, were so rich in talent that they could manage such a demonstration themselves, and much less do I believe it impossible to comprehend Scripture's teaching without hearing of the quarrels of Isaac, the counsels which Achitophel gave to Absalom, the civil war between Judah and Israel, and other such accounts, or that the doctrine itself could not have been demonstrated to the earliest Jews who lived at the time of Moses equally readily from stories, as it could to those who lived in Ezra's day. I will say more about this later.

[18]   The common people, therefore, are required to know only those histories which can most move their hearts to obedience and devotion. But the people themselves are not sufficiently skilled to make judgments about them, since they get more pleasure from stories and from strange and unexpected events than from the actual doctrine of the histories. This is why, in addition to reading the histories, they also need pastors or church ministers to explain these to them, owing to the weakness of their understanding.

[19]   However, let us not wander from our purpose, but let us state the conclusion we set out to prove, namely that, whatever the nature of these histories, belief in them is not relevant to the divine law, nor do they make men happy in themselves, nor do they serve any purpose other than for their doctrine, and this is the only reason why some of them may be more important than others. It is due to the salutary opinions that follow from them that the narratives of the Old and New Testaments are superior to other, non-sacred legends, and even among these, some are superior to others. Hence if anyone reads the stories of holy Scripture and believes all of them without paying attention to the doctrine that the Bible uses them to teach, and without amending his life, he might just as well read the Koran or the dramatic plays of the poets, or at any rate the common

chronicles, with the same attention that the common people usually give to their reading. On the other hand, as we have said, he who is completely ignorant of them, and nevertheless has salutary opinions and a true conception of living, is truly happy and truly has within him the spirit of Christ.

However, the Jews hold completely to the opposite view. They think that true opinions and a true conception of life make no contribution to happiness whenever people receive them by the natural light of reason alone and not as teachings prophetically revealed to Moses. Maimonides dares openly to assert this (*Kings*, ch. 8, Law 11)[12] in these words: 'Everyone who accepts the seven precepts[13] and diligently practises them is among the pious of the nations and an heir of the world to come; that is, if he accepts them and practises them because God prescribed them in the Law and revealed to us through Moses that the same requirements had been prescribed to the sons of Noah before. But if he practises them because he has been convinced by reason that he should, he is not one of us, nor does he belong to the pious or learned of the nations'. These are the words of Maimonides. Rabbi Joseph ben Shem Tov, in his book entitled *Kevod Elohim*, or *Glory of God*,[14] adds that Aristotle (who he supposes has written the supreme *Ethics*, and whom he esteems above all others) missed nothing that was relevant to true morality and expounded it all in his *Ethics* and would have put it all conscientiously into practice. Nevertheless, he adds, this would not have helped him towards salvation, since he did not receive these teachings as divine doctrine prophetically revealed, but derived them from the dictate of reason alone. I think it is evident to anyone who reads this attentively that all this is mere fabrication and does not rest upon the authority of the Bible, and hence one need only expound it in order to refute it.

Neither do I intend at this point formally to refute the opinion of those who are convinced that the natural light of reason can yield no sound

80

---

[12] Maimonides, *Mishneh Torah* [*Code of Law*], Book of Kings, ch. 8, law 11.

[13] Spinoza's footnote: N.B. the Jews think that God gave seven commandments to Noah, and the nations are bound only by these; to the Hebrew people alone he gave many other commandments, in order to render them happier than the rest.

[14] *Kevod Elohim* printed at Ferrara in 1556, was written in 1442 by Joseph ben Shem Tov Ibn Shem Tov (*c*.1400–*c*.1460), a Spanish Jewish physician and philosopher who, in that work, rejects the equivalence between biblical and Aristotelian ethics argued by Maimonides; nevertheless, he too was a great admirer of Aristotle and, at Segovia, in 1455, wrote a detailed commentary on the Hebrew version of Aristotle's *Nicomachean Ethics*.

teaching about what relates to true salvation. For those who insist that there is no sound reason in them are prevented from proving this by means of reason. And if they claim that they have something within them which is above reason, it is a mere fiction and far beneath reason, as their usual way of life has already proved clearly enough. But there is no need to speak more candidly about these things.

[20]   I would add just this, that we can know no one except from his works. Anyone therefore who abounds in the fruits of love, joy, peace, long-suffering, kindness, goodness, faithfulness, gentleness and self-control, against whom (as Paul says in his Epistle to the Galatians 5.22) there is no law, he, whether he has been taught by reason alone or by Scripture alone, has truly been taught by God, and is altogether happy. With this I have said everything that I proposed to say about the divine law.

On miracles

[1]   Just as men habitually call that knowledge which surpasses human understanding 'divinity', so they likewise classify any phenomenon whose cause is unknown by the common people 'divine' or a work of God. For the common people imagine that the power and providence of God are most clearly evident when they see something happen contrary to the usual course of things and their habitual views about nature, especially should it turn out to their benefit or advantage. They also suppose the existence of God is proven by nothing more clearly than from what they perceive as nature failing to follow its normal course. For this reason they suppose that all those who explain or attempt to explain phenomena and miracles by natural causes, are doing away with God or at least divine providence. They evidently hold that God is inactive whilst nature follows its normal course and, conversely, that the power of nature and natural causes are superfluous whenever God is active. Hence, they imagine that there are two powers, distinct from each other, the power of God and the power of natural things, and that the latter is determined by God in some way or, as most men think in our day, created by him. But what they understand by these powers, and what they understand by God and nature, they certainly do not know, except that they imagine the power of God to be like the authority of royal majesty, and the power of nature to be like a force and impetus.

The common people therefore call unusual works of nature miracles or works of God and do not want to know the natural causes of things, partly from devotion and partly from zeal to oppose those who pursue natural philosophy. They desire only to hear about that of which they are most ignorant and consequently about which they marvel most. Evidently, this is because they can only adore God, and ascribe all things to his will and governance, by ignoring natural causes and evincing wonder at what is outside the normal course of nature, and revere the power of God best when they envisage the power of nature as if it were subdued by God. This attitude seems to originate among the first Jews. They narrated miraculous stories to convince the pagans of their day, who adored visible gods, like the sun, the moon, water, air, and so on, that those gods were weak and inconstant or mutable, and subordinate to the invisible God. They also wanted to show that the whole of nature was directed by the governance of the God whom they adored solely for their own benefit. People have always been so drawn to this idea that to this day they have not ceased to invent miracles, in order to foment the belief that they are dearer to God than others and are the ultimate reason for God's creation and continual governance of all things. What will the common people not arrogate to themselves in their foolishness! They have no sound conception of either God or nature and, confusing God's decrees with human decisions, consider nature to be so limited that they believe men are its most important part.

[2] But this is quite enough about the opinions and prejudices of the common people regarding nature and miracles. We should now put this question into proper order. I will show:

(1) that nothing happens contrary to nature, but nature maintains an eternal, fixed and immutable order, and at the same time demonstrate what should be understood by the term 'miracle'

(2) that from miracles we cannot know about either the essence or the existence or the providence of God, but rather that all three are much better grasped from the fixed and unchangeable order of nature.

(3) I will show from some examples in the Bible that by the decrees, volitions and providence of God, Scripture itself means nothing other than the order of nature which necessarily follows from his eternal law.

(4) Finally, I will discuss the method required for [correctly] interpreting the miracles narrated in the Bible and what we should particularly notice in such miracle narratives. These are the chief points in the argument of this chapter, and I think that they are also very relevant to the aim of the work as a whole.

[3] (1) The first point is easily demonstrated from what we proved in chapter 4 about the divine law, namely, that all that God wills or determines involves eternal necessity and truth. From the fact that God's understanding

is not distinct from God's will, we showed that we are asserting the same thing when we say that God wills something as when we say that God understands it. Hence by the same necessity by which it follows from the divine nature and perfection that God understands some thing as it is, it also follows that God wills it as it is. But since nothing is necessarily true except by divine decree alone, it most clearly follows that the universal laws of nature are simply God's decrees and follow from the necessity and perfection of the divine nature. If anything therefore were to happen in nature that contradicted its universal laws, it would also necessarily contradict the decree and understanding and nature of God. Or if anyone were to assert that God does anything contrary to the laws of nature, he would at the same time be compelled to assert that God acts contrary to his own nature, than which nothing is more absurd. The same thing can also easily be shown from the fact that the power of nature is the divine power and virtue itself, and the divine power is the very essence of God, but this I am happy to leave aside for the time being.

[4]   Consequently, nothing happens in nature[1] that contradicts its universal laws; and nothing occurs which does not conform to those laws or follow from them. For whatever happens, happens by God's will and his eternal decree, i.e., as we have already shown, whatever happens, happens according to laws and rules which involve eternal necessity and truth. Nature therefore always observes laws and rules which involve eternal necessity and truth – albeit not all are known to us – and therefore also a fixed and immutable order. No sound reasoning convinces us that we should attribute only a limited power and virtue to nature or believe its laws are suited to certain things only and not to all. For, since the virtue and power of nature is the very virtue and power of God and the laws and rules of nature are the very decrees of God, we must certainly believe that the power of nature is infinite, and its laws so broad as to extend to everything that is also conceived by the divine understanding. For otherwise what are we saying but that God has created a nature so impotent and with laws and rules so feeble that He must continually give it a helping hand, to maintain it and keep things going as He wills; this I certainly consider to be completely unreasonable.

---

[1] Spinoza's footnote: note that here I mean not only matter and its properties, but other infinite things besides matter.

[5] From these premises therefore – that in nature nothing happens which does not follow from its laws, that its laws extend to all things conceived by the divine understanding, and finally that nature maintains a fixed and unchangeable order – it most evidently follows that the term 'miracles' can be understood only with respect to human beliefs, and that it signifies nothing other than a phenomenon whose natural cause cannot be explained on the pattern of some other familiar thing or at least cannot be so explained by the narrator or reporter of the miracle.

I could in fact say that a miracle is something whose cause cannot be explained from the principles of the natural things known to us by the natural light of reason. But since miracles were produced according to the capacity of the common people who were completely ignorant of the principles of natural things, plainly the ancients took for a miracle whatever they were unable to explain in the manner the common people normally explained natural things, namely by seeking to recall something similar which can be imagined without amazement. For the common people suppose they have satisfactorily explained something as soon as it no longer astounds them. Hence, for the ancients and the vast majority of men down to our own time, this was the only criterion for defining what was miraculous. Clearly, many things are therefore related as miracles in the Bible whose causes may readily be explained from the known causes of natural things, as we have already suggested in chapter 2 above, when we spoke of the incident of the sun's standing still in the time of Joshua[2] and its moving backwards in the time of Ahaz.[3] But we will consider these passages at greater length below, when we discuss the interpretation of miracles which I promised to deal with in this chapter.

[6] (2) It is now time for me to pass to the second issue and show that we cannot infer from miracles either the essence or the existence, or the providence, of God, but on the contrary that these are far better inferred from the fixed and immutable order of nature. To demonstrate this I proceed as follows. Since the existence of God is not known of itself,[4] it must necessarily be deduced from concepts whose truth is so firm and unquestionable that no power capable of changing them can exist, or be conceived. At any rate they must appear so to us from the moment we infer God's existence from them, if we want to derive this from them

---

[2] Joshua 10.   [3] Isaiah 38:7–8.   [4] Spinoza's footnote: see Annotation 6.

without risk of doubt. For if we could conceive that the axioms themselves might be modified by whatever power then we could doubt their truth, and hence also our conclusion concerning God's existence, and could never be certain about anything. Furthermore, we know nothing conforms to nature or conflicts with it, except what we have shown to agree or conflict with those [evident] principles. Therefore if we could conceive that anything in nature could be brought about by any power (whatever power that might be) which conflicts with nature, it would be in conflict with those primary principles and therefore would have to be rejected as absurd, or else there would be doubts about those primary principles (as we have just shown) and, consequently, about God and about all our perceptions of whatever kind. It is far from true, therefore, that miracles – in so far as the word is used for a phenomenon that conflicts with the order of nature – prove for us the existence of God. On the contrary, they would make us call into doubt that very point, since, without them, we could be absolutely certain of it, because we know that all things follow the certain and unchangeable order of nature. 85

[7] But let it be supposed that a miracle is something that cannot be explained by natural causes. This can be understood in two ways: either it does indeed have natural causes though they cannot be discovered by human understanding, or it admits no cause but God or the will of God. But because all things that happen by natural causes also happen by the sole power and will of God, we must necessarily conclude, finally, that whether a miracle has natural causes or not, it is a phenomenon that cannot be explained by a cause, that is, it is a phenomenon that surpasses human understanding. But we can understand nothing of a phenomenon, or of anything at all, that surpasses our understanding. For whatever we understand clearly and distinctly, must become known to us either by itself or by means of something else that is understood clearly and distinctly. Therefore, we cannot understand from a miracle, or work which surpasses our understanding, the essence of God or his existence, or anything about God and nature.

On the contrary, since we know that all things are determined and ordained by God, and that the operations of nature follow from the essence of God, and the laws of nature are the eternal laws and volitions of God, we must conclude, unconditionally, that we get a fuller knowledge of God and God's will as we acquire a fuller knowledge of natural things and more clearly understand how they depend on their first cause and how they behave according to the eternal laws of nature. From the perspective of our understanding, hence, we have much more right to term those phenomena which we understand clearly and distinctly works of God and attribute them to the will of God, than works of which we are wholly ignorant, however strongly they grip the imagination and make us mar-

86 vel. For it is only the phenomena of nature we understand clearly and distinctly that enhance our knowledge of God and reveal as clearly as possible the will and decrees of God. Therefore, those who have recourse to the will of God when they are ignorant of something are clearly talking nonsense: what a ridiculous way to acknowledge one's ignorance!

[8]   Furthermore, even if we could draw conclusions from miracles, we certainly could not derive [from them] the existence of God. Given that a miracle is a limited phenomenon, and never reveals anything more than a fixed and limited power, it is certain that from such an effect we cannot infer the existence of a cause whose power is infinite, but at most a cause whose power is fairly large. I say 'at most', for a phenomenon may also fol-low from several simultaneously concurring causes whose force and power is less than the power of all these causes together but much greater than that of each individual cause. Whereas the laws of nature (as we have already shown) extend to infinity, and are conceived by us as having some-thing of the character of eternity and nature proceeds according to them in a fixed and unalterable order, so that they themselves to that extent give us some indication of the infinity, eternity and immutability of God.

We therefore conclude that we cannot come to know God and his exis-tence and providence from miracles, the former being much better infer-red from the fixed and unalterable order of nature. In reaching this conclusion I am speaking of a miracle understood simply as a phenomenon which surpasses, or is thought to surpass, human understanding. For in so far as it is conceived to destroy or interrupt the order of nature or conflict with its laws, to that extent (as we have just shown) not only would it give us no knowledge of God, it would actually take away the knowledge we natu-rally have and make us doubt about God and all things.

[9]   Neither do I acknowledge any difference between a phenomenon which is contrary to nature and a phenomenon which is above nature (i.e., as some define it, a phenomenon that does not conflict with nature

but cannot to be made or produced by it).[5] For since a miracle does not occur outside of nature but within nature itself, even if it is said to be above nature, it must still necessarily interrupt the order of nature which otherwise we conceive to be fixed and unalterable by God's decrees. If therefore something happened in nature which did not follow from its laws, this would necessarily conflict with the order that God established in nature for ever by the universal laws of nature; it would hence be contrary to nature and its laws and, consequently, it would make us doubt our faith in all things and lead us to atheism. 87

Hence, I think that I have proved with sufficiently strong arguments the second point that I proposed to discuss, and thus we may conclude again on additional grounds that a miracle, whether contrary to nature or above nature, is a plain absurdity. Therefore, the only thing that we can understand by a miracle in Holy Scripture is, as I have said, a phenomenon of nature that surpasses human understanding, or is believed to do so.

[10] Now, before turning to my third point, I should like first to confirm my claim that we cannot achieve a knowledge of God from miracles with Scripture's authority. Even though Scripture nowhere explicitly tells us this, it may readily be inferred, especially from the command of Moses in Deuteronomy 13 to condemn a false prophet to death even if he performs miracles. He says: (even though) 'the sign and the wonder that he foretold to you shall come to pass, etc., do not' (nevertheless) 'listen to the words of that prophet, etc., for the Lord your God is testing you', etc. It plainly follows from this that miracles can also be performed by false prophets, and that unless men are duly strengthened by a true knowledge and love of God, they may just as easily embrace false gods as a consequence of miracles as the true God; for he adds: 'since Jehovah your God is testing you so as to know whether you love him with all your heart and with all your soul'. The Israelites, moreover, were unable to form a sound conception of God despite all those miracles, as experience itself testified. For when they were convinced Moses was away, they asked Aaron for visible gods, and the idea of God which they finally arrived at

[5] It was basic to Spinoza's system that nothing can be postulated to be 'above' nature or 'above' reason which is not also 'contrary to nature' and 'contrary to reason'; in this he is closely followed by Bayle but directly opposed by Locke, Leibniz and Malebranche, who all accept the principle that there are 'mysteries' above reason and 'above nature' which, however, are not contrary to nature or to reason.

as a result of so many miracles was a calf. This was shameful! Asaph despite having heard of so many miracles, nevertheless still doubted God's providence and would have turned from the true path had he not finally understood the true happiness (see Psalm 73). Solomon too, in whose time the affairs of the Jews were at their most flourishing, suspects all things happen by chance: see Ecclesiastes 3:19–21, 9:2–3 etc. Finally, it was thoroughly obscure to most prophets how the order of nature and human affairs was consistent with the conception of God's providence which they had formed. However, this was always entirely clear to the philosophers who seek to understand things not from miracles but from clear concepts, or at any rate to those [philosophers] who place true happiness in virtue and peace of mind alone, and do not attempt to make nature obey them but rather strive to obey nature themselves. They have certain knowledge that God directs nature not as the particular laws of human nature urge but as its universal laws require and, hence, that God takes account not just of the human race but of nature in its entirety.

[11]   It is thus also evident from Scripture itself that miracles do not yield true knowledge of God and do not clearly demonstrate the providence of God. The incidents frequently encountered in the Bible where God performs wonders to make himself known to men (as in Exodus 10.2 where God deceived the Egyptians and gave signs of himself so that the Israelites might know that he was God), do not show that the miracles really proved this; they only show that the beliefs of the Jews were such that they could readily be convinced by these miracles. We clearly proved above in chapter 2 that prophetic arguments, or arguments derived from revelation, are not drawn from universal and basic concepts but from the preconceptions and beliefs, no matter how absurd, of those to whom the revelations are made or whom the holy spirit seeks to convince. We illustrated this by many examples and by the testimony of Paul, who was a Greek to the Greeks and a Jew to the Jews.

While these miracles could persuade the Egyptians and Hebrews because of their prior beliefs, yet they could not yield any true idea and knowledge of God. Miracles could only bring them to acknowledge that there is a deity more powerful than all things known to them, and that he watched over the Hebrews, for whom at that point in time everything had succeeded beyond their expectations. Miracles could not demonstrate to them that God cares equally for all men: only philosophy can teach this.

This is why the Jews and all who adopted their notion of God's providence only from the varying condition of human affairs and men's unequal fortunes, persuaded themselves that the Israelites were dearer to God than other men, even though they did not surpass other men in human perfection, as we showed above in chapter 3.

[12] (3) I now turn to my third point: I will show from Scripture that the edicts and commands of God, and hence of providence, are nothing other than the order of nature. That is, when the Bible says that this or that was done by God or by the will of God, it simply means that it was done according to the laws and order of nature, and not, as most people think, that nature ceased to operate for a time or that its order was briefly interrupted. But the Bible does not directly teach things which do not concern its doctrine; nor is it its intention (as we have already shown with regard to divine law) to explain things by natural causes or teach purely philosophical things. Consequently our point has to be derived by inference from certain narratives in Scripture which, as it happens, are given at some length and in considerable detail. I will cite some of them.

[13] 1 Samuel 9.15–16 tells us that God revealed to Samuel that he would send Saul to him. But God did not send Saul to him as human beings are accustomed to send one man to another; this sending by God occurred simply according to the order of nature. Saul was searching (as is mentioned in the previous chapter) for the asses he had lost, and last, as he was wondering whether to return home without them, his servant advised him to approach the prophet Samuel, so as to learn from him where he could find them. Nowhere in the story is it evident that Saul received any other command from God apart from this natural procedure of approaching Samuel. In Psalm 105.24 it is stated that God turned the hearts of the Egyptians to hate the Israelites; this too was a natural change, as emerges from the first chapter of Exodus which reports the urgent reason that motivated the Egyptians to reduce the Israelites to slavery. At Genesis 9.13 God informs Noah that he will put a rainbow in the clouds. This action of God's is assuredly no other than the refraction and reflection affecting sun rays seen through drops of water. At Psalm 147.18 the natural action and heat of the wind by which frost and snow are melted is termed the word of God, and in verse 15 wind and cold are called the utterance and word of God. In Psalm 104.4 wind and fire are

styled the the envoys and ministers of God, and there are many other things in the Bible to this effect, showing very clearly that the decree of God, his command, his utterance, his word are nothing other than the very action and order of nature. Without doubt, therefore, everything narrated in Scripture actually happened naturally, and yet it is all ascribed to God, since it is not the intention of the Bible, as we have shown, to explain things in terms of natural causes but only to speak of things that commonly occupy people's imaginations, and to do so in a manner and style calculated to inspire wonder about things and thus impress devotion upon the minds of the common people.

[14]   Consequently, if we find certain things in the Bible for which we cannot attribute a cause, and which seem to have occurred beyond or even contrary to the order of nature, these things should not represent a problem for us; rather we should be fully persuaded that whatever really happened, happened naturally. This is also confirmed by the fact that some of the details of miracles are sometimes omitted in the telling, especially in a poetic narrative. These details of such miracles, however, plainly show that they involve natural causes. For instance, in order for the Egyptians to be afflicted with boils, it was necessary for Moses to throw ashes up into the air (see Exodus 9.10). The locusts reached the land of Egypt by a natural command of God, namely by means of a wind from the east that blew for a whole day and a night; later they left because of a very strong wind from the west (see Exodus 10.14, 19). It was by the same command of God that the sea opened up a path for the Jews (see Exodus 14.1), namely because of an east wind that blew very strongly for a whole night. To raise the boy who was believed to be dead, Elisha needed to lie over him for some time, until he first grew warm and finally opened his eyes (see 2 Kings 4.34–35). Lastly, in the Gospel of John ch. 9, circumstances are mentioned of which Christ made use to heal the blind man. We find many other things in Scripture which all evidently show that miracles require something other than what is called the absolute command of God. This is also clear from Exodus 14.27, where it is merely stated that the sea rose again, at a mere gesture from Moses, and there is no mention of any wind whereas, in the Song of Songs (15.10), we learn that it happened because God blew with his wind (i.e., with a very strong wind); this detail is omitted in the first telling, and owing to that it appears to be a greater miracle.

[15] Yet someone may perhaps object that we find a whole host of things in Scripture which do not seem capable of being explained by natural causes at all, for example, that men's sins and prayers can be a cause of rain or of the earth's fertility, or that faith can heal the blind, and other things of this sort narrated in the Bible. But I think I have already answered this; for I showed that Scripture does not explain things by their immediate causes, but rather relates things in a style and language that will encourage devotion, especially among the common people. For this reason, it speaks in a wholly inexact manner about God and things precisely because it is not seeking to sway men's reason but to influence and captivate their fancy and imagination. For if Scripture related the destruction of an empire in the way political historians do, it would not appeal to the common people; but it is very appealing to them when everything is narrated poetically and all things are ascribed to God, as the Bible normally does. When therefore Scripture says that the earth was sterile due to men's sins, or that blind men were healed by faith, it should move us no more than when it says that God is angry or saddened by men's sins or repents of a promise or favour he has given, or that God remembers his promise because he sees a sign – and a whole host of other things which are either expressed poetically or have been related according to the author's beliefs and preconceptions.

Thus, we conclude without reservation that all things that are truly reported to have happened in Scripture necessarily happened according to the laws of nature, as all things do. If anything is found which can be demonstrated conclusively to contradict the laws of nature or which could not possibly to follow from them, we must accept in every case that it was interpolated into the Bible by blasphemous persons. For whatever is contrary to nature, is contrary to reason, and what is contrary to reason, is absurd, and accordingly to be rejected.

[16] (4) It remains only to make a few remarks about the interpretation of miracles, or rather to recapitulate these (for the major points of this have already been given), and illustrate them with one or two examples, as I promised to do here as my fourth goal. I need to do this, so that no one giving a defective interpretation of some miracle, will leap to the unfounded conclusion that he has hit on something in Scripture that does contradict the light of nature.

[17]   It happens very rarely that men report something straightforwardly, just as it occurred, without intruding any judgment of their own into the telling. In fact, when people see or hear something new, they will, unless very much on their guard against their own preconceived opinions, usually be so biased by these that they will perceive something quite different from what they actually saw or heard had happened, especially if the event is beyond the understanding of the reporter or his audience, and most of all if it is in his interest that it should have happened in a certain way. This is why authors of chronicles and histories speak more about their opinions than about the actual events, and one and the same event can be so differently narrated by two persons with different beliefs that they seem to be reporting two different events. And, finally, it is often not very difficult to trace the beliefs of the chroniclers and historians just from their histories.

I could offer many examples confirming this, both from philosophers who have written natural histories, and from chroniclers, except that I think this would be superfluous. I will just give one from the Bible; the reader may then judge for himself of others.

[18]   In Joshua's time (as we have already mentioned above) the Hebrews, along with everyone else, believed that the sun moves by its so-called own diurnal motion while the earth remains at rest, and they adapted to this preconceived belief a miracle that occurred to them when they were fighting the five kings. They did not simply say that that day was longer than usual, they said that the sun and the moon stood still or ceased their motion. This greatly helped them at the time to confirm by experience, and persuade the gentiles who adored the sun, that the sun operates under the government of another deity at whose command it had to change its natural regular movement. Thus partly owing to religion, and partly from preconceived beliefs, they conceived of the thing happening in a totally different way from how it actually occurred, and that is how they reported it.

[19]   Hence, to interpret the biblical miracles correctly, and to understand from the reports of them how these things really happened, it is essential to know the beliefs of those who first reported them and have left them to us in writing and to distinguish their beliefs from what their senses could represent to them. For otherwise we shall confuse their beliefs and judgments with the miracle as it really happened.

But this is not the sole reason why it is necessary to know their beliefs. We must also know them so that we will not confuse what really happened with imaginary things and prophetic visions. For many things are reported in Scripture as real, and were actually believed to be real, though they were nothing but apparitions and imaginary things, for instance that God (the supreme being) came down from heaven (see Exodus 19.18 and Deuteronomy 5.19), and that Mount Sinai was smoking because God had descended upon it surrounded by fire, and that Elijah went up to heaven in a fiery chariot with fiery horses. All these were undoubtedly only visions, adapted to the beliefs of those who passed them on to us as they appeared to them, namely as actual events. For anyone whose knowledge rises even slightly above the common level knows that God does not have a right hand or a left hand, and does not move or stay still, and is not in space but is absolutely infinite, and all perfections are contained in him. These things, I say, are known to those who judge things from what is gathered by pure intellect, and not as the imagination is affected by the external senses, as the common people do, who therefore imagine God as corporeal and as holding royal power and seated on a throne which they suppose is in the dome of the sky above the stars, whose distance from the earth they do not think to be very great. Many events in the Bible have been adapted to these and similar beliefs (as we have said), and accordingly they must not be accepted as real by philosophers.

[20]   Finally for understanding miracles as they really happened one must know the phrases and figures of speech of the Hebrews. Anyone who does not pay sufficient attention to this will find numerous miracles in the Bible which its authors never intended to be understood as such, and therefore will be completely ignorant not only of the events and the miracles as they really occurred but also of the mentality of the authors of the sacred books. For example, Zechariah 14.7, speaking of some future war, says: 'And there shall be one day, known only to God', (for it will) 'not' (be) 'day or night, but in the evening time there shall be light'. By these words he seems to predict a great miracle, and yet he means to convey merely that the war will be doubtful throughout the whole day, its outcome known only to God, but that in the evening they will obtain the victory. For it was with such language that the prophets were accustomed to foretell and describe the victories and disasters of nations.

In the same way, we find Isaiah depicting the destruction of Babylon in chapter 13: 'For the stars of heaven and their constellations will not illuminate with their light, the sun will be dark at its rising and the moon will not give out the splendour of its light'.[6] I certainly do not think that anyone believes that these things actually happened at the fall of that empire, nor what he adds just after: 'therefore I will make the heavens tremble, and the earth shall be moved from its place'.[7] So too in Isaiah 48, in the last verse but one: 'And they did not thirst, he led them through the desert, he made water flow for them from the rock, he cleft the rock, and the waters gushed out'. By these words assuredly he simply means to say that the Jews will find springs in the desert (as sometimes happens) to assuage their thirst; for when they made their way to Jerusalem, with Cyrus' consent, it is agreed that no such miracles occurred. There are any number of things like this in the Bible which were merely figures of speech of the Hebrew, and there is no need to detail them here.

I would though like to make the general point that the Hebrews were not only accustomed to use these phrases for rhetorical adornment but also and particularly for the sake of devotion. This is why we even find in Scripture, 'bless God' for 'curse God' (see 1 Kings 21.10 and Job 2.9). It was for the same reason that they ascribed all things to God, and this is why the Bible appears to relate nothing but miracles even when it is talking of the most natural things, of which we have already given some examples above. So when Scripture says that God hardened the heart of Pharaoh, we have to understand that it simply means that Pharaoh was inflexible.[8] And when it is said that God opened the windows of the heavens, it just means that a lot of rain fell, and so on.[9] If one attends carefully to such details and notes that many things are reported in Scripture only very briefly, without detail, almost in an abbreviated manner, one will find virtually nothing in the Bible that can be shown to contradict the light of nature. On the contrary, in this way one will be able to grasp and readily interpret, with just a modest intellectual effort, many things which at first seem extremely obscure. With this I think I have fully enough demonstrated what I proposed.

[21]   But before ending the chapter, there is something more I need to mention: I have used a very different method here than I followed in the case of prophecy. There I asserted nothing concerning prophecy which

---

[6] Isaiah 13.10.   [7] Isaiah 13.13.   [8] Exodus 4.21; 7.3.   [9] Genesis 7.11.

I could not infer from principles revealed in Scripture. But here I have drawn particular conclusions only from principles known by the natural light of reason and done this deliberately. Since prophecy is beyond human understanding and is a purely theological issue, I could not say or know what it is in itself, as such, except on the basis of revealed principles. I was therefore obliged there to construct a history of prophecy and to derive certain dogmas from it which would show me its nature and characteristics, so far as that can be done. But with regard to miracles, the question we are investigating (namely, whether we may concede that something happens in nature which contradicts its laws or which does not conform to them) is wholly philosophical. Therefore I did not need a similar approach. I thought it more advisable to elucidate this question from principles known by the natural light of reason since these are the best known. I say that 'I thought it more advisable'; for I could also readily have dealt with it solely on the basis of biblical dogmas and principles, and I will expand on this here in a few words, so that it will be clear to everyone.

[22]   In some passages Scripture says of nature in general that it preserves a fixed and immutable order, as in Psalm 148.6 and Jeremiah 31.35–6. Furthermore, the philosopher in his book of Ecclesiastes 1.10 very clearly explains that nothing new happens in nature; and in verses 11 and 12, in illustration of the same thing, he says that, although sometimes something happens which appears to be new, it is actually not new but occurred in past times of which there is no memory. For, as he himself says, there is no remembrance of former things among those who live today, nor will there be any memory of today's affairs among those who are to come. Then, at 3.11, he says that God has ordered all things properly, in their time, and at verse 14 he says that he knows that whatever God does endures for ever, nor can anything be added to it nor anything taken away. All this evidently proves that nature maintains a fixed and immutable order, that God has been the same in all ages known and unknown to us, and that the laws of nature are so perfect and so fruitful that nothing can be added to or detracted from them, and miracles only seem to be new owing to men's ignorance. This, then, is what is explicitly taught in Scripture; nowhere does it teach us that anything happens in nature that contradicts nature's laws or cannot follow from them; and we should not attribute any such doctrine to it. 96

In addition, miracles require causes and circumstances (as we have already shown). They do not follow from the kind of autocratic government the common people ascribe to God but rather from divine decree and government which (as we have also shown from Scripture itself) signifies the laws of nature and its order. Finally, miracles may also be performed by impostors, as is proved from Deuteronomy 13 and Matthew 24.24.

It follows, further, and with the utmost clarity, that miracles were natural events and therefore must be explained so as not to seem 'new' (to use Solomon's word) or in conflict with nature, but as close to natural realities as possible; and I have given some rules derived from Scripture alone in order that anyone should be capable of doing this fairly easily.

[23]   Although I say that Scripture teaches these things, however, I do not mean that the Bible promotes them as doctrines necessary for salvation, but only that the prophets embraced them just as we do. Therefore it is up to every man to hold the opinion about them that he feels best enables him to subscribe with all his mind to the cult and religion of God. This is also the opinion of Josephus. Here is what he writes at the end of book 2 of his *Antiquities*: 'Let no one disbelieve this talk of a miracle occurring among men of the distant past, innocent of evil as they were, for whom a path to safety opened through the sea, whether this happened by God's will or of its own accord. For in more recent times the Pamphylian sea divided for the troops of Alexander, king of Macedon, and afforded them a passage through it when they had no other way to go, since it was God's will to destroy the Persian kingdom by means of him. This is admitted by everyone who has written about the deeds of Alexander; everyone therefore should think as he pleases about these things'.[10] These are Josephus' words and his judgement about belief in miracles.

---

[10] Josephus, *Antiquities of the Jews*, 2.347–8. We have rendered the Greek text of Josephus, since the Latin translation used by Spinoza is unintelligible at one point (*antiquitus a resistentibus*). The final clause of the quotation is a phrase which Josephus uses several times when recounting an extraordinary event.

On the interpretation of Scripture

[1]   All men are ready to say that Holy Scripture is the word of God that teaches us true happiness or the way of salvation, but their actions betray a quite different opinion. For the common people, the last thing that they appear to want is to live by the teaching of Scripture. We see them advancing false notions of their own as the word of God and seeking to use the influence of religion to compel other people to agree with them. As for theologians, we see that for the most part they have sought to extract their own thoughts and opinions from the Bible and thereby endow them with divine authority. There is nothing that they interpret with less hesitation and greater boldness than the Scriptures, that is the mind of the Holy Spirit. If they hesitate at all, it is not because they are afraid of ascribing error to the Holy Spirit or straying from the path of salvation, but rather of being convicted of error by others and seeing themselves despised and their authority trodden underfoot.

If people truly believed in their hearts what they say with their lips about Scripture, they would follow a completely different way of life. There would be fewer differences of opinion occupying their minds, fewer bitter controversies between them, and less blind and reckless ambition to distort our interpretation of the Bible and devise novelties in religion. On the contrary, they would not dare to accept anything as biblical teaching which they had not derived from it in the clearest possible way. Sacrilegious persons, who have not been afraid to corrupt the Scriptures in so many places, would have been careful to avoid committing such a dreadful offence and kept their impious hands off them. But vice and ambition have in the end exercised so much influence that religion has been made to consist in defending purely human delusions

rather than in following the teachings of the Holy Spirit. Far from con-
sisting of love, it has been turned, under the false labels of holy devotion
and ardent zeal, into the promotion of conflict and dissemination of
senseless hatred.

These bad things have been aggravated by superstition, which teaches
people to despise reason, and nature, and revere and venerate only such
things as conflict with these both. So it is hardly surprising that to
enhance their admiration and reverence for scripture, men seek to interpret it in such a way that it seems to conflict altogether with reason and
with nature. They imagine that the most profound mysteries are hidden
in Holy Scripture and put all their energy into investigating these absurd
issues while neglecting other matters which are useful. The fantasies they
come up with they ascribe to the Holy Spirit, attempting to defend them
with all the force and power of their passions. For this is how human
beings are constructed: whatever they conceive purely with their intellects, they also defend purely with intellect and reason while, on the
other hand, whatever opinions they derive from their passions, they
defend with their passions.

[2]   To extricate ourselves from such confusion and to free our minds
from theological prejudices and the blind acceptance of human fictions
as God's teaching, we need to analyse and discuss the true method of
interpreting Scripture. For if we do not know this, we can know nothing
for certain regarding what the Bible or the Holy Spirit wishes to teach. To
formulate the matter succinctly, I hold that the method of interpreting
Scripture, does not differ from the [correct] method of interpreting
nature, but rather is wholly consonant with it. The [correct] method of
interpreting nature consists above all in constructing a natural history,
from which we derive the definitions of natural things, as from certain
data. Likewise, to interpret Scripture, we need to assemble a genuine
history of it and to deduce the thinking of the Bible's authors by valid
inferences from this history, as from certain data and principles.
Provided we admit no other criteria or data for interpreting Scripture
and discussing its contents than what is drawn from Scripture itself
and its history, we will always proceed without any danger of going
astray, and we shall have the same assuredness in discussing things that
surpass our understanding as in discussing things that we learn by the
natural light of reason.

[3]   But in order to be perfectly clear that this method is not only the sure way but also the only way, and is consistent with the method of interpreting nature, we should note that the Bible is very often concerned with things that cannot be deduced from principles known by the natural light of reason. For the greater part of it is composed of historical narratives and revelations. In particular, these histories contain miracles, that is (as we showed in the previous chapter), narratives of things unknown to nature adapted to the beliefs and judgments of the chroniclers who compiled them. Revelations likewise are adjusted to the beliefs of the prophets, as we showed in the second chapter, and really do transcend human understanding. Consequently, knowledge of all these things, that is, of almost everything in Scripture, must be sought from the Bible itself, just as knowledge of nature has to be sought from nature itself.

[4]   As for the moral teachings contained in the Bible, these can indeed be demonstrated from general concepts, but it cannot be demonstrated from general concepts that Scripture teaches them; this can only be made evident from Scripture itself. In fact, if we want to attest the divine character of Scripture objectively, we must establish from the Bible alone that it offers true moral doctrines. This is the only ground on which its divine character can be proven. For we have shown that this is principally what the assurance of the prophets derived from, that their minds were attuned to the right and the good; and this is what we need to be convinced of ourselves, if we are to have confidence in them. We have also already proven that God's divinity cannot be attested by miracles, not to mention the fact that miracles could also be performed by false prophets. Hence, the divine character of the Bible must needs be established by this one thing alone, that it teaches true virtue, something which can only be established from Scripture itself. Were this not the case, we could not acknowledge the Bible and its divine character without massively prejudging the issue. All of our knowledge of the Bible, hence, must be derived only from the Bible itself. Finally, Scripture does not offer definitions of the things which it speaks of, any more than does nature. Such definitions must be drawn from the various narratives about different things in Scripture just as definitions of natural things are deduced from the different actions of nature.

[5]   The universal rule then for interpreting Scripture is to claim nothing as a biblical doctrine that we have not derived, by the closest possible

scrutiny, from its own [i.e. the Bible's] history.[1] What sort of thing a history of Scripture needs to be and what are the principal things it must deal with have now to be explained.

(1) Firstly, such a history must include the nature and properties of the language in which the biblical books were composed and which their authors were accustomed to speak. We can then investigate all the possible meanings that every single phrase in common usage can admit; and because all the writers of both the Old and the New Testament were Hebrews undeniably the history of the Hebrew language is more essential than anything else not only for understanding the books of the Old Testament which were first written in this language, but also those of the New Testament. For while the latter were propagated in other languages, they are full of Hebrew idioms.

(2) [Such a history] must gather together the opinions expressed in each individual book and organize them by subject so that we may have available by this means all the statements that are found on each topic. We should then make note of any that are ambiguous or obscure or seem to contradict others. By obscure expressions I mean those whose sense is difficult to elicit from the context of a passage while those whose meaning is readily elicited I call clear. I am not now speaking of how easily or otherwise their truth is grasped by reason; for we are concerned here only with their meaning, not with their truth. Moreover, in seeking the sense of Scripture we must take care especially not to be blinded by our own reasoning, in so far as it is founded on the principles of natural knowledge (not to mention our preconceptions). In order not to confuse the genuine sense of a passage with the truth of things, we must investigate a passage's sense only from its use of the language or from reasoning which accepts no other foundation than Scripture itself.

To make all this more clearly understood, I will give an example. Moses' statements, 'God is fire' and 'God is jealous' are as plain as possible so long as we attend exclusively to the meaning of the words, and therefore I class them as clear expressions, even though, with respect to truth and reason, they are exceedingly obscure. Moreover even though their literal sense conflicts with the natural light of reason, unless it is also clearly in conflict with the principles and fundamentals derived from investigating the history of Scripture we must still stick to this, the literal sense. Conversely, if the literal sense of these expressions is found to conflict with the principles drawn from Scripture, even if they are fully in agreement with reason, they will nevertheless need to be interpreted differently (i.e., metaphorically).

---

[1] Ex ipsius historia.

In order to know whether or not Moses believed that God is fire, we certainly must not argue on the basis of whether this statement agrees or conflicts with reason but only from other statements made by Moses himself. For example, since Moses also plainly teaches, in many passages, that God has no similarity with visible things in the sky or on earth or in the water, we must conclude that either this statement or all the others have to be interpreted metaphorically. But we should depart as little as possible from the literal sense, and therefore we must first ask whether this unique expression, 'God is fire', admits any but a literal sense, i.e., whether the word 'fire' has any other meaning apart from natural fire. If we do not find it signifying anything else in normal linguistic usage, that is how we must interpret the expression, however much it may conflict with reason. All the others, however much they agree with reason, will have to be accommodated to this one. Where linguistic usage does not permit this, such statements are irreconcilable, and hence we must suspend judgment about them. Now the word 'fire' also stands for anger and jealousy (see Job 31.12), and therefore Moses' statements are readily reconciled, and we are justified in concluding that they are one and the same. Again, Moses plainly teaches that God is jealous and nowhere teaches that God lacks emotions or mental passions. Hence, we must evidently deduce that this is what Moses believed, or at least what he wanted to teach, however much we may think this statement conflicts with reason. For, as we have already shown, we are not permitted to adjust the meaning of Scripture to the dictates of our reason or our preconceived opinions; all explanation of the Bible must be sought from the Bible alone.

(3) Finally our historical enquiry must explain the circumstances of all the books of the prophets whose memory has come down to us: the life, character and particular interests of the author of each individual book, who exactly he was, on what occasion he wrote, for whom and in what language. Then the fate of each book: namely how it was first received and whose hands it came into, how many variant readings there have been of its text, by whose decision it was received among the sacred books, and finally how all the books which are now accepted as sacred came to form a single corpus. All this, I contend, has to be dealt with in a history of the Bible.

It is important to know of the life, character and concerns of each writer, so that we may know which statements are meant as laws and which as moral doctrine; we are more readily able to explain someone's words, the better we know his mind and personality. It is also crucial to know on what occasion, at what time and for what people or age the various texts were written so that we may not confuse eternal doctrines with those that are merely temporary or useful only to a few people. It is essential, finally, to know all the other things mentioned above, so that, apart from the question of authorship, we may also discover, for each book, whether it may have been contaminated with spurious passages or not; whether mistakes have crept in, and whether the mistakes have been corrected by unskilled or untrustworthy hands. It is vital to know all this, so that we will not be carried away by blind zeal or just accept whatever is put in front of us. We must acknowledge exclusively what is certain and unquestionable.

[6]   Only when we have this history of Scripture before us and have made up our minds not to accept anything as a teaching of the prophets which does not follow from this history or may be very clearly derived from it, will it be time to begin investigating the minds of the prophets and the Holy Spirit. But this also requires a method and an order like we use for explaining nature on the basis of its history. In setting out to research natural history, we attempt first of all to investigate the things that are most universal and common to the whole of nature, *viz.* motion and rest and their laws and rules which nature always observes and by which it continually acts; from these we proceed by degrees to others that are less universal. Similarly we must first seek from the biblical history that which is most universal, the basis and foundation of the whole of Scripture, something affirmed by all the biblical prophets as eternal doctrine of supreme value for all men: for example, that there is a God, one and omnipotent, who alone is to be adored and cares for all men, loving most those who worship Him and love their neighbour as themselves, etc. These and similar things, I contend, Scripture teaches so plainly and so explicitly throughout that no one has ever called its meaning into question in these matters. But Scripture does not teach expressly, as eternal doctrine, what God is, and how he sees all things and provides for them, and so on. On the contrary, as we have already seen above, the prophets themselves have no agreed view about these matters, so that on these questions nothing can regarded as the teaching of the Holy Spirit, even if they can be decided very well by the natural light of reason.

103

[7]   Once we have adequately got to know this universal doctrine of Scripture, we should then proceed to other less universal things which concern matters of daily life, flowing like rivulets from the universal teaching. Such are all the particular external actions of true virtue which can only be done when the opportunity arises. Anything found in the

Scriptures about these things which is obscure and ambiguous, should be explained and decided only by the Bible's universal doctrine, and where such passages are self-contradictory, we must consider on what occasion, when, and to whom they were written.

When Christ says, 'blessed are those who mourn, for they shall receive consolation', for example, we do not know from the text what he means by 'those who mourn'. But later he teaches that we should be anxious about nothing but the kingdom of God alone and its justice, and this is what he commends as the supreme good (see Matthew 6.33). From this it follows that by 'those who mourn' he means only those who mourn that the kingdom of God and justice are neglected by men; for only those can mourn this who love nothing but God's kingdom and justice, and wholly despise all fortune besides.

So too when he says, 'but to him who strikes you on your right cheek, turn to him the other also', etc. Had Christ given these commands to judges as a legislator, he would have destroyed the Law of Moses by this edict. But he openly commends that Law (see Matthew 5.17); consequently, we must examine who it was exactly that said these things, to whom and at what time. Certainly, it was Christ who uttered them, but he was not laying down ordinances as a legislator. Rather he was offering doctrine as a teacher, because (as we showed above) it was less external actions that he sought to correct than people's minds. He pronounced these words to people who were oppressed and living in a corrupt state where justice was completely neglected, and he saw that the ruin of that state was imminent.

This very doctrine that Christ taught at a time when the city's desolation was imminent, we see that Jeremiah had also expounded at the time of the first destruction of the city (see Lamentations 3, letters Tet and Yod[2]). Hence, the prophets offered this teaching only at a time of oppression, and it is nowhere promulgated as a law. On the contrary, 104 Moses (who did not write at a time of oppression, but, it should be noted, was striving to construct a well-ordered state) issued the edicts to pay an eye for an eye, even though he too condemned vengeance and hatred of one's neighbour. Thus, it most evidently follows from the very principles of Scripture itself, that the doctrine of suffering injury and giving way to impious men in everything, is appropriate only in places

---

[2] *Lamentations* 3.25–30.

where justice is neglected and in times of oppression, but not in a well-ordered state. Indeed in a viable state, where justice is protected, everyone is obliged, if he wants to be considered just, to prosecute wrongs before a court (see Leviticus 5.1), not so as to secure revenge (see Leviticus 19.17–18) but to defend justice and his country's laws and to ensure that wrongdoing does not pay. All of this fully accords with natural reason. I could give many other examples pointing in the same direction, but consider these sufficient to explicate my meaning and the usefulness of this method, which is what concerns me at present.

[8]   So far we have explained only how to explore the meaning of biblical statements about questions of daily life. These are issues which are relatively easy to investigate since none of this was ever a subject of controversy for biblical writers. But other matters to be found in the Bible concerning purely philosophical questions, cannot be so easily resolved. The path to be followed here is thus more arduous. As we have already seen, the prophets disagreed among themselves in philosophical matters, and their narratives of things are very much adapted to the presuppositions of their respective times, and therefore we may not infer or explain the meaning of one prophet from clearer passages in another, unless it is absolutely evident that they both held exactly the same opinion. I will therefore now briefly explain how the mind of the prophets in such matters is to be investigated by an enquiry into Scripture.

Here too we must again begin from the most universal things, by inquiring first of all, from the clearest scriptural expressions, what prophecy or revelation is, and what it chiefly consists in. Then we must ask what a miracle is, and continue thus with the most general questions. From these we must descend to the opinions of each individual prophet, and from these in turn proceed finally to the sense of each particular

105   revelation or prophecy, of each narrative and miracle. We have given many examples above, in the appropriate places, showing how much care is needed not to confuse the minds of the prophets and historians with the mind of the Holy Spirit, so I do not think I need to discuss this at greater length. I should remark, however, with regard to the meaning of revelations, that our method only teaches us to investigate what the prophets actually saw or heard, not what they intended to signify or represent by these visions; that we can only conjecture, since we certainly cannot deduce it from the principles of Scripture.

[9]   We have offered a method for interpreting Scripture and at the same time demonstrated that this is the most certain and only way to uncover its true meaning. I grant that certainty about this last is easier to find for those, if they exist, who possess a solid tradition or a true exegesis inherited from the prophets themselves, such as the Pharisees claim to have, or those who possess a Pope who cannot err in the interpretation of scripture, as Roman Catholics proclaim. Since, however, we cannot be certain either about that tradition or papal authority, nothing certain can be grounded on either of these. The latter was denied by the earliest Christians and the former by the most ancient Jewish sects; further, if we then examine the chronology (apart from any other arguments) which the Pharisees inherited from their rabbis by which they trace this tradition back to Moses, we shall find that it is false, as I show in another place.[3]

This is why such a tradition should be altogether suspect to us. And although we are obliged, by our method, to consider one Jewish tradition as uncorrupt, namely the meaning of words in the Hebrew language we have received from them, we can still fairly have doubts about the former tradition while accepting the latter. For it could never have been of any use to change a word's meaning, but it might quite often have been useful to someone to alter the meaning of a passage. In fact it is extremely difficult to alter the meaning of a word; anyone who tried it would have at the same time to interpret in his own way and manner all the authors who have written in that language using that term in its accepted sense, or else with the greatest wariness corrupt the text. Again, the learned share with the common people in preserving a language, but the learned alone preserve books and the meanings of texts. Accordingly, we can easily conceive that the learned could have altered or perverted the sense of a passage in a very   106 rare book which they had under their control, but not the significance of words. Anyone who attempts to change the meaning of a word to which he is accustomed will have great difficulty in afterwards sticking consistently to the change in his speech and writing. We are thus wholly convinced, for these and other reasons, that it could never have entered into anyone's head to corrupt a language but might certainly occur to someone to misrepresent the meaning of a writer by doctoring his texts or interpreting them wrongly.

---

[3] See chapter 10 para. 17 below. pp. 153–4.

[10] Since our method, based on the principle that knowledge of the Bible is to be sought from Scripture alone, is the only true method, wherever it is unable to yield what is needed for a complete knowledge of Scripture, we must simply give up. I must now therefore point out the limitations and difficulties in this method's capacity to guide us towards a full and certain knowledge of the sacred books.

[11] Firstly, a major obstacle in this method is that it requires a perfect knowledge of the Hebrew language. But where is this to be sought? The ancient scholars of Hebrew have left nothing to posterity about the principles and structure of the language; at least we have absolutely nothing from them: no dictionary, no grammar, no book of rhetoric. The Jewish people have lost all their cultural and artistic accomplishments – no wonder, after suffering so many massacres and persecutions – and have held on to nothing but a few fragments of their language and a few books. Almost all the names of fruits, birds, fish, and very many other words, have perished through the ravages of time. Thus the meaning of many nouns and verbs occurring in the Bible is either completely unknown or disputed. Not only do we lack all this but, worst of all, we have no phrase-book of the language; for almost all the idioms and modes of speech peculiar to the Hebrew people have been erased from man's memory by all-devouring time.[4] We cannot therefore always discover, as we should, all the meanings of each and every phrase which usage of the language might yield, and there will be many statements expressed in distinctly known words whose sense will nevertheless still be highly obscure or utterly incomprehensible.

[12] Besides our inability fully to reconstruct the history of Hebrew, the very nature and structure of the language create so many uncertainties 107 that it is impossible to devise a method[5] which will show us how to uncover the true sense of all the statements of Scripture with assurance. For besides the usual causes of ambiguity common to all tongues, there are certain other features of this language that procduce a whole host of ambiguities. I think it is worth mentioning them here.

Firstly, a frequent source of vagueness and obscurity of expression in the Bible arises from the fact that all the letters of each single organ of speech are used interchangeably. Hebrew divides all the letters of the alphabet into

---

[4] Cf. Ovid, *Metamorphoses* 15.234 tempus edax rerum.   [5] Spinoza's footnote: see Annotation 7.

five classes, according to the five organs of the mouth involved in pronunciation, i.e. the lips, the tongue, the teeth, the palate and the throat. For example, *alef, het, 'ayin* and *hē* are called gutturals, and one is used for another without any distinction, at least so far as we know. Similarly, *el*, which means 'to', is often used for *'al*, which means 'above', and vice versa. This often renders all the parts of a phrase ambiguous or turns them into sounds devoid of meaning.

A second major source of ambiguity of phrases arises from the fact that conjunctions and adverbs have multiple significations. For instance, *vav* serves indifferently as a conjunction and disjunction: it can mean 'and', 'but', 'because', 'moreover' and 'then'. *ki* has seven or eight meanings: 'because', 'although', 'if', 'when', 'just as', 'that', 'burning', etc. It is the same with nearly all the particles.

The third ambiguity, that generates many others, is that verbs in the indicative have no present, imperfect, pluperfect, future perfect or other tenses which are usual in other languages; in the imperative and the infinitive they lack all but the present tense, and in the subjunctive they have no tenses at all. All these deficiencies of tense and mood can indeed be compensated for, very readily and neatly, from basic features of the language, following certain rules. But the earliest writers completely ignored them, and indifferently used the future tense for the present and past, and the past for the future, as well as the indicative for the imperative and subjunctive, and this has caused a good deal of uncertainty.

[13] Besides these three causes of obscurity in Hebrew, two others should be noted both of which are far more important. The first of these is that Hebrew has no letters for vowels. The second is that the Hebrews 108 did not use punctuation marks to separate clauses or for any kind of expression or emphasis. While both these things (both vowels and signs) are normally indicated by points and accents, we cannot accept these uncritically because they were invented and inserted by critics of a later period, whose authority ought not to weigh with us. It is clear from an abundance of evidence that the ancient writers wrote without points (i.e., without vowels and accents). Later generations added these two features in accordance with their own interpretations of the biblical books. Hence, accents and points which we now have are merely recent interpretations, and deserve no more credit or authority than other explanations of these authors.

Those who do not know this criticize the author of the Epistle to the Hebrews (11.21) for giving an interpretation of the text of Genesis 47.31 which is very wide of the reading of the pointed Hebrew text – as if the apostle should have learned the meaning of Scripture from those who inserted the points. My view is that it is, rather, the 'pointers' who are to blame. I will give both interpretations here, so that everyone may see this, and realize that the difference arises specifically from the lack of vowels. The 'pointers' interpreted this text, their points show, as meaning: 'and Israel leaned over' (or, changing *'ayin* into *alef* which is a letter of the same organ of speech, 'towards') 'the head of the bed'. But the author of the Letter interprets: 'and Israel leant over the head of the stick', because he is reading *mate* where others read *mita*, a difference arising solely from the vowels. Now this narrative is about the old age of Jacob, not about his sickness which comes in the next chapter, and it therefore seems more likely that the historian meant that Jacob leaned on the head of the stick (which of course very old people use to support themselves) and not of the bed, especially since in this way there is no need to suppose any substitution of letters. My aim in giving this example is not just to reconcile the passage of the Letter to the Hebrews with the text of Genesis, but, more importantly, to show how little we should trust modern points and accents. Consequently, anyone who sets out to interpret Scripture without preconceptions is obliged to be sceptical about them and to study the text with fresh eyes.

[14]   To return to our point, one may easily discern from the structure
109 and nature of the Hebrew language that numerous ambiguities are inevitable, and that no method will resolve them all. We cannot hope for this to be completely achieved by comparing expressions with each other which we have shown is the only way of distinguishing the true sense from the many senses which an expression may admit in ordinary usage. This is because comparison of expressions can only throw light on an expression accidentally, since no prophet wrote with the intention of deliberately explaining either another's words or his own. It is also because we can only infer the mind of one prophet, Apostle etc. from the mind of another in common, everyday matters, as we have already clearly shown but not when they speak about philosophical things or when they narrate miracles or historical events. I could also give some examples to show that many expressions that occur in Holy Scripture are inexplicable, but I prefer to

pass this over for the present, and proceed to make some further remarks about the difficulties and limitations of this the true method of interpreting Scripture.

[15] A further problem with this method is that it requires a history of the vicissitudes of all the biblical books, and most of this is unknown to us. For either we have no knowledge whatever of the authors, or (if you prefer) the compilers, of many of the books – or else we are uncertain about them, as I will demonstrate fully in the next chapters. Also, we do not know under what circumstances these books whose compilers are unknown were composed or when. Nor do we know into whose hands all these books subsequently came, or in whose copies so many variant readings occur, nor whether there may not have been many additional readings in others. I touched upon the need to know all this at one point but purposely omitted a few things which we should deal with now. If we read any book that contains incredible or incomprehensible things, or is written in very obscure language, and if we do not know its author or when and under what circumstances he wrote it, our efforts to get at its true sense will be fruitless. For if all this is unknown, we cannot ascertain what the author intended or might have intended. When, on the other hand, all these things are adequately known, we determine our thoughts so as not to make prejudicial judgments or attribute to the author, or person on whose behalf he wrote, either more or less than is correct, or take anything else into consideration but what the author could have had in mind, or what the period and context demanded.

110

This I think will be clear to everyone. It frequently happens that we read very similar stories in different books, about which we make quite contrasting judgments, depending on the different views we have of the writers. I remember once reading in a certain book that a man whose name was Orlando Furioso[6] was wont to drive a winged monster through the air and fly over any regions he wished, single-handedly killing large numbers of men and giants, and other fantasies of this kind, which are totally incomprehensible to our intellect. I have read a similar story in Ovid about Perseus,[7] and another in the books of Judges and Kings[8] about Samson (who alone and unarmed killed a thousand men) and Elijah,[9] who flew

[6] Ariosto, *Orlando Furioso* 10.66.   [7] Ovid, *Metamorphoses* 4.600ff.   [8] Judges 15.9–16.
[9] 2 Kings 2.11.

through the air and finally went off to heaven in a fiery chariot and horses. Yet although these stories, as I say, are very much alike, we nevertheless make a very different judgment about each of them. We persuade ourselves that the first writer intended to write only fables, the second poetical themes,[10] and the third sacred matters, and the only reason for such [differentiation] is the opinion we have about the writers. Thus it is vitally important to have some knowledge of the authors who have written things which are obscure or incomprehensible to the intellect, if we want to interpret their writings. For the same reasons, it is likewise vital, if we are to be able, when a passage is unintelligible, to reach a true reading from all the variants, to know in whose copy these readings were found and whether other readings have ever been encountered in the copies of other scribes of greater authority.

[16]   Another and final difficulty in interpreting some biblical books by our method is that we do not now have them in the same language in which they were originally written. The Gospel of Matthew and without doubt also the Letter to the Hebrews are commonly believed to have been composed in Hebrew, but these versions are not extant. There is also some doubt in what language the book of Job was written. Ibn Ezra[11] asserts in his commentary that it was translated into Hebrew from another language and that this is the cause of its obscurity. I will not discuss the apocryphal books, since they are of very different authority.

[17]   All these, then, are the difficulties of this method of interpreting Scripture on the basis of its own history which I undertook to describe. I think these difficulties are so great that I do not hesitate to affirm that in numerous passages either we do not know the true sense of Scripture or can only guess at it without any assurance. However, we must also stress that all these problems can only prevent our understanding the minds of the prophets in matters that are incomprehensible and which we can only imagine, and not those topics that are accessible to the intellect and of which we can readily form a clear conception.[12] For matters that by their nature are easily grasped can never be so obscurely phrased that they cannot be readily understood, according to the saying, a word is enough for

---

[10] Accepting the emendation 'res poeticas' for 'res politicas'.
[11] Ibn Ezra, *Commentary on Job*, 2.11.   [12] Spinoza's footnote: see Annotation 8.

a wise man.[13] Euclid, who wrote nothing that was not eminently straightforward and highly intelligible, is easily explained by anyone in any language. In order to see his meaning and be certain of his sense there is no need to have a complete knowledge of the language in which he wrote, but only a very modest, even schoolboy, acquaintance with it, nor does one need to know the life, interests and character of the author, nor in what language he wrote, to whom and when, nor the subsequent fate of his book or its variant readings, nor how or by what Council it was authorized.

What is true of Euclid we may also say about all who have written about things that are intelligible via their own nature. We thus conclude that we can readily discover the meaning of the Bible's moral teaching from the history of it that we are able to reconstruct, and can be certain about its true sense. For the teachings of true piety are expressed in the most everyday language, since they are very common and extremely simple and easy to understand. And since true salvation and happiness consists in our intellect's genuine acquiescence [in what is true] and we truly acquiesce only in what we understand very clearly, it most evidently follows that we can securely grasp the meaning of Scripture in matters necessary for salvation and happiness. Consequently, there is no reason why we should be concerned to the same extent about the rest, given that for the most part we are unable to grasp it by reason or the intellect and it is therefore something more curious than useful.

112

[18] I have now explained, I think, the true method for interpreting Scripture, and sufficiently expounded my view of it. Moreover, I do not doubt that everyone now sees that this method requires no other light than that of natural reason. For the special character and excellence of this light chiefly consists in deducing and concluding by valid inferences from things known or accepted as known, matters that are imperfectly understood and this is all that our method requires. Admittedly, this procedure does not suffice to achieve certainty about everything in the biblical books, but this is due not to any defect in our methodology but because the path it shows to be the true and right one was never cultivated, or even ventured on, by men, so that owing to the passage of time, it became arduous and almost impassable, as is eminently clear, I think, from the difficulties that I have pointed out.

[13] Terence, *Phormio* 541, Plautus, *Persa* 729.

[19] It remains now to examine the views of those who disagree with us. First, I shall consider the opinion of those who hold that the natural light of reason does not have the power to interpret Scripture and that for this a supernatural light is absolutely essential.[14] What this light is which is beyond nature, I leave to them to explain. I, for my part, can only surmise that they have been trying to admit, in very obscure terms, that they are generally in doubt about the true sense of Scripture; for if we examine their interpretations, we shall find that they contain nothing supernatural, indeed nothing more than mere conjectures. Compare them if you will with the interpretations of those who frankly admit that they have no light beyond the natural light – they will be found to be entirely comparable to them; that is, they are just human conceptions, the result of hard work and much thought.

As for their claim that the natural light of reason is not adequate for this task, it is evident that this is false. We have already proved that none of the difficulties in the interpretation of Scripture arises from the inadequacy of the natural light, but only from human carelessness (not to mention malice) in neglecting to construct the history of the Bible when it would have been possible to do so. It is also due (as everyone, I think, would admit) to this supernatural light being a divine gift bestowed only on the faithful. But the prophets and Apostles used to preach not only to the faithful but, primarily, to unbelievers and impious persons, who were thus enabled to understand the meaning of the prophets and Apostles. Otherwise the prophets and Apostles would have appeared to be preaching to little children and infants, not to people endowed with reason; it would have been pointless for Moses to make laws if they could be understood only by the faithful who need no law. Hence those who postulate the need for a supernatural light to interpret the minds of the prophets and Apostles truly seem to be lacking in natural light themselves; so I am very far from believing that such men have a divine supernatural gift.

[20] Maimonides' view, though, was very different. He thought that every passage of Scripture yields various, even contradictory, senses and that we cannot be certain of the truth of any of them unless we know that

---

[14] Presumably, Spinoza is chiefly thinking here of such Dutch Collegiant Bible critics as Petrus Serrarius (1600–9), Jan Pietersz. Beelthower (*c.* 1603–*c.* 1669), and his close friend Jarig Jelles (*c.* 1620–83), all of whom he knew well since his early years in Amsterdam and with whom he had doubtless often debated.

that passage which we are interpreting, contains nothing that is contrary to or that does not accord with reason. If its literal sense is found to conflict with reason, no matter how evident that may seem to be in itself, he insists it should then be construed differently. He makes this absolutely plain in his *More Nebuchim*[15] Part II, Chapter 25, where he says: 'Know that we do not refrain from saying that the world has existed from eternity on account of texts in Scripture about the creation of the world. For the passages teaching that the world was created are no more numerous than those which teach that God is corporeal. None of the ways by which we might explain the texts on the creation of the world are barred to us or even obstructed; indeed, we could have used the same method to interpret these as we used to reject the corporality of God. It might even have been much easier. We might have been able to explain these texts more naturally and find more support [in Scripture] for the eternity of the world than we found for the view that the blessed God is corporeal, which, on our interpretation, Scripture excludes. But two reasons persuade me not to do this and not to believe this' (namely, that the world is eternal). 'Firstly, because there is clear proof that God is not corporeal, and it is necessary to explain all the passages whose literal sense is in conflict with this proof, for it is certain that they will have an explanation' (other than the literal one). 'But there is no proof of the eternity of the world; and therefore it is not necessary, in quest of such a conception, to do violence to Scripture for the sake of an apparent opinion since we would accept its contrary if we found a convincing argument for it. The second reason is that to believe that God is incorporeal is not in conflict with the fundamentals of the Law, etc. But to believe in the eternity of the world in the manner in which Aristotle held destroys the Law from its foundations, etc.'

These are the words of Maimonides, from which what we have just said plainly follows. For if it was clear to him on the basis of reason that the world was eternal, he would not hesitate to bend Scripture to devise an interpretation that would ultimately render it saying apparently the same thing. In fact, he would be immediately convinced that Scripture intended to teach the eternity of the world, despite the fact that it everywhere says the opposite. Hence, it is impossible for him to be certain of the Bible's true meaning, however plain it may be, as long as he can doubt the truth of

114

---

[15] Maimonides, *Guide of the Perplexed* II.25.

what is stated there, or as long as its truth is not fully evident to him. For while the truth of a thing is not evident we will not know whether it agrees with reason or contradicts it and, consequently, will also not know whether the literal sense is true or false. Were this approach indeed the correct one, I absolutely agree that we would then need something beyond the natural light for interpreting Scripture. For there is almost nothing in the Bible that can be deduced from principles known by the natural light of reason (as we have already shown), and therefore we simply cannot be certain about their truth by means of the natural light. Hence, we could not be certain about the true meaning and sense of Scripture either, and we would necessarily need another light.

Again, were this conception [of Maimonides] correct, it would follow that the common people, who for the most part do not understand proofs or do not have time to examine them, will only be able to reach any conclusion at all about Scripture on the sole authority and testimony of philosophers, and consequently would have to suppose that philosophers cannot err in interpreting Scripture. This would surely produce a new ecclesiastical authority and a novel species of priest or pontiff, which would more likely be mocked than venerated by the common people.

While our method requires a knowledge of Hebrew and the common people likewise have no time to study that, no such objection weakens our position. For the Jewish and gentile common people for whom in their day the prophets and Apostles preached and wrote, understood their language so that they also grasped the prophets' meaning. Yet they did not understand the reasons for what the prophets preached, though, according to Maimonides, they needed to know them if they were going to grasp their meaning. Under our methodological scheme, hence, it need not follow that the common people must accept the testimony of interpreters. I can point to the common people who understood very well the language of the prophets and Apostles, but Maimonides will not be able to point to any common people who understand the causes of things and grasp their meaning on that basis. As far as the common people of today, are concerned, we have already shown that they can readily grasp in any language everything necessary for salvation as this is all entirely normal and familiar, even if they are ignorant about the reasons for what is required; and the common people rely on this understanding, and certainly not on the testimony of interpreters. As for everything else, there they are in the same position as the learned.

[21]   But let us return to Maimonides' stance and look at it more carefully. Firstly, it presupposes that the prophets agreed among themselves
in everything and were consummate philosophers and theologians; for
he insists that they reached conclusions from the truth of things which
we showed in chapter 2 to be false. Then his position assumes that the
sense of Scripture cannot be established from the Bible itself; for the
truth of things is not established from Scripture since it offers no demonstration of anything, and does not teach the things about which it speaks by
means of definitions and their own first causes. According to Maimonides,
therefore, its true sense cannot be established from itself and should not be
sought from the Bible itself. But it is evident from this chapter that this too
is incorrect. We have shown by both reason and examples that the sense of
Scripture is established from the Bible itself and, even when it speaks
about things known by the natural light of reason, is to be sought from the
Bible alone. Finally, his view assumes that we are permitted to explain and
distort the words of Scripture according to our own preconceived opinions, and to reject the literal sense, even when it is perfectly lucid and
explicit, and bend it to some other sense. Apart from the fact that such
liberty is diametrically opposed to what we have proved in this and other
chapters, nobody can fail to see that it is excessively audacious.

But suppose we granted such great freedom, what does it achieve?
Assuredly, nothing at all. For those things that are indemonstrable and
which compose the larger part of Scripture cannot be investigated by
this procedure nor explained or interpreted by this approach. Whereas,   116
on the other hand, by following our method, we can explain many such
things and discuss them with assurance, as we have already shown both
by reason and by the fact itself. As for whatever is comprehensible from
its nature, its sense, as we have already shown, can readily be derived
from the context of what is said. Hence the method [of Maimonides] is
plainly useless. It also utterly deprives the common people of the assurance they derive from conscientious reading and which everyone can have
of the sense of Scripture by following a different method. This is why we
dismiss this opinion of Maimonides as harmful, useless and absurd.

[22]   As for the tradition of the Pharisees, we have already noted above
that it is inconsistent with itself while the authority of the Roman Popes
requires clearer evidence, and for this reason alone I reject it. For if they
could prove [their authority] to us from Scripture itself and with the same

certainty as the Hebrew high priests could once do, it would not worry me that among the Roman Popes there have been a number of heretics and impious men. For formerly among the Hebrews heretics and impious men were also to be found who acquired the supreme pontificate by dubious means and yet nevertheless wielded, by edict of Scripture, the supreme power of interpreting the law. See Deuteronomy 17.11–12 and 33.10 and Malachi 2.8. But as they produce no such testimony, their authority remains wholly suspect.

In case anyone is misled by the example of the Hebrew High Priest to believe that the Catholic religion too requires a high priest, one must remark that the laws of Moses were the public laws of a country and necessarily needed therefore a public authority for their preservation. If every individual had the liberty to interpret the public laws at his own discretion, no state could survive; it would immediately be dissolved by this very fact, and public law would be private law. It is wholly different with religion. Since it does not consist so much in external actions as in simplicity and truth of mind, it does not belong to any public law or authority. For simplicity and truth of mind are not instilled in men by the power of laws or by public authority, and absolutely no one can be compelled to be happy by force of law. It requires rather pious and fraternal advice, a proper upbringing and, more than anything else, one's own free judgment. Since therefore the supreme right of thinking freely, about religion also, belongs to each and every individual, and it cannot be conceived that anyone could surrender this right, every individual will also possess the supreme right and authority to judge freely about religion and to explain it and interpret it for himself. The reason why the supreme authority in interpreting the laws and the supreme judgment on public questions lie with the magistrate is simply because they are matters of public right. For the same reason the authority to interpret religion and make judgments about it, will lie with each individual man, because it is a question of individual right.

It is therefore far from being the case that the authority of the Roman Pontiff to interpret religion can be inferred from the authority of the Hebrew High Priest to interpret the laws; on the contrary, one may more readily conclude from this that it is principally the individual who possesses this authority. And as the highest authority to interpret Scripture rests with each individual, the rule of interpretation must be nothing other than the natural light of reason which is common to all men, and not some light above nature or any external authority. The criterion should not be so difficult that it cannot be applied by any but the most acute philosophers, but should be adapted to the natural and common intelligence and capacity of [all] human beings, as we have shown that our norm is; for we have seen that the difficulties which it continues to present have their origin not in the nature of the method but in men's carelessness.

CHAPTER 8

In which it is shown that the Pentateuch and the books of Joshua, Judges, Ruth, Samuel and Kings were not written by the persons after whom they are named.[1] The question is then asked whether they were written by several authors or by one, and who they were

[1] In the previous chapter we dealt with the foundations and principles of knowledge of Scripture, and proved that these amount to nothing more than assembling an accurate history of it. We also showed that the ancients neglected this form of enquiry, essential though it is, or if they did write anything about it and handed it down, it has perished through the injury of time, and thus most of the foundations and principles of this knowledge have disappeared. Now we could live with this if later writers had kept within proper limits and faithfully passed on to their successors what little they had received or discovered and not contrived novelties out of their own heads. For this is how it has come about that the history of the Bible has remained not only incomplete but also rather unreliable, that is, the existing basis of our knowledge of the Scriptures is not just too sparse for us to construct an adequate history, it also teems with errors.

[2] My aim is to correct this situation and remove our prevailing theological prejudices. But my attempt, I am afraid, may be too late. For the situation has now almost reached the point that men will not allow themselves to be corrected on these questions but rather obstinately defend

---

[1] *Autographa.*

118

whatever position they have taken up, in the name of religion. There seems to be no room left for reason except perhaps among a very few persons (few in relation to the rest), so completely have these prejudices taken over men's minds. I will however make the attempt and not give up on the task, since there is no reason for complete despair.

[3] In order to demonstrate these things in due order, I commence with the false assumptions generally made about the real authors of the sacred books, and first with the author of the Pentateuch, whom nearly everyone has believed to be Moses. Indeed the Pharisees so vigorously defended this supposition that they considered anyone who took a different view a heretic. This is why Ibn Ezra, a man of quite liberal disposition and considerable learning, who was the first of all the writers I have read to call attention to this assumption, did not dare plainly to state his view but merely hinted at it with some rather obscure words which I shall not be afraid to render clearer here in order to make the point itself quite evident.

Here are Ibn Ezra's words from his commentary on Deuteronomy: "'Beyond the Jordan etc": If you understand the mystery of the twelve and of "Moses wrote the Law" and "the Canaanite was then in the land" and "it will be revealed on the mountain of God" and also "behold his bed, a bed of iron", then you will know the truth'.[2] In these few words he discloses and, at the same time, demonstrates that it was not actually Moses who wrote the Pentateuch but some other person who lived much later, and that the book Moses wrote was a different work.

In order to prove this, he notes:

(1) that the preface of Deuteronomy could not have been composed by Moses, since he did not cross the Jordan.

(2) that the entire book of Moses was inscribed very distinctly on the face of a single altar (see Deuteronomy 27, Joshua 8.37, etc.), an altar which consisted of only twelve stones according to the report of the rabbis, from which it follows that the book of Moses was a much more slender volume than the Pentateuch. This is what I think our author wished to signify by referring to 'the mystery of the twelve', though he might have meant the twelve curses mentioned in the same chapter of Deuteronomy. For it could be that he believed that they had not been included in the book of the Law, because, Moses not only commanded the Levites to inscribe the Law but also to recite these curses in order to bind the

---

[2] *Commentary on Deuteronomy*, 1.5.

people by oath to observe the inscribed laws. Or perhaps he meant to allude to the final chapter of Deuteronomy, about the death of Moses, a chapter that has only twelve verses. But it is not relevant to examine these and other such conjectures here.

(3) Ibn Ezra then notes that Deuteronomy 31.9 says, 'and Moses wrote the Law'. These words cannot be the words of Moses but come from another writer who is narrating the acts and writings of Moses.

(4) He notes the passage at Genesis 12.6, where in telling how Abraham was surveying the territory of the Canaanites, the historian adds that 'the Canaanite at that time was in that land', and thus clearly excludes the time at which he wrote it. This must therefore have been written after Moses' death, at a time when the Canaanites had been expelled and no longer possessed that territory. This is what Ibn Ezra, in his note on this passage, is indicating in the words: 'and the Canaanite was then in that land; it seems that Canaan' (a grandson of Noah) 'took the land of the Canaanite which was in the hands of another; if this is not true, there is a mystery in this thing, and he who understands it should be silent'. That is, if Canaan invaded those regions, then the sense will be that 'the Canaanite was already in that land at that time' – as distinct from a previous period when it was inhabited by another people. But if Canaan was the first to cultivate those regions (as follows from Genesis ch. 10), then the text excludes the present time, i.e. the time of the writer, which is not therefore the time of Moses, because in his time they still possessed that territory. This is the mystery about which Ibn Ezra recommends silence.

120   (5) He notes that at Genesis 22.14 Mount Moriah[3] is called the mountain of God, but did not have this name until after it had been dedicated to the building of the Temple and the choice of this mountain had not yet been made in Moses' time. Moses does not specify any place as chosen by God. On the contrary, he predicts that one day God will choose a place which will be given the name of God.

(6) Finally, Ibn Ezra notes that in Deuteronomy, chapter 3, the following is inserted into the story of Og, king of Bashan: 'Only Og, king of Bashan, remained of the rest[4] of the giants; behold, his bed was a bed of iron, the [bed] surely, which is in Rabbah of the sons of Ammon, nine cubits in length', etc. This parenthesis plainly indicates that the writer of these books lived long after Moses. The manner of speaking is appropriate only to someone referring to very ancient times, and pointing to relics of things to establish his credibility; without a doubt this bed was first discovered in the time of David, who subdued this city, as 2 Samuel 12.30 tells us.

---

[3] Spinoza's footnote: see Annotation 9.
[4] Spinoza's footnote: N.B. the Hebrew *rephaim* means 'condemned', and seems also, from 1 Chronicles 20.4, to be a proper name. I think therefore that here too it signifies some family.

But it is not only there but also a few lines further down[5] that the same historian interpolates some words of Moses: 'Jair, son of Manasseh, took the whole territory of Argob right up to the border of the Geshurites and the Mahacathites, and called those places, together with Bassan, by his own name "the villages of Jair", as it is to this day'. These things, I contend, the historian added in order to explain the words of Moses which he had just reported, namely, 'And the rest of Gilead and the whole of Bashan, the kingdom of Og, I gave to the half-tribe of Manasseh, the whole territory of Argob with the whole of Bassan, which is called the land of the giants'. Undoubtedly in the writer's time the Hebrews knew what the villages of Jair of the tribe of Judah were but did not know them as 'the territory of Argob' or 'the land of the giants'. He had to explain what these places were which had been so called long ago, and at the same time needed to give a reason why in his day they were denoted by the name of Jair, who was of the tribe of Judah, not of Manasseh (see 1 Chronicles 2.21 and 22).

[4] This is how we explain the opinion of Ibn Ezra and the passages of the Pentateuch he cites to support it. But he has not said everything, nor even the most important things. There are other, more powerful points to be made:

(1) The writer of these books not only refers to Moses in the third person but also makes affirmations about him. For instance, 'God spoke with Moses'.[6] 'God used to speak to Moses face to face'.[7] 'Moses was the most humble of all men' (Numbers 12.3). 'Moses was seized with anger against the commanders of the army' (Num. 31.14); 'Moses the divine man' (Deut. 33.1). 'Moses the servant of God died'.[8] 'Never was there a prophet in Israel like Moses',[9] etc. By contrast, when the Law which Moses had expounded to the people and written down, is set out in detail in Deuteronomy, Moses speaks and narrates his actions in the first person, for instance, 'God has spoken to me' (Deuteronomy 21, 17, etc.), 'I prayed to God',[10] etc. Later, however, at the end of the book, when he has finished recording the words of Moses, the historian reverts to the third person, proceeding to tell how Moses, having finished his exposition of the Law, gave it to the people in writing, then admonished them for the last time, and finally died. All of this – the manner of speaking, the testimony,

---

[5] Deuteronomy 3.14.   [6] E.g. Exodus 30.22, 31.1.   [7] Exodus 33.11.   [8] Deuteronomy 34.5.
[9] Deuteronomy 34.10.   [10] Deuteronomy 9.26.

and the very structure of the whole history – fully persuade us that these books were not written by Moses but by someone else.

(2) This account not only tells how Moses died and was buried, and was mourned by the Hebrews for thirty days, it should be noted, but also compares him with all those prophets who lived later, claiming he excelled them all. 'There has never arisen a prophet in Israel', it is there stated, 'like Moses, whom God knew face to face'.[11] Obviously Moses could not give this testimony about himself, nor could anyone who came immediately after him. It must have been someone who lived many generations later, especially as the historian speaks in the past tense, viz., 'there has never arisen a prophet' etc. And of his place of burial he says, 'no one knows it to this day'.[12]

(3) It is worth noting also that certain places are not called by the names which they had in Moses' lifetime but those by which they were known long afterwards. For example, 'Abraham pursued' (the enemy) 'as far as Dan' (see Genesis 14.14); Dan was not thus called until long after the death of Joshua (see Judges 18.29).

(4) The story is sometimes carried down until well after the end of Moses' life. Exodus 16.34, for instance, states that the sons of Israel ate manna for forty years, until they came to the border of the land of Canaan, i.e. down to the time specified in the book of Joshua 5.12. In the book of Genesis 36.31, it is said, 'These are the kings who reigned in Edom, before a king ruled over the sons of Israel'. Here, evidently, the chronicler is enumerating the kings of Idumaea before David conquered them[13] and appointed governors in Idumaea itself (see 2 Samuel 8.14).

[5] From all this it is plainer than the noonday sun that the Pentateuch was not written by Moses but by someone else who lived many generations after Moses. But now we should perhaps consider the books cited in the Pentateuch which Moses himself did write. From these themselves, it is evident that they were something different from the Pentateuch.

For it emerges, first, from Exodus 17.14 that Moses, by the command of God, wrote an account of the war against Amalek. Alhough it is not clear from that chapter in which book it occurs, at Numbers 21.12 we find mentioned the 'The Book of the Wars of God' and it is doubtless there that the war against Amalek is narrated, along with an account of all the places where the Israelites encamped on their journey which the author of the Pentateuch, at Numbers 33.2, testifies were also described by Moses.

Moreover, Exodus 24.4 and 7 gives evidence of another book, called 'The Book of the Covenant'[14] which Moses read out to the Israelites when

---

[11] Deuteronomy 34.10.   [12] Deuteronomy 34.6.   [13] Spinoza's footnote: see Annotation 10.
[14] Spinoza's footnote: *sepher* in Hebrew quite often means 'letter' or 'writing'.

God first entered into the covenant with them. This book, or letter, contained very little: simply the laws, or commands of God which are set out in Exodus from ch. 20.22 to ch. 24, as no one will deny who reads the chapter cited above impartially and with an ounce of sound judgment. According to that chapter, as soon as Moses understood the feeling of the people about entering into a covenant with God, he immediately wrote down the pronouncements and laws of God, and in the first light of morning, after completing certain ceremonies, read out to the assembled multitude the conditions for entering into the covenant. When he had finished reading these and the multitude had understood them, the people bound themselves to them with full consent. From the shortness of the time in which it was written and from its purpose of making the covenant, it follows that this book contained nothing but the few things just mentioned.

It is evident finally that in the fortieth year after the exodus from Egypt Moses expounded all the laws he had made (see Deuteronomy 1.5), and renewed the people's commitment to them (see Deuteronomy 29.14); he then wrote a book which contained the laws he had set out and the new covenant (see Deuteronomy 31.9). This book was entitled 'The Book of the Law of God' and is the book that Joshua subsequently expanded by adding the account of the people's renewal of the covenant again in his day, when they entered into covenant with God for the third time (see Joshua 24.25–6). But since we have no book extant which contains this covenant of Moses and the covenant of Joshua together, we must concede that it has perished – unless we adopt the desperate device of Jonathan, author of the Aramaic Paraphrase[15] and twist the words of Scripture to suit ourselves. Faced by this difficulty, Jonathan preferred to corrupt Scripture rather than admit his own ignorance. Joshua 24.26 says, 'and Joshua wrote these words in the Book of the Law of God'; Jonathan translated this into Aramaic as, 'and Joshua wrote these words and kept them with the Book of the Law of God'. What can one do with people who see nothing but what they want to see? What is this but to deny the real Scripture and concoct a new one in one's head?

We hence conclude that this Book of the Law of God which Moses wrote, was not the Pentateuch, but an entirely different work which the author of the Pentateuch inserted at an appropriate place in his own work.

[15] That is Jonathan ben Uziel, reputed author of the Aramaic Targum of the prophets, which, as Professor Fokke Akkerman has noted, was included in the Buxtorf Bible which Spinoza used. Spinoza writes 'Chaldean' for 'Aramaic', a common 17th-century usage.

This conclusion follows very clearly from the evidence we have given, as well as from the following. When it is stated in the passage of Deuteronomy just cited that Moses wrote the Book of the Law, the narrator adds that Moses gave it to the priests and commanded them to read it out to the whole people at stated times.[16] This shows that this book was much smaller than the Pentateuch, since it could be read through at one assembly and be understood by all.

Nor should we overlook the fact that of all the books Moses wrote, he ordered only this book of the second covenant to be preserved and guarded with religious care along with the 'Song' which he also wrote down afterwards so that the whole people might learn it by heart.[17] It was because the first covenant obliged only the people who were actually present while the second also obligated all their descendants (see Deuteronomy 29.14,15), that he ordered this book of the second covenant to be scrupulously preserved for future generations, and also the 'Song', as we have said, since it chiefly concerns future generations.

As there is hence no solid evidence that Moses wrote any works apart from these, and commanded that only 'The Book of the Law' and the 'Song' be religiously preserved for posterity, and since there are several things in the Pentateuch which Moses could not have written, evidently there is no justification for asserting that Moses was the author of the Pentateuch. Rather it is entirely contrary to reason to do so.

[6] But here someone may ask whether, besides this book, Moses did not also write down the laws when they were first revealed to him? In the space of forty years did he not write down any of the laws he promulgated other than the few contained, as I said, in the book of the first covenant? Although it might seem to stand to reason that Moses would also have written down the laws at the very time and place that he actually announced them, I nevertheless deny that we may definitely assert this. For we should not draw conclusions about such matters, as we showed above, unless they are evident from Scripture itself or may be legitimately inferred from its principles. For it is not enough that they stand to reason. In this case, reason itself does not drive us to this conclusion. Perhaps the elders communicated Moses' edicts to the people in writing which the narrator later collected and inserted into his account of Moses' life at

---

[16] Deuteronomy 31.9–11.   [17] The 'Song of Moses', Deuteronomy 31.30–32.47.

the appropriate place. So much for the Five Books of Moses; it is time now to examine the other books.

[7]   For similar reasons, the Book of Joshua also can be shown not to have been written by Joshua.[18] It is another person who testifies that Joshua's fame had spread throughout the earth (see 6.27), that he omitted none of the commandments of Moses (see the last verse of ch. 8 and ch. 11.15), that he grew old, that he summoned them all to an assembly,[19] and finally that he died.[20] Then too some things are told that happened after his death, for example, that after his death the Israelites worshipped God as long as the old men who knew him remained alive.[21] It is said at 16.10 that Ephraim and Manasseh 'did not drive out the Canaanite that dwelt in Gezer, but' (it adds) 'the Canaanite has dwelt in the midst of Ephraim to this day and has paid them tribute'. This is exactly what is said in the book of Judges, ch. 1, and the expression 'to this day' shows that the writer was speaking of something from the past. Similar is the text in the last verse of chapter 15 about the sons of Judah, as well as the story of Caleb which begins at verse 13 of the same chapter. The incident related at ch. 22.10 ff. about the two tribes and the half tribe that built 125 the altar beyond Jordan also seems to have occurred after Joshua's death: there is no mention of him in the whole account, and it is the people alone who debate the question of war, send out envoys, await a response and make the final decision for war. Finally, it plainly follows from 10.14 that this book was composed many generations after Joshua; for it says: 'there has been no day like that day either before or afterwards, on which God' (so) 'hearkened to any man', etc. If Joshua ever wrote a book, it was surely the one which is cited in this same narrative at 10.13.[22]

[8]   No sensible person, I believe, is persuaded that the Book of Judges was composed by the Judges themselves. For the summary of this whole history given in chapter 2 clearly proves that it was written entirely by one narrator alone. Moreover, it was undoubtedly written after the kings assumed the government, since its author often reminds us that 'in those days' there was no king in Israel.

---

[18] *Autographa*.   [19] Joshua 23.24.   [20] Joshua 24.29.   [21] Joshua 24.31.
[22] Joshua 10.13: 'Is this not written in the Book of Jashar?' (how the sun stood still in heaven).

[9]   As for the books of Samuel, there is no reason to tarry long as the narrative continues far beyond his lifetime. Here, I would merely want to note that this book too was composed many generations after Samuel. For in 1 Samuel 9.9 the narrator mentions in parenthesis, 'In the old days each man spoke thus in Israel when he went to consult God: "Come, let us go to the seer"; for he who today is called a prophet was in the old days designated a seer'.

[10]   Finally, the books of the Kings, as they themselves make clear, were excerpted from the books of the 'Acts of Solomon' (see 1 Kings 11.41), from the 'Chronicles of the Kings of Judah' (see 14.19, 29) and from the 'Chronicles of the Kings of Israel'.

[11]   We conclude therefore that all the books we have surveyed so far are derivative works,[23] and the events they describe are recounted as having happened long before. If we now turn to the unity of theme and structure of all these books, we shall readily conclude that all were writ-ten by one and the same chronicler, who set out to write the ancient history of the Jews from their earliest origins down to the first destruc-tion of the city.[24] These works are so closely joined to each other that we clearly discern from this alone that they consist of a single narrative by a single historian. As soon as he has finished relating the life of Moses, he passes to the history of Joshua with these words: 'And it happened, after Moses the servant of God died, that God said to Joshua' etc.[25] When this account is completed by the death of Joshua, he commences the history of the Judges with the same transitional phrase, even the same conjunc-tion: 'And it happened, after Joshua had died, that the sons of Israel sought from God', etc.[26] He annexes the book of Ruth to Judges, like an appendix, in this manner: 'And it happened in those days in which the Judges were judging that there was a famine in that land'.[27] He joins the first book of Samuel to Ruth in the same manner, and after completing that, proceeds, with his customary transition, to the second book of Samuel. Before the history of David is finished, he moves into the first book of Kings, where he continues his account of the history of David, and finally joins the second book of Kings to the first with the same connecting device.

---

[23] *Apographa*.   [24] The destruction of Jerusalem by the Babylonians in 587 BC (2 Kings 25).
[25] Joshua 1.1.   [26] Judges 1.1.   [27] Ruth 1.1.

The thematic structure and design of the histories also show that there was only one chronicler who had set himself a particular goal. For he begins by narrating the earliest origins of the Hebrew nation, then in due order tells on what occasions and at what times Moses issued laws and made many prophecies. Then he tells how, in accordance with Moses' predictions, they invaded the promised land (see Deuteronomy 7), and after they possessed it, abandoned the laws (Deuteronomy 31.16), as a result of which they suffered many ills (ibid. 17). He explains how, subsequently, they desired to choose Kings (Deuteronomy 17.14), who also fared well or ill according to their respect for the Laws (Deuteronomy 28.36 and the last verse), until finally he narrates the ruin of the state, just as Moses had predicted. Other matters that have nothing to do with supporting the Law, he either simply consigns to silence or else refers the reader to other historians. All these books therefore collude to one end: to teach the sayings and edicts of Moses, and illustrate them by the outcome of events.

[12] These three things, hence, taken together, namely unity of theme in all these books, their interconnectedness, and their being derivative works[28] written many centuries after the event, lead us to conclude, as we said above, that they were all composed by a single historian. Who this was, I cannot conclusively prove, though I suspect it was Ezra himself. Several substantial considerations concur to make me think this. The historian (whom we now know to have been only one man) takes his story down to the liberation of Jehoiachin, adding that he sat at the table of the king all 'his' life[29] (that is, either the life of Jehoiachin or the life of the son of Nebuchadnezzar, for the sense is completely ambiguous). It follows that no one before Ezra's time could have been this historian. But Scripture tells us of no one living at that time other than Ezra (see Ezra 7.10), who set himself zealously to reseach and explain the Law of God; it also relates that he was a writer (Ezra 7.6), well-versed in the Law of Moses. Hence, I cannot think that it was anyone but Ezra who wrote these books.

Ezra not only applied himself zealously to research the law of God, we see from this testimony, but also to elaborate it; and at Nehemiah 8.8[30] it is also said that 'they read the book of the Law of God as it was expounded and applied their intelligence to it and understood the

---

[28] *Apographa.*   [29] 2 Kings 25.27–30.   [30] Spinoza's text gives Nehemiah 8.9.

Scripture'. Now the book of Deuteronomy contains not only the book of the Law of Moses or the greater part of it, but also many things inserted into it to provide a fuller explanation. Hence, I infer that the book of Deuteronomy is this book of the Law of God written, elaborated and expounded by Ezra, and which they then read.

As for the many things inserted in parenthesis in the book of Deuteronomy to provide a fuller explanation, we gave two examples of this when we were explaining the views of Ibn Ezra. There are many others, for example 2.12: 'And the Horites formerly lived in Seir, and the sons of Esau drove them out, and destroyed them from their sight, and dwelt in their place, just as Israel did in the land of his inheritance which God gave him'. This explains verses 3 and 4 of the same chapter, namely that the mountain Seir, which had come to the sons of Esau as an inheritance, was not uninhabited when they occupied it, but they invaded it and dispossessed and destroyed the Horites who had lived there previously, just as the Israelites did to the Canaanites after the death of Moses. Verses 6–9 of chapter 10 are also inserted as a parenthesis into the words of Moses. It is obvious that verse 8, which begins 'at that time God set apart the tribe of Levi', must necessarily refer to verse 5, and not to the death of Aaron which Ezra seems to have inserted here merely because in the story of the calf which the people worshipped, Moses had said that he prayed to God for Aaron (see 9.20). Ezra then explains that, at the time of which Moses is here speaking, God chose for himself the tribe of Levi. He wants to show the reason for the choice and why the Levites were not called to share in the inheritance. Having done this, he picks up the thread of his story with the words of Moses. One may add also the preface of the book and all the passages that refer to Moses in the third person and many other passages that Ezra added or whose language he altered in ways that cannot now be traced, no doubt so as to render them more easily understood by the people of his time.

Had we Moses' own 'Book of the Law' itself, I do not doubt that we would find great discrepancies in the words as well as in the order and reasons for the commandments. For just by comparing the Decalogue as given in Deuteronomy with the version of the Decalogue in Exodus (which gives a full account), we find that it differs from Exodus in all these respects. The fourth commandment there is not only phrased differently but is also much longer, and the justification for it differs totally from the one given in the Decalogue in Exodus. And the order in which the tenth commandment is set out there also diverges from that in Exodus. These alterations, in this case and in others, were I think introduced by Ezra in the course of explaining the Law of God to his contemporaries, as I have said, and hence this is the 'Book of the Law of God' as explained and elaborated by him.

This is also, I think, the earliest of the books that I claimed he wrote. This I infer from the fact that it contains the laws of the country which is what the people most needs, and also because the book is not connected by any link with what comes before in the way that the others are but begins with the unconnected phrase, 'These are the words of Moses',[31] etc. After he had completed this book and taught the laws to the people, I believe he then turned his attention to writing a complete history of the Hebrew nation, from the foundation of the world to the final destruction of the city, into which he inserted this book of Deuteronomy in its place. Perhaps he called the first five books by the name of Moses, because it is here above all that his life is related: he took the title from the most prominent character. For the same reason he called the sixth book by the name of Joshua, the seventh by the Judges, the eighth by Ruth, the ninth and perhaps also the tenth by the name of Samuel, and the eleventh and twelfth by the name of the Kings. But whether Ezra produced a definitive version of this work and completed it as he intended to do, on this see the following chapter.

---

[31] Deuteronomy 1.1.

CHAPTER 9

Further queries about the same books, namely, whether Ezra made a definitive version of them, and whether the marginal notes found in the Hebrew MSS are variant readings

[1] How much the investigation we have made into who really wrote these books improves our understanding of them is readily seen merely from the passages cited above confirming our view of that question. Without it, anyone would certainly find them highly obscure. But apart from the question of authorship, there are other aspects of the books themselves which remain to be remarked on which popular superstition does not permit ordinary people to come to grips with. The foremost of these is that Ezra (whom I will continue to regard as their author until someone demonstrates a more certain candidate) made no final version of the narratives contained in them, but merely collected narratives from different writers, sometimes just copying them out as they were, and passed them on to posterity without examining them properly and setting them in due order. I cannot conjecture the reasons (except perhaps an early death) that prevented him from completing this task in every respect. But the fact itself is abundantly attested even though we lack the [works of] the ancient Hebrew historians, by the very few fragments of their works that remain to us.

[2] The history of Hezekiah (2 Kings 18.17 ff.) is related as it was found written in the 'Chronicles of the Kings of Judah'. For we find the whole of this history in the book of Isaiah, and the book of Isaiah itself was contained in the 'Chronicles of the Kings of Judah' (see 2 Chronicles

32.32).[1] It is word-for-word the same, with the exception of a few details,[2] from which we can only conclude that there were variant readings in Isaiah's narrative – unless someone wants to find imaginary mysteries in them, as is done in other cases.

Again, the last chapter of 2 Kings is contained in the final chapter of Jeremiah as well as in his chapters 39 and 40. We also find that 2 Samuel 7 corresponds to 1 Chronicles 17, though here the words are so noticeably altered[3] in various passages that it is easy to see these two chapters have been taken from two different versions of the story of Nathan. Finally, the genealogy of the kings of Idumea given at Genesis 36.31ff. also appears in the same words in the opening chapter of 1 Chronicles, even though the author of the latter plainly borrowed his account from other chroniclers and not the twelve books we attribute to Ezra.[4] If we possessed [the works of] these chroniclers, the thing itself [that we are asserting] would undoubtedly be immediately apparent. But since we lack them, as I said, our sole recourse is to examine the histories themselves – their order and connection, their discrepancies in repeated passages, and their differences in chronology – so as to enable us to make judgments about the other writings.

[3]   Let us therefore examine them, or at least the most striking of them, commencing with the story of Judah and Tamar which the historian begins at Genesis chapter 38 with the words, 'And it came to pass at that time, that Judah departed from his brothers'. That 'time' must necessarily be related to some other time[5] already mentioned, but it cannot be linked to the period of its immediate context in Genesis. For from the time when Joseph was taken into Egypt until the time when the patriarch Jacob also set out for Egypt with all his family, we can calculate no more than twenty two years. (For Joseph was seventeen years old when he was sold by his brothers, and when Pharaoh ordered him to be released from prison he was thirty years old; add the seven years of abundance and the two years of famine, and you will get twenty two years.) Yet no one can imagine that in this short period so many things could have happened. For Judah begat three children, one after the other, from one wife whom

130

---

[1] The two books of Chronicles in the Bible are distinct from the non-extant 'Chronicles of the Kings of Judah' and 'Chronicles of the Kings of Israel' which Spinoza discusses above, ch. 8 para 10, p. 126.
[2] Spinoza's footnote: see Annotation 11.   [3] Spinoza's footnote: see Annotation 12.
[4] The twelve books from Genesis to 2 Kings: see above, ch. 8 para 12, pp. 127–9.
[5] Spinoza's footnote: see Annotation 13.

he married at that time; the eldest of them grew up and took Tamar to wife; when he died, the second brother married her; he too died; and long after these events, Judah himself unwittingly had intercourse with his own daughter-in-law, Tamar, who bore him twin sons, one of whom became a parent – and all within the aforesaid period of twenty-two years! Since all these things cannot be ascribed to the period to which Genesis refers, it must necessarily be related to another time which came just before this in another book. It follows that Ezra simply transcribed this story too and inserted it among the others, without examining it.

[4] But we must also concede that not only this chapter but the whole
131 history of Joseph and Jacob has been taken and transcribed from different histories, so obviously riddled is it with inconsistencies. Genesis 47 narrates that when Jacob was first introduced to Pharaoh by Joseph, he was 130 years old. If we subtract the twenty-two years he spent in mourning because Joseph was away and, in addition, the seventeen years which was the age of Joseph when he was sold, and finally the seven years which he served for the sake of Rachel, it will be found that he had reached the advanced age of eighty-four when he married Leah. On the other hand Dinah was scarcely seven years old[6] when she was raped by Shechem, and Simeon and Levi were scarcely twelve and eleven respectively when they sacked his whole city and put all its citizens to the sword.[7]

[5] I need not go through every example in the Pentateuch. We have only to notice that everything in these five books, commandments and histories alike, is narrated in a confused manner, without order and without respect for chronology, and that stories are repeated, sometimes in different versions. We will then easily see that they were all collected and stored away, so that they would be available to be examined at a later date and reduced to order.

[6] But it is not only the material in the Five Books; the histories in the other seven books, which go down as far as the destruction of the city,[8] were collected in the same manner. Who does not see that at Judges 2.6 a new historian begins (the one who had also written the deeds of Joshua),

---

[6] Spinoza's footnote: see Annotation 14.   [7] Genesis 34.
[8] Destruction of Jerusalem in 587 BC.

and that his words have simply been transcribed? After our historian had told, in the final chapter of Joshua, how Joshua died and was buried, and promised in the first chapter of this book [Judges] to narrate what happened after his death, how could he have combined what he starts to tell[9] us here about Joshua himself with the preceding chapters, if he wished to follow the thread of his story? Similarly chapters 17 and 18 of 1 Samuel have been taken from a different chronicler, who thought there was another reason why David began to frequent the court of Saul, very different from that offered in chapter 16 of the same book. This other chronicler did not think David approached Saul because Saul invited him on the advice of his servants (as told in chapter 16), but because he happened to have been sent by his father to his brothers in the camp, became known to Saul through his victory over the Philistine Goliath, and was retained at court. I suspect the same thing about 1 Samuel 26;   132 the historian seems to be telling the same story there as in chapter 24, but following the version of another chronicler.

[7]   But I will leave this and turn to chronology. At 1 Kings 6 it is said that Solomon built the Temple 480 years after the exodus from Egypt, but from the chronicles themselves we extrapolate a larger number, as follows:

Moses governed the people in the desert	40 years
Joshua lived for 110 years but according to Josephus[10] and others his governance lasted no more than	26
Cushan-rishathaim held the people under his sway	08
Othniel son of Kenaz was judge[11]	40
Eglon king of Moab had power over the people	18
Ehud and Shamgar were judges	80
Jabin king of Canaan again held the people under his sway	20
After that the people had peace	40
After that they were in the power of Midian	07
At the time of Gideon they lived in liberty	40
And under the government of Abimelech	03
Tola the son of Puah was judge	23

---

[9] Spinoza's footnote: see Annotation 15.   [10] Josephus, *Antiquities of the Jews*, 5.117.
[11] Spinoza's footnote: see Annotation 16.

And Jair	03
The people were again in the power of the Philistines and of the Ammonites	18
Jephthah was judge	06
Ibzan of Bethlehem	07
Elon the Zebulunite	10
Abdon the Pirathonite	08
The people was again under the sway of the Philistines	40
Samson was judge[12]	20
And Eli	40
The people was again under the sway of the Philistines until it was liberated by Samuel	20
David reigned	40
Solomon before he built the temple	04
Add these up and the total number of years is	580

133 [8] To this we must add the years of the generation following the death of Joshua in which the Hebrew state flourished until conquered by Cushan-rishathaim. I believe it to have been many years. I cannot accept that immediately following Joshua's death, all those who had witnessed his prodigious deeds perished in a moment, or that their successors abandoned the laws at a single stroke falling from the highest virtue into the deepest wickedness and idleness, or that Cushan-rishathaim conquered them with a single blow.[13] Each one of these events requires almost a life-time in itself, and there is hence little doubt that Scripture compressed into Judges 2.7–10 the history of many years which it passed over in silence. We should add further the years when Samuel was judge, whose number is not given in Scripture, and also the years of Saul's reign which I omitted from my earlier calculation, because it is unclear from the account of him how many years he reigned.

[9] It is indeed asserted at 1 Samuel 13.1 that Saul reigned for two years, but that text has been mutilated and from the actual account given of him we obtain a larger number. That the text has been mutilated cannot be doubted by anyone who has even a passing acquaintance with Hebrew.

---

[12] Spinoza's footnote: see Annotation 17.   [13] 'Dictum factum': Terence, *The Self Tormentor*, 760.

134

It begins, 'Saul was . . . years old when he began to reign, and he reigned for two years over Israel'. Who does not see that Saul's age when he acquired the kingship has been omitted? It is also undeniable, I believe, that a larger number is implied by the history itself. For 1 Samuel 27.7 says that David remained among the Philistines, to whom he had fled on account of Saul, for one year and four months. By this reckoning everything else had to have happened in a space of eight months, which I do not suppose anyone believes. Josephus, at any rate, at the end of the sixth book of his *Antiquities*, corrected the text to: 'Therefore Saul reigned while Samuel was still alive for eighteen years, and for another two after his death'.[14]

As a matter of fact, the whole account in chapter 13 totally fails to fit with what comes before it. At the end of chapter 7 it was stated that the Philistines were so completely crushed by the Hebrews that they did not dare to approach the frontier of Israel in Samuel's life-time. But here we learn that in the life-time of Samuel the Hebrews were invaded by the Philistines, by whom they had been reduced to such misery and poverty that they lacked weapons with which to defend themselves and any means 134 to make them. I would certainly have my work cut out to try to reconcile all these stories in the first book of Samuel so that they could plausibly appear to have been written and put in order by a single chronicler.

[10]   But to return to my theme. The years of Saul's reign must be added to my calculation. I have also not included the years of anarchy among the Hebrews, because they are not consistently detailed in Scripture itself. It is not clear in my opinion, how long the period was in which the events recorded in the book of Judges from chapter 17 to the end took place. From all this it most evidently follows that a true chronology of these years cannot be legitimately compiled from the histories themselves, and that the histories do not agree with each other on one and the same chronology but assume very different ones. We must therefore conclude that these histories have been collected from different writers, without being [properly] examined or put in order.

[11]   There seems to have been no less a discrepancy between the chronology of the 'Chronicles of the Kings of Judah' and that of the 'Chronicles of the Kings of Israel'. In the 'Chronicles of the Kings of Israel',

[14] Josephus, *Antiquities of the Jews*, 6.378.

Jehoram the son of Ahab reportedly began to reign in the second year of the reign of Jehoram, son of Jehoshaphat (see 2 Kings 1.17). But the 'Chronicles of the Kings of Judah' stated that Jehoram, son of Jehoshaphat began to reign in the fifth year of the reign of Jehoram, son of Ahab (ibid., 8.16). Again, anyone who undertakes to compare the accounts in the book of Chronicles with those of the books of Kings will find many other similar discrepancies, which I do not need to survey here, and I certainly do not need to review the manoeuvres of those writers who try to reconcile them. The rabbis talk evident nonsense. The commentators I have read fantasize, fabricate and completely distort the language. For example, where 2 Chronicles[15] says, 'Ahaziah was forty-two years old when he began to reign,' some forge a fiction whereby these years have their beginning from the reign of Omri and not from the birth of Ahaziah. If they could show that this was the intent of the author of Chronicles, I would not hesitate to say that the latter did not know how to express himself. They make up a good many other such things. If they were true, I would state categorically that the ancient Hebrews were totally ignorant both of their own language and of the art of constructing an orderly narrative, and I would not accept that there is any method or rule for interpreting Scripture, but anyone could make up anything he liked.

135 [12]   If anyone thinks that I am speaking here too generally and without adequate grounds for what I say, I challenge him to try the thing himself and show us a genuine order in these histories which historians could emulate in writing chronological narratives without going astray. In interpreting the stories and attempting to reconcile them, I ask him to pay close attention to the specific language and to the ways in which things are expressed and the topics arranged and connected, explaining them in such a way that we too could emulate them in our own writing, following his explanation.[16] Should he succeed, I will without hesitation concede defeat, and for me he 'will be the great Apollo'.[17] I confess that I have not been able to find anything like this, despite a long search. I say nothing here that I have not long been pondering deeply, and despite being steeped in the common beliefs about the Bible from childhood on, I have not been able to resist my conclusion. But there is no reason to detain the reader longer on

---

[15] 2 Chronicles 22.2.   [16] Spinoza's footnote: see Annotation 18.
[17] Virgil, *Eclogues* 3.104: 'eris mihi magnus Apollo'.

this topic and challenge him to undertake an enterprise bound to fail. All I needed was to propose the thing, so as to set out my meaning more clearly. I now move on to the other issues I undertook to discuss, concerning the fate of these books.

[13]   For besides what we have just proved, we must also take account of the fact that these books have not been preserved by later ages with such care that no errors have crept in. Ancient scribes noticed several dubious readings and some mutilated passages, though not all of them. I am not here discussing whether the errors are serious enough to cause major difficulty for the reader though I do believe that they are of little significance at any rate for those who peruse the Scriptures with a more open mind. I can certainly say that I have not noticed any error or variant reading concerning moral doctrine which would render it obscure or ambiguous. But there are many people who do not allow that any fault has entered in even on other questions, adopting the stance that by a certain special providence God has preserved the entire Bible uncorrupted. They assert that variant readings are indications of the most profound mysteries, and maintain the same about the twenty-eight asterisks, all of which occur in the middle of a paragraph, and even insist that fabulous secrets are contained in the accents on the letters. I do not know whether they affirm this from foolishness and doddering devotion or from pride and malice, so that people would believe that they alone know God's secrets, but this I do know: I have read nothing in them that sounds like a deep secret, rather it is all very childish. I have also read, and personally know, some people who dabble in Cabbalism; the stupidity of whom is beyond belief.

[14]   As for the fact that errors have crept in, as we said, I think no sensible person can doubt it if he has read the passage about Saul (which I cited above from 1 Samuel 13.1) and also 2 Samuel 6.2, 'And David and the whole people that were with him arose and went from Judah, so that they might take the ark of God from there'. Anyone can see in this passage that the place they went to, Kirjat Jeharim,[18] from which they were to take the ark, has dropped out. We cannot deny that 2 Samuel 13.37 has also been scrambled and mutilated: 'And Absalom fled and went to Talmai, the son of Ammihud, king of Geshur, and mourned for his son

---

[18] Spinoza's footnote: see Annotation 19.

every day, and Absalom fled and went to Geshur and stayed there for three years'.[19] I remember noticing other such passages which will not come back to me at the moment.

[15]   That the marginal notes which occur throughout the Hebrew MSS were doubtful readings, cannot be questioned by anyone who sees that most of them have arisen owing to the great similarity of Hebrew letters with each other. I refer, for example, to the similarity of *kaf* and *bet*, *yad* and *vav*, *dalet* and *resh*, and so on. When 2 Samuel 5.24 gives, 'and at that' (time) 'at which you will hear', there is a note in the margin, 'when you will hear'. At Judges 21.22, 'and when their fathers or their brothers come to us in multitude' (i.e. 'often')' etc., there is a marginal note, 'in order to complain'. Many such errors have also arisen from the use of the letters which they call silent letters , i.e., letters whose pronunciation is often not felt and are confused with one another. For example, at Leviticus 25.30 the text is, 'and the house that is in the city which has no wall will be guaranteed', but in the margin we find, 'which has a wall', and so on.

[16]   But although these things are clear enough in themselves, we would like to answer the claims of certain Pharisees who try to persuade us that the marginal notes were added or indicated by the biblical writers themselves to signify some mystery. They take the first of these arguments (which I do not find very persuasive) from the custom of reading the Scriptures aloud. If, they say, these notes were put beside the text because there was a variety of readings and later generations were unable to delete either of them, why did it become the custom always to retain the marginal sense? Why, they say, did they write the sense that they wanted to retain in the margin? On the contrary, they should have written the scrolls themselves as they wanted them to be read instead of writing in the margin the sense and reading of which they most approved.

The second argument appears to have some plausibility, being taken from the actual nature of the phenomenon: namely, that errors creep into codices not by design but by chance and whatever happens in that way happens randomly. But in the Five Books of Moses the word 'girl' is invariably (with one exception) written defectively, contrary to the rules of grammar, without the letter *he* while, on the contrary, in the margin it

---

[19] Spinoza's footnote: see Annotation 20.

appears penned correctly following the general rule. Did this too occur because the hand slipped in writing it? By what stroke of fate could it happen that the pen was always in too much of a hurry whenever this word cropped up? They could easily and without scruple have completed the word and made the correction according to the rules of grammar. Since these readings are not co-incidental and such obvious faults were not amended, they hold that they were deliberately made by the earliest writers to convey something of special significance.

[17]   These arguments are easily answered. I am not going to spend time on the argument from the customary way of reading which they have adopted. Superstition may have had some influence, and perhaps that was the origin of it, because they judged both readings to be equally good or tolerable, and lest either of them be lost, they wanted one to be written and the other to be read. Being unsure, they were evidently afraid to exercise their judgement in so important a matter, in case they chose the false reading instead of the true one. They aimed to avoid giving preference to either one, which they would certainly have done had they ordered that only one be read out, especially as marginal notes are not written in the sacred scrolls. Or perhaps it derived from the fact that they wanted certain things, although correctly written, to be read out differently, following instructions in the margin. Hence they made it a general custom to read the Bible in accordance with the marginal notes.

[18]   I will now explain why the scribes were moved to note in the margin certain things that were to be read out. Not all marginal notes are doubtful readings; they also made a note about things that were foreign to everyday usage, for example obsolete words, and words that the current sense of propriety did not permit to be read in a public gathering. The ancient writers, without any sense of wrongdoing, called things by their proper names and did not resort to polite euphemisms. But after vice and debauchery established their reign, things that the ancients uttered without obscenity, 138 came to be thought obscene. This was not a sufficient reason to alter Scripture; but in order to humour the sensibility of the common people, they took to ensuring that decent versions of the terms for sexual intercourse and excrement were read out in public, as they had noted them in the margin.

In any case, whatever the reason why it became customary to read and interpret Scripture according to the marginal readings, it was not because the correct interpretation had to be in accord with them. For besides the fact that in the Talmud itself the Rabbis often differed from the Masoretes[20] and approved different readings, as I shall show in a moment, some of the material found in the margins does not appear to be linguistically correct. For example, in 2 Samuel 14.23 it is written, 'because the King has granted the request of his servant', a construction that is perfectly regular and agrees with that in verse 16 of the same chapter. But the marginal reading ('of your servant') does not agree [as it should] with the person of the verb. So too in the final verse of chapter 16 of the same book there is written, 'as when one consults' (i.e., 'there is a consultation of') 'the word of God', where the marginal note adds, 'anyone' as the subject of the verb. This does not seem to be quite right, for the regular construction is to put impersonal verbs in the third person singular active, as grammarians know very well. There are several marginal annotations of this sort which are in no way preferable to what is in the text itself.

[19]   As for the Pharisees' second argument, one can also readily reply to that from what we have just said, namely, that the scribes annotated obsolete words as well as doubtful readings. In Hebrew, unquestionably, as in other languages, subsequent developments rendered many words obsolete and antiquated. Many such are found in the Bible, and the most recent scribes, as we said, noted each of them, so that they would be read before the people in accordance with the accepted usage of the time. This is the reason why *na'ar* ['boy'] is noted on every occasion, because in old times it was of common gender and meant the same as *juvenis* ['young person'] in Latin. Likewise, the capital city of the Hebrews was normally called *Jerusalem* and not *Jerusalaim*. I take the same view of the pronouns 'he' and 'she': more recent writers changed the *vav* into *'yad* (a frequent change in Hebrew) when they wanted to indicate the feminine gender; but ancient writers distinguished the feminine of this pronoun from the masculine by the vowels alone. Equally, the irregular forms of certain verbs were different in earlier than in later writers, and, lastly, the ancients possessed the remarkably neat device of the paragogic letters *he, aleph, mem, nun, tav, yod*, and *vav*.[21] I could

[20] Although the names of a few of the Masoretes are known, the vast system of marginal notes and (divergent) methods of vocalization, punctuation and accentuation, collectively called the *Masorah* in Hebrew, remain essentially anonymous. The Masoretes were active from the end of the fourth down to the eleventh century CE.

[21] Suffixed letters or syllables to lend added emphasis or modify meaning.

illustrate all this here with numerous examples, but I do not want to annoy the reader with tedious reading. If anyone asks how I know these things, I reply that they are found in the most ancient writers, i.e., in the Bible, but later writers did not choose to imitate them, and imitation is the only reason why in other languages, even in dead languages, obsolete words can remain still known.

[20]   Since I have said that the majority of these marginal notes are doubtful readings, someone will perhaps ask next why there are never more than two readings found for each passage? Why not sometimes three or more? Again, certain expressions in the Scriptures which are correctly annotated in the marginal note, are so obviously contrary to grammar, that it is barely credible scribes could have hesitated or been in doubt which reading was correct. Here too the reply is readily given. To the first question, I answer that there were once more readings than the ones we find annotated in our codices. Several readings are noted in the Talmud which were neglected by the Masoretes, and in many passages they are so manifestly divergent that the superstitious editor of the Bomberg Bible[22] was finally compelled to admit in his preface that he did not know how to reconcile them: 'Here we do not know what answer to give,' he says, 'except to repeat what we said earlier', namely, that 'it is the habit of the Talmud to contradict the Masoretes'. Hence there is no justification for claiming there have never been more than two readings for each passage.

Even so, I readily concede, in fact believe, that no more than two readings were found for each passage and for two reasons:

(1) because the reason we offered for the survival of variant readings does not permit more than two: for we showed that, usually, these arose from the similarity between certain letters. The issue in the end thus nearly always came back to which of two letters one was to append – *bet* or *kaf*? *jod* or *vav*? *dalet* or *resh*? and so on. These are the most frequently used letters, and therefore it could often occur that both yield a tolerable sense. Equally, the question was often whether a syllable was long or short, where length is determined by the letters we have called 'silent'. Further, not all the annotations concern doubtful readings: as we said, many were included for the sake of decency, and to explain obsolete and antiquated words.

140

---

[22] The standard second edition of the Bomberg Bible was published by Daniel Bomberg at Venice in 1524–5, edited by Jacob ben Hayyim.

(2) The reason why I am convinced that no more than two readings are found for each passage is because I believe that the scribes found very few copies of the text, perhaps no more than two or three. In the *Treatise of the Scribes*,[23] chapter 6, only three are mentioned, which they maintain were found in the time of Ezra, claiming the notes were added by Ezra himself. In any case, if they had only three, we can readily conceive that two of them would always agree in any given passage. In fact it would surely be amazing if three different readings were found for one and the same passage in only three copies. Anyone who wonders by what mischance it came about that there was such a dearth of copies after Ezra should simply read the first chapter of 1 Maccabees, or Josephus' *Antiquities*, 12.7.[24] It seems something of a miracle that they could have preserved even these few copies through such a prolonged and powerful persecution. No one, I think, if he reads about this episode with any attention will doubt it. Hence, we see the reasons why there are never more than two doubtful readings. It is decidedly not the case, therefore, that because there are never more than two readings given, in these annotated passages of the Bible, we may deduce that they were deliberately written incorrectly as a way of indicating mysteries.

As for the other contention that some passages are so deficiently composed that there could never have been any doubt that they violate the grammatical rules of all periods, and that hence they should simply have corrected them instead of making notes in the margin – this contention carries no weight with me, and I am not obliged to ascertain what religious scruple persuaded them not to correct it. Perhaps it was simple sincerity, because they wanted to bequeath the Bible to posterity in the state in which it was found, in the few original surviving copies, pointing out discrepancies between the originals not as dubious but as variant readings. The only reason why I have called them 'doubtful' is because in truth I find nearly all of them to be so uncertain that I do not know which is to be preferred to the other.

[21] Finally, apart from these doubtful readings, the scribes have also
141 drawn attention to several truncated passages by putting an empty space in the middle of a paragraph. The Masoretes tell us how many: they enumerate twenty-eight places where a vacant space is left in the middle of a paragraph. I do not know whether they believe that some mystery lies concealed even in the number. The Pharisees, in any case, religiously

---

[23] *Sopherim*. In the Babylonian Talmud. [24] Josephus, *Antiquities*, 12.256 in modern editions.

preserve a space of a certain length. For an example of this see Genesis 4.8, where the text is written thus: 'And Cain said to Abel his brother . . . and it came to pass, while they were in the field, that Cain' etc., where a space is left empty at the point where we are expecting to know what it was that Cain said to his brother. There are twenty-eight such spaces preserved by the scribes (apart from those we have already noted). Many of them would not appear to be mutilated if the space had not been left there. But of all these points enough.

CHAPTER 10

Where the remaining books of the Old Testament are examined in the same manner as the earlier ones

[1]   I pass to the remaining books of the Old Testament. About the two books of Chronicles I have nothing to say that is certain and worth anything, other than that they were composed long after Ezra, perhaps even after Judas Maccabeus had restored the Temple.[1] For in 1 Chronicles 9 the historian tells us 'which families first (i.e., at the time of Ezra) lived in Jerusalem', and then in verse 17 records the names of the 'gatekeepers', two of whom are also mentioned in Nehemiah 11.19. This shows that these books were written long after the rebuilding of the city. But nothing seems to be established about their true author or their authority, utility or doctrine. In fact, I am extremely surprised that they were admitted among the sacred books by the same men who excluded the Book of Wisdom, Tobias and the other so called apocryphal books from the scriptural canon. However, it is not my intention to detract from their authority; as they have been universally accepted, I leave it at that.

[2]   The Psalms too were collected and divided into five books in the period of the Second Temple. According to Philo Judaeus,[2] Psalm 88 was published when King Jehoiakim was still in prison in Babylon, and Psalm 89 after the same king had regained his liberty, something I do not think

---

[1] Spinoza's footnote: see Annotation 21.

[2] Philo Judaeus (c. 20 BC–c. 50 AD), Hellenistic Jewish philosopher of Alexandria. The text Spinoza is citing (Philo Judaeus, *Breviarium de temporibus*, bk. 2), as several scholars have pointed out, is one of the forged texts written by Annius of Viterbo and published in his *Commentaria super opera diversorum auctorum de antiquitatibus loquentium* (Rome 1498).

Philo would have said, were it not either the received opinion of his time or had he not received it from others worthy of credence.

[3]   The Proverbs of Solomon were, I believe, also collected together at the same time, or at least in that of King Josiah, because in the first verse of chapter 25 it is said, 'These also are proverbs of Solomon which the men of Hezekiah, King of Judah, copied'. But here I cannot remain silent about the audacity of those rabbis who wanted to exclude this book, together with Ecclesiastes, from the canon of sacred writings, and lay it aside with the rest that have not come down to us. And they would certainly have done so, had they not found some passages where the Law of Moses is commended. It must truly be regretted that sacred and excellent things depended upon the judgment of such men. I congratulate them for their being willing to let us have these books, but cannot help doubting whether they passed them on to us in good faith. However I do not want to go deeply into that here.

[4]   I pass on therefore to the books of the Prophets. When I study these, I see that the prophecies they contain were redacted from other books, and that in those books they were not always composed in the same order in which they were spoken or written by the prophets themselves. Furthermore, they do not include all the prophecies but only those that could be found in one place or another. These books are thus nothing more than fragments of the prophets.

Isaiah began to prophesy when Uzziah was king, as the writer who transcribed them himself testifies in the opening verse.[3] But at this time he was not just a prophet; for he also wrote an account of all the achievements of King Uzziah (see 2 Chronicles 26.22), a book which no longer survives. What we do have derives from the Chronicles of the Kings of Judah and of Israel, as we have shown. In addition, the rabbis maintain this prophet also prophesied whilst Manasseh was king and that the latter had him put to death, and although this story seems to be a legend, they still apparently believed that not all of his prophecies are extant.

[5]   Jeremiah's prophecies, narrated as if they were a historical account, appear to be a collection of excerpts from several different chronicles.

---

[3] Isaiah 1.1.

They are set out in an unsystematic manner with no regard to chronological succession, and the same story is duplicated in several versions. Chapter 21, for example, explains the reason for the arrest of Jeremiah, namely, that he predicted the destruction of the city to [King] Zedekiah whilst the latter was consulting him. This narrative is then interrupted and chapter 22 moves on to the story of his denunciation of Jehoiachin (who reigned before Zedekiah), and his predicting his captivity. Chapter 25 then describes what had been revealed to the prophet earlier, in the fourth year of Jehoiakim's reign. The text then gives the prophecies from the first year of this king's reign, and proceeds in the same manner, accumulating prophecies with no regard to temporal order, until finally in chapter 38 he returns to the story which began to be narrated in chapter 21 (as if these 15 chapters were in parenthesis). For the connecting particle with which chapter 38 begins refers back to verses 8, 9, and 10 of chapter 21. Then, the text recounts Jeremiah's final arrest differently, providing a very different reason for his prolonged detention in the court of the guard than was given in chapter 37. Hence, it is clearly evident that these things have all been gathered from different chroniclers and cannot be accounted for in any other way.

The remaining prophecies in the closing chapters, where Jeremiah is speaking in the first person, appear to have been copied from the book Baruch wrote at Jeremiah's dictation. For that volume (as is clear from 36.2) contained only what was revealed to Jeremiah from the time of Josiah to the fourth year of Jehoiakim, which is where our book begins. Everything from chapter 45, verse 2 to chapter 51, verse 59 likewise seems to have been copied from the same volume.

[6]   The opening verses of the Book of Ezekiel plainly indicate that this too is but a fragment. The conjunction with which the book begins obviously refers to other things already said, connecting them with what is to come. Not just the conjunction, moreover, but the whole structure of the work presuppose other writings. For the thirtieth year with which the book begins indicates that the prophet is continuing rather than beginning his narrative. The writer also remarks in parenthesis in verse 3, 'there had often been a word of God to Ezekiel the priest, the son of Buzi, in the land of the Chaldeans' etc., as if he were saying that the words of Ezekiel which he had recorded down to this point referred to other things which had been revealed to him before this thirtieth year.

Again, Josephus in his *Antiquities* 10.7 relates that Ezekiel predicted that Zedekiah would not see Babylon, but we do not find this in his book as we have it. On the contrary, in chapter 17 we read that Zedekiah would be taken to captivity in Babylon.[4]

[7] Of Hosea, we cannot say for certain that he wrote more than is contained in the book which goes under his name. Yet I am surprised we do not possess more from him, as by the writer's own testimony, he prophesied 144 for more than eighty-four years. More generally, we know the writers of these books did not collect the writings of all the prophets that ever lived nor all the writings of the prophets that we have. Of the prophets who prophesied in the reign of Manasseh mentioned in a general way in 2 Chronicles 33.10, 18, 19, we possess no prophecies at all. Nor do we retain all the prophecies of the Twelve Prophets.[5] Of Jonah, only his prophecies concerning the Ninevites were copied down for us, though he did also prophesy to the Israelites; about which see 2 Kings 14.25.

[8] Regarding the Book of Job, and Job himself, there has been much controversy among the commentators. Some take the view that Moses wrote it and that the whole story is just a parable; this is what some of the Rabbis of the Talmud teach and Maimonides also advocates in the *Guide of the Perplexed*.[6] Others believed the story to be true and thought that Job lived in Jacob's time and married his daughter Dinah. Ibn Ezra, as I said above, affirms in his commentary on the book that it had been rendered into Hebrew from another language. I wish he had demonstrated this for us more conclusively, since we could deduce from it that the gentiles too possessed sacred books. I leave the question therefore in some doubt, surmising only that Job was a gentile and a man of the highest constancy, whose situation was initially favourable, then extremely adverse, and in the end full of good fortune; for so Ezekiel 14.14[7] speaks of him along with others. I believe Job's varied fortune and constancy of mind have given many the opportunity to disagree concerning divine providence, or at least gave the author of this book the opportunity to compose his dialogue. For its content and style seem to be not those of a man miserably ill on an ash-heap but rather someone

[4] Spinoza's footnote: see Annotation 22.   [5] The 'minor' biblical prophets from Hosea to Malachi.
[6] Maimonides, *Guide of the Perplexed*, 3.22–3.
[7] The Latin text has 14.12. Noah, Daniel and Job are named as three supremely righteous men.

meditating at leisure in an academy. I would also believe along with Ibn Ezra that this text was translated from another language, since it seems to aspire to emulate gentile poetry. The father of the gods twice calls a council, and Momus, here called Satan, criticizes God's words with the greatest freedom, etc.; but these are only conjectures and not solidly based.

[9]   I pass to the book of Daniel, which without doubt, from chapter 8 on, consists of writings by Daniel himself. I do not know where the seven earlier chapters were drawn from: since they were composed in Chaldaic (except chapter 1), we may suspect that they come from Chaldean chronicles. Were this clearly established, it would be the most convincing possible evidence proving that Scripture is sacred only in so far as we understand through it the things signified there, but not as regards the words, or language and forms of discourse, in which the things are expressed. Furthermore, it would prove that all books expounding and teaching the highest things are, no matter what language they are written in – or by whom, equally sacred. As it is, we can at least take note that these chapters were written in Chaldaic [i.e. Aramaic] and yet are as sacred as the rest of the Bible.

145

[10]   The opening book of Ezra is so closely connected with the book of Daniel that it is easy to tell that it is the same writer continuing his orderly narrative of the affairs of the Jews from the time of the first captivity. Likewise, the Book of Esther, I have no doubt, is connected with this book. The conjunction with which Esther begins can refer to no other text. For it is not credible that this is the book that Mordecai wrote. In 9.20–2, a third person, referring to Mordecai, records that he wrote letters and indicates what they contained. Then at verse 31 of the same chapter, he states that Queen Esther confirmed by edict the arrangements pertaining to the festival of the Lots (Purim), and that this was written in 'the book', i.e. (as the Hebrew expression implies) in a book that was known to everybody at that time to contain these things. Ibn Ezra concedes, as everyone must, that this book perished along with others. Finally, the chronicler refers us, for Mordecai's other activities, to the Chronicles of the Persian Kings. Hence, there is no doubt that Esther too was penned by the same narrator who wrote the books of Daniel and Ezra, as well as that of Nehemiah,[8] since that is called 'the second book of Ezra'. Consequently, these four

---

[8] Spinoza's footnote: see Annotation 23.

books – Daniel, Ezra, Esther and Nehemiah – we assert were written by one and the same author, though I cannot even guess who he was.

Whoever he was, we can discover how he obtained his knowledge of these histories and the source from which he probably transcribed the greater part of them. For we know that the governors or rulers of the Jews in the Second Temple period, had, like the kings of the First Temple period, scribes or chroniclers who wrote down their annals or histories in chronological order. The Chronicles or Annals of the Kings are cited frequently in the text of 1 and 2 Kings. The Annals and Chronicles of the rulers and priests of the Second Temple are cited first at Nehemiah 12.23 and later at 1 Maccabees 16.24. This, surely, is the book (see Esther 9.31) we referred to just now where Esther's edict and those of Mordecai were set out and which, we agreed with Ibn Ezra, had perished. Thus, from these Annals or Chronicles the whole content of these books appears to have been extracted or copied; for their author cites no other source and we know of no other recognized authority. 146

[11] It is certain, however, that these books were not written either by Ezra or Nehemiah since Nehemiah 12.10–11 gives a genealogy of the High Priests from Jeshua to Jaddua, the sixth high priest, who met Alexander the Great at the time the Persian empire was on the point of being conquered (see Josephus *Antiquities* 11.8), or, as Philo Judaeus calls him in his *Book of Times*,[9] the sixth and last Priest under the Persians. Indeed, the fact is plainly indicated again in this same chapter of Nehemiah, verse 22: 'the Levites', says the chronicler, 'in the time of Eliashab, Joiada, Johanan and Jaddua, were recorded' (i.e., in the 'Chronicles') above[10] the reign of Darius the Persian'. No one supposes, I imagine, that Ezra[11] or Nehemiah were so long-lived as to outlive the fourteen kings of Persia. For it was the first Persian king, Cyrus,[12] who gave the Jews permission to rebuild the Temple, and it was more than 230 years from his time to that of King Darius,[13] fourteenth and last king of the Persians.

I have no doubt, therefore, that these books were composed long after Judas Maccabeus restored worship in the Temple, and the reason why they

[9] *Breviarium de temporibus*: see n. 2.
[10] Spinoza's footnote: NB Unless 'supra' means 'beyond', this is an error of the copyist, who wrote 'above' instead of 'until'.
[11] Spinoza's footnote: see Annotation 24.   [12] Cyrus, reigned 559–529 BC.
[13] Darius III, reigned *c*. 380–330 BC.

were written was that spurious books of Daniel, Ezra and Esther were being published at that time by certain malcontents, who were doubtless of the sect of the Sadducees, since the Pharisees never accepted these books so far as I know. Although a number of fables are to be found in the book called 4 Ezra which we also read in the Talmud, we should not for that reason ascribe them to the Pharisees, for, aside from a few ignoramuses, they all accept that these stories were added by some concoctor of fables. This was done, so I believe, by certain persons to make the Pharisaic traditions look ridiculous.

Otherwise, possibly these books were transcribed and published at this time for this reason: to show the people that the prophecies of Daniel had been fulfilled and thus strengthen them in their religion, so that, amid all their calamities, they would not despair of future security and seeing better times. But truly, even though these books are so recent and new, numerous errors, unless I am mistaken, have crept into them owing to the haste of the copyists. For several marginal notes, like those we discussed in the previous chapter, are to be found in these books as in the others, and some passages cannot be explained in any other way, as I shall now show.

[12]   But before doing so, a word about the marginal readings in these books. Even if we must grant the Pharisees that the marginal readings are as ancient as the compilers of the books themselves, it is still essential to state that these editors (if there really were more than one) made these notes because they found that the chronicles from which they copied them were not written with sufficient care and while some errors were obvious, they did not dare to emend the writings of their elders and ancestors. Nor do I need to discuss this any further, and so will go on to point out a number of slips which are not noted in the margins.

[13]   (1) There are I do not know how many mistakes which have crept into Ezra chapter 2. Verse 64 states the total of all the people who are mentioned in separate groups throughout the chapter: there are said to be 42,360 of them. However if you add the totals for each group, you arrive at no more than 29,818. Therefore, there is a mistake here either in the final figure or the sub-totals. But it seems credible that the total would have been correctly transmitted, since doubtless everyone remembered it by heart as a memorable fact. The same cannot be said, though, of the partial figures. Had a mistake crept into the final total, it would have been

147

immediately obvious to everyone and readily put right. Moreover, this is fully confirmed by the fact that in Nehemiah 7, from which this chapter of Ezra (which is called the 'epistle of the genealogy') is copied, the final figure – as Nehemiah 7.5 explicitly says – tallies completely with that given in the book of Ezra whereas the sub-totals are widely discrepant, some being larger and others smaller than the numbers in Ezra. All these latter together amount to 31,089. Hence there can be no doubt that numerous errors have found their way into the sub-totals of both Ezra and Nehemiah.

Every single commentator who tries to reconcile these blatant contradictions, offers the best solution his intellectual ability allows. But, as I mentioned above, in worshipping the letters and words of Scripture in this way, they are simply exposing the editors of the holy books to 148 ridicule. They make it appear that these writers do not know how to express themselves or organize what they have to say. Furthermore, they are utterly obscuring the lucid simplicity of Scripture. For if it is permitted to interpret Scripture as they do throughout, there would surely not be a single phrase whose true sense we could not doubt. There is no reason to dwell on this topic any longer. For I am quite convinced that if any historian wished to imitate [in history-writing] all the things the commentators devoutly concede to the writers of the biblical books, they themselves would deride him in every way. If they deem it blasphemous to say that the Bible is erroneous in various places, what label should I affix to those who adorn the Scriptures in whatever fashion they please, who demean the sacred narrators and make them appear to utter nonsense and get everything muddled, and who deny the clearest and most evident sense of Scripture?

What is plainer in the Bible than that in the 'epistle of the genealogy' which has been inserted into chapter 2 of the book that goes under Ezra's name, Ezra and his companions enumerated all those who left for Jerusalem in groups, since these figures include not only the totals for those who could declare their genealogy but also of those who could not? What, I say, is clearer from Nehemiah 7.5 than that he has simply copied this epistle? Those who explain it otherwise are simply denying the true sense of Scripture and therefore the Bible itself.

As for considering it devout to adapt some passages of Scripture to fit others, this is nothing but a ridiculous notion of piety. For they alter clear passages to fit obscure ones and correct ones to fit mistaken ones using corrupt sections to pervert sound passages. However, I would not wish to label them blasphemous, since they have no intention to speak evil, and to err is indeed human.

[14] But I return to my theme. Besides the errors which must be conceded in both Ezra and Nehemiah in the calculations of the 'epistle of the genealogy', there are several other mistakes which should be noted. There are errors in the actual names of the families, more in the genealogies and histories, and, I am afraid, some even in the prophecies themselves. Assuredly, the prophecy of Jeremiah in chapter 22 about Jeconiah[14], and especially the wording of the last verse of that chapter, do not seem to agree at all with Jeconiah's history: see the end of the second Book of Kings,[15] and Jeremiah[16] and 1 Chronicles 3.17–19. I cannot see either how he could say 'you will die in peace' etc. about Zedekiah, whose eyes were torn out as soon as he had seen his sons killed (see Jeremiah 34.5). Were prophecies to be interpreted after the event, their names would need to be switched, and Jeconiah substituted for Zedekiah and vice versa. But this is too paradoxical and I prefer to leave the problem as something insoluble, especially since, if there is error here, it should be attributed to the editor and not to defects in the original texts.

[15] As for the other deficiencies I spoke of, I do not plan to detail them all here, since I could not do so without making this extremely tedious for the reader, especially as they have already been pointed out by others. For Rabbi Shlomo[17] was compelled by the very evident contradictions he observed in the genealogies I have discussed, to utter these candid words (in his commentary on 1 Chronicles 8): 'The fact that Ezra' (who he thinks wrote the books of Chronicles) 'calls the sons of Benjamin by other names, and gives him a different genealogy from the one we have in the book of Genesis, and finally lists most of the Levites' cities differently from Joshua, derives from the fact that he found his sources disagreeing'. Slightly further on, he adds: 'the fact that the genealogy of Gibeon and others is given twice, but differently each time', (is) 'because Ezra found

[14] Also [apparently] known as Coniah and Jehoiachin.   [15] 2 Kings 25.27.
[16] Jeremiah 52.31.
[17] I.e. Rabbi Solomon ben Isaac of Troyes (1040–1105) usually known by his acronym Rashi; he has subsequently remained the most widely cited and authoritative rabbinic commentator on virtually the whole Hebrew Bible, and especially the Pentateuch.

several divergent epistles of genealogy for each man, and in copying from them, followed the majority version, but when the number of discrepant genealogies was equal on either side, then he copied out both versions'.

He thus concedes without reservation that these books were compiled from originals which had not been adequately corrected or were less than altogether certain. Furthermore, the commentators themselves, when attempting to reconcile passages, very often do nothing but reveal how these errors arise. In any case, I do not think that anyone with a sound judgment believes that the sacred chroniclers had the deliberate intention of writing in such a way that they would be seen as continually contradicting themselves.

[16] Possibly someone will say that I am completely undermining Scripture by my manner of proceeding, since it may lead everyone to suspect that the Bible is everywhere full of mistakes. But, on the contrary, I have shown that my methodology works in favour of Scripture by preventing passages which are clear and pure from being corrupted to fit defective passages and simply because some passages are defective, we are not justified in placing every passage under suspicion. There has never ever been a book without mistakes: has anyone (I ask) therefore ever supposed that they were defective throughout? Of course not, especially when the expression is lucid and the meaning of the author is clearly evident.

[17] This completes what I wanted to say about the history of the books of the Old Testament. Our conclusion is evident: no canon of sacred books 150 ever existed before the time of the Maccabees.[18] The books we now possess were selected, in preference to many others, by the Second Temple Pharisees who also set out the forms for prayers, and these have been accepted purely as a consequence of their decisions. Hence, those who seek to demonstrate the authority of Holy Scripture must prove the authority of each individual book. It is insufficient to demonstrate the divine character of just one book, if one wishes to prove the divinity of all. Otherwise we would be obliged to suppose that the council of the Pharisees could not have erred in their selection of books, and no one will ever demonstrate that.

The reason driving me to assert it was the Pharisees alone who selected the books of the Old Testament, placing them in the canon of sacred

---

[18] Spinoza's footnote: see Annotation 25.

books, is that Daniel 12.2 affirms the resurrection of the dead which the Sadducees denied. Equally, the Pharisees themselves plainly tell us as much in the Talmud. For in the treatise *Sabbath* (ch. 2, folio 30, p. 2) 'Rabbi Jehuda, speaking in the name of Rab, said: the learned sought to suppress the book of Ecclesiastes, because its words are not consistent with the words of the Law' (n.b., the book of the Law of Moses). 'But why did they not withdraw it? Because it begins with the Law and ends with the Law'. Slightly further on he adds, 'and they also sought to suppress the book of Proverbs', etc. Finally (in ch. 1, folio 13, p. 2 of the same treatise) he remarks: 'Remember that man for his generous spirit, whose name was Neghunja, the son of Hiskia; for without him the book of Ezekiel would have been discarded, because its words contradicted the words of the Law', etc. It very clearly follows from this that the learned in the Law called together a council to determine what kind of books should be received as sacred and which should be excluded. Hence, anyone desirous of being sure about the authority of them all, must go through the entire deliberative process afresh seeking justification for each of them.

[18] Now it should be time likewise to examine in the same manner the books of the New Testament. However, I am well aware that this has already been done by men expert in the relevant fields of knowledge and especially the [requisite] languages whereas I myself do not have so accurate a knowledge of Greek that I would dare to enter this field; on top of which we lack the originals of the books originally composed in Hebrew. For all these reasons I prefer not to undertake this task, though I do want to note the things most relevant to my design and I shall do this in the following chapter.

151

Where it is asked whether the Apostles wrote their Epistles as apostles and prophets or as teachers, and the role of an Apostle is explained

[1] No one who peruses the New Testament can doubt that the Apostles were prophets. However, as we showed at the close of chapter 1, prophets did not always speak on the basis of revelation; indeed, they rarely did so. Hence, we may wonder whether the Apostles composed their Epistles as prophets on the basis of revelation, and by explicit command, like Moses and Jeremiah, and so on, or whether they wrote them as private individuals or teachers. This is open to question especially since Paul mentions in his First Epistle to the Corinthians 14.6. that there are two different forms of discourse, one based upon revelation and the other upon knowledge. This is why, I maintain, one needs to enquire whether in their Epistles the Apostles are prophesying or teaching.

The style of the Epistles, if we are ready to study it, we shall find to be very different from the style of prophecy. Whenever the prophets testified, they invariably declared that they were speaking at the command of God: 'Thus says God', 'the God of hosts says', 'the word of God', etc. This was apparently their style not only in their public proclamations, but also in those of their letters that contain revelations, as in that of Elijah to Jehoram (see 2 Chronicles 21.12), which begins, 'Thus says God'. We find nothing comparable in the Apostles' letters; on the contrary, at 1 Corinthians 7.40 Paul speaks according to his own opinion. Actually, ambiguous meanings and tentative expressions are found in many passages as, for example, 'we therefore think'[1]

---

[1] Spinoza's footnote: see Annotation 26.

(Epistle to the Romans 3.28), and 'for I think' (8.18), and many more. There are other turns of phrase which stand far removed from prophetic authoritativeness as, for example, 'and this I say as a weak man and not by command' (see 1 Corinthians 7.6), 'I give my advice as a man who by the grace of God is trustworthy' (see 1 Corinthians 7.25), and many others of the sort.

152

[2] Note too that when Paul remarks in the same chapter that he has, or does not have, an instruction or command from God, that he does not mean an instruction or command which God had revealed to him but simply the teachings which Christ gave to his disciples on the mountain. Moreover, if we now turn to the manner in which the Apostles convey the teaching of the Gospel in these Epistles, we shall see that this too diverges very widely from the prophetic manner. For the Apostles always employ arguments, so that they seem to be engaged in a debate rather than prophesying. By contrast prophecies contain nothing but dogmas and decrees, since in them it is God who is presented as speaking, and God does not engage in discussion but issues edicts on the absolute authority of his nature. Equally, prophetic authority does not permit participation in argument, for whoever seeks to confirm his dogmas by means of reason is thereby submitting them to the judgment of each individual for decision. This is what Paul seems to have done by engaging in debate, for at 1 Corinthians 10.15 he says, 'I speak to you as to intelligent men; judge for yourselves what I say'. Finally, as we showed in chapter 1, the prophets did not receive revelations by virtue of the natural light, i.e. by a process of reasoning.

[3] Although some conclusions in the Pentateuch appear to be reached by inference, anyone who studies them will see that they can in no way be taken as conclusive arguments. For example, when Moses admonished the Israelites (Deuteronomy 31.27), 'If you have been rebellious against God while I have lived with you, you will be much more so after I am dead', we should not see this as Moses attempting to convince the Israelites by a process of argument that they will necessarily turn away from the true worship of God after his death. For the argument would be false, as could be shown from Scripture itself. The Israelites remained constant in the time of Joshua and the elders and even later in the time of Samuel, David, Solomon, etc. For this reason these words of Moses

156

amount to no more than a conventional flourish with which he predicts the future defection of the people in a rhetorical manner and as vividly as he could imagine it. The reason why I claim Moses did not say these things on his own initiative in order to make his prediction probable to the people, but as a prophet on the basis of revelation, is that verse 21 of the same chapter says that God had revealed this very thing to Moses in other words. It was thus not necessary for Moses to be convinced of this prediction and decree of God by probable reasoning. It was necessary only that it be vividly impressed in his imagination, as we showed in chapter 1, and this could be done only by his imagining their present disobedience, which he had often experienced, as continuing. This is how all of Moses' arguments in the Pentateuch are to be understood; they are not drawn from the repertory of reason, they are simply turns of phrase by which he expressed God's edicts more effectively and imagined them more vividly.

[4]   I do not mean to say categorically that the prophets were incapable of presenting arguments on the basis of revelation. I affirm only that the more prophets argue cogently, the more their knowledge of what was revealed approximates to natural knowledge and that they are perceived to possess supernatural knowledge chiefly from their proclaiming pure dogmas, or decrees, or [unsupported] opinions. Likewise, it is on this account that Moses, the supreme prophet, put forward no orderly arguments. By contrast, the long deductions and arguments of Paul, such as are found in the Epistle to the Romans, were by no means written on the basis of supernatural revelation. Rather, the Apostles' modes of discourse and discussion in their Epistles reveal very plainly that they did not write them on the basis of divine command and revelation, but simply on that of their own natural judgment. For these letters contain nothing but brotherly advice mixed with courtesies (which of course are totally alien to prophetic authority), like Paul's excusing himself at Romans 15.15 by saying, 'Brethren, I have written to you rather too boldly'.

We may reach the same conclusion from another direction: for we nowhere read that the Apostles were commanded to write; they were ordered only to preach wherever they went and confirm their words with signs. Their presence and these signs were absolutely essential to convert the nations to religion and strengthen them in it, as Paul himself makes very clear at Romans 1.11: 'because I very much desire', he says, 'to see you, so that I may impart to you the gift of the spirit, that you may be strengthened'.

[5]   But here it might be objected that we could just as well infer that the Apostles did not preach as prophets either. For when they went to one place or another to preach, they did not do so by express command, as the prophets had done. We read in the Old Testament that Jonah went to Nineveh to preach, and read at the same time that he was expressly sent there, and what he was to preach there was revealed to him. Likewise, we learn, at some length, that Moses went to Egypt as God's envoy, and at the same time we are told what he was obliged to say to the Israelites and to Pharaoh, and also what miracles he was to perform among them to prove his credentials. Isaiah, Jeremiah and Ezekiel received explicit orders to preach to the Israelites. According to the testimony of Scripture, moreover, the prophets preached nothing that they had not received from God. But in the New Testament we very rarely read of anything comparable concerning the Apostles when they were about to journey to one place or another, to preach. On the contrary, we find some things that clearly reveal that the Apostles chose for themselves where they would preach, as in the case of the disagreement between Paul and Barnabas which led to their separation (see Acts 15.37, 38 etc.). We also find that they often wanted to go somewhere but were unable to do so, as Paul testifies in Romans 1.13: 'These many times have I tried to come to you and have been prevented'; and 15.22: 'This is the reason why I have been hindered many times from coming to you'; and the final chapter of 1 Corinthians, verse 12: 'Concerning my brother Apollos, I strongly urged him to come to you with the brethren; but he had no inclination at all to come to you; though when he has an opportunity', etc. Both from these expressions, thus, and the conflict between the Apostles, as well as from the fact that when they were going somewhere to preach, Scripture does not say, as it does of the ancient prophets, that they went at the command of God, it might seem that I should conclude that it was as teachers and not prophets that the Apostles preached.

However, this objection is readily removed, if we look at the difference between the Apostles' vocation and that of the Old Testament prophets. The latter were not called to preach and prophesy to all nations, but only to certain particular ones, and for that reason they required an express and particular command in each case. But the Apostles were summoned to preach to everyone without exception and to convert all men to religion. Therefore wherever they might go, they were following the command of Christ. Moreover, they did not need to have what they were to preach revealed to them before they went, for they were disciples of Christ to whom he had said, 'and when they deliver you up, do not be anxious how or what you will say; for what you will say will be given you in that hour,' etc. (see Matthew 10.19–20).   155

[6]   Hence, we conclude that the Apostles received by special revelation only what they preached with their own voices and, at the same time, confirmed by wonders (see what we demonstrated at the beginning of chapter 2). What they merely taught, either in writing or orally, without using signs as testimony, they spoke or wrote on the basis of knowledge (i.e. natural knowledge); on this see 1 Corinthians 14.6.

It is no objection to this that all the Epistles begin with a confirmation that they are Apostles. For as I shall show presently, the Apostles received not just the power of prophecy but also authority to teach. It is in this sense that we allow that they wrote their Epistles as Apostles, and that this is the reason each of them starts his preface with a confirmation of his Apostleship. Or perhaps, to win their readers' confidence more readily and seize their attention, they wanted above all to stress that they had won a reputation among all the faithful for their preaching and had also shown by plain testimony that they taught true religion and the way of salvation. For I find that whatever I see in these Epistles about the calling of the Apostles and their sacred and divine spirit, is ascribed to the preaching they had done, with the single exception of passages in which 'the spirit of God' and 'holy spirit' are intended to mean a healthy and happy mind, a mind dedicated to God, etc. (as we explained in chapter 1). For example, in 1 Corinthians 7.40 Paul says, 'in my view, she is blessed if she remains as she is, and I think that the spirit of God is in me'. Here by 'spirit of God' he means his own mind, as the context of the sentence indicates. What Paul is saying is: 'I judge ("in my view") that the widow who does not wish to marry a second time is blessed; for I am celibate myself by choice and consider myself to be blessed'. There are other passages like this that I do not think I need to cite here.

Since we must conclude that the Apostles' Epistles were composed using the natural light of reason alone, we should now ask how they could teach by means of natural knowledge alone things that are not within its scope. We will meet with no difficulty here, if we recall what we said about the interpretation of Scripture in chapter 7 of this treatise. For while the Bible's contents generally surpass our understanding, they can still be safely discussed provided we admit only principles drawn from Scripture itself. In the same way the Apostles could make many inferences and deductions from what they had seen and heard and received from revelation and could, if they chose, teach them to others. Equally, although religion, as the Apostles preached it by simply telling the story of Christ, does not come within the scope of reason, nevertheless everyone can acquire the essence of it by means of the natural light of reason, for, like the whole of Christ's teaching,[2] it consists primarily of moral doctrine. Lastly, the Apostles did not need supernatural light to adapt to the common understanding the religion which they had already confirmed by miracles so that everyone could easily accept it from his heart. Nor did they require supernatural light to teach men about it; and this is the purpose of the Epistles, to teach and admonish men in the way each of the Apostles judged best to strengthen them in religion.

Here we must add that the Apostles, as I said just now, had received not just the power to proclaim the story of Christ, as prophets, i.e., by confirming it with miracles, but also authority to teach and admonish in the way that each of them judged best. Paul clearly points to both of these gifts in the Second Epistle to Timothy 1.11 in these words: 'in which I have been appointed a preacher and Apostle and teacher'. Also in the First Epistle to Timothy 2.7, 'of which I have been appointed a preacher and Apostle (I speak the truth in Christ, I do not lie)', 'a teacher of the gentiles in faith and truth'. In these words, then, he plainly confirms both roles, i.e., his apostleship and his teaching mission; and in his Epistle to Philemon, verse 8, he proclaims his authority to admonish anyone at any time with these words: 'although I have much freedom in Christ to command you to do what is required, nevertheless' etc. Here we should note that if Paul had received from God the commands he was to give to Philemon, as a prophet, then surely he would not have been permitted to reduce God's command to a request. Hence, it definitely follows that he was speaking of the freedom of admonition vested in him as a teacher and not as a prophet.

---

[2] Spinoza's footnote: see Annotation 27.

[7] However, it is not entirely evident that each Apostle could choose the 157
path of instruction he judged best, but only that in virtue of their apostolic
office they were not just prophets but also teachers – unless we appeal to
reason which plainly shows that anyone with authority to teach also has
authority to choose the way he wishes to teach. But it will be better to
demonstrate all this from Scripture alone. From Scripture, it is clear that
each of the Apostles chose his own particular way, as in the words of
Paul in his Epistle to the Romans 15.20, 'Anxiously endeavouring not to
preach where the name of Christ was already invoked, lest I build on an
alien foundation.' Clearly, had they all the same style of teaching, and had
they established the Christian religion on the same foundation, Paul
would definitely not have termed another Apostle's foundations 'alien',
as his own would have been the same. Since he does pronounce them
alien, it necessarily follows that each of them constructed the edifice of
religion on a different foundation. In their capacity as teachers, the
Apostles were thus in the same position as other teachers: for teachers
have their own individual ways of teaching, and always prefer to teach
those who are wholly untutored, and have not begun to learn from anyone else, whether in languages or the sciences, even in the mathematical
sciences whose truths are indubitable.

[8] Furthermore, if we read through the Epistles themselves with some
care, we shall see that the Apostles do indeed agree about religion itself,
but widely disagree as to its foundations. Paul, for instance, to strengthen
men in religion and to show them that salvation depends upon the grace of
God alone, taught that no one may glory in their works but in faith alone,
and that no one is justified by works (see Epistle to the Romans, 3.27–8), as
well as the whole doctrine of predestination. On the other hand, James,
in his Epistle, teaches that a man is justified by works and not by faith
alone (see the Epistle of James 2.24); indeed, James sums up his whole
doctrine of religion in a very few words ignoring all of Paul's arguments.

[9] Finally, there can be no doubt that many disputes and schisms have
arisen because different Apostles constructed religion on different foundations. Disputes and schisms have ceaselessly disturbed the church ever
since apostolic times, and will surely never cease to trouble it, until reli- 158
gion is finally separated from philosophical theories and reduced to the
extremely few, very simple dogmas that Christ taught to his own. This was

impossible for the Apostles to accomplish, because the Gospel was unknown to people at that time and hence, to avoid offending them too much with the novelty of its teaching, they adapted it, so far as they could, to the minds of their contemporaries (see the First Epistle to the Corinthians 9.19–20), and built upon the basic principles that were most familiar and acceptable at the time. That is why none of the Apostles engaged with philosophy more than Paul who was summoned to preach to the gentiles while the others, who preached to the Jews, the despisers of philosophy, likewise adapted themselves to their minds (see the Epistle to the Galatians 2.11 etc.), and taught a religion devoid of philosophical theory. How happy our own age would surely be, were we to see it also free from all superstition.[3]

---

[3] I.e. via total separation of theology and philosophy.

CHAPTER 12

On the true original text of the divine law, and why Holy Scripture is so called, and why it is called the word of God, and a demonstration that, in so far as it contains the word of God, it has come down to us uncorrupted

[1]   Those who consider the Bible in its current state a letter from God, sent from heaven to men, will undoubtedly protest that I have sinned 'against the Holy Ghost'[1] by claiming the word of God is erroneous, mutilated, corrupt and inconsistent, that we have only fragments of it, and that the original text of the covenant which God made with the Jews has perished. However, if they reflect upon the facts, I have no doubt that they will soon cease to protest. For both reason and the beliefs of the prophets and Apostles evidently proclaim that God's eternal word and covenant and true religion are divinely inscribed upon the hearts of men, that is, upon the human mind. This is God's true original text, which he himself has sealed with his own seal, that is, with the idea of himself as the image of his divinity.

[2]   To the early Jews, religion was handed down in writing as law, evidently   159
because in those times they were looked on as if they were infants. Later, however, Moses (Deuteronomy 30.6) and Jeremiah (31.33) proclaimed to them that a time would come when God would inscribe his law in their hearts. It was therefore appropriate for the Jews alone, and especially for the Sadducees, in their time, to fight for the law written upon tablets, but it is not at all appropriate for those who have the law inscribed on their minds.

---

[1] Cp. Matthew 12.31, Mark 3.29, Luke 12.10.

Anyone willing to reflect on this, will find nothing in what I have said that is in conflict with God's word, or with true religion and faith, or anything that can lessen its authority; for, on the contrary, we are enhancing it, as we showed at the end of chapter 10. If this were not so, I would have resolved to remain silent about these topics. I would even – so as to avoid all difficulties – have gladly agreed that profound mysteries lie hidden in the Scriptures. However, since this belief has produced intolerable superstition and other disastrous consequences which I reviewed at the beginning of chapter 7, I realized that I simply could not ignore them, especially as religion requires no superstitious embellishment but, on the contrary, it loses all its splendour when it is adorned with these fictions.

[3]   But they [i.e. my adversaries] will insist that, even though the divine law is written on our hearts, the Bible is still the word of God, and therefore we may not say that it is mutilated and corrupt any more than we may say this of the word of God. Truly, though, I fear that they, on the contrary, try too hard to be pious. They are converting religion into superstition, indeed verge, unfortunately, on adoring images and pictures, i.e. paper and ink, as the word of God. I know I have said nothing unworthy of Scripture or of the word of God, since I have said nothing that I have not demonstrated to be true by the clearest reasoning. That is why I can also assert with confidence that I have said nothing that is irreligious or that smacks of impiety. I admit that some impious persons who find religion a burden, may discern an excuse for wrongdoing here and may infer, without any justification but merely to indulge their pleasures, that Scripture is thoroughly flawed and corrupted and consequently lacks authority. One can do nothing to help such people. It is a commonplace that nothing can be so well formulated that it cannot be perverted by wrong interpretation. Anyone who aspires to indulge in pleasures will readily find a pretext. Nor were those who in ancient times possessed the original texts themselves and the ark of the covenant, and indeed the prophets and the Apostles, any better or more obedient. All men alike, both Jews and gentiles, have always been the same, and in every age virtue has been very rare.

[4]   However, to remove every scruple, I must show on what grounds Scripture, or any inarticulate object, could be called sacred and divine. After that, I must prove what the word of God really is and that it is not contained in a certain number of books. Finally I must demonstrate that,

in so far as the Bible teaches what is requisite for obedience and salvation, it could not have been corrupted. Everyone will readily be able to see from this that we have said nothing against God's word, nor given any licence to impiety.

[5]   Something intended to promote the practice of piety and religion is called sacred and divine and is sacred only so long as people use it religiously. If they cease to be pious, the thing in question likewise, at the same time, ceases to be sacred. If they devote that thing to impious purposes, the very object that before was sacred will be rendered unclean and profane. For example, a certain place was called by the patriarch Jacob 'the house of God', because there he worshipped the God that had been revealed to him. But the very same place was called 'the house of iniquity' by the prophets (see Amos 5.5 and Hosea 10.5), because in their time, following the practice of Jeroboam, the Israelites were accustomed to sacrifice to idols there.

Here is another example that brings all this out very clearly. Words acquire a particular meaning simply from their usage. Words deployed in accordance with this usage in such a way that, on reading them, people are moved to devotion will be sacred words, and any book written with words so used will also be sacred. But if that usage later dies out so that the words lose their earlier meaning, or if the book becomes wholly neglected, whether from wickedness or because people no longer need it, then both words and book will then likewise have neither use nor sanctity. Lastly, if the same words are differently deployed or it becomes accepted usage to construe the [same] words in the contrary sense, then both words and book which were formerly sacred will become profane and impure. From this it follows that nothing is sacred, profane, or impure, absolutely and independently of the mind but only in relation to the mind.

[6]   This is entirely evident from many passages of Scripture. Jeremiah 7.4 (to take an example at random) holds the Jews of his time to be wrong in calling Solomon's temple the temple of God, for, as he goes on to say, in the   161 same chapter, God's name could only be present in that temple as long as it was frequented by men who worshipped him and defended justice. But once frequented by murderers, thieves, idolaters and other wrongdoers instead, it was then rather a den of sinners. I have often wondered why it is that Scripture says nothing about what became of the ark of the covenant.

It is certain, though, that it perished or was burnt along with the Temple, although there was nothing more sacred or venerated among the Hebrews.

Hence, Scripture too is sacred and its discourse divine in the same way, that is so long as it moves people to devotion towards God. Should it become completely neglected, as it once was by the Jews, it is thereby rendered nothing but ink and paper and becomes absolutely devoid of sanctity and subject to corruption. If it is then perverted or perishes, it is not true to say that God's word has deteriorated or perished, just as it would be false to say in Jeremiah's time that it was the Temple of God, as the Temple had been until then, that perished in the flames. Jeremiah himself says the same thing of the Law when rebuking the impious men of his time in these terms: 'How can you say, we are trained in the Law of God and are its guardians. Assuredly, it has been written in vain, vain is the scribe's pen!'[2] That is, even though the Scripture is in your hands, you are wrong to say that you are guardians of God's Law, now that you have rendered it ineffective.

So too when Moses broke the first tablets, it was not the word of God that he cast from his hands in anger and broke (who could imagine this of Moses or of God's word?) but only the stones. They had been sacred before because the covenant under which the Jews bound themselves to obey God was inscribed upon them. But as they subsequently negated that covenant by worshipping a [golden] calf, the stones no longer possessed any sanctity whatever. It is for the same reason that the second tablets[3] could perish with the ark. It is thus wholly unsurprising that Moses' original texts are no longer extant and the process we described in the preceding chapters could have happened to the books which we do possess, given that the true original of the divine covenant, the most sacred thing of all, has totally perished.

Let [my opponents] therefore cease accusing us of impiety. We have said nothing against the word of God, nor have we corrupted it. Let them rather turn their anger, if they have any justified anger, against the ancients whose wickedness profaned the ark of God, the Temple, the Law and all holy things, and rendered them liable to corruption. Equally, if as the Apostle says, in 2 Corinthians 3.3, they have a letter from God within themselves, written not in ink but by the spirit of God, not on tablets of stone but on tablets of flesh, on the heart, let them cease worshipping the

162

---

[2] Jeremiah 8.8.   [3] Exodus 34.

letter and being so concerned about it. This I think suffices to explain on what grounds the Bible should be considered sacred and divine.

[7] Now we must ascertain what precisely is to be understood by 'debar Jehova' (word of God). Now 'debar' means 'word', 'speech', 'edict' and 'thing'. We showed in chapter 1 the reasons why in Hebrew a thing is said to be of God and is ascribed to God; and from this we can readily grasp what Scripture means by word, speech, edict and thing of God. There is no need to repeat it all here, nor for that matter the third point we made, regarding miracles in chapter 6. It suffices to recall the substance of it, so that what we want to say about our present topic may be better understood.

When 'word of God' is predicated of a subject which is not God himself, it properly signifies the divine law which we discussed in chapter 4, that is, the religion which is universal or common to the whole human race. On this subject see Isaiah 1.10 etc., where Isaiah teaches the true way of living, that does not consist in ceremonies but in charity and integrity of mind, and calls it interchangeably God's law and the word of God. It is also used metaphorically for the order of nature itself and fate – since in truth this depends upon the eternal decree of the divine nature and follows it – and especially for what the prophets foresaw of this order. For they did not see future things by means of their natural causes but rather as the decisions or decrees of God. It is also used for every pronouncement of any prophet, in so far as he had grasped it by his own particular virtue or prophetic gift and not by the common natural light, and the primary reason for this is that the prophets were in truth accustomed to envisage God as a legislator, as we showed in chapter 4.

The Bible, consequently, is called the word of God for these three reasons: (1) because it teaches true religion of which the eternal God is the author; (2) because it offers predictions of future things as decrees of God; and (3) because those who were its actual authors for the most part taught these things, not by the common natural light of reason, but by a light peculiar to themselves, and portrayed God as saying them. Although there is much besides in Scripture which is merely historical and to be understood by the natural light, its designation as God's word is taken from its most important feature.

[8]   From this we readily see how God is to be understood as the author of the Bible. It is owing to the true religion that it teaches and not because he wanted to present human beings with a certain number of books. We may also see why the Bible is divided into the books of the Old and the New Testament. It is because before Christ's coming the prophets were accustomed to proclaim religion as the law of the country based upon the covenant entered into at the time of Moses; whereas after Christ's coming the Apostles preached religion to all people everywhere, as the universal law, based solely upon Christ's passion. It is not because the books of the Testaments differ in doctrine, nor because they were written as covenantal texts, nor, finally, because the universal religion, which is supremely natural, was anything new, except to those people who did not know it: 'he was in the world', says John the Evangelist 1.10, 'and the world did not know him'. Therefore, even if we had fewer books, whether of the Old or of the New Testament, we would still not be deprived of the word of God (by which is properly meant, as we have just said, true religion), just as we do not now regard ourselves as deprived of it, even though we do now lack many other excellent writings, like the Book of the Law which was zealously preserved in the Temple as the text of the covenant, and the Books of the Wars, the Books of the Chronicles, and many, many others, from which the books of the Old Testament which we now possess were selected and assembled.

[9]   All this is confirmed by many other arguments:

(1) In neither Testament were the books written at one and the same time, for all centuries, by express command but rather from time to time by specific individuals in the way their times and individual temperaments dictated. This is made clear by the callings of the prophets (who were called to admonish the impious men of their time) and by the Epistles of the Apostles.

(2) It is one thing to understand Scripture and the minds of the prophets and quite another to understand the mind of God which is the very truth of a thing as follows from what we showed about the prophets in chapter 2. This distinction applies no less to histories and to miracles, as we showed in chapter 6. But this same [vast difference] can not be said to be present in those passages which speak of true religion and true virtue.

(3) The books of the Old Testament were selected from among many   164
others, and collected and approved by a council of Pharisees, as we showed in
chapter 10. The books of the New Testament were also brought into the canon
by the decrees of certain councils, whose decrees discarded as spurious
numerous other texts which were widely held to be sacred. Now the member-
ship of these councils (both Pharisaic and Christian) did not consist of prophets but solely of teachers and learned men. Nevertheless we must
necessarily admit that in thus making this selection they took the word of
God as their criterion, and hence before approving any books, must necessarily have had a conception of God's word.

(4) The Apostles wrote not as prophets but as teachers (as we said in the
previous chapter) choosing the manner of teaching that they thought would
be easiest for the disciples whom they wanted to teach at the time. From this
it follows that there are many things in their writings (as we concluded at the
end of that chapter) which, from the point of view of religion, we are now able
to dispense with.

(5) Finally, there are the four evangelists of the New Testament. But who
will believe that God wanted to recount Christ's history and communicate it
to men in writing four times? Admittedly, there are some things in one
which are not found in another, and some passages help elucidate others. But
it does not follow from this that it was necessary for us to know everything the
four narrate or that God chose them to write so that the history of Christ
would be better grasped. For each preached his own gospel in a different
place, and each recorded what he had preached, doing so in a straightforward
fashion so as to tell Christ's history clearly. None wrote so as to explain [the
versions of] the others. If they are now sometimes more readily, and better,
understood by comparison with each other, that is accidental and occurs only
in a few passages; and were these passages unknown, the story would still be
just as evident and men no less happy.

[10]   These considerations prove that Scripture is properly termed
the word of God only with respect to religion, i.e., the universal divine
law.[4] It remains now to show that, in so far as it is properly so called, it is
not defective or distorted or truncated. Here, I call a text defective,

---

[4] It is typical of Spinoza to redefine the meaning of the term 'religion' in this way. In his philosophy
'true religion' means following the universal and absolute rules of morality, which can only be
demonstrated according to him, philosophically, and hence understood only by a few, but which
revealed religions do, or at least should, teach all men to 'obey'.

distorted or truncated which is so badly written and composed that its sense cannot be discerned from its use of language or elicited from Scripture itself. I refuse to grant that because Scripture contains the divine law, it has always preserved the same points, the same letters and the same words (I leave this for the Masoretes to prove and others who have a superstitious veneration of the letter). I assert only that the meaning, which alone entitles any text to be called divine, has come down to us uncorrupted, even though the words in which it was first expressed are deemed to have been frequently altered. As we said, this removes nothing from the dignity of Scripture; for Scripture would be no less divine even if written in other words or in a different language. Thus, no one can question that in this sense we have received the divine law, uncorrupted. For we see from Scripture itself, and without any difficulty or ambiguity, that the essence of the Law is to love God above all things and one's neighbour as oneself. And this cannot be adulterated nor penned in a slap-dash, error-prone manner. For if Scripture ever taught anything else than this, it would necessarily have had to teach everything else differently, since this is the foundation of all religion. Were this removed, the entire structure would immediately collapse. Such a Scripture as that would not be the same as the one we are discussing here but an altogether different book. It remains, then, indisputable that this is what Scripture has always taught and consequently that no error has occurred here affecting the sense, which would not have been noticed at once by everybody. Nor could anyone have corrupted it without immediately betraying his malicious intent.

[11] As this foundation is thus undeniably unadulterated, the same must be conceded about everything that flows indisputably from it and which is hence likewise fundamental: such as, that God exists, that he provides for all things, that he is omnipotent, that he has decreed that the pious will fare well and wrongdoers badly, and that our salvation depends upon His grace alone. For Scripture everywhere manifestly teaches all these things, and thus must always have taught them; otherwise all the rest would be meaningless and without foundation. We must insist also that all the [Bible's] moral precepts are equally free of corruption, since they most evidently follow from this universal foundation: to defend justice, assist the poor, not to kill, not to covet other men's property, etc. None of these things, I contend, can be corrupted by

human malice or destroyed by age. For if any of these was thus deleted, it would be immediately restored by their universal foundation, and espe- 166 cially by the principle of charity which in both testaments is everywhere what is commended the most.

Furthermore, while it is impossible to imagine a crime so appalling that it has not been committed by somebody somewhere, yet there is no one who would attempt to abolish the Law to excuse their own crimes or present a malicious thing as an eternal and salutary doctrine. For human nature is evidently so fashioned that anyone (whether king or subject) who has committed any wrong, tries to present their actions in such colours that it will be believed that they have done nothing contrary to right and justice.

[12]   We therefore conclude unreservedly that the entire divine universal law which Scripture teaches has come into our hands unadulterated. There are other things too that we cannot doubt have been passed down to us in good faith: for example, the outlines of the biblical histories because these were well known to everyone; at one time the common people of the Jews were accustomed to sing of the ancient deeds of the people in psalms. Likewise, the main points of Christ's deeds and passion were immediately reported throughout the Roman empire. Unless therefore most of mankind have engaged in a conspiracy together – which is not credible – one cannot believe that later generations have transmitted the main lines of these histories otherwise than as they received them from the earliest generation. Consequently, anything adulterated or spurious could only have occurred in the remaining material – whether in some circumstance of a historical narrative or prophecy designed to incite the people to greater devotion, or in some miracle intended to outrage philosophers, or in philosophical matters after [various] schismatics began to mingle these with religion and each of them strove to win support for his own fabrications by abusing divine authority in this way. But it is irrelevant to salvation whether things of this kind are corrupt or not, as I will show explicitly in the next chapter, although I think it is already evident from what we have already said, especially in chapter 2.

CHAPTER 13

Where it is shown that the teachings of Scripture are very simple, and aim only to promote obedience, and tell us nothing about the divine nature beyond what men may emulate by a certain manner of life

[1]   We proved in chapter 2 of this treatise that the prophets possessed extraordinary powers of imagination but not of understanding, and that it was not the deeper points of philosophy that God revealed to them but only some very simple matters, adapting Himself to their preconceived beliefs. We then showed in chapter 5 that Scripture explains and teaches things in such a way that anyone may grasp them. It does not deduce and derive them from axioms and definitions, but speaks simply, and to secure belief in its pronouncements, it confirms them by experience alone, that is, by miracles and histories narrated in a language and style designed to influence the minds of the common people: on this see chapter 6 (point 3).[1] Finally, we demonstrated in chapter 7 that the difficulty of comprehending the Bible lies solely in the language and not in the sublimity of its content. There is the further problem, though, that the prophets were not addressing the learned among the Jews but the entire people without exception, and the Apostles likewise were accustomed to proclaim the Gospel teaching in churches where there was a miscellaneous congregation of all types of people. From all this it follows that biblical teaching contains no elevated theories or philosophical doctrines but only the simplest matters comprehensible to even the very slowest.

---

[1] For point 3 in ch. 6, see pp. 89–92.

[2] I never cease to be amazed at the ingenuity of those I mentioned earlier who uncover in Scripture mysteries too profound to be explained in any human terms and hence imported into religion so many philosophical questions that the Church now resembles a university and religion a field of learning or, rather, ceaseless learned controversy. But, then, why should one be astonished if those who claim to have a supernatural light are unwilling to defer in knowledge to philosophers who claim nothing more than natural understanding? Rather it would be truly surprising had these men introduced anything novel, on any philosophical question, that had not long before been commonplace among pagan philosophers (despite which they claim the latter were 'blind'). For if you ask what mysteries they discover hidden in Scripture, you will find nothing but the fabrications of Aristotle or Plato or some like philosopher which mostly could be more readily dreamt up by some layman than derived from Scripture by even the most consummate scholar. 168

[3] We do not mean to lay it down as an absolute rule that nothing of a purely philosophic nature is inherent in the Bible. Indeed, we mentioned certain such things in the previous chapter as fundamental principles of Scripture. My point is that such things are very few and extremely simple. I propose now to demonstrate what these are and how they are defined. This will be straightforward for us now that we know that it was not the purpose of the Bible to teach any branch of knowledge. For from this we can readily infer that it requires nothing of men other than obedience, and condemns not ignorance but disobedience. Since obedience to God consists solely in love of our neighbour (for he who loves his neighbour, with the intention of obeying God, has fulfilled the Law, as Paul observes in his Epistle to the Romans, 13.8), it follows that the only knowledge commended in Scripture is that which everyone needs to obey God according to this command, that is if, lacking this knowledge, they must necessarily be disobedient or at least deficient in the habit of obedience. All other philosophical concerns that do not directly lead to this goal, whether concerned with knowledge of God or of natural things, are irrelevant to Scripture and must therefore be set aside from revealed religion.

[4] Anyone may now readily see this for himself, as I have said. Nevertheless, I want to set the whole thing out yet more carefully and explain it more clearly, since the entire question of what religion is depends on it.

For this purpose, we need to demonstrate, first and foremost, that an intellectual or precise knowledge of God is not a gift generally given to all the faithful, in the way that obedience is. Secondly, we must prove that that knowledge which God, via the prophets, required all men to possess universally and which every individual is obliged to possess, consists of nothing other than an understanding of God's justice and charity. Both of these points are readily demonstrated from Scripture itself.

[5] For (1), the first point, most evidently follows from Exodus 6.3, where in showing Moses the singular grace given to him, God says: 'And I was revealed to Abraham, to Isaac and to Jacob as *El Shaddai*, but I was not known to them by my name Jehovah.' To clarify this, we must note that *El Shaddai* in Hebrew signifies 'God who suffices' because he gives each person what suffices for him; and although *Shaddai* is often used on its own to refer to God, we should not doubt that the word *El* ('God') should always be silently understood. We should further note that no name is found in the Bible other than Jehovah to indicate the absolute essence of God without relation to created things. The Hebrews therefore claim this is the only proper name of God and that all the others are forms of address; and in truth the other names of God, whether they are nouns or adjectives, are attributes which belong to God in so far as He is considered in relation to his creatures or manifested through them. An example is *El* (or *Eloha*, if we insert the paragogical letter *He*), which means simply 'powerful', as is well-known since it belongs to God alone in a pre-eminent degree, just as when we speak of Paul as 'the Apostle'. Elsewhere the virtues of his power are given in full, as *El* ('powerful'), great, terrible, just, merciful, etc., or the word is used in the plural but with a singular meaning, as is very common in Scripture, in order to include all his virtues at the same time.

Hence, God tells Moses that he was not known to the patriarchs by the name of Jehovah. The patriarchs, it follows, knew no attribute of God disclosing his absolute essence, but only his acts and promises, i.e., his power in so far as it is manifest through visible things. However, God does not tell Moses this so as to charge the patriarchs with lack of faith but, on the contrary, to praise their faith and trust, by which they believed God's promises to be true and certain, despite their lacking the exceptional knowledge of God that Moses had. For while Moses possessed more elevated conceptions of God, he entertained doubts about the divine promises and complained to God that instead of the promised salvation the Jews' situation was getting worse and worse.

The patriarchs, then, were ignorant of the unique name of God, and God communicated it to Moses so as to extol their faith and the simplicity of their hearts, and also to emphasize the singular grace granted to Moses. From this, it follows most evidently, as we asserted in the first place, that people are not obliged by commandment to know God's attributes; this is a particular gift bestowed only on certain of the faithful. It is not worth adding further testimonies from the Bible to prove this; for who does not see that the knowledge of God has not been equal among all the faithful? and that no one can be wise by command any more than he can live or exist by command? All equally, men, women and children, can obey by command but cannot all be wise.

[6] But if anyone answers that there is indeed no need to understand God's attributes but only to believe them, quite simply, without demon- 170 stration, he is certainly talking nonsense. For invisible things which are objects of the mind alone can not be seen with any other eyes than through conceptual demonstrations. Those people therefore who do not grasp the demonstrations, see nothing at all of these things, and therefore whatever they report from hearsay about such questions, neither affects nor indicates their minds any more than the words of a parrot or a robot which speaks without mind and sense.

[7] Now, before going any further, I need to explain why it is often stated in Genesis that the patriarchs called God by the name of Jehovah. This appears to stand in straight contradiction with what I have just said. If we recall, however, what we proved in chapter 8, we shall readily be able to reconcile this [seeming contradiction]. In that chapter we showed that the compiler of the Pentateuch does not denote things and places with precisely the names they had at the time to which he refers but rather with those by which they were better known in his own time. God is hence recounted in Genesis as being called by the patriarchs by the name of Jehovah, not because he was known to them by that name, but rather because this was a name supremely revered by the Jews. This is the inference we must come to, I repeat, as we are expressly told in our text from Exodus[2]

---

[2] Exodus 6:3.

that God was unknown to the patriarchs by that title and, likewise, in Exodus 3.13 Moses desires to know God's name, whereas had it been previously known, he too would have known of it. One must therefore conclude, as I contend, that the faithful patriarchs were ignorant of this divine name, and that knowledge of God is God's gift but not his command.

[8] (2) We should now pass on to our second point and demonstrate that the only knowledge of Himself God requires of men, via the prophets, is knowledge of His divine justice and love, that is, those attributes of God that men may emulate by a sound rationale of life. Jeremiah teaches this in so many words. At 22.15–16 speaking of King Josiah, he says: 'Your father indeed ate and drank and passed judgment and administered justice, then it' (was) 'well with him, he defended the right of the poor and indigent, then it' (was) 'well with him, for' (N.B.) 'this is to know me, said Jehovah'. No less clear is 9. 23: 'but in this alone let each man glory, that he understands me and knows me, that I Jehovah practise charity, judgment and justice on earth, for in these things I delight, says Jehovah'. This is also the significance of Exodus 34.6–7 where when Moses desires to see and know God, God only reveals to him His attributes of justice and love. Lastly, a verse of John,[3] which I shall also discuss later, is particularly relevant. It explains God by love alone, since no one has seen him, and concludes that he who has love, truly has God and knows him.

We see, then, that Jeremiah, Moses and John very succinctly summarize the knowledge of God each man is obliged to have. They make it consist in this one single thing, as we argued, that God is supremely just and supremely merciful, or the one and only exemplar of the true life. Furthermore, the Bible gives no explicit definition of God, and does not decree that any attributes of God be accepted other than those we specified just now, and these are the only ones that it commends. From all of this, we conclude that intellectual knowledge of God, considering His nature as it is in itself, a nature which men cannot emulate by a certain rationale of living and cannot adopt as a paradigm for cultivating a true rationale of living, has no relevance whatsoever to faith and revealed religion, and consequently men may have totally the wrong ideas about God's nature without doing any wrong.

---

[3] 1 John 4.7–8.

[9] It is not in the least surprising, therefore, that God adapted Himself to the imaginations and preconceived opinions of the prophets and that the faithful have held conflicting views about God, as we showed with numerous examples in chapter 2. Nor is it at all surprising that the sacred books express themselves so inappropriately about God throughout, attributing hands and feet to him, and eyes and ears, and movement in space, as well as mental emotions, such as being jealous, merciful, etc., and depicting him as a judge and as sitting on a royal throne in heaven with Christ at his right hand. They are here manifestly speaking according to the [utterly deficient] understanding of the common people, whom Scripture strives to render not learned but obedient.   172

However, theologians as a rule have contended that whatever they could discern with the natural light of reason is inappropriate to the divine nature and must be interpreted metaphorically and whatever eludes their understanding must be accepted in the literal sense. But if everything of this sort which is found in the Bible had necessarily to be construed and explained metaphorically, then Scripture would have been composed not for common folk and uneducated people, but exclusively for the most learned and philosophical. Moreover, were it really impious, to attribute to God piously and in simplicity of heart those characteristics we have just mentioned, the prophets would certainly have been particularly scrupulous about phrases of this sort given the intellectual limitations of ordinary people, if for no other reason. They would have made it their principal aim to teach God's attributes clearly and explicitly as everyone is obliged to accept them. But nowhere do they in fact do this.

We should certainly not accept, therefore, that beliefs considered as such, in isolation and without regard to actions, entail anything of piety or impiety at all. We must rather assert that a person believes something piously or impiously only in so far as they are moved to obedience by their beliefs or, as a result of them, deem themselves free to offend or rebel [against God's word]. Hence, if anyone is rendered disobedient by believing the truth, he truly has an impious faith; in so far, on the other hand, as he becomes obedient through believing what is false, he has truly a pious faith. For we have shown that true knowledge of God is not a command but a divine gift, and God requires no other knowledge from men than that of his divine justice and charity, knowledge required not for intellectual understanding but only for obedience [to the moral law].

CHAPTER 14

What faith is, who the faithful are, the foundations of faith defined, and faith definitively distinguished from philosophy

[1] For a true knowledge of faith it is above all necessary to acknowledge that the Bible is adapted to the understanding not only of the prophets but also of the fickle and capricious common people among the Jews. No one who studies this point even casually can miss this. Anyone who accepts everything in Scripture indifferently as God's universal and absolute doctrine and cannot correctly identify what is adapted to the notions of the common people, will be incapable of separating their opinions from divine doctrine. He will put forward human beliefs and fabrications as God's teaching and thereby abuse the authority of the Bible. Who does not see that this is the principal reason why sectaries teach so many mutually contradictory beliefs as doctrines of faith, and support them with many examples from Scripture, so much so that the Dutch long ago produced a saying about it: 'every heretic has his text'? For the sacred books were not written by one man alone, nor for the common people of a single period, but by a large number of men, of different temperaments and at different times, and if we calculate the period from the earliest to the latest, it will be found to be around two thousand years and possibly much longer.

We do not mean to charge these sectarians with impiety for adapting the words of the Bible to their own beliefs. Just as it was once adapted to the understanding of the common people, so also anyone may adapt it to his own beliefs if he sees that in this way he can obey God with fuller mental assent in matters concerning justice and charity. We do accuse them, however, of refusing to grant the same liberty to others. They persecute all who do not think as they do as if they were enemies of God, even though they may be the most honourable of men and dedicated to true virtue while they esteem those who agree with them as the elect of God, even if they are the most violent of men. Surely nothing could be devised which is more pernicious and dangerous to the state.

[2] Hence, in order to determine how far each person possesses freedom to think whatever they wish about faith and who we should 174 regard as the true faithful even if their beliefs differ from ours, we must [correctly] define faith and its fundamental principles. This is what I propose to do in this chapter, and at the same time I propose to separate faith from philosophy which, indeed, has been the principal purpose of the whole work.

[3] To do this in an orderly manner, let us restate the supreme purpose of the whole of the Bible, for that will guide us to the true criterion for defining faith. We said in the last chapter that the sole aim of Scripture is to teach obedience [to the moral law]. This no one can contest. Who does not see that both testaments are nothing but a training in such obedience? And that both testaments teach men this one single thing, to obey in all sincerity? For, not to repeat the evidence I offered in the last chapter, Moses did not attempt to persuade the Israelites with reason but rather to bind them with a covenant, by oaths and with benefits; he then constrained the people to obey the law by threatening them with penalties and encouraging them with rewards. These are all methods for inculcating obedience not knowledge. Likewise, the Gospel's teaching contains nothing other than simple faith: to believe in God and to revere him, or, which is the same thing, to obey him. To demonstrate something so obvious, I do not need to accumulate texts of Scripture commending obedience; for these abound in both testaments.

Similarly, the Bible teaches us itself, in numerous passages and with utter clarity, what each of us must do to obey God. It teaches that the entire Law consists in just one thing, namely love of one's neighbour. No one can deny that the person who loves his neighbour as himself by God's command, is truly obedient and blessed according to the Law, whereas anyone who hates his neighbour and neglects him, is rebellious and disobedient. Finally it is universally acknowledged that Scripture was written and published not just for the learned but for all people of every age and sort. From these things alone it most evidently follows that we are not obliged by Scripture to believe anything other than what is absolutely necessary to fulfil this command. Hence, this decree alone is the one and only rule of the entire universal faith; it alone must govern all dogmas of faith, that is, all dogmas that everyone is obliged to believe.

175 [4] Since this is entirely obvious and everyone can see that everything can properly be deduced from this foundation alone or by reason alone, how could it have happened that so many dissensions have arisen in the church? Could there have been other causes than those we set out at the beginning of chapter 7? This is what compels me to explain at this point the correct method and means of defining the dogmas of faith on the foundation we have discovered. Unless I do this, and define the matter by certain rules, I shall rightly be thought not to have got very far. For anyone will be able to introduce any novelty they like by insisting it is a necessary means to obedience, especially when it is a question of the divine attributes.

[5] In order to set the whole thing out in proper order, I will begin with the definition of faith. On the basis of the foundation we have laid down, faith can only be defined by, indeed can be nothing other than, acknowledging certain things about God, ignorance of which makes obedience towards him impossible and which are necessarily found wherever obedience is met with. This definition is so evident and follows so plainly from what we have just demonstrated that it requires no commentary.

[6] I will now explain in a few words what follows from it.

(1) It follows that faith does not lead to salvation in itself, but only by means of obedience, or, as James says at 2.17, faith by itself without works is dead; on this subject see the whole of this chapter of James.

[7] (2) It follows that whoever is truly obedient [to the moral law] necessarily possesses the true faith which leads to salvation. For, as we said, if obedience is met with, faith too is necessarily found, as the same Apostle explicitly states (2.18): 'Show me your faith apart from your works, and I will show you my faith from my works'. John likewise affirms in his first Epistle (1 John 4.7–8): 'Whoever loves' (i.e. his neighbour), 'is born of God and knows God; he who

does not love, does not know God; for God is love'. From this it follows that we can only make the judgement whether someone is faithful or unfaithful from his works. If his works are good, he is one of the 'faithful', even if he differs from the other 'faithful' in matters of belief. On the other hand, if his works are bad, he is unfaithful, even if he agrees with the wording of what they believe. For if obedience is met with, faith is necessarily found, but faith without works is dead.

The same John also teaches this explicitly in verse 13 of the same chapter: 'By this', he says, 'we know that we abide in Him and He abides in us, because He has given us of His own spirit', namely love. For he had already stated that God is 176 love, hence he concludes (from the principles he had already accepted) that anyone who has love, truly has the spirit of God. He even concludes, because no one has seen God, that no one recognises God or is aware of him other than through love of his neighbour, and hence that the only attribute of God that anyone can know is this love, so far as we share in it. If these arguments are not decisive, they nevertheless explain John's meaning clearly enough, but chapter 2, verses 3 and 4, of the same Epistle explain it still more clearly, where he tells us in explicit terms what we intend to say here. 'And by this', he affirms, 'we are sure that we know him, if we keep his commandments. He who says, I know him, and does not keep his commandments, is a liar, and the truth is not in him.' From this it likewise follows, that the true antichrists are those who persecute honest men and lovers of justice because they differ from them in doctrine and do not adhere to the same tenets of belief as themselves. For we know that those who love justice and charity are faithful by this measure alone, and he who persecutes the faithful is an antichrist.

[8] (3) It follows, finally, that faith requires not so much true as pious dogmas, that is, such tenets as move the mind to obedience, even though many of these may not have a shadow of truth in them. What matters is that the person who embraces them does not realize that they are false – otherwise, he is necessarily in revolt against [true piety]: for how can anyone eager to love justice and obey God adore as divine what that person knows to be alien to the divine nature? People may indeed err in their simplicity of heart, but the Bible does not condemn ignorance, only wilful disobedience, as we have already shown. Indeed, this necessarily follows from the only possible definition of faith itself, all parts of which must be derived from its universal foundation which we have already laid out and from the sole intent of the whole of the Bible, unless we are willing to contaminate it with our own opinions. This definition does not expressly require dogmas that are true but only such as are necessary for inculcating obedience, i.e. those that confirm the mind in love towards our neighbour, by means of which alone each person is in God (to use John's language) and God is in each person.

[9]   Each person's faith therefore must be deemed pious or impious by reason of their obedience or disobedience alone, and not in relation to truth or falsehood. Besides which, there is no doubt that man's common nature is extremely diverse. People do not agree about everything; rather opinions govern men in different ways such that doctrines that move one person to devotion provoke another to derision and contempt. It follows that in the true universal and general faith pertain no dogmas capable of giving rise to controversy amongst honest people. For doctrines of this nature may be pious in one person and impious in another, given that they are to be judged by works alone. The only tenets that belong to universal faith therefore are those that are absolutely required for obedience to God, ignorance of which makes obedience quite impossible. As for the rest, every person, knowing himself better than anyone else, should believe whatever he considers best for strengthening his love of justice. On this basis, I think no scope is left for disputes within the church.

[10]   Nor will I any longer hold back from listing the dogmas of universal faith or the fundamentals of the intent of the whole of Scripture, which (as follows very clearly from what we have shown in these two chapters) all tend towards this: that there exists a supreme being who loves justice and charity, and that, to be saved, all people must obey and venerate Him by practising justice and charity towards their neighbour. From this principle all the specific points are readily derived, and there are no others beside these:

(1) There is a God (that is, a supreme being) who is supremely just and merciful, or an exemplar of the true life, whom no one who does not know or who does not believe that He exists can obey or acknowledge as judge.

(2) He is one; for no one can doubt that that this too is absolutely required for supreme devotion, admiration and love towards God. Devotion, admiration and love, will arise only from the pre-eminence of one above all others.

(3) He is everywhere present and all things are manifest to Him; for if things were believed to be hidden from him, or if it were not known that he sees all things, there would be doubts about the equity of his justice by which he directs all things, or it would even be unknown.

(4) He possesses supreme right and dominion over all things; nor is anything that He does compelled by laws, but He does all things at His absolute pleasure and by His unique grace. For all men are obliged to obey Him absolutely but He is obliged to obey no one.

(5) Worship of God and obedience to Him consist solely in justice and charity, or in love of one's neighbour.

(6) All who obey God in this rationale of living, and only they, are saved; those who live under the sway of pleasures are lost. If people did not firmly believe this, there would be no reason why they should obey God rather than their own pleasures.

(7) Finally, God forgives the repentant their sins; for there is no one who does not sin, and therefore if this were not clearly established, all would despair of their salvation and would have no reason to believe that God is merciful. But anyone who firmly believes that God forgives men's sins with the mercy and grace with which he directs all things and is more fully inspired with the love of God for this reason, truly knows Christ according to the spirit, and Christ is within him.

[11]   No one can fail to recognize that all these things absolutely need to be known, so that all men without exception may be able to love God by command of the Law explained above, for if any of these is removed, obedience too is gone. But what God, or the exemplar of the true life, is, e.g. whether he is fire or spirit or life or thought, etc. is irrelevant to faith, as are questions about the manner in which he is the exemplar of the true life: for example, is it because He has a just and merciful mind? or is it because all things exist and act through Him and therefore we understand them through Him and see what is true, right and good through Him? Whatever one's views on these questions, it makes no difference.

Furthermore, it has nothing to do with faith whether one believes that God is everywhere in essence or in potential, whether He governs all things from liberty or from the necessity of nature, whether He issues edicts like a prince or teaches them as eternal truths, whether man obeys God of his own free will or by the necessity of the divine decree, or whether reward of the good and punishment of wrongdoers takes place naturally or supernaturally. It makes no difference, I contend, with regard to faith how anyone understands these questions and others like them, provided no one draws conclusions with an eye to having greater licence for wrongdoing or becoming less obedient towards God.

Indeed everyone, as we have already said, must adapt these doctrines of faith to his own understanding and to interpret them for himself in whatever way seems to make them easier for him to accept unreservedly and with full mental assent. For, as we have pointed out, faith was once revealed and written according to the understanding and beliefs of the

178

179 prophets and of the common people of their time, and in the same manner everyone in our day must adapt faith to their own views so that they may accept it without any mental reservation or hesitation. For faith, as we showed, requires not so much truth as piety; and since faith is pious and apt for salvation only by way of obedience, no one is faithful except on the ground of obedience. It is, therefore, not the man who advances the best reasons who necessarily manifests the best faith but rather the man who performs the best works of justice and charity. How salutary and necessary this doctrine is in a society if we wish people to live in concord and peace with each other! How many of the causes of wrongdoing and disorder it abolishes, I submit to everyone's judgment.

[12]   Before going any further, it is worth noticing that we can, from what we have just shown, readily answer the objections mentioned in chapter 1 where we referred to God speaking to the Israelites from Mount Sinai. For while the voice heard by the Israelites could yield no philosophical or mathematical certainty about God's existence, still it sufficed to overwhelm them with awe of God, such as they had formerly known Him, and rouse them to obedience, which indeed was the purpose of this awesome display. For God did not intend to teach the Israelites the absolute attributes of His essence (for on that occasion he revealed none), but rather break their wilful spirit and bring them to obedience; and hence He approached them not with reasons but with the roar of trumpets, thunder and lightning (see Exodus 20.20).

[13]   It remains only to show that there is no interaction and no affinity between faith or theology, on the one side, and philosophy, on the other. By now this must be obvious to anyone who knows the aim and the foundations of these two disciplines, which are certainly as different from each other as any two things could be. For the aim of philosophy is nothing but truth, but the aim of faith, as we have abundantly demonstrated, is simply obedience and piety. The foundations of philosophy are universal concepts, and philosophy should be drawn from nature alone. But the foundations of faith are histories and language and are to be drawn only from Scripture and revelation, as we showed in chapter 7. Faith therefore allows
180 every person the greatest liberty to think, so that they may think whatever they wish about any question whatever without doing wrong. It only

condemns as heretics and schismatics those who put forward beliefs for the purpose of promoting disobedience, hatred, conflict and anger. On the other hand, faith regards as faithful only those who promote justice and charity as far as their reason and abilities allow.

[14]   Finally since the things we have demonstrated here are the cardinal points I proposed to make in this treatise, I desire, before going any further, to make an earnest request of my readers, to read these two chapters with some attention and take the trouble to reflect on them again and again, and to understand that we have not written them simply to make some novel remarks, but to correct abuses, and indeed we hope one day to see them corrected.

CHAPTER 15

Where it is shown that theology is not subordinate to reason nor reason to theology, and why it is we are persuaded of the authority of Holy Scripture

[1] Those who do not know how to distinguish philosophy from theology dispute as to whether Scripture should be subject to reason or whether, on the contrary, reason should be the servant of Scripture: that is to say, whether the sense of Scripture should be accommodated to reason or whether reason should be subordinated to Scripture. The latter position is adopted by sceptics who deny the certainty of reason, and the former defended by dogmatists. But from what we have previously said it is obvious that both are absolutely wrong. For whichever position we adopt, we would have to distort either reason or Scripture since we have demonstrated that the Bible does not teach philosophical matters but only piety, and everything in Scripture is adapted to the understanding and preconceptions of the common people. Hence, anyone who tries to accommodate the Bible to philosophy will undoubtedly ascribe to the prophets many things that they did not imagine even in their dreams and will construe their meaning wrongly. On the other hand, anyone who makes reason and philosophy the servant of theology will be obliged to accept as divinely inspired the prejudices of the common people of antiquity and let his mind be taken over and clouded by them. Thus both will proceed senselessly, albeit the latter without reason and the former with it.

[2] The first of the Pharisees [i.e. in the rabbinic tradition] who openly took
181 the position that Scripture must be adapted to reason was Maimonides (whose stance we reviewed in chapter 7 and refuted with many arguments).

Although this author has been a great authority among the rabbis, on this particular question most of them have deserted him and gone over to the opinion of a certain Rabbi Jehuda Al-Fakhar,[1] who in attempting to avoid Maimonides' error has fallen into the opposite one. He took the position[2] that reason should be subordinate to Scripture and indeed wholly subjected to it. He did not believe that anything in the Bible should be explained metaphorically merely because the literal sense is in conflict with reason but only where it conflicts with Scripture itself, that is, with its evident dogmas. Hence he formulates the universal rule that anything that Scripture teaches dogmatically[3] and affirms in explicit words, we must accept as true unreservedly solely on the basis of its authority. Furthermore, he maintained, no dogma will be found in the Bible which contradicts it directly but only by implication, because Scripture's modes of expression often seem to assume something other than what it teaches directly, and these are the only passages that need to be explained metaphorically.

For example, Scripture expressly teaches that God is one (see Deuteronomy 6.14), and there is no passage anywhere directly asserting that there is more than one God. However, there are several passages where God speaks of himself in the plural, as also do the prophets. This is a manner of speaking which seemingly implies there are several gods, though the intent of the expression does not assert it. All such passages should therefore be explained metaphorically, not because they are in conflict with reason but because Scripture itself directly asserts that there is one God. Likewise, because Scripture, at Deuteronomy 4.15, according to Al-Fakhar, flatly asserts that God is incorporeal, we must believe, on the basis of this passage alone – and not of reason, that God has no body, and consequently, on the authority of Scripture alone, we must lend a metaphorical interpretation to all passages which attribute to God hands and feet and so on, whose phrasing by itself seems to imply a corporeal God.

[3] This is the contention of al-Fakhar, and in so far as it seeks to explain Scripture solely via Scripture, I applaud it. But I am surprised that someone endowed with reason should try so hard to destroy reason. It is

---

[1] I.e. Jehuda al-Fakhar, a physician in early thirtheenth-century Toledo who was among the leading rabbinic opponents of Maimonides' Aristotelian rationalism.

[2] Spinoza's footnote: N. B. I remember that I once read this in the letter against Maimonides, which occurs among the so called 'Letters of Maimonides'.

[3] Spinoza's footnote: see Annotation 28.

182 indeed true that Scripture must be explained by Scripture, so long as we are only deriving the sense of the passages and the meaning of the prophets, but after we have arrived at the true sense, we must necessarily use our judgment and reason before giving assent to it. If reason must be entirely subject to Scripture despite its protests against it, I ask whether we should do this in accordance with reason or, like blind men, without reason. If the latter, then we are certainly acting stupidly and without any judgment. But what of the former? We are in that case accepting Scripture solely at the command of reason, and therefore we would not accept it where it is in conflict with reason. I also ask, who can accept anything with his mind if his reason protests against it? For what is it to reject something with your mind but a protest of reason?

Assuredly, I am utterly amazed that men should want to subject reason, the greatest gift and the divine light, to ancient words which may well have been adulterated with malicious intent. I am amazed that it should not be thought a crime to speak disparagingly of the mind, the true text of God's word, and to proclaim it corrupt, blind and depraved, while deeming it the highest offence to think such things of the mere letter and image of God's word. They consider it pious not to trust their reason and their own judgment and deem it impious to have doubts concerning the reliability of those who have handed down the sacred books to us. This is plain stupidity, not piety. But I ask, why does the use of reason worry them? What are they afraid of? Can religion and faith not be defended, unless we make ourselves ignorant of everything and reason is totally dispensed with? If they believe that, then surely such people fear Scripture more than they trust it. Religion and piety should not wish to have reason for a servant nor should reason wish to have religion for a servant. Both should be able to rule their own realms in the greatest harmony. I will explain this directly, but I want first to examine the rule of this rabbi [i.e., R. Al-Fakhar].

[4] As we said, he wants us to be bound to accept as true everything that Scripture affirms and reject as false everything Scripture denies, and he holds that the Bible never affirms or denies in explicit terms anything contrary to what it affirms or denies in another passage. Yet everyone must see how very rash these two positions are. I will omit here what he did not remark, that Scripture consists of a variety of different books, of different periods and for different men, and compiled by a variety of authors; I will also pass over the point that he makes these assertions on

his own authority and that neither reason nor Scripture assert anything comparable. He ought to have shown from the character of the language and the purpose of the passage, that all passages that are in conflict with others only by implication, can be properly construed metaphorically as well as that Scripture has come down to us uncorrupted.

But let us examine the issue methodically and consider the first point: what if reason protests? Are we still obliged to accept as true what Scripture affirms and reject as false whatever Scripture denies? Perhaps he will say that nothing is found in Scripture which is in conflict with reason. But Scripture, I contend, expressly affirms that God is jealous (namely in the Ten Commandments and at Exodus 24.14 and Deuteronomy 4.24 and several other passages). This is in conflict with reason, despite which we should supposedly regard this as true. Any passages in Scripture implying that God is not jealous would then necessarily have to be explained metaphorically, so that they would not appear to assume anything of the sort. Likewise, the Bible expressly states that God descended to Mount Sinai (see Exodus 19.20, etc.), and ascribes other local motions to Him, and nowhere explicitly asserts that God does not move. Thus, this too would have to be admitted by all men as true while Solomon's assertion that God is not contained in any place (see 1 Kings 8.27), not being a direct statement but just a consequence of deducing that God does not move, will therefore have to be explained in such a way that it does not deny local motion to God. Equally, the heavens would have to be considered the dwelling-place and throne of God since Scripture expressly affirms it. There are very many things phrased in this way, in accordance with the beliefs of the prophets and the common people, which reason and philosophy, though not Scripture, reveal to be false. Yet all of them, in the view of al-Fakhar, must be accepted as true, since there is no consultation with reason concerning these questions.

[5] Secondly, he is mistaken in claiming that one passage contradicts another passage only by implication, and never directly. For Moses directly asserts that 'God is fire' (see Deuteronomy 4.24) and flatly denies God has any similarity to visible things (see Deuteronomy 4.12). If he responds that the latter does not deny God is fire directly but only by implication, and that we must reconcile it with the other passage, so that it may not seem to deny it, well then, let us concede that God is fire, or rather, in order not to participate in such nonsense, let us discard this example and proceed

184   to another. Samuel clearly denies[4] that God repents of his decisions (see 1 Samuel 15.29) while Jeremiah by contrast maintains that God repents of the good and evil which he has decreed (see Jeremiah 18.8–10). Now, are these two passages not plainly contradictory to each other? Which then of the two propositions does he propose to interpret metaphorically? Both are universal but contrary to the other; what one plainly affirms, the other directly denies. Thus, by his rule he must both accept the fact as true and reject it as false.

But again, what does it matter that a passage does not contradict another directly but only by implication, if the implication is clear and the context and nature of the passage does not admit metaphorical interpretation? There are very many such passages in the Bible. See chapter 2 (where we showed that the prophets held different and contrary opinions), and especially look at the numerous contradictions we pointed out in the histories (in chapters 9 and 10).

[6]   I need not go through them all again here, for what I have said suffices to demonstrate the absurdities that follow from this opinion and such a rule, how false these are and how superficial the author.

We must therefore dismiss both this theory and that of Maimonides. We have established it as absolutely certain that theology should not be subordinate to reason, nor reason to theology, but rather that each has its own domain. For reason, as we said, reigns over the domain of truth and wisdom, theology over that of piety and obedience. For the power of reason, as we have shown, cannot extend to ensuring that people may be happy by obedience alone without understanding things, while theology tells us nothing other than this and decrees nothing but obedience. Theology has no designs against reason, and cannot have any. For the dogmas of faith (as we showed in the previous chapter) determine only what is necessary for obedience, and leave it to reason to determine how precisely they are to be understood in relation to truth. Reason is the true light of the mind without which it discerns nothing but dreams and fantasies.

By theology here I mean precisely revelation in so far as it proclaims the purpose which we said that Scripture intends, namely the method and manner of obedience that is the dogmas of true piety and faith. This is

---

[4] Spinoza's footnote: see Annotation 29.

what is properly termed the word of God, which does not consist in a 185
specific collection of books (on this see chapter 12). If you consider the
commands or moral advice of theology understood in this way, you will
find that it agrees with reason, and if you look at its intent and purpose,
you will see that in fact it does not conflict with reason in anything. Hence,
it is universal to all men.

As regards Scripture generally, when considered as a whole, we have
already shown in chapter 7 that its sense must be determined solely from
its own history and never from the universal history of nature which is
the sole ground of philosophy. If we find, after we have investigated its
true sense in this way, that in places it conflicts with reason, this should
not trouble us at all. For we know for certain that nothing of this sort
encountered in the Bible, and nothing men can be ignorant of without
loss of charity, has the least effect on theology or on the word of God.
Consequently, everyone may think whatever they like about such matters
without doing wrong. We conclude therefore without hesitation that
Scripture is not to be accommodated to reason nor reason to Scripture.

[7]   Yet since we are unable to prove by means of reason whether the
fundamental principle of theology – that men are saved by obedience
alone – is true or false, are we not open to the question: why therefore do
we believe it? If we accept it without reason, like blind men, are we not
acting stupidly and without judgment? If on the other hand we try to assert
that this principle can be proved by reason, theology will then become part
of philosophy and could not be separated from it. To this I reply that I hold
categorically that the fundamental dogma of theology cannot be discovered by the natural light, or at least that no one has yet proven it, and
that is why revelation was absolutely indispensable. Nevertheless, we can
use our judgment to accept it with at any rate moral certainty now that it
has been revealed. I say 'with moral certainty', since it is impossible for us
to be more certain of it than the prophets themselves were to whom it was
first revealed, and theirs, as we showed in chapter 2 of this treatise, was
solely a moral certainty.

It is therefore wholly erroneous to try to demonstrate the authority of
Scripture by mathematical proofs. For the Bible's authority depends
upon that of the prophets, and therefore cannot be demonstrated by
stronger arguments than those with which the prophets in their time 186
were accustomed to convince the people of their authority. Indeed,

certainty here can rest only on the foundation on which the prophets rested their assuredness and authority. We showed that the assuredness of the prophets consisted in three things: (1) a clear and vivid imagination, (2) a sign and (3) finally and especially, a mind devoted to justice and goodness. These were their only grounds, and therefore these are also the only grounds on which they could prove their authority to those to whom in their time they spoke with their living voices or can prove it to us whom they address in writing.

Now the first thing, the vivid imagination of things, could only be available to the prophets themselves, and therefore all of our certainty about revelation can and should rest solely upon the other two things, namely the sign and their teaching. Moses too asserts this explicitly. At Deuteronomy chapter 18 he commands the people to obey a prophet who has given a true sign in the name of God, but to condemn to death **any** who made false declarations even in the name of God, as well as any who attempted to seduce the people from true religion, even where they confirmed their authority with wonders and portents. On this question see Deuteronomy 13, from which it follows that a true prophet is distinguished from a false one by both teaching and miracles. For Moses declares that such a man thus distinguished is a true prophet, and bids the people believe him without any fear of deception, while those who have proclaimed false teachings even in the name of God, or who have taught false gods, even if they have wrought true miracles, are false prophets and deserve death.

This is why we too are obliged to believe in Scripture, i.e., the prophets themselves, on precisely the same grounds: teaching confirmed by miracles. Since we see that the prophets commend justice and charity above all things and plead for these alone, we deduce they were sincere and not deceitful in teaching that men are made happy by obedience and faith; and because they also confirmed this with signs, we are convinced they were not speaking wildly or madly when they prophesied. We are further persuaded of this when we note that they offered no moral teaching which is not in accord with reason. Nor is it coincidental that the word of God in the prophets agrees completely with the actual word of God speaking in us [through reason]. These things, then, we infer from the Bible with just as much certainty as the Jews in their time 187 understood them from the living voice of the prophets. For we showed above, at the end of chapter 12, that the Bible has descended to us unadulterated as regards its [moral] doctrine and the main historical narratives.

So it is a sound judgment to accept this fundamental principle embracing the whole of theology and Scripture, even though it cannot be demonstrated by mathematical proof. For it is indeed ignorance to refuse to accept something just because it cannot be mathematically demonstrated when it is confirmed by the testimonies of so many prophets, is a source of great solace for those whose capacity to reason is limited, is of great value to the state, and may be believed unreservedly without danger or damage. As if we should admit nothing as true, for the prudent conduct of our lives, which can be called into question by any method of doubt, or as if so many of our actions were not highly uncertain and full of risk!

[8] Admittedly, those who believe that philosophy and theology contradict each other and think that we should banish one or the other and get rid of one of them, are well-advised to try to lay solid foundations for theology and attempt to prove it mathematically. For no one who is not without hope or insane would want to abolish reason completely or totally reject the arts and sciences and deny the certainty of reason. And yet we cannot altogether excuse them [for attempting to prove theology mathematically]: for they are attempting to use reason to reject reason and hence search for a certain reason to render reason uncertain. But in fact, as they strive to prove the truth and authority of theology by mathematical demonstration, and deprive reason and the natural light of authority, what they are really doing is bringing theology itself under the rule of reason. For underneath, they seem evidently to suppose that theology's authority will have no impact unless it is illuminated by the natural light of reason.

If on the other hand they claim totally to acquiesce in the internal testimony of the Holy Spirit, and to make use of reason only for the sake of unbelievers, so as to convince them, we should still not trust what they say. We can readily demonstrate straight off that they assert this from passion or vanity. For it very clearly follows from the previous chapter that the Holy Spirit gives testimony only about good works, which Paul too calls the fruits of the spirit (Galatians 5.22), and the spirit is in truth 188 simply the mental peace which arises in the mind from good actions. But no spirit other than reason gives testimony about the truth and certainty of things that are purely matters for philosophy, and reason, as we have already shown, claims the realm of truth for itself. If therefore they pretend to have any other spirit that makes them certain of the truth, they are making a false claim. They are merely speaking from their emotional prejudices or trying to take refuge in sacred things because they are afraid of being defeated by philosophers and publicly exposed to ridicule. But in vain; for what altar of refuge can a man find for himself when he commits treason against the majesty of reason?

[9] And now I dismiss them for I think that I have done sufficient justice to my own case in showing how philosophy is to be separated from theology, and what both essentially are: neither is subordinate to the other; each has its own kingdom; there is no conflict between them. Finally, I have also demonstrated, as opportunity arose, the absurdities, harm and danger, caused by men's amazing confusion of these two branches and their not knowing how to distinguish accurately between them and separate the one firmly from the other.

[10] But before I go on to other things, I must emphasize very strongly here,[5] although I have mentioned it before, the usefulness and necessity of Holy Scripture or revelation, which I hold to be very great. For given that we cannot discern by the natural light alone that simple obedience is the path to salvation,[6] and revelation alone teaches us that it comes from a singular grace of God which we cannot acquire by reason, it follows that Scripture has brought great consolation to mortal men. Everyone without exception can obey, not merely the very few – very few, that is, in comparison with the whole human race – who acquire the habit of virtue by the guidance of reason alone. Hence, if we did not possess this testimony of Scripture, we would have to consider the salvation of almost all men to be in doubt.

---

[5] Spinoza's footnote: see Annotation 30.   [6] Spinoza's footnote: see Annotation 31.

On the foundations of the state, on the natural and civil right of each person, and on the authority of sovereign powers

[1] Hitherto our concern has been to separate philosophy from theology and to establish the freedom to philosophize which this separation allows to everyone. The time has now come to enquire how far this freedom to think and to say what one thinks extends in the best kind of state. To consider this in an orderly fashion, we must first discuss the foundations of the state but, before we do that, we must explain, without reference to the state and religion, the natural right (*jus*) which everyone possesses.

[2] By the right and order of nature I merely mean the rules determining the nature of each individual thing by which we conceive it is determined naturally to exist and to behave in a certain way. For example fish are determined by nature to swim and big fish to eat little ones, and therefore it is by sovereign natural right that fish have possession of the water and that big fish eat small fish. For it is certain that nature, considered wholly in itself, has a sovereign right to do everything that it can do, i.e., the right of nature extends as far as its power extends. For the power of nature is the very power of God who has supreme right to [do] all things. However, since the universal power of the whole of nature is nothing but the power of all individual things together, it follows that each individual thing has the sovereign right to do everything that it can do, or the right of each thing extends so far as its determined power extends. And since it is the supreme law of nature that each thing strives to persist in its own state so far as it

can, taking no account of another's circumstances but only of its own, it follows that each individual thing has a sovereign right to do this, i.e. (as I said) to exist and to behave as it is naturally determined to behave.

Here we recognize no difference between human beings and other individual things of nature, nor between those human beings who are endowed with reason and others who do not know true reason, nor between fools or lunatics and the sane. For whatever each thing does by the laws of its nature, that it does with sovereign right, since it is acting as it was determined to by nature and can not do otherwise. Hence as long as people are deemed to live under the government of nature alone, the person who does not yet know reason or does not yet have a habit of virtue, lives by the laws of appetite alone with the same supreme right as he who directs his life by the laws of reason. That is, just as a wise man has a sovereign right to do all things that reason dictates, i.e., [he has] the right of living by the laws of reason, so also the ignorant or intemperate person possesses the sovereign right to [do] everything that desire suggests, i.e., he has the right of living by the laws of appetite. This is precisely what Paul is saying when he acknowledges that there is no sin before law is established,[1] i.e., as long as men are considered as living under the government of nature.

[3] Each person's natural right therefore is determined not by sound reason but by desire and power. For it is not the case that all men are naturally determined to behave according to the rules and laws of reason. On the contrary, all men are born completely ignorant of everything and before they can learn the true rationale of living and acquire the habit of virtue, a good part of life has elapsed even if they have been well brought up, while, in the meantime, they must live and conserve themselves so far as they can, by the sole impulse of appetite. For nature has given them nothing else, and has denied them the power of living on the basis of sound reason, and consequently they are no more obliged to live by the laws of a sound mind than a cat is by the laws of a lion's nature. Anyone therefore deemed to be under the government of nature alone is permitted by the sovereign right of nature to desire anything that he believes to be useful to himself, whether brought to this by sound reason or by the impulse of his passions. He is permitted to take it for himself by any

---

[1] Romans 7.7.

means – by force, by fraud, by pleading – whatever will most easily enable him to obtain it, and thus he is permitted to regard as an enemy anyone who tries to prevent his getting his way.

[4] From this it follows that the right, and the order of nature, under which all human beings are born and for the most part live, prohibits nothing but what no one desires or no one can do;[2] it does not prohibit strife or hatred or anger or fraud or anything at all that appetite foments. This is unsurprising since nature is not bound by the laws of human reason which aim only at the true interest and conservation of humans, but rather by numberless other things that concern the eternal order of the whole of nature (of which human beings are but a small part), and all individual things are determined to live and behave in a certain way only by the necessity of this order. When therefore we feel that anything in nature is ridiculous, absurd or bad, it is because we know things only in part. We wish everything to be directed in ways familiar to our reason, even though what reason declares to be bad, is not bad with respect to the order and laws of universal nature but only with respect to the laws of our own nature.

191

[5] Nevertheless, no one can doubt how much more beneficial it is for men to live according to laws and the certain dictates of reason, which as I have said aim at nothing but men's true interests. Besides there is no one who does not wish to live in security and so far as that is possible without fear; but this is very unlikely to be the case so long as everyone is allowed to do whatever they want and reason is assigned no more right than hatred and anger. For there is no one who does not live pervaded with anxiety whilst living surrounded by hostility, hatred, anger and deceit and who does not strive to avoid these in so far as they can. If we also reflect that without mutual help, and the cultivation of reason, human beings necessarily live in great misery, as we showed in chapter 5, we shall realize very clearly that it was necessary for people to combine together in order to live in security and prosperity. Accordingly, they had to ensure that they would collectively have the right to all things that each individual had from nature and that this right would no longer be determined by the force and appetite of each individual but by the power and will of all of them together.

---

[2] One of the key doctrines of Spinoza's moral philosophy and one which, in effect, goes well beyond Hobbes in eliminating the whole basis of natural law as generally understood in medieval and early modern thought.

They would, however, have had no hope of achieving this had they confined themselves only to the promptings of desire – for, by the laws of appetite, everyone is drawn in different directions. Thus, they had to make a firm decision, and reach agreement, to decide everything by the sole dictate of reason (which no one dares contradict openly for fear of appearing perfectly mindless). They had to curb their appetites so far as their desires suggested things which would hurt someone else, and refrain from doing anything to anyone they did not want done to themselves. Finally, they were obliged to defend other people's rights as their own.

[6] Now we must consider *how* this agreement has to be made if it is to be accepted and endure. For it is a universal law of human nature that no one neglects anything that they deem good unless they hope for a greater good or fear a greater loss, and no one puts up with anything bad except to avoid something worse or because he hopes for something better. That is, of two good things every single person will choose the one which he himself judges to be the greater good, and of two bad things he will choose that which he deems to be less bad.[3] I say expressly what appears to him the greater or lesser good when he makes this choice, since the real situation is not necessarily as he judges it to be. This law is so firmly inscribed in human nature that it may be included among the eternal truths that no one can fail to know. It necessarily follows that no one will promise without deception[4] to give up his right to all things, and absolutely no one will keep his promises except from fear of a greater ill or hope of a greater good.

To understand this better, imagine that a highwayman forces me to promise to give him all I have, at his demand. Since my natural right is determined by my power alone, as I have already shown, it is certain that if I can free myself from him by deceit, by promising whatever he wants, I may by the law of nature do so, i.e., I may fraudulently agree to whatever he demands. Or suppose that I have made a promise to someone in good faith not to taste food or any sustenance for a space of twenty days and only later realize that my promise was stupid and that I cannot keep it without doing myself a great deal of harm. Since I am obliged by natural right to choose the lesser of two evils, I have a sovereign right to break the bond of

---

[3] This doctrine, developed more fully in Spinoza's *Ethics*, functions consistently throughout his work as a fundamental principle of his psychology, his moral philosophy and his political thought.

[4] Spinoza's footnote: see Annotation 32.

such an agreement and render what was said to be unsaid. This, I say, is allowed by natural right, whether I see it by true and certain reason or whether it is out of mere belief that I appear to grasp that I was wrong to make the promise. For whether I discern things truly or falsely, it is the greater harm that I shall fear and, by nature's design, strive by every means to avoid.

[7] We conclude from this that any agreement can have force only if it is in our interest, and when it is not in our interest, the agreement fails and remains void. For this reason, we also conclude that it is foolish to call for someone else to keep faith with oneself, in perpetuity, if at the same time one does not try to ensure that violating the agreement will result in greater loss than gain for the violator. This principle should play the most important role in the formation of a state. For if everyone were readily led by the guidance of reason alone and recognized the supreme advantage and necessity of the state, everyone would utterly detest deceit and stand fully by their promises with the utmost fidelity because of their concern for this highest good of preserving the state, and, above all things, they would keep faith, which is the chief protection of the state; but it is far from being the case that everyone can easily be led by the 193 sole guidance of reason.

For everyone is guided by their own pleasure, and the mind is very often so preoccupied with greed, glory, jealousy, anger, etc., that there is no room for reason. Accordingly, even if people promise and agree to keep faith by offering sure signs of sincerity, no one can be certain of another person's good faith, unless something is added to the promise. For everyone can act with deceit by the right of nature and is not obliged to stand by promises except where there is hope of a greater good or fear of a greater evil. Now we have already shown that natural right is determined solely by each person's power. If, therefore, willingly or unwillingly someone surrenders to another a portion of the power they possess, they necessarily transfer the same amount of their own right to the other person. Likewise, it follows that the person possessing the sovereign power to compel all men by force and restrain them by fear of the supreme penalty which all men universally fear, has sovereign right over all men. This person will retain this right, though, for only so long as he retains this power of doing whatever he wishes; otherwise his command will be precarious, and no stronger person will be obliged to obey him unless he wishes to do so.

[8] Human society can thus be formed without any alienation of natural right, and the contract can be preserved in its entirety with complete fidelity, only if every person transfers all the power they possess to society, and society alone retains the supreme natural right over all things, i.e., supreme power, which all must obey, either of their own free will or through fear of the ultimate punishment. The right of such a society is called democracy. Democracy therefore is properly defined as a united gathering of people which collectively has the sovereign right to do all that it has the power to do. It follows that sovereign power is bound by no law and everyone is obliged to obey it in all things. For they must all have made this agreement, tacitly or explicitly, when they transferred their whole power of defending themselves, that is, their whole right, to the sovereign authority. If they had wanted to keep any right for themselves, they should have made this provision at the same time as they could have safely defended it. Since they did not do so, and could not have done it without dividing and therefore destroying its authority, by that very fact they have submitted themselves to the sovereign's will. They have done so without reservation (as we have already shown), compelled as they were by necessity and guided by reason. It follows that unless we wish to be enemies of government and to act against reason, which urges us to defend the government with all our strength, we are obliged to carry out absolutely all the commands of the sovereign power, however absurd they may be. Reason too bids us do so: it is a choice of the lesser of two evils.

[9] It was not difficult, moreover, for each person to take this risk of submitting himself absolutely to the power and will of another. For sovereigns, we showed, retain the right to command whatever they wish only so long as they truly hold supreme power. If they lose it, they at the same time also lose the right of decreeing all things, which passes to the man or men who have acquired it and can retain it. This is why it can very rarely happen that sovereigns issue totally absurd commands. To protect their position and retain power, they are very much obliged to work for the common good and direct all things by the dictate of reason; for no one has maintained a violent government for long, as Seneca says.[5] Furthermore, there is less reason in a democratic state to fear absurd proceedings. For it is

[5] Seneca, *The Trojan Women*, 258–9.

almost impossible that the majority of a large assembly would agree on the same irrational decision. In addition, there is its foundation and purpose which is precisely, as we have also shown, to avoid the follies of appetite and as much as possible to bring men within the limits of reason, so that they may dwell in peace and harmony. Without this foundation, the whole structure soon disintegrates. It is the duty of the sovereign alone to provide for these things, and it is the subjects' duty, as we have said, to carry out its command, and acknowledge no law other than what the highest power proclaims as law.

[10] Perhaps someone will think that in this way we are turning subjects into slaves, supposing a slave to be someone who acts on command, and a free person to be one who behaves as he pleases. But this is not true at all. In fact, anyone who is guided by their own pleasure in this way and cannot see or do what is good for them, is him or herself very much a slave. The only [genuinely] free person is one who lives with his entire mind guided solely by reason. Acting on command, that is, from obedience, does take away liberty in some sense, but it is not acting on command in itself that makes someone a slave, but rather the reason for so acting. If the purpose of the action is not his own advantage but that of the ruler, then the agent is indeed a slave and useless to himself. But in a state and government where the safety of the whole people, not that of the ruler, is the supreme law,[6] he who obeys the sovereign in all things 195 should not be called a slave useless to himself but rather a subject. The freest state, therefore, is that whose laws are founded on sound reason; for there each man can be free whenever he wishes,[7] that is, he can live under the guidance of reason with his whole mind. Similarly, though children are obliged to obey all their parents' commands, they are nonetheless not slaves, since a parent's commands are mostly directed to the good of the children. We thus recognize a vast difference between a slave, a child and a subject, and we distinguish them on these grounds as follows. A slave is someone obliged to obey commands from a master which look only to the advantage of the master; a child is one who at the command of a parent does what is advantageous for himself; and a subject is one who does by command of the sovereign what is useful for the community and consequently also for himself.

[6] Cicero, *On the Laws*, 3.3.8.   [7] Spinoza's footnote: see Annotation 33.

[11] With this, I think, the fundamentals of the democratic republic are made sufficiently clear, this being the form of state I chose to discuss first, because it seems to be the most natural and to be that which approaches most closely to the freedom nature bestows on every person. In a democracy no one transfers their natural right to another in such a way that they are not thereafter consulted but rather to the majority of the whole society of which they are a part. In this way all remain equal as they had been previously, in the state of nature. Also, this is the only form of government that I want to discuss explicitly, since it is the most relevant to my design, my purpose being to discuss the advantage of liberty in a state. Accordingly, I disregard the foundations of the other forms of government. To understand their right, we do not need now to know how they have arisen and often still arise, since that is clear enough from what we have just proved. Whether the holder of sovereign power is one or a few or all, indubitably the supreme right of commanding whatever they wish belongs to him or them. Besides, anyone who has transferred their power of defending themselves to another, whether freely or under compulsion, has clearly surrendered his natural right and has consequently decided to obey the other absolutely, in all things; and they are wholly obligated to do so as long as the king, nobility, or people preserves the supreme power they received, given that this was the ground for the transfer of jurisdiction. We do not need to say more.

[12] Now that we have established the foundations and right of the state, it will be easy to show what, in the civil state, is the civil right of the citizen, what an offence is and what justice and injustice are; we can also readily explain who is an ally, who an enemy, and what the crime of treason is.

196

[13] We can mean nothing by the civil right of the citizen other than the freedom of each person to conserve themselves in their own condition, which is determined by the edicts of the sovereign power and protected by its authority alone. For as soon as someone has transferred to another their right to live by their own free will as determined solely by their own authority, that is, once they have transferred their liberty and their power to defend themselves, they must live solely by the judgment of the other and be defended exclusively by his forces.

[14] An offence is committed when a citizen or subject is compelled by another person to suffer a loss, contrary to the civil law or the edict of the

sovereign; for an offence can be conceived as occurring only in the civil state. No offence can be committed against subjects by sovereigns, since they are of right permitted to do all things, and therefore offences occur only between private persons obliged by law not to harm one another.

[15]   Justice is a fixed intention to assign to each person what belongs to them[8] in accordance with civil law. Injustice is to take away from someone, on a pretext of right, what belongs to them by a correct interpretation of the laws. Justice and injustice are also called equity and inequity, because those who are appointed to settle legal disputes are obliged to have no respect of persons, but to treat all as equal, and equally to defend the right of each individual, not begrudging the rich or despising the poor.[9]

[16]   Allies are members of two states who, to avoid the danger of a war or for any other advantage, make a mutual agreement not to harm one another, and to give assistance to each other when need arises, while each side retains its own independence. This agreement will be valid as long as its foundation, the source of the danger or advantage, persists. No one makes an agreement, and no one is obligated to honour a pact, except in the hope of some good or apprehension of some adverse consequence. When this ground is removed, the agreement automatically lapses. Experience very clearly confirms this. For while different governments make compacts between themselves not to harm each other, they also strive so far as possible to prevent the other outstripping them in power. They do not trust the other's word unless they see very clearly the interest and advantage for both parties in making the agreement. Otherwise they fear being deceived, and not without reason. For who will acquiesce in the words and promises of one who holds sovereign power and has the right to do anything he wishes, whose highest law must be the security and advantage of his own rule, unless he is a fool who is ignorant of the right of sovereigns? Besides if we take piety and religion into account, we shall also see that it is criminal for anyone who holds power to keep their promises if this involves loss of their power. For they cannot fulfil any promise which they see will result in loss of their power, without betraying the pledge that

197

[8] Justinian, *Institutes*, 1.1.
[9] Equality is the essential principle of justice, for Spinoza, but also of his (secularized) moral philosophy and of what he regards as the best kind of state, namely democracy.

they gave to their subjects. This pledge is their highest obligation, and sovereigns normally swear the most solemn oaths to uphold it.

[17]   An enemy is someone who lives outside a state in the sense that he does not recognize the authority of the state either as its ally or as its subject. For it is not hatred but right that defines an enemy of a state's authority, and a state's right against someone who does not recognize its authority by any agreement is the same as its right against someone who actively damages it. It has the right to compel him either to surrender or to enter into an alliance by whatever means it can.

[18]   Finally, the crime of treason occurs only among subjects or citizens who by a tacit or express agreement have transferred all their power to a state. A subject is said to have committed such a crime if he has attempted to seize the right of supreme power in some way or to transfer it to someone else. I say 'has attempted', for if it were the case that such persons could only be condemned after the deed was done, a state would generally be seeking to do this too late, after its right had been seized or transferred to someone else. I am speaking of anyone, I emphasize again, who by whatever means attempts to seize the right of supreme power. I do not accept that it makes any difference whether the state as a whole would lose or gain even in the most obvious way from it. For whatever reason anyone makes this attempt, he has done injury to the majesty[10] of the state and it is right to condemn him, just as everyone admits it is perfectly right to do in warfare. Any soldier who does not stay where he is posted, but attacks the enemy without his commander's knowledge, even if his tactics are good and he succeeds in driving the enemy off while yet still doing so as a personal venture of his own, is rightly condemned to death, since he has violated his oath and the right of his commander. Not everyone sees with equal clarity that all citizens, without exception, are equally always bound by this right, but the reasoning remains absolutely the same. For the state must be protected and directed by the counsel of the sovereign power only and all have agreed without reservation that this right belongs to him alone. Should anyone, therefore, by his own decision and without the knowledge of the sovereign power, seek to carry out a public negotiation,

---

[10] 'majestatem laesit' picks up the phrase 'crimen laesae majestatis', translated 'crime of treason' above.

even if the state would certainly gain from it, they have, as we have said, 198
violated the right of the sovereign power and harmed its majesty, and are
thus deservedly condemned.

[19]   It remains, so as to remove every last scruple, to answer the
question whether what we said above namely, that everyone who does not
have the use of reason lives in a state of nature by the laws of his desire,
and that this is a sovereign natural right, does not directly conflict with
revealed divine law. For every person without exception (whether they
have the use of reason or not) is equally obliged by divine command to
love their neighbour as themselves, and therefore we cannot do harm to
another person without doing wrong and living by the laws of appetite alone.

We can easily deal with this objection simply by examining the state of
nature more closely. For this is prior to religion both by nature, and in
time. No one knows from nature[11] that he is bound by obedience
towards God. Indeed, he cannot discover this by reasoning either; he can
only receive it from a revelation confirmed by miracles. Hence, prior to a
revelation, no one is obligated by divine law, which he simply cannot
know. The state of nature is not to be confused with the state of religion,
but must be conceived apart from religion and law, and consequently
apart from all sin and wrongdoing. This is how we have conceived it, and
have confirmed this by the authority of Paul. It is not only owing to this
ignorance that we consider the state of nature to be prior to revealed
divine law and apart from it, but also because of the freedom in which all
men are born. For if men were bound by nature to the divine law, or if
the divine law were a law of nature, it would be superfluous for God to
enter into a covenant with men and bind them with an oath. We must
therefore admit unreservedly that divine law began from the time when
men promised to obey God in all things by an explicit agreement. With
this agreement they surrendered their natural liberty, so to speak, transferring their right to God, and this, as we have said, occurred in the civil
state. I will discuss this more fully in the following chapters.

[20]   But it may still be urged that sovereign powers, like subjects, are
equally bound by this divine law, despite the fact that they retain, as we
said, the natural right and are [in that respect] permitted to do anything.

---

[11] Spinoza's footnote: see Annotation 34.

This difficulty arises not so much from the notion of the state of nature as from that of natural right. To remove it completely, I maintain that in the state of nature everyone should live by the revealed law for the same reason as they ought to live by the dictates of sound judgment, and that is because it is advantageous to them and essential to their security. They may refuse to do so if they wish, but they do this at their own peril. Everyone is therefore obliged to live solely by their own decisions and not by someone else's, and they are not bound to acknowledge anyone as judge or as the rightful defender of religion. I affirm that the sovereign has retained this right. While he may consult advisors, he is not obliged to recognize anyone as judge or any mortal except himself as defender of any right, other than a prophet expressly sent by God who has proved this by incontrovertible signs. Even then it is not a man whom he is compelled to recognize as judge but rather God himself. Should the sovereign refuse to obey God in his revealed law, he may do so, but at his own peril and to his own loss. No civil or natural law forbids him. For the civil law derives solely from his own decree, while natural right derives from the laws of nature, and the laws of nature are not accommodated to religion, which is concerned solely with human good, but to the order of universal nature, that is, to the eternal decree of God, which is unknown to us. Others seem to have conceived a rather obscure notion of this, in saying that man can sin against the revealed will of God, but not against his eternal decree by which he predestined all things.

[21]   One may also inquire: what if the sovereign commands something which is against religion and the obedience which we have promised to God by an explicit agreement? Should we obey the divine or the human commandment? I shall discuss this at greater length in later chapters. Here I will just say briefly that we must above all obey God when we have a certain and undoubted revelation but that people are very prone to go astray in religion and make many dubious claims that result from the diversity of their understanding, and generate serious conflict, as experience clearly testifies. It is therefore certain that if no one were obliged by law to obey the sovereign power in matters that he thinks belong to religion, then the law of the state would depend upon the different judgments and passions of each individual person. For no one would be obligated by the law if he considered it to be directed against his faith and superstition, and on this pretext everyone would be able to claim licence to do anything.

Since by this means the law of the state is wholly violated, it follows that the supreme right of deciding about religion, belongs to the sovereign power, whatever judgment he may make, since it falls to him alone to preserve the rights of the state and to protect them both by divine and by natural law. All men are obliged to obey his decrees and commands about 200 religion, on the basis of the pledge given to him, which God commands to keep scrupulously.

[22] If those who hold the sovereign power are pagans, one of two things follows. Either we must not make any compact with them but be willing to suffer death rather than transfer our right to them, or, if we have made an agreement and transferred our right to them, we must obey them and keep faith with them, or be compelled to do so, since by that act, we have deprived ourselves of the power of[12] defending ourselves and our religion. This is the case for all except he to whom God has promised, by a particular revelation, assistance against tyrants or specifically granted an exemption. Thus, among all the many Jews who were in Babylon, we see that only three young men who did not doubt the assistance of God, refused to obey Nebuchadnezzar.[13] The rest, except for Daniel, who was revered by the king himself, rightly and unhesitatingly obeyed when compelled to do so, reflecting perhaps that they had been made subject to the king by God's decree and that the king possessed supreme power and retained it by God's providence. Eleazar[14] on the other hand wanted to give an example of constancy to his own people while his country was still more or less independent. He wanted them to follow him in bearing anything rather than allow their right and power to be transferred to the Greeks, and suffer anything to avoid being forced to swear allegiance to the pagans.

The general rule, however, is confirmed by daily experience. Rulers of Christian countries do not hesitate to make treaties with Turks and pagans in order to enhance their own security. They take care, though, to forbid those of their subjects who go and live in those countries to assume more freedom in their religious or moral practices than has been expressly agreed or than that government permits, something evident in the agreement mentioned earlier which the Dutch made with the Japanese.

---

[12] *Se potentia*, added by Akkerman.   [13] Daniel 3.   [14] 2 Maccabees 6.18–31.

CHAPTER 17

Where it is shown that no one can transfer all things
to the sovereign power, and that it is not necessary
to do so; on the character of the Hebrew state in
the time of Moses, and in the period after his
death before the appointment of the kings; on its
excellence, and on the reasons why this divine state
could perish, and why it could scarcely exist
without sedition

[1] The conceptualization offered in the previous chapter of the right
of sovereign powers to all things and the transfer of each person's natural right to them, agrees quite well with practice, and practice can be
brought very close to it, yet in many respects it will always remain
merely theoretical. No one will ever be able to transfer his power and
(consequently) his right to another person in such a way that he ceases
to be a human being; and there will never be a sovereign power that
can dispose of everything just as it pleases. In vain would a sovereign
command a subject to hate someone who had made himself agreeable
by an act of kindness or to love someone who had injured him, or forbid him to take offence at insults or free himself from fear, or many
other such things that follow necessarily from the laws of human nature. Experience itself also teaches this very clearly, I think. People have
never given up their right and transferred their power to another in
such a way that they did not fear the very persons who received their
right and power, and put the government at greater risk from its own
citizens (although bereft of their right) than from its enemies. If people

could be so thoroughly stripped of their natural right that they could undertake nothing in the future[1] without the consent of the holders of sovereign power, then certainly sovereigns could dominate their subjects in the most violent manner. However, I believe no one would accept that. Hence we must admit that each person retains many aspects of his right, which therefore depend upon no one's will but their own.

[2]   To understand more precisely how far the right and power of the state extend, we should note that state power does not consist merely in compelling people, through fear, but also of the use of every means available to   202
it to ensure obedience to its edicts. It is not the reason for being obedient that makes a subject, but obedience as such. There are numerous reasons why someone decides to carry out the commands of a sovereign power: fear of punishment, hope of reward, love of country or the impulse of some other passion. Whatever their reason, they are still deciding of their own volition, and simultaneously acting at the bidding of the sovereign power. Just because someone does something by their own design, we should not immediately infer that they do it of their own right and not that of the state. Whether moved by love, or compelled by fear, to avoid some bad consequence, they are always acting under their own counsel and decision. Hence, either there is no sovereignty nor any right over subjects or else sovereignty must necessarily extend to everything that might be effective in inducing men to submit to it. Thus whatever a subject does that complies with the sovereign's commands, whether elicited by love or forced by fear, or whether (as is more common) from hope and fear mingled, or reverence, a sentiment composed of mixed fear and admiration, or whatever motive, he still does so by right of the sovereign, not his own.

This also very clearly emerges from the fact that obedience is less a question of an external than internal action of the mind. Hence he is most under the dominion of another who resolves to obey every order of another wholeheartedly. Consequently, those exert the greatest power who reign in the hearts and minds of their subjects. By contrast, were it true that it is those who exert the greatest power who are the most feared, then these would surely be the subjects of tyrants, since they are very much dreaded by the tyrants who rule over them. And while it is impossible, of course, to control people's minds to the same extent as their tongues, still minds too

---

[1] Spinoza's footnote: see Annotation 35.

are to some degree subject to the sovereign power, which has various ways to ensure that a very large part of the people believes, loves, hates, etc., what the sovereign wants them to. Our conclusion from this has to be that whilst this result does not ensue from a direct edict of the government, it nevertheless does follow from the effect of the sovereign's power and leadership, that is, by virtue of its right, as experience abundantly proves. Thus, without any logical contradiction, we can conceive of men who believe, love, hate, despise, or exhibit any passion whatever, owing to the power of the state alone.

203 [3] Although we can envisage a quite extensive power and right of government, therefore, it will still never be so great that those who hold it will exert all the power they need to do whatever they want, as I think I have shown plainly enough. I have already said it is not my intention to show how, despite this, a state could be formed that would be securely preserved for ever. Rather, so as to reach my own goal, I will point out what divine revelation formerly taught Moses in this connection, and then we shall examine the history and vicissitudes of the Hebrews. We shall see from their experience what particular concessions sovereign powers must make to their subjects for the greater security and success of their state.

[4] Durability of a state, reason and experience very clearly teach, depends chiefly upon the loyalty of its subjects, their virtue and their constancy in executing commands; but it is not so easy to ascertain in what way they can be helped to keep up their loyalty and virtue consistently. Both rulers and ruled are human, that is, beings 'always inclined to prefer pleasure to toil'.[2] Anyone with any experience of the capricious mind of the multitude almost despairs of it, as it is governed not by reason but by passion alone, it is precipitate in everything, and very easily corrupted by greed or good living. Each person thinks he alone knows everything and wants everything done his way and judges a thing fair or unfair, right or wrong, to the extent he believes it works for his own gain or loss. From pride they condemn their equals, and will not allow themselves to be ruled by them. Envious of a greater reputation or better fortune which are never equal for all, they wish ill towards other men and delight in that.

[2] Terence, *Andria* [*The Woman of Andros*], 77–78: ingenium est omnium hominum ab labore proclive ad lubidinem 'human nature being always inclined to prefer pleasure to toil' (Terence, *The Woman of Andros, The Self-Tormentor, The Eunuch*, ed. and trans. John Barsby (Cambridge, MA, 2001)).

There is no need to survey all of this here, as everyone knows what wrongdoing people are often moved to commit because they cannot stand their present situation and desire a major upheaval, how blind anger and resentment of their poverty prompt men to act, and how much these things occupy and agitate their minds. To anticipate all this and construct a state that affords no opportunity for trouble-making, to organize everything in such a way that each person, of whatever character, prefers public right to private advantage, this is the real task, this the arduous work.[3] The necessity for this has compelled people to seek many stratagems. But they have never succeeded in devising a form of government that was not in greater danger from its own citizens than from foreign foes, and which was not more fearful of the former than of the latter.

204

[5] An example of this is the Roman state, wholly undefeated by its enemies, but so often overwhelmed and wretchedly oppressed by its own citizens, especially in the civil war of Vespasian against Vitellius; on this see Tacitus, at the beginning of book 4 of the *Histories*, where he paints a most miserable picture of the city. Alexander, more simply, (as Curtius says at the end of book 8) rested his reputation on his enemies' judgment rather than that of his own citizens, believing his greatness could be more readily ruined by his own men, etc.[4] Fearing his fate, he makes this prayer to his friends: 'Only keep me safe from internal treachery and the plots of my court, and I will face without fear the dangers of war and battle. Philip was safer in the battle line than in the theatre; he often escaped the violence of the enemy, he could not avoid that of his own citizens. Look at the ends of other kings, you will find that they were more often killed by their own people than by the foe' (see Quintus Curtius, 9.6).[5]

[6] This is why in the past kings who usurped power tried to persuade their people they were descended from the immortal gods, their motive surely being to enhance their own security. They evidently believed their subjects would willingly allow themselves to be ruled by them and readily submit only if their subjects and everyone else regarded them not as equals but as gods. Thus, Augustus persuaded the Romans that he

---

[3] Virgil, *Aeneid*, 6.129.   [4] Quintus Curtius, *History of Alexander*, 8.14.46.
[5] Quintus Curtius, *History of Alexander*, 9.6.25–6.

derived his origin from Aeneas, the son of Venus and one of the gods. 'He wanted to be worshipped in temples with statues of himself as a god and with flamens and priests' (Tacitus, *Annals*, bk. 1).[6] Alexander wished to be hailed as son of Jupiter which he seemingly did from policy rather than pride, as his response to the invective of Hermolaus indicates. 'It was almost ridiculous', he says, 'what Hermolaus demanded of me, that I should argue with Jupiter, whose oracle acknowledged me. Are the gods' responses also in my power? Jupiter offered me the name of "son"; to accept this did no harm [N.B.] to our enterprise. Would that the Indians too believed me to be a god! Wars hinge upon reputation; often a false belief has had the same effect as the truth' (Curtius, 8.8). With these few words he cleverly seeks to persuade ignorant men to accept his pretence while at the same time indicating the reason for it. Cleon too did this in the speech in which he tried to convince the Macedonians to humour the king. After lending some semblance of truth to the pretence by singing Alexander's praises and recounting his merits in tones of admiration, he passes in this way to the usefulness of the strategy: 'the Persians worshipped their kings as gods not merely from piety but also from policy, for the majesty of the state is the preservation of security', and concludes, 'that when the king entered the banqueting-hall, he himself would prostrate his body to the ground. Others should do the same, especially those who are gifted with good sense' (see 8.5 of the same book).

205

But the Macedonians were too sensible [to do the like] and it is only where men become wholly barbarous that they allow themselves to be so openly deceived and become slaves useless to themselves rather than subjects. Others, though, have been more easily able to persuade people that majesty is sacred and fulfils the role of God on earth and has been instituted by God rather than by the consent and agreement of men, and is preserved and defended by a special providence and divine assistance. Likewise, monarchs have devised other stratagems of this sort for preserving their states, but I will omit them so as finally to get on to the topics I want to deal with. I will just note and discuss, as I undertook to do, the stratagems divine revelation formerly taught Moses.

---

[6] Tacitus, *Annals*, 1.10.6: 'se templis et effigie numinum per flamines et sacerdotes coli vellet'. Spinoza quotes these words exactly.

[7]   After the Hebrews departed from Egypt, we have already noted above in chapter 5, they were no longer obligated by the law of any other nation, but it was up to them to institute new laws as they pleased and occupy whatever lands they wanted. Once liberated from the intolerable oppression of the Egyptians, they were not bound by compact to anyone; rather they regained the natural right to all that they could get, and everyone was once again free to decide whether they wanted to retain this right or give it up and transfer it to another person. Being in this natural state, they resolved, on the advice of Moses in whom they all had the greatest trust, to transfer their right to no mortal man but rather to God alone. Without hesitation, all equally with one shout promised to obey God absolutely in all his commands, and to recognize no other law but that which He himself conferred as law by prophetic revelation. This undertaking or transfer of right to God was made in the same way that we conceived above it is made in an ordinary society, whenever men make up their minds to surrender their natural right. For they gave up their right freely, not compelled by force or frightened by threats, and transferred it specifically to God with an agreement (see Exodus 24.7) and an oath. In order that the agreement should be accepted and settled without any suspicion of fraud, God made no agreement with them until after they had experienced his astounding power, by which alone they had been saved and by which alone they could be redeemed in the future   206 (see Exodus 19.4–5). Believing they could be saved by God's power alone, they transferred to Him all their natural power of preserving themselves – which previously perhaps they thought they had from themselves – and hence transferred all their right.

[8]   Consequently, God alone held the government of the Hebrews, and it was thus rightly called the kingdom of God owing to the covenant, and God was aptly called also king of the Hebrews. Hence, the enemies of this state were the enemies of God, citizens who attempted to usurp power were guilty of treason against God's majesty and the laws of the state were the laws and commands of God. For this reason, civil law in this state and religion (which as we have shown consists solely in obedience to God) were one and the same thing. That is, religious dogmas were not doctrines but rather laws and decrees, piety being regarded as justice, and impiety as crime and injustice. Anyone who defected from this religion ceased to be a citizen and for this reason alone was held to

be an enemy, and anyone who died for religion was deemed to have died for his country; thus, no distinction at all was made between civil law and religion. For that reason this state could be called a theocracy, since its citizens were bound by no law but the Law revealed by God. Even so, the fact of the matter is that all these things were more opinion than reality. For in reality the Hebrews retained absolutely the right of government, as will be clear from what I am about to say: it is evident from the manner and method by which this state was governed, which I propose to explain here.

[9]   The Hebrews did not transfer their right to another person but rather all gave up their right, equally, as in a democracy, crying with one voice: 'We will do whatever God shall say' (making no mention of an intermediary). It follows that they all remained perfectly equal as a result of this agreement. The right to consult God, receive laws, and interpret them remained equal for all, and all equally without exception retained the whole administration of the state. This is why, on the first occasion, they all equally approached God to hear what he wished to decree. But in this first encounter they were so exceedingly terrified and astonished when they heard God speaking that they thought their final day had come. Gripped by terror, they approached Moses again, saying: 'Behold we have heard God speaking in the fire, and there is no reason why we should wish to die. This great fire will surely consume us. If we must again hear the voice of God, we shall surely die. You approach therefore, and hear all the words of our God, and you' (not God) 'will speak to us. We shall revere everything God tells you, and will carry it out'.[7] By proceeding thus, they plainly abolished the first covenant and absolutely transferred their right to consult God and interpret His edicts to Moses. For they did not promise here, as before, to obey all that God said to them but rather everything God would say to Moses (see Deuteronomy 5, after the Ten Commandments,[8] and 18.15–16). Hence, Moses remained the sole maker and interpreter of the divine laws. He was also therefore the supreme judge whom no one else could judge and who alone among the Hebrews acted for God, i.e., he held sovereign majesty. For he alone had the right of consulting God, of transmitting God's answers to the people and compelling them to act on them. Alone, indeed, for if while Moses lived, anyone else

207

---

[7] Deuteronomy 5.23–7; cf. also Exodus 20.18–21.   [8] Deuteronomy 5.23–7.

had attempted to make any pronouncement in God's name, even were he a true prophet, he would be charged with usurping the sovereign right (see Numbers 11.28).[9]

[10]   Here we should note that although the people chose Moses, they did not possess the right to choose Moses' successor. For no sooner had they transferred their right of consulting God to Moses, and unconditionally promised to regard him as the divine oracle, they lost absolutely every right and had to accept anyone whom Moses should choose as his successor just as if chosen by God.

Now had he chosen someone to exercise the entire administration of the state, as he had done, including the right to consult God alone in his tent, and hence authority to make and to repeal laws, to decide about war and peace, send ambassadors, appoint judges, choose a successor, and carry out all the functions of supreme power, it would have been a purely monarchical government. The sole difference would have been that, ordinarily, monarchical power results from God's decree with this remaining hidden from the monarch himself, whereas in the case of that of the Hebrews, the monarchy was in a certain manner ruled, or should have been ruled, by God's decree which was revealed only to the monarch. However, this difference does not diminish the dominion and right of the monarch over the people but on the contrary increases it. In the case of both kinds of state the people are equally subject and equally ignorant of the divine decree; both depend upon the words of the monarch, and understand right and wrong from him alone. But the fact that they believe all his commands derive from revelation of God's decree to him renders the people more, not less, subject to him.

Moses, however, chose no such successor, but rather left a form of state to his successors that could not be called democratic, aristocratic or monarchical, but rather theocratic. For the right to interpret the laws and communicate God's responses was assigned to one man while the right and power of administering government according to the laws interpreted by the first and the responses he communicated was given to another. On this see Numbers 27.21.[10] So that this may be better understood, I will provide an orderly account of the whole system of government.

[9] Spinoza's footnote: see Annotation 36.   [10] Spinoza's footnote: see Annotation 37.

[11] First the people were commanded to construct a building to be as it were the palace of God, i.e., the palace of the supreme authority of this state. This was to be built at the expense of all the people, not of one man, so that the house where God was to be consulted should belong to all. The Levites were chosen as the officials and administrators of this divine palace. Aaron, Moses' brother, was chosen as the highest of these, and to be second, as it were, to God the king; and his sons legitimately succeeded him. As the man closest to God, therefore, he was the supreme interpreter of the divine Laws; he issued the responses of the divine oracle to the people and prayed to God on their behalf. If along with these powers he had also possessed the right of command, nothing would have distinguished him from an absolute monarch. But he was not given this power, and the whole tribe of Levi was so lacking the ordinary powers of government that it did not even have a portion of land, as the other tribes did, as its own rightful possession and means of subsistence. Moses ordained rather that this tribe should be maintained by the rest of the tribes, so that it would always be held in the greatest honour by the common people since it alone was dedicated to God.

[12] An armed force was formed from the other twelve tribes and ordered to invade the territory of the Canaanites and divide it into twelve parts and distribute it by lots among the tribes. For this task twelve chiefs were chosen, one from each tribe, and they were given the right, along with Joshua and the high priest Eleazar, to divide the territories into twelve equal parts and distribute them by lot. Joshua was chosen supreme commander of the armed force. He alone had the right to consult God in times of crisis – not, however, like Moses, alone in his tent or in the tabernacle, but rather through the high priest to whom alone the responses of God were given. Likewise, he had the right to proclaim God's commands which had been communicated through the high priest, of compelling the people to obey them, and of devising and applying means for carrying them out. He also had the right to choose from the army as many men as he wished and whoever he wished and to send out envoys in his name; broadly, every right of war depended upon his decree alone. No one automatically succeeded to his position, nor was his successor directly chosen by anyone except God, and then only when a crisis affecting the whole people required it. Apart from this, all matters of war and peace were administered by the chiefs of the tribes, as I shall shortly show.

209

[13] Finally, he ordered all men from the age of twenty to sixty to take up arms for military service, and to make up their expeditionary forces from the people alone. They were to swear allegiance not to their commander or the high priest but to religion and God. They were therefore called the forces or armies of God, and among the Hebrews God for his part [was called] the God of armies. For this reason, in great battles, on whose outcome depended either victory or disaster for the whole people, the ark of the covenant went in the midst of the army, so that the people seeing their king virtually present should fight with all their strength.

[14] From these instructions issued by Moses to his successors, we readily deduce that he chose people to be administrators of the state rather than absolute rulers. He gave no one the right to consult God alone whenever he wished, and consequently gave no one the authority he had himself possessed of making and repealing laws, deciding war and peace, of choosing both temple and state officials. All of these functions belong to one who holds sovereign power. The supreme priest, for example, had the right of interpreting the Law and transmitting God's responses, not, like Moses, whenever he wished, but only when requested by the general or the supreme council or such like. The supreme commander of the army and the councils, on the other hand, could consult God whenever they wished, but could receive God's responses only from the high priest. Thus, God's pronouncements in the mouth of the high priest were not decrees but just responses; they gained the force of commands and decrees only when accepted by Joshua and the supreme councils. This high priest, who received the divine responses from God, neither controlled an armed force nor exercised government by right; on the other hand those who possessed territories by right had no power to make laws.

Both Aaron and his son Eleazar were chosen by Moses as high priest; after the death of Moses, no one had the right to choose the priest, and the son legally succeeded his father. The commander of the army was likewise chosen by Moses, and assumed the role of commander not by the high priest's authority but by that conferred on him by Moses. Hence, when Joshua died, the high priest chose no one in his place, nor [210] did the chiefs of the tribes consult God about a new commander. Rather each chief retained Joshua's right with respect to the armed forces of his own tribe, and all collectively retained Joshua's right regarding the general armed forces. They only needed a supreme commander, it seems, when they had to join forces to fight a common enemy. This was especially the case in Joshua's time when they did not yet all have a fixed abode, and all things were held in common right. But after all the tribes had divided among themselves the lands they possessed by right of war and the additional territory they were commanded to annex, no longer did all things belong to all men. This is why there was no longer any basis for a common commander, since, owing to the division, the different tribes needed to be thought of not so much [as bodies of] fellow citizens but confederates. With respect to God and religion indeed they still had to be thought of as fellow citizens, but only as confederates with regard to the right one had over another.

This much resembles the situation of the States General of the United Netherlands – apart from the common Temple. For the division of a common thing into parts simply means that each now possesses his part alone, and the rest give up the right which they had to that part. This was why Moses chose chiefs for the tribes, so that after the division of the state, each would have responsibility for his portion, in consulting God through the high priest about the affairs of his own tribe, commanding his militia, founding and fortifying cities, appointing judges in each city, attacking the enemy of his own individual territory, and generally in handling all issues of war and peace. He was not obliged to recognize any judge other than God[11] or someone whom God had expressly delegated as a prophet. Otherwise, if he defected from God, the other tribes would be obliged not to judge him as a subject but attack him as an enemy who had violated his treaty obligations.

We have examples of these things in scripture. When Joshua died, it was the children of Israel, not a new supreme commander, who consulted God. When it became clear that the tribe of Judah had to attack an enemy of its own for the first time, it made an agreement of its own with Simeon to attack the enemy with the joint forces of both; the other tribes were not included in this league (see Judges 1.1–3). Each tribe waged war separately (as narrated in the previous chapter) against their own enemies and accepted into submission and allegiance whichever they wished, even though there was a commandment not to spare any of them via any kind of agreement, but to exterminate them all. For this transgression they were indeed rebuked but not brought to justice by

211

---

[11] Spinoza's footnote: see Annotation 38.

anyone. But this is not the reason why the tribes began to engage in wars against each other and meddle in each other's affairs. Rather they launched a hostile attack against the tribe of Benjamin which had offended the others and so seriously dissolved the bond of peace that none of the confederates could feel safe in dealing with them. After fighting three battles, they finally defeated them and slaughtered all of them indiscriminately, guilty and innocent alike, by right of war, and afterwards lamented their action, though their repentance came too late.[12]

[15]   These examples confirm what we said just now about the right of each individual tribe. But perhaps someone will ask who chose the successor to the leader of each tribe? I can ascertain nothing certain about this from Scripture itself, but conjecture that, as each tribe was divided into families, the heads of which were chosen from the older members of the family, the oldest of [the heads of families] duly succeeded to the position of leader. It was from the older men that Moses chose the seventy associates who formed the supreme council with him; those who held the reins of government after the death of Joshua, are called 'elders' in Scripture; finally 'elders' was very often used among the Hebrews to mean 'judges', as I think is well-known.

Our purpose does not require us to settle this for certain. It suffices that after the death of Moses no one person, as I have shown, held all the offices of the supreme commander. For nothing depended on the decision of one man or one council, or of the people, but rather some things were administered by one tribe, others by the others, all with equal rights; thus, it is entirely clear that, after the death of Moses, the state was neither monarchical nor aristocratic nor democratic, but as we said, theocratic. This was, firstly, because the palace of the government was the Temple, and it was only by virtue of the Temple that all the tribes were fellow citizens, as we have shown. The second reason was that all the citizens had to swear allegiance to God as their supreme judge, and promised to obey him alone in all things absolutely; and finally, the supreme commander of them all, when one was needed, was chosen by no one but God alone. Moses clearly prophesies this to the people in the name of God at Deuteronomy 18.15, and the choice of Gideon, Samson and Samuel testifies to it in practice. Hence we should not doubt that the   212

---

[12] Judges, chs. 20–1.

other faithful chiefs were chosen in a similar way, though this is not clear from their history.

[16]   Now that all this has been established, it is time to see how much this way of organizing the state could guide men's minds, and discourage both rulers and ruled from becoming either tyrants or rebels.

[17]   Those who administer a state or hold power inevitably try to lend any wrong they do the appearance of right and try to persuade the people that they acted honourably; and they often succeed, since the whole interpretation of right or law is entirely in their hands. For there is no doubt that they assume, due to this, the greatest liberty to do whatever they want and whatever their desires prompt them to do, and conversely, lose much of this freedom whenever the right to interpret the laws devolves upon others, and likewise if the true interpretation of them is so plain to all that no one can be in any doubt about it. From this it is evident that the Hebrew leaders were deprived of a great opportunity for wrongdoing in that the right to interpret the laws was given wholly to the Levites (see Deuteronomy 21.5), who held no responsibility for government and had no portion [of territory] along with the others and whose entire fortune and position depended upon a true interpretation of the laws. [It also helped] that the whole people was ordered to congregate in a certain place once every seven years to learn the Laws from the priests, and, in addition, that everyone had an obligation to read and reread the book of the Law by himself continually and attentively (see Deuteronomy 31.9 ff. and 6.7). The leaders therefore had to take very good care, if only for their own sakes, to govern entirely according to the prescribed laws, which were quite clearly understood by all, if they wanted to be held in the highest honour by the people who at that time revered them as ministers of God's government and as having the place of God. Otherwise they could not escape the most intense kind of hatred, among their subjects, as intense as theological hatred tends to be.

[18]   An additional means, plainly, and something invariably of the utmost importance for curbing the boundless licentiousness of princes, was that the military was formed from the whole body of the citizenry (with no exemptions between the ages of twenty and sixty), and that the leaders could not hire foreign mercenaries. This, unquestionably, was a

very powerful restraint, for it is certain that princes can oppress a people 213 simply by making use of a mercenary armed force, and they fear nothing more than the liberty of their soldier-citizens, whose courage, toil and expenditure of blood have won the state its freedom and glory. When Alexander was about to encounter Darius in battle for the second time, Parmenio offered him [unacceptable] advice;[13] Alexander did not rebuke Parmenio who had given this advice but Polyperchon who supported Parmenio. For as Curtius says at 4.13, he did not dare to rebuke Parmenio again, since he had recently chastised him in stronger terms than he would have wished. Neither was he able to suppress the liberty of the Macedonians which he very much feared, as we have already said, until he had more captives in his army than native Macedonians. Only then could he give rein to his own headstrong temperament, which had long been restrained by the liberty of the best citizens. If therefore this liberty of citizen-soldiers restrains the leaders of a merely human state, accustomed to appropriate for themselves all the credit for victories, how much more must it have restrained the leaders of the Hebrews, whose soldiers fought not for the glory of their leaders but the glory of God, and engaged in battle only when they had received a response from God.

[19]   To this should be added that all the Hebrew leaders were united only by the bond of religion. If any of them therefore rejected it and began to violate the divine right of each person, the others would consider him an enemy on this ground alone and rightly suppress him.

[20]   There was also, thirdly, the fear of a new prophet. If a man who lived a blameless life showed by certain accepted signs that he was a prophet, he had by this fact alone the supreme right of command like that of Moses – which he exercised in the name of God who was revealed to him alone – and not merely like the chiefs, who consulted God through the high priest. There is no doubt that such men could easily draw the oppressed people to themselves, and persuade them of whatever they wanted even by trivial signs. On the other hand, if things were well-run, the leader could stipulate beforehand that any prophet should first appear before him so as to be examined by him, as to

---

[13] On this occasion Alexander rejected the advice of Parmenio, his senior general, but thought it more politic to rebuke one of Parmenio's junior supporters for offering bad counsel, rather than risk rebuking Parmenio himself.

whether he was of good morals, whether he had certain and indubitable signs of his mission, and whether what he wanted to say in God's name agreed with accepted doctrine and the common laws of the country. If the signs were unsatisfactory or the doctrine was new, he could rightly condemn him to death, but if all was well, he was accepted solely on the authority and testimony of the leader.

214

[21] There is also, fourthly, the fact that the leader did not surpass the rest in nobility, nor by right of blood. The government of the state belonged to him only because of his age and his virtue.

[22] There is, finally, also the advantage that the leaders and body of the armed forces could not be carried away by a desire for war rather than peace. For the armed forces, as we said, consisted only of citizens, and therefore matters of war as well as of peace were handled by these same men. The man who was a soldier in the camp was a citizen in the assembly; the officer in the camp was a judge in the council of elders; and the general in the camp was a leader in the state. Hence no one could desire war for war's sake, but only for the sake of peace and the protection of freedom. Perhaps also a leader abstained from novelties so far as he could, so that he would not be obliged to come before the high priest and suffer the indignity of standing in his presence. So much for the factors that kept political leaders within bounds.

[23] We must now see by what means the people were held in check, and this too is clearly indicated by the principles of their government. Anyone willing to pay any attention to these will immediately see that they must have aroused in the minds of the citizens such a unique love that it would be the hardest thing in the world to induce them to betray their country or defect from it. On the contrary, they must all have been ready to suffer death rather than tolerate a foreign power. For having transferred their right to God, they believed their kingdom was the kingdom of God, that they alone were the children of God and that other nations were enemies of God, whom for that reason they regarded with extreme hostility (believing as they did that this was pious: see Psalm 139.21–2). Nothing was more abhorrent to them than to swear loyalty to a foreigner and to promise allegiance to him. No greater disgrace, nothing more detestable could be imagined than to betray their country, the very kingdom of God. Just to go and live outside the country was

thought to be an outrage, since the worship of God by which they were for ever bound, could be practised, all agreed, only on their native soil, as it was held to be the only holy land, all others being unclean and polluted. When David was forced into exile, he grieved before Saul in these words: 'If those who incite you against me are men, they are accursed, because they banish me from walking in the inheritance of God, and say, "Go, and worship other gods".'[14] For the same reason, we must especially note here, no citizen was condemned to exile: for a transgressor deserves punishment but not disgrace.   215

Thus the love of the Hebrews for their country was not simple love but piety, which along with hatred of other nations, was so nourished and inflamed by daily worship that it must have become second nature. For their daily worship was not only completely different (which made them altogether unique and utterly distinct from others) but absolutely contrary to that of other peoples. As a consequence of which these daily expressions of reproach were bound to generate a ceaseless hatred, and one more firmly entrenched in their minds than any other, given that such a detestation born of great devotion and piety, was itself viewed as pious, and no hatred is greater or more persistent than this type. Nor was the usual cause of hatred lacking either, that is, of course, reciprocal abhorrence becoming more and more inflamed, because other nations were bound to react by developing an extreme hatred for them.

[24]   Freedom from human government, devotion to their country, an absolute right over all others, a hatred which was not only permitted but pious, a perception that all men are enemies, a unique system of morals and worship: reason teaches clearly, and experience itself testifies, how much all these things served to harden the minds of the Hebrews in bearing all things with singular constancy and courage on behalf of their country. Never while the city was standing, could they bear to be under alien rule, and therefore Jerusalem was often called a rebellious city (see Ezra 4.12–15). The second commonwealth was scarcely a shadow of the first, after the priests had usurped the authority of civil government, but even so the Romans experienced very great difficulty in destroying it, as Tacitus himself remarks with these words in *Histories*, book 2:[15] 'Vespasian had almost completed the Jewish war, the siege of Jerusalem alone being

---

[14] 1 Samuel 26.19.   [15] Tacitus, *Histories*, 2.4.

left, but that was a great and arduous task more because of the character of the nation and the obstinacy of their superstition than because there remained sufficient strength in the besieged to bear their dire situation'.

[25] Apart from these factors, whose impact stemmed from opinion alone, there was another aspect to this state, a very solid factor unique to them which must have very much discouraged the citizens from thinking about defection or ever conceiving a desire to desert their country. This is consideration of their interest which is the life and strength of all human actions. It was I say uniquely powerful in this state. For nowhere else did citizens hold their possessions with a stronger right than this state's subjects. They held an equal portion of the lands and fields with the leader, and each one was the perpetual owner of his share. If anyone was compelled by poverty to sell his estate or field, he had to be restored to it again when the Jubilee came around, and there were other customs of this kind to ensure that no one could be dispossessed of his allotted property. Nowhere could poverty be more tolerable, than where it was a matter of the highest piety to practise charity towards one's neighbour, that is, towards one's fellow-citizen, so that God their king would continue to look with favour upon them. Hebrew citizens therefore could live well only within their own land; outside of it there was nothing [for them] but loss and shame.

Other significant factors helped to retain the citizens on their native soil, as well as obviate civil wars and remove causes of conflict. No one was subject to his equal, each being subject only to God. Charity and love towards one's fellow citizen were esteemed as the highest piety and considerably reinforced by the shared animosity with which they viewed other nations and vice versa. But the most potent factor was the strong discipline of obedience in which they were brought up. Every single thing they had to do according to a specific prescript of the Law. They could not plough as and when they pleased, but could only do so at certain times and in particular years, and with only one kind of beast at a time; they could sow and reap only in a certain way and at a particular time; their lives without exception were a continual practice of obedience (on this issue see chapter 5 on the use of ceremonies). To people wholly accustomed to this, it must have appeared to be freedom rather than slavery; surely no one could have desired what was forbidden, only what was prescribed.

Another key factor seems to have been that at certain times of the year they were under obligation to devote themselves to leisure and cheerfulness, not to do whatever they pleased but obey God with all their hearts. Three times in the year they feasted with God (see Deuteronomy 16); they had to cease from all work on the seventh day of the week and allow themselves to rest; and, besides these, other times were designated when honest enjoyment and feasting were not so much allowed as prescribed. I do not think anything can be devised which is more effective than this for swaying men's minds. Nothing captivates minds more effectively than the cheerfulness arising from devotion, i.e., from love and wonder together. They were unlikely to become bored with it all through famil-   217 iarity, as the worship reserved for festival days was exceptional and varied.

On top of this, there was the supreme reverence for the Temple they always scrupulously kept up owing to its unique cult and rituals that worshippers were required to perform before being allowed to enter. Even today they cannot read, without a shudder of horror, of the scandalous act of Manasseh in daring to place an idol in the Temple itself.[16] The people felt no less reverence for the laws kept with religious care within the innermost sanctum. Popular prejudices and murmuring hardly posed a threat here, since no one dared offer a judgment about divine questions. They had to do whatever they were commanded by the authority of the divine response received in the Temple or via the Law delivered by God without consulting reason. I have now, I think, explained briefly but clearly the essential design of this state.

[26]   It remains now to inquire into why the Hebrews so often lapsed from the Law, why they were so often overrun, and why in the end their state could be utterly destroyed. Perhaps someone will assert at this point that it happened due to the wilful disobedience of this people. But this is childish. How was this nation more disobedient than others? Was it by nature? Nature certainly does not create peoples, individuals do, and individuals are only separated into nations by differences of language, law and morality. It can only be from these latter factors, namely law and morality, that each nation has its unique character, its unique condition, and its unique prejudices. If therefore one had to grant that the Hebrews were more wilfully disobedient than other people, this would have to be imputed to a fault in its laws or in their morality. The truth is that had God wished their state to last longer, He would have organized their

----

[16] 2 Kings 21.1–9.

rights and laws differently and instituted a different form of state. What else can be said, then, than that their God was angry with them not merely, as Jeremiah 32.31 says, from the foundation of the city but right from the laying down of the Laws. Ezekiel too attests to this at 20.25 saying, 'I also gave them statutes which were not good and edicts by which they might not live; I made them impure by their very gifts by rejecting every first opening of the womb' (i.e., the first-born), 'so that I might destroy them, so that they would know that I am Jehovah'.

218   So as to understand these words and the cause of the destruction of the state, one should note that the original intention was to entrust the sacred ministry to the first-born, and not to the Levites (see Numbers 8.17). But after everyone but the Levites had worshipped the golden calf, the first-born were rejected and declared unclean and the Levites chosen in their place (Deuteronomy 10.8). The more I ponder this, the more I must exclaim, in Tacitus' words, that at that time 'God did not wish to save them but to punish them'.[17] Nor can I sufficiently express my amazement that there was so much anger in the divine mind,[18] that He should actually make laws (which are normally designed to protect the honour, safety and security of all the people) to avenge himself and punish them, and thus the laws seemed to be not laws (i.e., a protection for the people) but penalties and punishments. Everything always reminded them of their impurity and rejection: all the gifts they were obliged to donate to the Levites and the priests, their obligation to redeem their first-born and pay a poll-tax in silver to the Levites, the exclusive privilege of the Levites to approach whatever was sacred.

Furthermore, the Levites always gave them opportunities for criticism. For undoubtedly, among so many thousands of Levites, there must have been numerous narrow-minded clerics who made a nuisance of themselves. In retaliation, the people kept an eye on the activities of the Levites who, after all, were only men, and would blame them all for the misdeeds of just a few: that is the way of things. Thus, there would constantly be protests – especially if the price of corn was high – and unwillingness to continue supporting a non-labouring elite whom they resented and were not even related to them by blood. What wonder, then, if in times of peace when manifest miracles had ceased and there were no men of outstanding authority, people became indignant and envious, and began to grow stale

---

[17] Tacitus, *Histories*, 1.3.   [18] An echo of Virgil, *Aeneid*, 1.11: 'tantaene animis coelestibus irae?'

in their worship which, though divine, was demeaning to them as well as suspect in itself, and if they looked around for a new cult. What wonder too if the leaders, who always alone hold the sovereign right to rule, gave in to the people and introduced new cults, in order to win their allegiance for themselves and turn them away from the priests.

[27]   But if their republic had been set up according to its first design, all the tribes would have retained equal right and honour, and everything would have proceeded in complete security. For who would wish to violate the sacred right of his kin? What would they want more than to support those of their own blood, their brothers and parents, as religious piety required? What would they have wanted more than to learn from them how to interpret the Law and hear from them the divine respon- 219 ses? In this way, all the tribes would have remained far more closely bound to each other, that is, if all had had an equal right to administer the sacred things. Indeed, there would have been nothing to fear had His choosing the Levites had any other cause than anger and vengeance. But as we said, God was angry, and he made them impure by their gifts, to repeat again the words of Ezekiel, by rejecting the first opening of the womb in order to destroy them.

[28]   This is confirmed by the histories. No sooner had the people, still in the desert, found they had some time to spare, than many of them (not from the common folk) began to resent this priestly election and to foment the view that Moses was setting up these institutions not by divine command but simply as he pleased, since he had chosen his own tribe over the others and conferred the right of priesthood for ever on his own brother. So they instigated a commotion and went to see him, claiming they were all equally sacred and that it was not right that he should be elevated above all the rest.[19] Nor was there any way that he could pacify them; however, via a miracle which he invoked as a token of his high standing with God, they were all annihilated. From this arose a new and more general sedition of the whole people; for the people believed that those men had been destroyed not by God who was their judge but rather by the craft of Moses. He did not finally subdue them until a terrible disaster, that is a pestilence, left them so worn down that

---

[19] Numbers 16.

they preferred to die rather than to live. It was thus at that time more a case of sedition lapsing than of harmony being established. Scripture testifies to this at Deuteronomy 31.21, where God assures Moses, after predicting that after the latter's death the people would lapse from the worship of God: 'I know what they want and what they are plotting today, while I have not yet brought them to the land that I swore to give them'. A little later Moses directly addressed the people: 'I know your rebellion and your disobedience. If while I have lived among you, you have been unruly against God, how much more will you be so after my death?'[20]

[29] Actually, this is what was to happen, as is well known. Great changes occurred, voluptuousness, luxury and idleness surged up among them, and everything deteriorated, until, after being conquered many times, they openly violated the divine Law and demanded to have a man as their king; and thus the chief edifice of the state was no longer the Temple but a royal court, and all the tribes were no longer fellow citizens under the divine law and the priesthood but under kings. This was a major cause of further subversion, which in the end brought about the fall of the entire state. For what could be more insupportable to kings than to reign on sufferance, or have to put up with a state within the state?

220

The earliest kings, selected from among private men were content with the degree of dignity conferred upon them. But once their sons obtained the kingship by right of succession, they gradually began to change everything, so as to possess the entire power of the state for themselves which, for the most part, they lacked as long as the authority of the Laws depended not on them but on the high priest, who kept the Laws in the sanctuary and interpreted these to the people. Like their subjects, they were bound by the Laws, and had no right to repeal them, or make new ones carrying similar authority. The right of the Levites forbade kings, as secular persons, no less than their subjects, from handling sacred matters. And, lastly, they sought more power because the whole security of their government was dependent on the will of one man who was regarded as a prophet. Of this dependence they had seen ample proof in the example of Samuel who, with great liberty gave Saul his orders and, afterwards, was easily able, owing to one fault of Saul's, to transfer his authority to rule to David. In this way they faced a government within a government, holding their title on sufferance.

---

[20] Deuteronomy 31.27.

To overcome this, they permitted temples to be dedicated to other gods, so that there might be no more consultation of the Levites. Then, they sought out more men to prophesy in the name of God, so as to have other prophets to counter the veritable ones. But whatever they tried, they were never able to obtain what they wanted. The true prophets were ready for everything. They awaited the opportune moment which is the reign of a new king, something always precarious whilst recollection of the previous king remains strong. At such a moment they could easily instigate against the new king, on divine authority, a rival well-known for his courage to vindicate the divine law and take over the government or his part of it by right.

But even the prophets could not bring about any true improvement by this means. For even if they deposed a tyrant, the causes of tyranny still remained, and so all they achieved was to bring in a new tyrant at the expense of much citizens' blood. Consequently, there was no end to strife and civil war, and the reasons why the divine law was violated remained always the same; these reasons could only be removed by overthrowing the state entirely.

[30]   With this we have seen how religion was introduced into the Hebrew republic and how the latter could have continued for ever if the just anger of the Law-giver had permitted it to continue in the same way. But this could not be and hence it had to perish. Here I have been speaking only about the first state, for the second was scarcely a shadow of the first, since by that time they were bound by the law of the Persians   221 whose subjects they were, and after they obtained their freedom, the high priests usurped the right of leadership and obtained absolute control of the state. Consequently, the high priests aspired to possess both government and priesthood together, and this is why there has been no need to say more about this second Commonwealth. The next chapters will show whether the first state is as imitable as we think it to have been durable, or whether it is pious to imitate it, so far as this can be done.

[31]   Finally, I should just like to repeat the statement we made above, that what we have shown in this chapter demonstrates that divine law, or the law of religion, arises from a covenant, and without a covenant there is no law but the law of nature. It follows that by the ties of religion the Hebrews were bound in piety only towards their fellow citizens and not towards the nations who were not party to the Covenant.

CHAPTER 18

Some political principles are inferred from the Hebrew state and its history

[1] The Hebrew state, as we analysed it in the last chapter, might have lasted for ever, but no one can now imitate it, and it would not be wise to try to do so. For if anyone wished to transfer their right to God, they would have to make an explicit covenant with God, just as the Hebrews did, and this would require not only the will of those who were transferring their right, but also the will of God to whom it was to be transferred. But God has revealed through the Apostles that His covenant is no longer written in ink or on stone tablets but rather on the heart by the spirit of God.[1] Moreover, such a form of state would probably only be useful to those desirous of living without interacting with others, shutting themselves up within their own borders and separating themselves from the rest of the world, but not to those who need to have commerce with others. There are very few who would find such a form of state advantageous to them. Yet though it cannot be emulated as a whole, it nevertheless has numerous features that are at least well worth noticing, and which it would perhaps be very wise to imitate.

[2] Since, as I said above, it is not my intention to discuss the state systematically, I will leave out a great many things and specify only what is relevant to my purpose. First, it is not contrary to God's rule to choose a supreme magistrate who will have the sovereign right of government. After the Hebrews transferred their right to God, they handed over the

---

[1] 2 Corinthians 3.3.

supreme right of command to Moses. He alone therefore possessed authority to make and unmake laws, choose ministers of sacred worship, judge, teach, punish, and govern all the people in all things absolutely. Equally, while the ministers of sacred worship were the interpreters of the laws, it was not their responsibility to judge citizens or excommunicate anyone. Such powers belonged only to the judges and to the leaders chosen from the people (see Joshua 6.26, Judges 21.18 and 1 Samuel 14.24).

[3]   Furthermore, if we are willing to study Hebrew history, we shall discover other things deserving of notice:

[4]   (1) Firstly, there were no sects in their religion, until the high priests obtained the authority to issue decrees and manage the business of government in the second Commonwealth, usurped control of the state and finally even wanted to be called kings, so that their authority might be rendered permanent. The reason for this is obvious. In the first state, no decree could be issued in the name of a high priest, since priests had no power to issue decrees, but only the right to give the responses of God, when requested to do so by the leaders or councils. At that time, accordingly, they could have no wish to promulgate new decrees but merely administered and safeguarded the existing edicts. By no other means than keeping the laws uncorrupted could they safely preserve their liberty against the will of the secular leaders. But after acquiring the power to manage the business of government and the right of leadership, as well as the priesthood, each of them began seeking glory for his own name in religion and in everything else, by using priestly authority to settle issues by every day promulgating fresh edicts about belief, ceremonies and everything else, and by attempting to lend such rulings as much authority as the Laws of Moses had. As a result religion degenerated into fatal superstition, and the true sense and interpretation of the Laws was perverted. Similarly, as the high priests insinuated themselves into the leadership at the beginning of the restoration, they went along with anything that would draw the common people in their wake. They lent their approval even to impious actions by the common people, and twisted Scripture to accommodate their base morality. Malachi testifies to this in so many words. He rebuked the priests of his time by calling them despisers of the name of God and proceeded to castigate them thus: 'The lips of a priest preserve knowledge, and the law is sought from his mouth, for he is the messenger of God. But you have fallen from the way, so that the Law is a stumbling-block to many; you

223

have corrupted the covenant of Levi, says the Lord of hosts'.[2] After this, he continued with further accusations, charging them with interpreting the Laws as they wished and showing respect only for persons and not for God. But the high priests could assuredly never have accomplished all this, however cunningly they proceeded, without this being noticed by the wiser sort, and without their insisting, as the high priests' audacity mounted, that only the written laws should be considered binding. All the other rulings called 'traditions of the fathers' by the deluded Pharisees – who, according to Josephus, in his *Antiquities*,[3] mostly came from among the common people – should be set aside.

But however that may have been, there can be no doubt whatever that adulation of the high priests, corruption of religion and the laws, and an incredible proliferation in the number of rulings, afforded ample and frequent occasion for commotions and disputes which could never be settled. For when men are driven by the ardour of superstition and begin to quarrel and where the magistrates then take sides, it is impossible to quieten the people down. Rather they inevitably divide into factions.

(2) The prophets, who, of course, were private individuals, had more success, it should be noted, in antagonizing than reforming people by means of the liberty which they usurped to admonish, scold and rebuke; on the other hand, those admonished or punished by kings, were readily corrected. Actually, the prophets were frequently insupportable even to pious kings, owing to the authority they had to judge which actions were pious or impious and rebuke even the kings themselves, if they persisted in any public or private activity contrary to the prophets' view of what was correct. King Asa, who by the testimony of Scripture ruled piously, put the prophet Hananiah on the treadmill (see 2 Chronicles 16) for daring to reprove and admonish him freely following the agreement Asa had come to with the king of Aramaea. There are also other examples, apart from this, showing that religion lost more than it gained as a consequence of such licence, not to mention the fact that serious civil wars arose because the prophets retained so much authority for themselves.

(3) Also worthy of note is the fact that whilst the people held the sovereign power, they experienced only one civil war, and this conflict was brought to a complete end, the victors evincing so much compassion for the vanquished that they made every effort to restore them to their former dignity and power. But after the people, despite having no experience of kings, exchanged their original [republican] form of government for monarchy, there was practically no end to civil wars, and the Hebrews engaged in battles of unparalleled ferocity. In one such encounter – this is almost impossible to believe – 500,000

224

---

[2] Malachi 2.7–8. [3] Josephus, *Jewish Antiquities*, 18.12–15.

men of Israel were slaughtered by those of Judah. In another, the Israelites killed many of the men of Judah, captured their king, virtually demolished the walls of Jerusalem and (to let everyone know that there was no limit to their fury) totally devastated the Temple itself. Then, laden with great quantities of spoil taken from their brothers and sated with their blood, they took hostages and left the king his almost utterly ruined kingdom. Finally, they laid down their arms, having built their security not on the edifice of good faith but the drastic weakening of the men of Judah. Some years later, when Judah's strength had revived, they engaged again in battle, and again the Israelites emerged victorious, annihilating 120,000 men of Judah, taking as many as 200,000 women and children captive, and once again seizing immense booty. But when their resources were consumed in these and other conflicts mentioned in passing in the histories, they themselves finally likewise fell prey to their enemies.

[5]   If we try to calculate the periods in which the Israelites were allowed to enjoy complete peace, we shall find a significantly vast difference [between the periods without and with kings]. In the time before the kings, they often passed forty and even, on one occasion (you may hardly believe this), eighty years, in concord, without foreign or internal wars. But as soon as the kings took control, the reason for going to war was no longer, as before, peace and liberty but rather glory, and we read that all the kings fought wars except only Solomon whose virtue, i.e. wisdom, flourished better in peace than in war. Deadly lust for power took over, rendering the path to the throne very bloody for many of them. Finally, the laws remained uncorrupted as long as the rule of the people continued, and were more faithfully observed: for prior to rule by kings, there were very few prophets to counsel the people. But once monarchy was opted for, there was always a large number of prophets: Obadiah saved a hundred of them from death by hiding them so that they would not be liquidated with the rest of the prophets. Nor do we find the people being deceived by any false prophets until after power passed to kings many of whom they strove to flatter. Besides, the people whose resolve is generally high or low according to their situation, readily disciplined themselves in disasters, prior to kings, and turned to God and restored the laws, and in this manner extricated themselves from every danger. By contrast, afterwards, their kings, since monarchical minds are always proud, and cannot back down without feelings of humiliation clung obstinately to their faults, until the final destruction of the city.

[6]   We see very clearly from this:

(1) How pernicious it is both for religion and the state to allow ministers of things sacred to acquire the right to make decrees or handle the business of government. Rather everything proceeds with much more stability, we see, if they are so tightly restricted that they may not give responses on any subject on which questions have not been put to them, and in the meantime are allowed to teach and practise only what is generally received and usual.

(2) How dangerous it is to refer purely philosophical questions to divine law, and to make laws about opinions which men can or do dispute. Government is bound to become extremely oppressive where [dissident] opinions which are within the domain of each individual, a right which no one can give up, are treated as a crime. Where this happens, the anger of the common people tends to prevail. Pilate knew that Christ was innocent but ordered him to be crucified so as to appease the fury of the Pharisees. In order to strip those who were richer than themselves of their offices, the Pharisees aimed to stir up controversies about religion and accuse the Sadducees of impiety. Following the example of the Pharisees, all the worst hypocrites everywhere have been driven by the same frenzy (which they call zeal for God's law), to persecute men of outstanding probity and known virtue, resented by the common people for precisely these qualities, by publicly reviling their opinions, and inflaming the anger of the barbarous majority against them. This aggressive licence cannot easily be checked because it hides itself under the cloak of religion, especially when the sovereign authorities have introduced a cult of which they themselves are not the heads. Where that occurs, the authorities are not regarded as the interpreters of divine law but as members of the church, that is, as people who accept the doctors of the sect as the interpreters of divine law. In this situation, the authority of the magistrates usually has very little influence with the common people; rather the authority of the theologians (to whose interpretations they think that even kings must submit), acquires overwhelming weight. In order to avoid these difficulties, the safest policy is to regard piety and the practice of religion as a question of works alone, that is, as simply the practice of charity and justice, and to leave everyone to his own free judgment about everything else; but we will speak about this more fully presently.[4]

(3) We see how necessary it is both for the state, and for religion, to assign the authority to decide what is religiously right or not to the sovereign power alone. For if authority to make this distinction in practice cannot without great harm to both state and religion be left to God's prophets themselves, much

---

[4] See pp. 238ff. and 250ff.

less can it be assigned to men unable to foretell the future or work miracles. But I will discuss this formally in the next chapter.

(4) Finally, we see how disastrous it is for a people unaccustomed to live under kings and already possessing settled laws, to appoint a monarch. For the people will be unable to endure so powerful an authority, while the royal majesty will find equally insupportable the laws or rights of the people, introduced as they were by an authority lower than its own. Still less will the monarch be inclined to defend these laws, especially since when they were first introduced no doctrine of kingship applied, but only of the council or popular assembly which regarded itself as holding power. Hence, when defending their ancient rights, the king would appear to be the people's servant rather than its master. A new monarch will put all his efforts into making new laws and transforming the powers of the state to his own advantage and reducing the people to the point where they cannot take the king's position away as easily as they gave it to him.

[7]   But I cannot fail to say here that it is equally dangerous to depose a monarch, even if it is clear by every criterion that he is a tyrant. A people accustomed to royal authority and held in check only by it, will despise any lesser authority and hold it in contempt. Accordingly, if they depose a king, it will be as indispensable for them, as for the prophets in the past, to select another monarch in place of the previous one, and he will then be a tyrant, not of his own choosing but of necessity. For how will he inevitably regard citizens whose hands are stained with royal blood, citizens glorying in parricide as in a noble act, an act which cannot fail to be an ominous example for him? If he wishes to be king and refuses to accept the people as a judge of kings, and his master, and if he is not to reign at their plea-sure, he must certainly avenge the death of his predecessor and provide a   227 counter-example for his own sake, so that the people will not commit the same crime again. It will not, however, be easy to avenge the death of a tyrant by killing citizens, without at the same time defending the cause of the former tyrant, approving his actions and following in all his footsteps. This is why a people have often been able to change tyrants but are never able to get rid of them or change the monarchical form into another form of state.

[8]   The English people have provided a fatal example of this truth. They looked for reasons that would seem to justify their deposing their

monarch.[5] But once they had deposed him, they could do no less than change their form of state. However, after spilling a great deal of blood, they succeeded merely in installing a new monarch[6] with a different title (as if the whole thing had been about nothing but a title). The new ruler could remain in power only by destroying the entire royal line, and by killing the friends of the king or those suspected of his friendship, and starting a war in order to put an end to the inactivity of peaceful times, which affords an opportunity for murmurings of discontent to arise. He contrived to turn the thoughts of the common people away from the execution of the king by keeping them intent and occupied with new challenges.[7] By the time the people realized that they had done nothing for the safety of their country except violate the right of a legitimate king and change everything for the worse, it was too late [to correct the damage]. Consequently, as soon as they had the chance, they decided to retrace their steps, and did not rest until they saw everything restored to its former state.

[9]   Someone may perhaps put forward the example of the Romans to show that a people can easily remove a tyrant from their midst. But actually I think that this example fully confirms our position. Admittedly, the Roman people could much more easily get rid of a tyrant and change their form of government [than the English], with the right of choosing the king and his successor residing in the hands of the people, and they themselves (a notoriously rebellious populace) not yet having learned to obey kings. Indeed, of the six kings they had in earlier times, they slaughtered three. Yet all they achieved thereby was to choose many tyrants in place of one, and these kept them in ceaseless wretched strife in foreign and civil wars until finally, the form of state once again became monarchical except only, as in the case of England, for the change of name.

[10]   As for the States of Holland, they did not, to our knowledge, ever have kings but only Counts, to whom the right of government was never

---

[5] Spinoza is referring to the English Civil War and the dethroning of King Charles I (reigned: 1625–49).

[6] I.e. Oliver Cromwell, Lord Protector of England.

[7] Spinoza is referring here to the First Anglo-Dutch War (1652–4) which he is suggesting Cromwell started in order to distract the attention of the English from their internal politics.

transferred. For as the sovereign States of Holland publicly state, in the 228
resolution published by them in the time of the Earl of Leicester,[8] they
had always reserved to themselves the authority to remind these Counts
of their duty, retaining the power to defend their authority and the liberty
of the citizens, and rescue themselves from them should they become
tyrants, and generally keep a check on them, so that they could do
nothing without the permission and approval of the States. The right of
sovereignty, it follows, was always vested in the States. This was what the
last Count of Holland [i.e. Philip II of Spain] strove to usurp. Hence it is
by no means true that they rebelled against him when they recovered
their original power which they had by then almost lost. These examples
thus confirm what we have said, namely, that the form of each state must
necessarily be retained and cannot be changed without risking the total
ruin of the state. These are the points that I thought worth noticing here.

---

[8] Robert Dudley, earl of Leicester (1533–88), was sent over by Queen Elizabeth and accepted by the
Dutch as 'governor-general' of the United Provinces, a position which he held during the years
1585–7.

CHAPTER 19

Where it is shown that authority in sacred matters
belongs wholly to the sovereign powers and that
the external cult of religion must be consistent
with the stability of the state if we wish to obey
God rightly

[1]   When I said above that only those who hold sovereign power
have jurisdiction over everything, and that all authority depends on their
decree alone, I had in mind not just civil jurisdiction but also that over
sacred matters. For they must be both the interpreters and guardians of
things sacred. I want to put a particular emphasis on this point con-
centrating on it in this chapter, because very many people vigorously
deny that this right (i.e. jurisdiction over sacred matters) belongs to the
sovereign authorities, and refuse to recognize them as interpreters of
divine law. From this they also arrogate to themselves licence to accuse
and condemn sovereigns and even to excommunicate them from the
church (as Ambrose long ago excommunicated the emperor Theodosius).
We shall see below in this present chapter that what they are in effect
doing is dividing the sovereign power and attempting to devise a path to
power for themselves.

[2]   I intend first to show that religion has the power of law only by decree
of those who exercise the right of government and that God has no special
kingdom among men except through those who exercise sovereignty. I also
wish to demonstrate that religious worship and pious conduct must be
229   accommodated to the peace and interests of the state and consequently
must be determined by the sovereign authorities alone.

[3]   I speak expressly of pious conduct and formal religious worship and
not piety itself or private worship of God or the means by which the
mind is internally directed wholeheartedly to revere God. For internal
veneration of God, and piety, as such are under everyone's individual
jurisdiction (as we showed at the end of ch. 7), and cannot be transferred
to another. Furthermore, what I mean by 'kingdom of God' here is plain
enough, I suppose, from chapter 14. We showed there that a person fulfils
the law of God by practising justice and charity at God's command, from
which it follows that a kingdom of God is a kingdom in which justice and
charity have the force of law and command. I cannot see that it makes
any difference here whether God teaches and commands the true practice of justice and charity by the natural light of reason or by revelation.
It makes no difference how such practice is revealed[1] to men, provided
that it possesses supreme authority and serves men as their highest law.

Justice and charity I must therefore now show can only receive the
force of law and command via the authority of the state, and then I will
easily be able to conclude (since the right of government belongs only to
the sovereign authorities) that religion has the force of law exclusively by
decree of those who possess the right to exercise government. It follows
that God has no special kingship over men except through those who
exercise government.

[4]   That the practice of justice and charity has the force of law only via
the authority of the state is clear from what was said above. We have
proved in chapter 16 that, in the natural state, reason has no more right
than has appetite; both those who live by the laws of appetite and those
who live by the laws of reason there possess the right to do everything
they can. This is why, in the state of nature, men were not able to conceive of wrong nor of God as a judge punishing men for wrongdoing, but
rather recognized that all things happen according to the common laws
of universal nature and that the same chance (to use Solomon's words)[2]
affects the just and the unjust, the pure and the impure, and so on, and
there is no room for justice or charity. And if the teachings of true reason, which are the divine teachings themselves (as we showed in ch. 4 on

---

[1] Spinoza means here that it makes no difference whether men base their conduct on justice and
charity because they think religion teaches this, or whether they grasp that this is the highest morality through use of their reason.

[2] Ecclesiastes 9.2.

the divine law), are to have the full force of law, it is necessary that each
230   person should give up his own natural right and that all should transfer
their right to all men, or else some men, or else one man; and it was then
and only then that we first learned what justice and injustice, equity and
inequity are.

[5] Justice therefore and all the doctrines of true reason without
exception, including charity towards our neighbour, receive the force of law
and command from the authority of the state alone, that is (as we showed
in the same chapter) solely from the decree of those who have the right to
rule. Now because, as I have already shown, the kingdom of God consists
solely in the law of justice, charity and true religion, it follows that God has
no kingdom over men except through those who hold power. This is what
we have been seeking to demonstrate. It makes no difference, I say, whether
we conceive of religion as revealed by the natural light of reason or by the
light of prophecy. The demonstration is universal, since religion is the
same and equally revealed by God, whichever way men are supposed to
have learned it.

[6]   Therefore, in order that even prophetically revealed religion should
have the force of law among the Hebrews, each of them had first to give
up his natural right, and all had to decide by common consent to obey
solely what was prophetically revealed to them by God. This is exactly
the same thing as we have shown occurs in a democratic state, where all
decide by common consent to live by the dictate of reason alone.
Although the Hebrews also transferred their right to God, they could
only do this in intention rather than reality, for in fact (as we saw above)
they retained the absolute right of government until they transferred this
to Moses. Thereafter, Moses remained absolute ruler, and it was through
him alone that God ruled over the Hebrews. For the same reason also,
namely because religion receives the force of law by the authority of the
state alone, Moses could not punish those who violated the sabbath
before the covenant since they then, in consequence, still possessed their
own right (see Exodus 16.27). After the covenant, on the other hand (see
Numbers 15.36), i.e., after each one gave up their natural right, the
sabbath received the force of command by virtue of the right of the state.
   On the same grounds, revealed religion no longer possessed the force of
law after the destruction of the Hebrew state. For there can be no doubt

that as soon as the Hebrews transferred their right to the king of Babylon, the kingdom of God and the divine law immediately ceased to be effective. For, by that very fact, the covenant with which they undertook to obey everything that God ordained, and which had been the 231 foundation of the kingdom of God, was utterly abolished. They could no longer continue to observe it since from that moment onwards they were no longer under their own jurisdiction (as when they were in the desert or in their own country) but under that of the Babylonian ruler whom they were obliged to obey in everything (as we showed in chapter 16). This is also what Jeremiah expressly teaches at chapter 29.7: 'Strive', he says, 'for the peace of the state, to which I have brought you as captives; for its well-being will be your well-being'. They could not strive for the salvation of that state as participants in government do, being captives, but rather had to as slaves do. This meant observing the ordinances and laws of the state, even though they were very different from those to which they had been accustomed in their own country and being obedient in everything, so as to obviate all cause of sedition.

It most evidently follows from all of this that religion among the Hebrews assumed the force of law only from the authority of the state, and when this was obliterated, religion could no longer be regarded as the prescription of a particular state but as a universal religion of reason. I say 'of reason' because the universal religion was not yet known by revelation.

[7] We conclude, therefore, absolutely, that religion, whether revealed by the natural light of reason or by prophetic light, receives the force of a commandment solely from the decree of those who have authority to govern, and that God has no special kingdom over men except through those who hold power.

[8] This follows also from what we said in chapter 4 and is further clarified by it. We proved there that all God's decrees involve eternal truth and necessity, and God cannot be conceived as a prince or legislator enacting laws for men. For this reason divine teachings, whether revealed by natural or by prophetic light, necessarily acquire the force of a decree not directly from God, but from those who exercise the right of governing and issue edicts or by their mediation. Hence, we can only conceive of God ruling over men and directing human affairs in accordance with justice and equity as effected by their mediation. This is also

confirmed by experience itself. For we find no traces of divine justice except where just men rule. Elsewhere, to use Solomon's words once again,[3] we see the same chance affecting the just and the unjust, pure and impure, which has rendered many people doubtful concerning divine providence, since they thought God ruled over men directly and directed the whole of nature for their benefit.

232 [9] It is clear from both experience and reason, then, that divine law depends solely upon the decree of the sovereign authorities, and hence also that they are its interpreters. We shall now see how they do this. For it is time to demonstrate that external religious worship and every expression of piety must, if we wish to obey God rightly, be consistent with the stability and conservation of the commonwealth. With this proven, we shall easily be able to understand why sovereign authorities are the [sole] interpreters of religion and piety.

[10] It is certain that piety towards one's country is the highest piety that anyone can show, for if the state is dissolved, nothing good can exist; everything is put in danger; anger and impiety are the only powers, and everyone is terrified. It follows that any pious act that one can perform for a neighbour becomes impious if it entails harm to the whole state, and, conversely, there can be no impious act against a neighbour which is not to be deemed pious if done for the preservation of the state. It is pious, for instance, if I hand over my cloak to someone who is in dispute with me and aspires to take my tunic, also.[4] But in a situation where this is judged prejudicial to the preservation of the commonwealth, the pious thing, rather, is to bring him before a court, even if he will be condemned to death. This is why Manlius Torquatus is celebrated because he valued the safety of the people more than piety towards his son.[5] Given this, it follows that the people's safety is the supreme law[6] to which all other laws both human and divine must be accommodated. However, it is the duty of the sovereign authority alone to determine what is necessary for the security of the whole people and of the state, and lay down what it deems necessary. It follows that it is also the duty of the sovereign authority alone to lay down how a person should behave with

---

[3] Ecclesiastes 9.2.   [4] Matthew 5.40, Luke 6.29.   [5] See Livy, *History of Rome*, 8.6–7.
[6] Cicero, *On the Laws*, 3.3.

piety towards their neighbour, that is, to determine how one is obliged to obey God.

[11] From this, it emerges very evidently in what sense the sovereign authorities are interpreters of religion; we also understand that no one can rightly obey God, if they do not adapt pious observance to which everyone is bound, to the public interest, and if, as a consequence, they do not obey all the decrees of the sovereign power. For we are obliged by God's decree to treat with piety all persons, without exception and inflict harm on no one. Accordingly, no one is permitted to give assistance to 233 anyone who seeks to cause loss to another, much less to the whole state. Hence, no one can behave piously toward his neighbour according to God's decree, unless he accommodates piety and religion to the public interest. But no private person can know what *is* in the interest of the state other than from the decrees of the sovereign authorities, who alone have the responsibility to transact public business. Consequently, no one can rightly cultivate piety or obey God, without obeying all edicts of the sovereign authority.

[12] This is likewise confirmed in practice. No subject is permitted to aid anyone whom the sovereign authorities have condemned to death or declared an enemy [of the state], whether a citizen or a foreigner, a private man or a ruler of another state. Although the Hebrews were commanded that everyone should love his neighbour as himself (see Leviticus 19.17–18), they were still obliged to denounce to a judge anyone who committed an offence against the stipulations of the Law (see Leviticus 5.1 and Deuteronomy 13.8–9) and slaughter that person if condemned to death (see Deuteronomy 17.7). Equally, it was necessary for the Hebrews, as we showed in chapter 17, to accommodate their religion uniquely to their state and separate themselves from all other peoples so as conserve the liberty they had acquired and retain absolute dominion of the lands they had occupied. They were thus admonished: 'Love your neighbour and hate your enemy' (see Matthew 5.43). Again, after they had lost their state and been taken captive to Babylon, Jeremiah taught them that they should strive for the well-being of the country into which they had been brought captive. Later, when Christ saw that they were going to be scattered throughout the whole world, he taught them to cultivate piety towards all men without distinction. All of this most

evidently shows that religion has always been adapted to the interest of the state.

[13] If anyone asks what right the disciples of Christ had to preach religion, since they were indubitably private men, I answer that they preached by right of the power which they had received from Christ to drive out impure spirits (see Matthew 10.1). At the end of chapter 16 above, I insisted that all men are obliged to keep faith even with a tyrant, unless God has promised a person special help against a tyrant by a separate revelation. Consequently, nobody may use [the example of the disciples] as a precedent, unless he too possesses the power to work miracles. This is likewise evident from the fact that Christ also admon-
234 ished his disciples not to fear those who kill the body (see Matthew 10.28). If this were addressed to everyone, governments would be established to no purpose, and Solomon's instruction (Proverbs 24.21), 'My son, fear God and the king', would be quite impious, which it assuredly is not. We must therefore necessarily admit that the authority that Christ conferred upon his disciples was dispensed uniquely, to them alone, and cannot serve as a precedent for others.

[14] I will not waste time on the arguments of my opponents where they strive to separate sacred law from civil law and to maintain that only the latter belongs to the sovereign authorities while the former adheres to the universal church. Their arguments are so flimsy that these do not deserve to be refuted. However, there is one thing here which I must mention and show that they are miserably mistaken in maintaining their seditious view (I beg pardon for the rather harsh expression), by taking as an example the Hebrew high priest who at one time had the right to handle sacred affairs. For the high priests received this right from Moses who, as we showed above, alone retained the sovereign power, and, equally, they could also be deprived of it by his decree. For he himself chose not only Aaron but also his son Eleazar and his grandson Phinehas, and conferred on them authority to administer the priesthood. Thereafter, the high priests retained this authority exclusively as evident substitutes for Moses, that is, for the sovereign power. As we have already shown, Moses chose no successor to his government, but rather distributed its duties in such a way that those who came after him were seen to be substitutes for him, administering the state as if the king were

absent rather than dead. Then, in the second commonwealth the priests held this authority absolutely, having acquired control of the government as well as the priesthood. Therefore, the right of the priesthood always rested upon the edict of the sovereign power, and the priests never held it except in conjunction with [their own] control of the government. Earlier, authority over sacred matters was in fact absolutely in the hands of the kings (as will be clear from what we shall say presently at the end of this chapter) with only one exception: they were not allowed to turn their hand to performing the sacred rites in the temple, because everyone who was not in the genealogy of Aaron was held to be profane. This sole exception clearly has no place in any Christian state.

[15]   We cannot doubt, therefore, that in our day sacred matters remain under the sole jurisdiction of sovereigns. (The prime requisite for administering sacred matters is not a person's family line but rather outstanding moral qualities; accordingly, one cannot exclude those who hold power on the ground that they are secular persons.) No one has the right and power 235 without their authority or consent, to administer sacred matters or choose ministers, or decide and establish the foundations and doctrines of a church, nor may they [without that consent] give judgments about morality and observance of piety, or excommunicate or receive anyone into the church, or care for the poor.

[16]   All this has been demonstrated not only to be true, as we have just shown, but also absolutely essential both to religion itself and to conservation of the state. Everyone knows how much influence right and authority in sacred matters have with the common people and how much everyone listens to someone who possesses such authority. I may say that whoever has this power has the greatest control over the people's minds. Therefore, any body which attempts to remove this authority from the sovereign power, is attempting to divide the government. Conflict and discord, like that which occurred between the kings and priests of the Hebrews in the past, will inevitably ensue and will never be resolved. Indeed, as I said before, anyone who strives to appropriate this authority from the sovereign powers is, in effect, preparing a road to power for himself. For what decisions can sovereigns make if they do not possess this authority? They can assuredly make no decision whatever about war or peace or anything else, if they are obliged to wait upon the opinion of

245

another person to tell them whether the policy they judge to be in the interests of the state is pious or impious. On the contrary, everything will depend upon the decision of the one who possesses the right to judge and decree what is pious and what is impious, what is holy and what is sacrilegious.

[17]   Every age has witnessed examples of this kind of dissension. I will adduce just one which is, however, typical of them all. Because this right was conceded to the Pope of Rome without restriction, he gradually began to bring all the kings under his control until finally he ascended to the very pinnacle of supreme power. Henceforward, any ruler who sought to lessen his authority even a little, and especially the German emperors, entirely failed to achieve this; in fact, on the contrary, by attempting it, they enormously further enhanced his authority. However, what no monarch could achieve by fire and the sword, ecclesiastics proved able to accomplish by the sole power of the pen. From this instance alone one readily appreciates the strength and power of this right and how vital it is for sovereigns to retain this authority for themselves alone.

[18]   If we also properly reflect on some remarks we made in the last 236 chapter,[7] we shall see that all this actually contributes substantially to the enhancement of [true] religion and piety. We observed above that while the prophets themselves were endowed with divine virtue, they were still private individuals, and that therefore the warnings, rebukes and denunciations which they took the liberty to deliver to men merely antagonized them and failed to set them on the right path. However, when men were warned or punished by kings, they were easily disciplined. Kings themselves, we also saw, very often turned away from religion for the very reason that this right did not adhere to them absolutely, and then the entire population followed them. Plainly, this [kind of thing] has also happened very frequently in Christian states.

[19]   Here perhaps someone will inquire: who shall have the right to champion piety, if those who hold power choose to be impious? Or are they to be still regarded, even then, as interpreters of piety? I reply to this

[7] See p. 232.

objection with a question: what if ecclesiastics (who are also men and private individuals whose duty is to look after their own business alone) or others to whom someone may wish to entrust authority in sacred matters, choose to be impious? Are they then still to be regarded as interpreters of piety?

It is indeed certain that if those who exercise power aspire to go their own way, whether they possess authority in sacred matters or not, everything, both sacred and secular, will rapidly deteriorate, and all the faster if private men make a seditious attempt themselves to champion divine right. Therefore, absolutely nothing is achieved by denying this right to sovereigns. On the contrary, the situation is rendered very much worse. For this very circumstance necessarily renders them impious (just like the Hebrew kings to whom this right was not granted without restrictions), and the consequent damage to the whole state is no longer merely possible or probable but certain and inevitable. Whether we consider the truth of the matter, or the security of the state, therefore, or the enhancement of piety, we are obliged to conclude that the divine law, or the law about sacred matters, depends entirely on the decree of the sovereign authorities and that these are its interpreters and defenders. It also follows from this that the ministers of the word of God are those who teach the people piety by the authority of the sovereign powers and adapt it by their rulings to the public interest.

[20]   It remains now to explain why there has always been controversy about this right in Christian states, whereas, so far as I know, the Hebrews never had any doubts about it. It may seem rather extraordinary that there has always been a problem about something so obvious and essential or 237 that sovereigns have never held this authority undisputedly and without great risk of subversion and harm to religion. Were we unable to provide a clear explanation for this, I might easily be persuaded that everything I have proposed in this chapter is merely theoretical or the kind of speculation that can never be useful. However, if we reflect on the earliest beginnings of the Christian religion, the reason for this situation leaps out at us.

It was not kings who first taught the Christian religion, but rather private individuals, who were acting against the will of those who exercised political power, whose subjects they were. For a long time they were accustomed to meet in private assemblies or churches, to set up sacred offices, and manage, regulate and decide everything without having any rationale of government. After the passage of many years, though, when their religion was first introduced into the government, churchmen had to instruct the emperors in the religion that they themselves had fashioned. Hence, they were easily able to ensure that they themselves were recognized as this religion's professors and interpreters, as well as being pastors of the church and vicars, so to speak, of God. Subsequently, to prevent Christian kings from arrogating this authority for themselves, ecclesiastics made the very effective move of prohibiting the highest ministers of the church and supreme interpreter of religion from marrying. Besides this, they vastly increased the number of religious dogmas and so utterly intertwined these with philosophy that its highest interpreter had to be both a consummate philosopher and theologian, and busy himself with an immense number of useless speculations, something which is only possible for private men and those with a great deal of free time.

[21] Among the Hebrews the situation had been completely different. Their church began at the same time as their state, and Moses, who held absolute power, taught the people religion, organized the sacred ministries and selected the ministers. Thus, it came about among them that it was the royal authority, by contrast, that had most influence with the people and that in the main kings exercised authority in sacred matters. After Moses' demise no one exercised government absolutely, but the leader had the right to determine both sacred and other matters (as we have already shown), and for their part the people were obliged to go to the supreme judge rather than a priest to be instructed in religion and piety (see Deuteronomy 17.9–11). Finally, although the [Israelite] kings did not possess authority to the same extent as Moses, almost the whole organization of the sacred ministry and the selection of ministers depended upon their decree.

238

It was actually David who designed the structure of the Temple (see 1 Chronicles 28.11–12, etc.). Afterwards, he assigned 24,000 Levites to chant psalms, 6000 Levites from among whom the judges and officers were to be chosen, and then 4000 more as porters and another 4000 to play musical instruments (see 1 Chronicles, 23.4–5).[8] He also divided

---

[8] 1 Chronicles 23.4–5: '"Twenty-four thousand of these," David said, "shall have charge of the work in the house of the Lord, six thousand shall be officers and judges, four thousand gatekeepers, and four thousand shall offer praises to the Lord with the instruments which I have made for praise."'

these men into companies and chose leaders for them, so that each company might perform its service at the proper time in a regular rotation (see 1 Chronicles 23.5). Likewise, he divided the priests into so many companies, but I do not want to review every single detail one after the other, and I refer the reader to 2 Chronicles 8.13, which says 'the worship of God as Moses instituted it was practised in the Temple by the command of Solomon' and, in verse 14, 'that he himself' [i.e. Solomon] 'established the companies of the priests in their ministries and the companies of the Levites . . . according to the command of David, the man of God'. Finally in verse 15, the historian testifies 'that they did not turn aside from what the king had commanded the priests and Levites in any matter, nor in the management of the treasuries'.

[22] From all of this and from other histories of the kings, it most evidently follows that the entire practice of religion and the sacred ministry ensued from the commands of kings. I said above that they did not possess the right that Moses had, of choosing the high priest, of consulting God directly or of condemning prophets who prophesied while they were still alive. I mention this simply because the authority which the prophets had gave them the right to choose a new king, and to pardon parricide, but not to summon a king to court, if he dared violate the law, or take legal proceedings against him.[9] That is why if there had been no prophets who could safely grant pardon to parricide by a special revelation, the kings would have had complete authority over all things, both sacred and civil, without restriction. Consequently, sovereigns today, who do not have prophets and are not obliged by law to accept them (for they are not bound by the laws of the Hebrews), have and always will retain this authority [over sacred matters] absolutely, even though they are not celibate, provided they do not allow religious dogmas to proliferate or become confused with knowledge.

---

[9] Spinoza's footnote: see Annotation 39.

CHAPTER 20

Where it is shown that in a free state everyone is allowed to think what they wish and to say what they think[1]

[1] Were it as easy to control people's minds as to restrain their tongues, every sovereign would rule securely and there would be no oppressive governments. For all men would live according to the minds of those who govern them and would judge what is true or false, or good or bad, in accordance with their decree alone. But as we noted at the beginning of chapter 17, it is impossible for one person's mind to be absolutely under another's control. For no one can transfer to another person his natural right, or ability, to think freely and make his own judgments about any matter whatsoever, and cannot be compelled to do so. This is why a government which seeks to control people's minds is considered oppressive, and any sovereign power appears to harm its subjects and usurp their rights when it tries to tell them what they must accept as true and reject as false and what beliefs should inspire their devotion to God. For these things are within each person's own right, which he cannot give up even were he to wish to do so.

[2] A person's judgment, admittedly, may be subjected to another's in many different and sometimes almost unbelievable ways to such an extent that, even though he may not be directly under the other person's command, he may be so dependent on him that he may properly be said to be under his authority to that extent. Yet however much skilful methods may accomplish in this respect, these have never succeeded in altogether

---

[1] Tacitus, *Histories*, 1.1.

suppressing men's awareness that they have a good deal of sense of their own and that their minds differ no less than do their palates. Moses very much subjected his people's judgment to himself, not by trickery but rather by his divine virtue, as he was believed to be a man of God and to speak and do all things by divine inspiration. But even he could not prevent malicious rumours and innuendoes. Much less can other rulers. In so far as such subjugation of judgment were to be considered possible, it would be most likely under a monarchical government and least probable under a democratic one where all the people, or a large part of them, hold power collectively. The reason for this difference, I think, will be evident to everybody.

[3]   However much therefore sovereign authorities are believed to have a   240
right to all things and to be the interpreters of right and piety, they will never be able to ensure that people will not use their own minds to judge about any matter whatever and that, to that extent, they will not be affected by one passion or another. It is indeed true that they can by natural right regard as enemies everyone who does not think absolutely as they do in all things, but we have moved on from arguing about right, and are now discussing what is beneficial. So while conceding that they may by natural right employ a high degree of violence in governing, and arrest citizens or liquidate them for the most trivial reasons, nevertheless everyone will agree that this is not consistent with the criteria of sound reason. Indeed, rulers cannot do such things without great risk to their whole government, and hence we can also deny that they have absolute power to do these and similar things and consequently that they possess any complete right to do them. For as we have proved, the right of sovereign authorities is limited by their power.

[4]   No one, therefore, can surrender their freedom to judge and to think as they wish and everyone, by the supreme right of nature, remains master of their own thoughts. It follows that a state can never succeed very far in attempting to force people to speak as the sovereign power commands, since people's opinions are so various and so contradictory. For not even the most consummate statesmen, let alone the common people, possess the gift of silence. It is a universal failing in people that they communicate their thoughts to others, however much they should [sometimes] keep quiet. Hence, a government which denies each person freedom to speak and to communicate what they think, will be a very violent government whereas a state where everyone is conceded this freedom will be moderate.

[5]   However, we cannot altogether deny that treason may be committed as much by words as by deeds. Consequently, if it is impossible altogether to deny subjects this freedom, it is, on the other hand, likewise very dangerous to concede it without any restriction. For this reason we must now ask how far this freedom can and ought to be granted to each person, so as to be consistent with the stability of the state and protecting the sovereign's authority. This, as I explained at the beginning of chapter 16, has been my principal goal.

[6]   It very clearly follows from the fundamental principles of the state which I explained above that its ultimate purpose is not to dominate or control people by fear or subject them to the authority of another. On the contrary, its aim is to free everyone from fear so that they may live in security so far as possible, that is, so that they may retain, to the highest possible degree, their natural right to live and to act without harm to themselves or to others. It is not, I contend, the purpose of the state to turn people from rational beings into beasts or automata, but rather to allow their minds and bodies to develop in their own ways in security and enjoy the free use of reason, and not to participate in conflicts based on hatred, anger or deceit or in malicious disputes with each other. Therefore, the true purpose of the state is in fact freedom.

[7]   Furthermore, when constituting a state one thing which we noted was indispensable was that the entire power of decision-making should be lodged in all the people, or else in some, or else just one. But people's free judgments are very diverse and everyone thinks they know everything themselves, and it can never happen that everyone will think exactly alike and speak with one voice. It would have been impossible therefore for people to live in peace, unless each one gave up his right to act according to his own decision alone. Each one therefore surrendered his right to act according to his own resolution, but not his right to think and judge for himself. Thus no one can act against the sovereign's decisions without prejudicing his authority, but they can think and judge and consequently also speak without any restriction, provided they merely speak or teach by way of reason alone, not by trickery or in anger or from hatred or with the intention of introducing some alteration in the state on their own initiative. For example, suppose someone shows a law to be contrary to sound reason and voices the opinion that it should be repealed. If at the same

time they submit their view to the sovereign power and in the meantime do nothing contrary to what that law commands, they surely deserve well of their country, as every good citizen does. If, on the other hand, they make use of this freedom to accuse the magistrate of wrongdoing and render him odious to the common people or make a seditious attempt to abolish the law against the magistrate's will, then they are nothing more than agitators and rebels.

[8]   Here we can see how the individual may say and teach what he thinks without infringing the right and authority of the sovereign power, that is, without disturbing the stability of the state. The key is to leave decisions about any kind of action to the sovereign powers and do nothing contrary to their decision, even if this requires someone acting in a way contrary to what he himself judges best and publicly expresses. This he can do without prejudice to either justice or piety, and this is what he should do, if he wants to show himself a just and good man.

As we have already shown, justice depends solely upon the sovereigns' 242 decree, and thus only someone who lives according to their official decrees can be just. The highest form of piety too (as we showed in the previous chapter) is that which is practised with respect to the peace and tranquillity of the state, and that stability could not be maintained if everyone lived according to his own judgment. Consequently, it is also impious to undertake anything on the basis of one's own judgment contrary to the decree of the sovereign whose subject one is since, were everyone allowed to do so, the ruin of the state would inevitably follow. Furthermore, so long as one behaves according to the decrees of the sovereign authorities, one cannot act contrary to the decree and dictate of one's own reason. For it was the individual's own reason that made him decide wholly to transfer his right to live according to his own judgment to the sovereign. We can also confirm this in practice. For in any kind of council, whether it is sovereign or subordinate, it is rare for an action to be taken by a unanimous vote of all members; nevertheless, resolutions to act are taken by the common decision of all the councillors, as much by those who voted against as by those who voted in favour.

[9]   But I return to my topic. We have seen from the principles of the state how everyone may enjoy liberty of judgment without prejudice to the right of the sovereign power. On the basis of the same principles, we can also

readily determine which opinions are subversive in a given state. It is those views which, simply by being put forward, dissolve the agreement by which each person surrenders their right to act according to their own judgment. For example, it is seditious for anyone to hold that a sovereign power does not have an autonomous right or that one should not keep a promise or that everyone should live according to their own judgment, and other views of this kind which are directly contrary to the aforesaid agreement. It is subversive not so much because of the judgments and opinions in themselves as because of the actions which such views imply. By the very fact that someone thinks such a thing, they are tacitly or explicitly breaking the pact that they made with the sovereign. Accordingly, all other opinions which do not imply such an act as breaking an agreement or vengeance or anger, etc., are not subversive – except perhaps in a state which is corrupt in some way, where superstitious and ambitious people who cannot tolerate free-minded persons, have achieved such reputation and prominence that their authority exerts greater influence with the common people than that of the sovereign powers. However, we would not wish to deny that there are some views which can be published and propagated with malicious intention though in themselves they appear to be purely concerned with truth and falsehood. But we have already determined what these are in chapter 15 and in a way that ensured that reason would nevertheless remain free.

243

If finally we remember that everyone's loyalty to the state, like their faith in God, can only be known from their works, that is, from their charity towards their neighbour, it will not be doubted that the best state accords everyone the same liberty to philosophize as we showed that faith likewise allows.

[10] Undeniably, there are sometimes some disadvantages in such freedom. But what was ever so cleverly designed that it entailed no disadvantages at all? Trying to control everything by laws will encourage vices rather than correcting them. Things which cannot be prevented must necessarily be allowed, even though they are often harmful. How many evils arise from extravagance, from envy, greed, drunkenness, and so on! These are nevertheless tolerated because they cannot be prevented by authority of the law, even though they really are vices. How much more should liberty of judgment be conceded, which is without question a virtue and cannot be suppressed. Further, the disadvantages which do arise from

it can all be avoided by the authority of the magistrates (as I shall show directly). I should also add further that this liberty is absolutely essential to the advancement of the arts and sciences; for they can be cultivated with success only by those with a free and unfettered judgment.

[11] But let us suppose that such liberty can be suppressed and that people can be so controlled that they dare not say anything but what the sovereign power requires them to say. Now it will certainly never happen that they think only what the authorities want, and thus it would necessarily follow that men would be continually thinking one thing and saying something else. This would undermine the trust which is the first essential of a state; detestable flattery and deceit would flourish, giving rise to intrigues and destroying every kind of honest behaviour. For in reality it is far from possible to make everyone speak according to a script. On the contrary, the more one strives to deprive people of freedom of speech, the more obstinately they resist. I do not mean greedy, fawning people who have no moral character – their greatest comfort is to think about the 244 money they have in the bank and fill their fat stomachs – but those whom a good upbringing, moral integrity and virtue have rendered freer.

There are many men who are so constituted that there is nothing they would more reluctantly put up with than that the opinions they believe to be true should be outlawed and that they themselves should be deemed criminals for believing what moves them to piety towards God and men. They therefore proceed to reject the laws and act against the magistrate. They regard it as very honourable and not at all shameful to behave in a seditious manner, on this account, or indeed attempt any kind of misdeed. It is a fact that human nature is like this, and therefore it follows that laws to curb freedom of opinion do not affect scoundrels but rather impinge on free-minded persons. They are not made to restrain the ill-intentioned so much as persecute well-meaning men, and cannot be enforced without incurring great danger to the state.

[12] Furthermore, such laws are completely useless. Those who believe doctrines condemned by law to be true will be unable to obey while those who reject them as false will celebrate edicts condemning them as their own special privileges and glory in them so that the sovereign will be powerless to abolish such edicts afterwards even should he wish to. To these points should be added the second conclusion we derived from the

history of the Hebrews in chapter 18.[2] Finally, how many schisms have arisen in the *ecclesia* (Church and community)[3] principally because the magistrate tried to settle controversies among the learned by means of the law? For if men had not nurtured hopes of aligning the law and government on their side, and thereby triumphing to the applause of the common people over their opponents, and winning high positions for themselves, they would never have fought one another so unrestrainedly; and such fanaticism would never have swayed their minds. Not only reason but also experience teaches us these things with new instances every day. Such decrees as these, laying down what everyone must believe and forbidding anything from being said or written against this or that dogma, were often introduced to appease, or rather surrender to, the fury of those who cannot tolerate free minds and who, with their stern authority, easily *convert* the zeal of the volatile common people into rage and turn this against whoever they please.

[13]   How much better it would be to restrain the indignation and fury of the common people than issue useless decrees which cannot but be broken by those who love virtue and the arts, and render the state so narrowminded that it cannot subsequently tolerate men with free minds. What greater ill can be devised for any commonwealth than for honest men to be banished like outlaws because they think differently from the rest and do not know how to hide this? What is more dangerous, I contend, than for people to be treated as enemies and led off to death, not for misdeeds or wrongdoing, but because they make a free use of their intelligence, and for the scaffold which should be the terror only of wrongdoers to become a magnificent stage on which to exhibit to all a supreme exemplum of constancy and virtue while casting the deepest reproach on the sovereign? Those who know themselves to be honest, do not fear death as wrongdoers fear it and plead to escape punishment. Their minds are not tormented by remorse for shameful actions. On the contrary they consider it not a punishment but an honour to die in a good cause: they deem it glorious to die for freedom. And what an example to give! Executing men whose cause the just love, the seditious-minded detest and of which the ignorant and feeble-minded

245

---

[2] See p. 234 above.

[3] The Spinoza expert and classicist Wim Klever has pointed out that although the word *ecclesia* in Latin normally means 'church', Spinoza here seems more likely to be using it in the original Greek sense of the community of all the people including the public cult.

understand nothing. Surely no one could find anything else in such an exemplum than a desire to emulate or at least to extol it?

[14] In order, then, for loyalty to be valued rather than flattery, and for sovereigns to retain their full authority and not be forced to surrender to sedition, freedom of judgment must necessarily be permitted and people must be governed in such a way that they can live in harmony, even though they openly hold different and contradictory opinions. We cannot doubt that this is the best way of ruling, and has the least disadvantages, since it is the one most in harmony with human nature. In a democratic state (which is the one closest to the state of nature), all men agree, as we showed above, to act – but not to judge or think – according to the common decision. That is, because people cannot all have the same opinions, they have agreed that the view which gains the most votes should acquire the force of a decision, reserving always the right to recall their decision whenever they should find a better course. The less people are accorded liberty of judgment, consequently, the further they are from the most natural condition and, hence, the more oppressive the regime.

[15] Examples are easily available to offer further confirmation [of our thesis that] that no disadvantages stem from such freedom, something which cannot be suppressed simply by the authority of the sovereign but which can, of itself, readily keep men from injuring each other, even where they maintain different opinions. I do not need to go far to find instances of this. Amsterdam is a fine example of a city which enjoys the fruits of this 246 liberty, with its great growth being the admiration of all nations. In this flourishing republic, this superb city, people of every sect and nation live together in the greatest harmony. Before they make a loan to someone, they just want to know whether he is rich or poor and whether he is known to behave with good faith or deceitfully. For the rest, religion or sect does not come into it because this does not help to win or lose a case before a court, and no sect is so hugely resented by others that its members (provided they harm no one and give each man his due and live honestly)[4] are not defended by the public authority and under the protection of the magistracy.

On the other hand, when the controversy about religion between the Remonstrants and Counter-Remonstrants began to agitate office-holders

---

[4] Justinian, *Institutes*, 1.1.

and the Dutch provincial assemblies earlier this century, it led after a time to a complete split.[5] This schism demonstrated in all sorts of ways that decrees designed to regulate religion which were intended to put an end to [theological] disputes, actually have quite the opposite effect, stirring people up rather than disciplining them while other men deem themselves authorized by such laws to arrogate a boundless license to themselves. Besides, such schisms do not arise from an intense passion for truth (which is the fount and origin of amity and gentleness), but from a great lust for power. It is thus plainer than the noonday sun that the real schismatics are those who condemn other men's books and subversively instigate the insolent mob against their authors, rather than the authors themselves, who for the most part write only for the learned and consider reason alone as their ally. Hence, the real agitators are those who attempt to do away with freedom of judgment in a free republic – a freedom which cannot be suppressed.

[16]   We have thus demonstrated:

(1) that it is impossible to deprive men of the liberty of saying what they think.

(2) that this liberty may be accorded to everyone without danger to the right and authority of the sovereign powers, and each person may retain this liberty without risk to their authority so long as no one arrogates to himself licence to promulgate in the state any alteration of the law or act in any way contrary to the existing laws.

(3) that each person may possess such liberty without danger to the stability of the state, and that it causes no disadvantages which cannot be easily checked.

(4) that each person may possess this liberty without prejudice to piety.

247   (5) that issuing decrees about doctrinal issues is completely useless.

(6) Finally, we have proven that not only may this liberty be granted without risk to the peace of the republic and to piety as well as the authority of the sovereign power, but also that to conserve all of this such freedom must be granted. For when, contrary to this, efforts are made to strip men of this liberty, and those with dissenting views are summoned to court (albeit not

---

[5] The bitter dispute between the Dutch Remonstrants (Arminians) and strict Calvinist Counter-Remonstrants began over purely theological issues, especially the question of free will, but became more and more political and eventually brought the United Provinces to the verge of civil war, leading directly to the downfall of Oldenbarnevelt and the Orangist *coup-d'etat* of 1618.

for their inner thoughts which alone could offend), then an example is made of honest men which is viewed rather as martyrdom [than justified punishment]. This antagonizes rather than frightens people, and moves them to compassion, or even incites them to take revenge. Finally, upright dealing and trust are undermined, flatterers and traitors are encouraged, and the foes [of those with dissenting views] triumph, since their indignation has been surrendered to: they have turned the sovereign powers into adherents of their dogmas of which they are recognized as the interpreters. As a consequence, they dare usurp the authority and right of the high officers of the state and are not ashamed to boast that they have been directly appointed by God and that their own decrees are divine whereas those of the sovereign authorities are merely human ones and, accordingly, they then require that sovereigns should defer to these divine – that is to say to their own – decrees. No one can fail to see that all this is utterly destructive of the common good of the republic.

[17]   For this reason we reach the same conclusion here as we did above, in chapter 18, that the state is never safer than when piety and religion are taken to consist solely in the practice of charity and justice, when the right of the sovereign authorities, whether in sacred or secular matters, is concerned only with actions, and when everyone is allowed to think what they wish and to say what they think.

[18]   This completes what I proposed to discuss in this treatise. It remains only to say explicitly that I have written nothing in it that I would not very willingly submit to the examination and judgment of the sovereign authorities[6] of my own country. If they judge that anything I have said here conflicts with the laws of the land or is prejudicial to the common good, I wish it unsaid. I know that I am human and may have erred. However, I have taken great pains not to err, and to ensure above all that whatever I have written should be entirely consistent with the laws of the land, with piety, and with morality.

---

[6] 'Sovereign authorities' means here the States General of the United Provinces together with the States of Holland, which formally held sovereignty and legal jurisdiction over all of Spinoza's places of residence (Amsterdam, Rijnsburg, Voorburg and The Hague).

Annotations: Spinoza's supplementary notes to the Theological-Political Treatise

In the years after the publication of the *Tractatus Theologico-Politicus*, Spinoza gradually added a number of supplementary notes in the margins of his own personal copy which we know he wished to see added to the published version. 'I should like you', he wrote to Henry Oldenburg, in September 1675, 'to point out to me the passages in the *Tractatus Theologio-Politicus* which have proved a stumbling-block to learned men. For I want to clarify this treatise with some additional notes and, if possible remove the prejudices which have been conceived against it.'[1] The copy furnished with these *Adnotationes* was sent from The Hague to his publisher, Jan Rieuwertsz, in Amsterdam, after Spinoza's death, in 1677, along with the rest of his manuscripts and papers. Although this original version subsequently disappeared without trace, most of the notes appeared in the French version of the *Tractatus*, in 1678, while the remainder, and nearly all those previously known only in the French version, were rediscovered in modern times. They were found, in their Latin versions, as hand-written explanatory notes on various manuscripts and printed copies of the book. The fullest version, a list of 36 Latin *Adnotationes* compiled by Prosper Marchand (1675–1756), survives today in a manuscript kept in the Leiden University Library. However, there remains a certain amount of disagreement among scholars as to whether all or only most of these notes were actually written by Spinoza himself.

---

[1] Spinoza, *The Letters*, 322; see also Fokke Akkerman, 'Aantekeningen' to Spinoza, *Theologisch-Politiek Traktaat* (ed.) F. Akkerman (Amsterdam, 1997), p. 438.

[Chapter 1]

Annotation 1: (p. 13) '*nabi*': If the third root letter of a word, in Hebrew, is one of those called 'quiescent', it is normally omitted, and instead the second letter of the stem is reduplicated. Thus from *khilah*, omitting the quiescent *hé*, we get *kholél* and hence *khol*, and from *nibah* we get *nobéb*, and thence *nib sepataim*, 'utterance' or 'speech'. Similarly, from *baza* we get *bazaz* or *buz* (*shagag, shug, misgéh* come from *shagah*; *hamam* from *hamah*; *belial, balal* from *balah*). Rabbi Solomon Jarghi [Rashi] has therefore interpreted this term *nabi* very well, and is wrongly criticized by Ibn Ezra, who does not have quite so perfect a knowledge of Hebrew. Note also that the noun *nebuah* ('prophecy') is a general term which includes every kind of prophecy, while other words are more restricted and refer to a particular kind of prophecy, as I believe is well-known to scholars.[2]

Annotation 2: (p. 14) 'its practitioners cannot be called prophets': That is to say, interpreters of God. For an interpreter of God is someone who interprets the decrees of God[3] to others to whom these have not been revealed and who, in accepting them, are relying solely on the authority of the prophet and the credit which he enjoys. However, if those who listen to prophets became prophets in the same way as those who listen to philosophers become philosophers, a prophet would then not be an interpreter of divine decrees, since his hearers would be relying not on the testimony and authority of the prophet but on the actual[4] revelation and internal testimony just as the prophet does. In the same way, sovereign authorities are the interpreters of the law of their state, because the laws which they make are upheld exclusively by the authority of the sovereigns themselves and rely upon their testimony alone.

Annotation 3 (p. 25) 'that the prophets had a unique and extraordinary virtue': although some men have certain abilities that nature does not bestow on others, we do not say that they surpass human nature unless the capacities they uniquely possess are such that these cannot be understood from the definition of human nature. Gigantic size, for instance, is uncommon but it is still human; likewise, very few people possess the gift of composing poems extempore but this too is nevertheless human;[5] as is

---

[2] 'Since they do not suggest anything else' [in Dutch].   [3] 'That have been revealed to him'.
[4] 'Divine' [in French].   [5] 'And there are some who do it easily' [in French].

the ability, while awake, to imagine something as vividly as if one had the object in front of one. But if there were anyone who possessed a different means of perception and a different basis of cognition, he would undoubtedly surpass the limits of human nature.

[Chapter 3]

Annotation 4: (p. 47) 'to the patriarchs': Genesis ch. 15 tells how God told Abraham that he was his defender and would give him a very great reward; to which Abraham replied, that he had nothing very much to expect since in extreme old age he remained still childless.

Annotation 5 (p. 47) 'security of life': It is clear from Mark 10.21 that to win eternal life it is not enough to keep the commandments of the Old Testament.

[Chapter 6]

Annotation 6 (p. 84) 'Since the existence of God is not known of itself': as long as our idea of Him is confused, and not clear and distinct, we are in doubt about the existence of God, and consequently about everything. For just as someone who does not comprehend a triangle properly does not know that its three angles are equal to two right angles, so anyone with a confused conception of the divine nature does not see that it belongs to the nature of God to exist. In order to conceive the nature of
253 God clearly and distinctly, we must take notice of certain very simple ideas that are called common notions and connect the things that belong to the divine nature with them. It will become evident to us, first, that God necessarily exists and is everywhere, secondly, at the same time, that all the things that we conceive involve the nature of God in themselves and are conceived by means of it, and, finally, that everything that we adequately conceive is true. On this point, see the Introduction to the book entitled *The Principles of Philosophy Demonstrated by the Geometrical Method.*[6]

---

[6] That is, Benedict de Spinoza, *Descartes's Principles of Philosophy Demonstrated by the Geometrical Method* (Amsterdam, 1663).

[Chapter 7]

Annotation 7 (p. 106) 'it is impossible to devise a method': For us, that is, who are unfamiliar with this language and ignorant of its idioms.

Annotation 8 (p. 110) 'conception': By intelligible things I mean not only things which are correctly demonstrated but also those that we regularly accept with moral certainty and hear without surprise. Everyone comprehends the propositions of Euclid before they are demonstrated. I would also say that accounts of things relating to the future and the past which are not beyond men's belief, as well as laws, practices and customs, are also intelligible and clear, even though they cannot be mathematically demonstrated. But sacred signs and stories that seem to exceed what is believable, I call unintelligible. Even so, they offer a good deal that can be investigated by our method and enable us to understand the mind of the author.

[Chapter 8]

Annotation 9 (p. 120) 'Mount Moriah': That is, by the historian, not by Abraham; for he says that the place which today is called, 'it shall be revealed on the mountain of God', was called by Abraham 'God will provide'.

Annotation 10 (p. 122) 'conquered': From this time until the reign of Joram when they revolted from him (2 Kings 8.20), the Idumaeans did not have kings. Governors appointed by the Jews took their place (see 1 Kings 22.48),[7] and that is why the governor of Idumaea (2 Kings 3.9) is called a 'king'. But it may be questioned whether the last of the Idumaean kings began to reign before Saul was made king or whether in this chapter of Genesis Scripture meant only to speak of kings who were unconquered.[8] It is absolute nonsense to include Moses in the list of the kings: by his divine inspiration he instituted a form of state for the Hebrews that was at the opposite pole from monarchy.

254

---

[7] 1 Kings 22.47 in RSV.   [8] 'And glorious' [in Dutch].

[Chapter 9]

Annotation 11 (p. 131) 'with the exception of a few details': For example, 2 Kings 18.20 says, in the second person, *amarta*, 'you have said it, but with your mouth only', etc., whereas Isaiah 36.5 has *amarti*, which means, 'I have said it, these are certainly my words, that war needs strategy and courage'. Again, 2 Kings 18.22 reads 'but perhaps you will say' in the plural, whereas, in Isaiah's version, it is in the singular. Moreover, in the text of Isaiah these words (from 2 Kings 18.32) are not found: 'a land of olive oil and honey, so that you may live and not die; and do not listen to Hezekiah'.[9] Many more such variant readings are encountered, and no one will be able to decide which one is to be preferred.

Annotation 12 (p. 131) 'noticeably altered': For example, 2 Samuel 7.6 reads, 'and I have been constantly travelling in a tabernacle and a tent' whereas 1 Chronicles 17.5 has, 'and I have gone from tent to tent and from tabernacle . . .', where obviously *mithalek* has been changed to *méohél*, *ohél* to *el-ohél* and *bemishkan* to *mimishkan*. Again, 2 Samuel 7.10 has 'to afflict him', whereas 1 Chronicles 17.9 says 'to waste him'. Even on a first reading of these chapters, anyone who is not completely obtuse or utterly mad will see many discrepancies of this kind, including some of still greater significance.

Annotation 13 (p. 131) 'That "time" must necessarily be related to some other time': It is clear from the context of the phrase itself that the text refers to the time when Joseph was sold and no other. It may also be inferred from the actual age of Judah, who at that point was in his twenty-second year at the most, if we calculate from the story about him which comes just before. For it emerges from the final verse of Genesis 29 that Judah was born in the tenth year after the patriarch Jacob began to serve Laban and Joseph[10] was born in the fourteenth year. Since Joseph himself was hence 17 when he was sold, Judah at that point in time was 21 years old, and no more. Those who believe that this long absence of Judah from home occurred before Joseph's sale are simply trying to calm their own anxieties and have more worries than certainties about Scripture's divinity.

Annotation 14 (p. 132) 'On the other hand Dinah was scarcely seven years old': the view of some commentators that Jacob spent eight or ten years

---

[9] 'That is why I do not doubt that they are substituted words' [in French].   [10] 'At a very advanced age'.

travelling between Mesopotamia and Bethel is, I would say, quite absurd despite the authority of Ibn Ezra. He hurried as much as he could not only because he must have been longing to see his parents who were very old, but especially to fulfil his vow (see Genesis 28.20 and 31.13).[11] But if these points appear to be conjectures rather than sound reasons, let us grant that Jacob spent eight or ten or, if you like, even more years on this short journey, which would make his fate worse than Ulysses'. Even so, they [such commentators] could certainly not deny that Benjamin was born in the final year of this journey, i.e., on their hypothesis, when Joseph was fifteen or sixteen or thereabouts. For Jacob left Laban in the seventh year after the birth of Joseph and from the time when Joseph was seventeen to the year in which the patriarch himself went down into Egypt, we cannot, as we have shown in this very chapter, count more than twenty-two years. Therefore, when Benjamin set out for Egypt he was at most twenty-three or twenty-four years old, and at this young age it is clear that he must have had grandsons (see Genesis 46.21, and compare it with Numbers 26.38–40 and with 1 Chronicles 8.1ff.).[12] This is assuredly no less contrary to reason than [to insist] that Dinah was raped when she was seven years old or than the other things we have deduced from the chronology of this story. Hence, it is sufficiently evident that as these unscholarly commentators try to solve these knotty problems, they merely create others and make it all still more complicated and incoherent.

256

Annotation 15 (p. 133) 'starts to tell'

'That is to say, in different terms and in a different order than they are found in the book of Joshua.'[13]

Annotation 16 (p. 133) 'Othniel son of Kenaz was judge'

Rabbi Levi ben Gerson[14] and others believe that these forty years which Scripture says they spent in liberty begin with Joshua's death and

---

[11] 'And God had also reminded him to pay his vow' (Genesis 31.3 and 13) and promised him his help to bring him back to his country'.

[12] 'For Bela, the first-born of Benjamin, had begotten two sons, Ard and Naaman'.

[13] This Annotation exists in French only.

[14] Gersonides (1288-*c*. 1344),(or Levi ben Gershom) whose acronym was Ralbag lived in Provence, in southern France. Writing in Hebrew, he was an eminent mathematician, astronomer, Bible exegete and philosophical commentator on Aristotle, Euclid and Averroes.

therefore include the eight previous years when the people was under the sway of Cushan-rishathaim, while the following eighteen years should be included in the total of 80 years in which Ehud and Shamgar were judges. Similarly, they also believe that the other periods of slavery are always included in those which Scripture affirms they spent in freedom. But Scripture states an explicit number for the years when the Hebrews languished in slavery and for the years when they were in liberty, and Judges 2.18 expressly tells us that their affairs always flourished while the judges were alive. It is therefore quite clear that while attempting to unravel such knots, the rabbi (who is otherwise a very learned man), and those who follow in his footsteps, are just amending rather than explaining Scripture.

257

The same mistake is made by those who insist Scripture means to refer, in its usual reckoning of years, solely to periods of settled government among the Jews without including in the total the periods of anarchy[15] and servitude since they regarded these as unhappy, interregnal times.[16] Scripture does indeed pass over periods of anarchy in silence but nevertheless narrates the years of slavery no less than the years of liberty, making no attempt to erase these from their Annals, as such people imagine.

It is also perfectly obvious that in 1 Kings chapter 6, Ezra[17] wished to include in the total he gives for the number of years since the exodus from Egypt every single year without exception,[18] and no scholar of the Bible has ever doubted this. For leaving aside for a moment the exact wording of the text, the genealogy of David, which is given at the end of the book of Ruth and at 1 Chronicles 2, hardly allows for so large a number of years ['that is, 480' (in the French)]. For in the second year after the exodus from Egypt Nahshon was leader of the tribe of Judah (see Numbers 7.11–12), and therefore died in the desert[19] and his son Salmon crossed the Jordan with Joshua. But according to this genealogy of David,[20] Salmon was

---

[15] 'As they call them in their aversion to popular government' [in French].

[16] 'For to say that the Hebrews did not wish to note in their Annals the periods when their Commonwealth flourished, because these were times of misfortune and of interregnum, so to speak, or that they erased from their Annals the years of servitude, if this is not an insult, it is a chimerical fiction and an absolute absurdity' [in French].

[17] 'Who is the author of these books, as we have shown' [in French].

[18] 'Down to the fourth year of the reign of Solomon' [in French].

[19] 'With all those who had reached the age of twenty years and were capable of bearing arms' [in French].

[20] See Ruth, 4.18–22.

David's great-great-grandfather.[21] If from the total of 480 years we deduct   258
4 for the reign of Solomon, 70 for the life of David, and 40 spent in the
desert, it will be found that David was born 366 years after the passage of
the Jordan, and[22] therefore it is necessary that his father, grandfather,
great-grandfather, and great-great grandfather[23], each one of them, begat
children[24] when ninety years old.[25]

Annotation 17 (p. 134) 'Samson was judge': Samson was born after the
Philistines had conquered the Hebrews.[26]

Annotation 18 (p. 136) 'we too could': Otherwise, one is revising the
words of Scripture rather than explaining them.

Annotation 19 (p. 137) 'Kirjat Jeharim': Kirjat Jeharim is also called
Baale-judah, hence Kimchi[27] and others think that Baale-judah, which
I have here translated 'from the people of Judah', was the name of the   259
town; but they are mistaken because *baale* is plural. Moreover, if this text
of Samuel is compared with the version in 1 Chronicles, we shall see that
David did not arise and leave Baal but went there. If the author of
2 Samuel intended to name the place from which David took the ark,
then to express that in Hebrew, he would have said: 'and David arose,
and set out . . . from Baale-judah, and took the ark of God from there'.

---

[21] 'Thus it is not necessary to claim that this Salmon was at least 91 years old when he begat Boaz, and
that the latter was of a similar age when David was born. For on the assumption that year 4 of
Solomon's reign is the one referred to in 1 Kings 6, the 480th year after the exodus from Egypt,
David by this count was born in the 366th year after the passage of the Jordan' [in French].

[22] 'supposing therefore that Salmon, the ancestor of David, was born during the actual passage of the
Jordan' [in French].

[23] 'Salmon, Boaz, Obed and Jesse' [in French].

[24] 'In succession in their extreme old age' [in French].

[25] 'And consequently that there could hardly be 480 years from the exodus from Egypt to year 4 of the
reign of Solomon, if Scripture had not explicitly said so' [in French].

[26] 'One may doubt whether these twenty years should belong to the years of liberty, or whether they
are included in the forty which immediately precede during which the people was under the yoke
of the Philistines. For myself, I confess that I think it is more likely and credible that the Hebrews
recovered their liberty when the princes of the Philistines perished with Samson. Thus I have
included only these twenty years of Samson among those during which the yoke of the Philistines
lasted, because Samson was born while the Philistines held the Hebrews in subjection, apart from
the fact that in the treatise on the Sabbath, mention is made of a certain book of Jerusalem, where
it is said that Samson judged the people for forty years; but the question is not about those years
only' [in French].

[27] David Kimchi (*c.* 1160–1235) noted grammarian, lexicographer and biblical commentator.

Annotation 20 (p. 138) 'and stayed there for three years':

[French only.] Those who have troubled to comment on this text, have emended it as follows: 'and Absalom fled and took refuge with Talmai, the son of Hammihud, king of Geshur, where he remained for three years, and David mourned for his son all the time he was at Geshur'. But if that is what you call interpretation, and if it is permitted to give oneself this much license in explicating Scripture and transpose entire clauses like this, adding one thing and supp-ressing another, then surely it is permitted to corrupt Scripture and give it as many shapes as one wishes, like a piece of wax.[28]

[Chapter 10]

Annotation 21 (p. 144) 'perhaps even after Judas Maccabaeus had restored the Temple': This suggestion, if anything of the sort can be called a suggestion, derives from the genealogy of king Jeconiah given at 1 Chronicles 3[29] which continues as far as the sons of Elioenai who were the thirteenth generation on from him.[30] We should note that this Jeconiah did not have any children at the time of his imprisonment. To judge from the names he gave them, he seemingly begat[31] his children in the prison and seems to have had his grandchildren, so far as can also be conjectured from their names, after he was freed. Thus Pedaiah (which means 'God has freed') who is said, in this chapter, to have been 'the father of Zerubbabel', was born' in the year 37 or 38 of Jeconiah's captivity, i.e., 33 years before king Cyrus gave the Jews leave [to return]. Consequently Zerubbabel, whom Cyrus made governor of the Jews, seems to have been at most 13 or 14 years old. But I would have preferred to pass over all this in silence for reasons which our difficult times[32] do not allow me to explain. For the informed reader, it is enough just to mention this. Those who are willing to go through the whole list of the descendants of Jeconiah given in 1 Chronicles 3 from verse 17 to the end of the chapter, with some attention, and to compare the Hebrew text with the translation which is called the Septuagint, will without difficulty be able to see that these books were revised after the second restoration of the city

260

---

[28] This Annotation exists in French only. [29] 1 Chronicles 3.17–24.
[30] 'In the direct line' [in French]. [31] 'Two' [in French].
[32] Instead of 'our difficult times', Spinoza originally wrote here 'iniuriae et superstitio regnans' [injustice and the prevailing superstition]. The caution Spinoza signals here presumably has to do with the Scriptural genealogy of Christ which is hereby brought into question.

achieved by Judas Maccabeus. By that time the descendants of Jeconiah had lost the leadership, but not before.

Annotation 22 (p. 147) 'taken': And so no one would have suspected that his prophecy contradicted the prophecy of Jeremiah, though Josephus' account made everyone believe it did, until they knew from the actual event that both men predicted the truth.

Annotation 23 (p. 148) 'Nehemiah': The historian himself tells us (Nehemiah 1.1) that the greater part of this book was taken from the book which Nehemiah himself wrote. It is certain, though, that the narrative from 8.1 to 12.26 is an interpolation, and so are the two final verses of chapter 12, which are inserted as a parenthesis into the words of Nehemiah.

Annotation 24 (p. 149) 'Ezra': Ezra was the uncle of the first High Priest Joshua (see Ezra 7.1 and 1 Chronicles 6.13–15), and set out from Babylon to Jerusalem with Zerubbabel (see Nehemiah 12.1). But it seems that when he saw that the affairs of the Jews were in chaos, he returned to Babylon, as 261 others did also; this is clear from Nehemiah 1.2. He remained there until Artaxerxes' reign when, after obtaining what he wanted, he set out a second time for Jerusalem: see Ezra 2.2 and 63, and compare with Nehemiah 10.2 and 12.1. Though translators render *Hatirschata*, by 'envoy', they give no example to prove it, and on the other hand it is certain that new names were given to Jews who had to frequent the court. Thus Daniel was called Balteshazzar, and Zerubbabel was called Sheshbazzar (see Daniel 1.7, Ezra 1.8 and 5.14) and Nehemiah was called Hatirschata. Due to his office, though, he was habitually addressed as 'procurator' or 'governor': see Nehemiah 5.14 and 12.26.[33]

Annotation 25 (p. 153) 'that no canon of sacred books ever existed before the time of the Maccabees': The so-called 'Great Synagogue' did not begin until after the conquest of Asia by the Macedonians.[34] The opinion of Maimonides, Rabbi Abraham ben David and others that the presidents of this council were Ezra, Daniel, Nehemiah, Haggai, Zechariah and so

[33] 'It is therefore certain that Atirśatha is a proper name, like Hatselephoni, Hatsobeba (1 Chronicles 4.3,8), Halloghes (Nehemiah 10.25), and so on' [in French].

[34] Elsewhere Spinoza dates this conquest from the death of Darius III in 330 BC. See p. 149.

on, is a ridiculous fiction, and rests on no other foundation than rabbinical tradition, which insists that the Persian empire lasted a mere thirty-four years. This is the only way they can argue that the decrees of this Great Synagogue or Synod which was composed solely of Pharisees[35] were accepted by the prophets,[36] who had received them from other prophets, and so on right back to Moses, who received them from God himself and handed them on to posterity by word of mouth not in writing. The Pharisees [i.e., the rabbis] may persist in believing these things with their usual obstinacy; but experts, who know the reasons for councils and synods and who are also aware of the controversies between the Pharisees and the Sadducees will readily be able to infer the reasons why this Great Synagogue or Council was called. It is certain in any case that no prophet participated in this Council, and that the decrees of the Pharisees which they call traditions,[37] received their authority from this Council.

262

[Chapter 11]

Annotation 26 (p. 155) 'we think': Translators render *logizomai* in this passage 'conclude' and argue that Paul is using it in much the same sense as *sullogizomai*, despite the fact that the Greek word *logizomai* has the same meaning as *hashab*, which is 'reckon', 'think', 'estimate'. Taken in this sense *logizomai* agrees very well with the Syriac (i.e. Aramaic) text. For the Syriac translation (if indeed it is a translation, which may be doubted, since we know neither the translator nor the time of publication, and the native language of the Apostles was actually Syriac)[38] renders this text of Paul as *methrahgenan hachil*, which Tremellius[39] properly translates as 'we therefore think'. For *rehgjono*, the noun which is formed from this verb, means 'thought'; for *rehgjono* is *rehgutha* in Hebrew ('will'); hence 'we want' or 'we think'.

---

35 'Which were rejected by the Sadducees' [in French].
36 According to this tradition, the Presidents of the Grand Synagogue were the three latest prophets, Haggai, Zechariah and Malachi.
37 'About which they have made such a noise' [in French].
38 The language Spinoza calls 'Syriac' is now generally called Aramaic.
39 Tremellius prepared an edition of the New Testament in which he set out in four columns the Greek text, the Syriac text and Latin translations of both. Spinoza generally relies upon Tremellius' Latin translation of the Syriac text, which he suggests here was the original text.

Annotation 27 (p. 160) 'like the whole of Christ's teaching': 'That is to say, the teaching that Jesus Christ gave on the mountain which St. Matthew reports (ch. 5 ff.) [French only].

[Chapter 15]

Annotation 28 (p. 187) 'anything that Scripture teaches dogmatically': See [Lodewijk Meyer] *Philosophy, the Interpreter of Holy Scripture* [*Philosophia S. Scripturae Interpres*], p. 75.[40]

Annotation 29 (p. 190) 'Samuel' see [Meyer] *Philosophy the Interpreter*, p. 76.

Annotation 30 (p. 194) 'I must emphasize very strongly here': see [Meyer] *Philosophy the Interpreter*, p. 115.

Annotation 31 (p. 194) 'that simple obedience is the path to salvation': In other words,[41] it is not reason but rather revelation that can teach us that it suffices for salvation or happiness to accept the divine decrees as laws or commandments and that there is no need to understand them as eternal truths. This is clear from what we proved in chapter 4.

[Chapter 16]

Annotation 32 (p. 198) 'will promise without deception': In the civil state where the common law determines what is good and what is bad, deception is rightly divided into good and bad. In the state of nature, however, where everyone[42] is judge of his own [affairs] and has the supreme right to prescribe laws for himself and interpret them and even to abolish them if he judges it to be advantageous to himself, it is not possible to conceive that anyone deliberately acts deceitfully.

Annotation 33 (p. 201) 'for there each man can be free whenever he wishes': A person can be free in any civil state whatsoever. For a person is

---

[40] Lodewijk Meyer's important book, declaring [Cartesian] 'philosophy' to be the 'true interpreter' of Scripture, appeared in Latin at Amsterdam in 1666 and in its slightly longer Dutch version at Amsterdam the following year. There are a number of places in the text of the *Theological-Political Treatise* where Spinoza appears to be carrying on a silent dialogue with his friend and ally.
[41] 'Which we do not know naturally' [in French].   [42] 'Of right' [in French].

certainly free to the extent that he is guided by reason. However, (contrary to what Hobbes says) reason recommends peace without reservation, and peace cannot be had unless the general laws of the state are maintained inviolate. Hence, the more a person is led by reason, i.e. the freer he is, the more resolutely he will uphold the laws and obey the commands of the sovereign authority whose subject he is.

264   **Annotation 34** (p. 205) 'For no one knows from nature': when Paul says that men are 'without a way out',[43] he is speaking in a human manner. For in chapter 9 'verse 18' of the same Epistle, he expressly states that God pities whom he will and hardens whom he will, and that men are without excuse simply because they are in God's power like clay in the hands of a potter who from the same lump makes one vessel for beauty, and another for menial use; it is not because they have been warned beforehand. As for the divine natural law whose highest precept we have said is to love God, I have called it a law in the sense in which philosophers apply the word law to the common rules of nature according to which all things[44] happen. For love of God is not obedience but a virtue necessarily present in someone who rightly knows God. Obedience on the other hand, concerns the will of someone who commands, not the necessity and truth of a thing. Since we do not know the nature of God's will but do certainly know that whatever happens happens solely by God's power, we can never know except via revelation whether God wishes men to observe a cult revering him like a worldly ruler. Furthermore, divine commandments seem to us like decrees or enactments only so long as we are ignorant of their cause. Once we know this, they immediately cease to be edicts and we accept them as eternal truths, not as decrees, that is, obedience immediately turns into love which arises from true knowledge as inevitably as light emanates from the sun. By the guidance of reason therefore we can love God but not obey him, since we cannot accept divine laws as divine so long as we do not know their cause, nor by reason can we conceive of God as issuing decrees like a prince.

---

[43] The reference seems to be to Epistle to the Romans 1.20.   [44] 'Necessarily' [in French].

[Chapter 17]

Annotation 35 (p. 209) 'that they could undertake nothing in the future': 'Two common soldiers undertook to transfer the government of the Roman people, and they did so' (Tacitus, *Histories*, 1).[45]

Annotation 36 (p. 215) 'see Numbers 11.28': In this passage[46] two men[47]   265
are accused of having prophesied in the camp,[48] and Joshua advises that they should immediately be arrested. He would not have done this,[49] had it been permissible for anyone to give divine responses to the people without Moses' permission. Even so, Moses decided to acquit them, and rebuked Joshua for his urging him to seek royal power for himself at a time when he was so very tired of ruling that he would prefer to die rather than govern alone, as is evident from verse 14[50] of the same chapter. This is his reply to Joshua:[51] 'Are you angry on my account? Would that the whole people of God were prophets.' That is,[52] would that the right of consulting God would succeed in placing the government in the hands of the people themselves.[53] Joshua therefore was not ignorant of the law[54] but of the requirements of the time and this is why he was reproached by Moses, just as Abishai was by David when he advised the king to condemn Shimei to death, who was certainly guilty of treason; see 2 Samuel 19.22–3.

Annotation 37 (p. 215) ' On this see Numbers 27.21': The translators (that I happen to have seen) make a bad job of verses 19 and 23 of this chapter. These verses do not signify that he gave Joshua orders or instructions, but rather that he made or appointed him leader, as often in Scripture, e.g., Exodus 18.23, 1 Samuel 13.14, Joshua 1.9, and 1 Samuel 25.30, etc.[55]

---

[45] Tacitus, *Histories*, 1.25.2.   [46] 'In Numbers' [in French].
[47] 'Whose names are given ch. 11 verse 28 of this book' [in French].
[48] 'The news of it came immediately to Moses' [in French].
[49] 'And one would not have hesitated to report it to Moses as a criminal action' [in French].
[50] 'And 15' [in French].   [51] Numbers 11.29.
[52] 'You would wish that there was only me to rule; as for myself, I would wish that the right of consulting God would return to each individual and they would all rule together, and let me go'. [in French].
[53] 'And they would let me go' [in French].   [54] 'And the authority' [in French].
[55] 'The harder translators try to render verses 19 and 23 of this chapter literally', adds the (very competent) original French translator of Spinoza's text, either Gabriel de Saint-Glain (*c.* 1620–84) or Jean-Maximilian Lucas (1646–97) 'the less intelligible they make it, and I am convinced very few people understand the true sense of it. Most imagine that God commands Moses in verse 19 to instruct Joshua in the presence of the Assembly, and in verse 23 that he laid his hands upon him

266 **Annotation 38:** (p. 218) 'He was not obliged to recognize any judge other than God': The rabbis claim that what is commonly called the Great San-hedrin[56] was instituted by Moses, and not merely the rabbis but also the majority of Christians, who are as absurd about this as the rabbis. Moses did indeed select for himself seventy associates to share the cares of gov-ernment with him, since he could not carry the burden of the whole people by himself. However, he never issued a decree setting up a Council of Seventy. On the contrary, he issued orders that each tribe should appoint judges in the cities which God had given him, to settle disputes in accor-dance with the laws he had made,[57] and if the judges themselves should be in doubt concerning the law, that they should consult the High Priest (who was thus the supreme interpreter of the laws) or the [superior] judge to whom they were subordinate at the time (who had the right of consulting the High Priest), in order to settle the dispute in accordance with the High Priest's interpretation.

If it happened that a subordinate[58] judge claimed not to be bound to give his verdict according to the High Priest's decision whether received from him or from his sovereign, he was sentenced to death by the supreme

267 judge in office at the time, through whom the subordinate judge had been appointed: see Deuteronomy 17.9. This might be either someone like Joshua, the supreme commander of the whole people of Israel or it might be a leader of one of the tribes, who, after the division into tribes, had the right of consulting the priest about the affairs of his tribe, of deciding about war and peace, of fortifying cities, of appointing judges,[59] etc. Alternatively, it might be a king to whom all or some of the tribes had transferred their right.

I could offer a good many instances from history to confirm all this, but I will mention just one which seems a particularly striking instance. When the prophet of Shiloh chose Jeroboam as king, by that very fact he gave him the right of consulting the High Priest and of appointing judges, and

and instructed him, because they fail to notice that this turn of phrase is very common among the Hebrews when declaring the election of a prince legitimate and confirming him in his charge. It is thus that Jethro speaks when counselling Moses to choose associates to help him judge the people, "if you do this," he says, "then God will command you", as if he were saying that his authority will be sound, and that he will be able to maintain himself in power, on which see Exodus 18.23, 25.30, 1 Samuel 13.15, 25.30, and especially Joshua 1.9, where God says to him, "have I not commanded you, have courage, and show yourself a man of heart", as if God were saying to him, "is it not I who have made you leader? Do not be afraid then of anything, for I will be with you everywhere".'

[56] 'The great gathering' [in Dutch].   [57] 'And punish law-breakers' [in French].
[58] 'The lesser' [in Dutch].   [59] 'In his own towns, which were subject only to him' [in French].

Jeroboam obtained all and every right over the ten tribes that Rehoboam retained over the two tribes. Jeroboam could therefore appoint a supreme council in his palace with the same right by which Jehoshaphat had done so at Jerusalem (see 2 Chronicles 19.8ff.). For, undoubtedly, since Jeroboam was king by command of God, neither he nor his subjects were obliged by the law of Moses to submit to Rehoboam as judge since they were not Rehoboam's subjects. Even less were they obliged to submit to the court at Jerusalem which had been set up by Rehoboam and was subordinate to him. Since the Hebrew state remained divided, there were as many supreme councils[60] as there were states. Those who do not pay attention to the different political arrangements of the Hebrews, at different times, but rather imagine them all to be one,[61] thus become entangled in all sorts of difficulties.

[Chapter 19]

Annotation 39 (p. 249) 'or take legal proceedings against him': Here we must pay special attention to what we said about right in chapter 16.

---

[60] 'Different and independent the one from the other' [in French].

[61] 'As if it was all the same' [in French].

Index

philosopher xlvi, 37, 110, 119, 120, 121, 128, 147, 148, 149, 261, 265
improvement of human life (by weakening 'superstition') 185, 197–8, 255
individual liberty xx, xxii, xxvii, xxix, xxx, 202, 252, 258
Inquisition xxxvii, 250–1
intellectual knowledge of God 59–60, 61, 66–7, 176, 177
Isaiah 18, 23, 24, 28, 31, 32, 34, 35, 38, 50, 68, 70, 94, 145, 158, 167
Islam xi, xix, xvii, xix, xxi, xxii, 5, 7, 78
Israel, ancient state of the Hebrews 11
Israelites 16, 37, 38, 43–56, 63, 87–8, 156–7, 179, 184

James the Apostle, disagrees with Paul 161, 180
Japan 75, 207
Jelles, Jarig (c. 1620–1683), Collegiant ally of Spinoza xx, 112
Jeremiah 29, 31, 40, 50, 53, 71, 103, 145–6, 158, 163, 166, 176, 190, 241, 243, 269
Jesus, see Christ
Jews, in post-biblical times 55, 71, 79, 106
Job, book of 41, 49, 110, 147
John the Apostle 176, 180–1
Jonah xxx, 39, 49, 50, 147, 158
Jonathan ben Uziel (first-century AD), disciple of Hillel and translator of the prophets into Aramaic 123
Joshua 18, 33, 34, 35, 123, 125, 129, 132, 133, 134, 152, 216, 217, 273, 274
  Book of Joshua 125
Josiah 145
Joseph 18, 22, 131, 132, 264, 265
Josephus, Flavius (first-century AD) Jewish historian 40, 96, 133, 135, 142, 147, 149, 232, 269
Judaism xi, xxi, xxii, 7, 74–5
justice and charity, as the essence of true religion and the Bible xviii, xxiv, 10, 11, 58, 103, 104, 170, 174, 176, 177, 178, 181, 182, 183, 184, 185, 192, 203, 239, 240, 253, 259
justification by works 64, 161, 180

Kimchi, David (c. 1160–1235), Jewish grammarian 267
Koerbagh, Adriaen (1632–69), Dutch radical thinker xv, xxvi, xxxvi
Koran, see Islam
Kuhnraht, Heinrich (1560–1605), German mystical writer 1

La Court, Johan de (1622–80) Dutch republican writer xxxvi, 6
La Court, Pieter de (1618–85) Dutch republican writer xxx
La Peyrère, Isaac (1596–1676) French Millenarian and Bible critic xi
Law of Moses xlv, 9, 15, 17, 21, 23, 29, 39, 60, 70, 71, 103, 116, 128, 145, 275
Leibniz, Gottfried Wilhelm (1646–1716) German philosopher xviii, xxxii, xxxvii, 87
Leicester, Robert Dudley, earl of (1533–88), governor-general of the United Provinces 237
Leiden University xxxvi, 260
Levites, priestly tribe of the Hebrews 216, 226–7, 228, 229, 231, 245, 248, 249
liberty of the press, see freedom to publish
literal sense (sensus literalis) 100–1, 113, 114, 115, 177
Locke, John (1632–1704) English philosopher xv, xvi, xxi, xxii, xxiii, xxvi, xxvii, xxix, xxxiii, 87

Machiavelli, Niccolò (1469–1527) Florentine political thinker ix
Maimonides, Moses (1135–1204) the pre-eminent medieval Jewish philosopher and rabbinic authority, xlvi, 18, 79, 112, 113, 114, 115, 147, 186, 187, 190, 269
Malachi 48, 231, 270
Marchand, Prosper (1675–1756), Huguenot editor and erudit 260
Masoretes, (i.e. scribes involved in the early written transmission of the Old Testament Hebrew text) 140, 141, 170
mathematical, as opposed to moral, certainty 28, 29, 30, 191, 193
Maurice of Nassau (1567–1625), Dutch Stadholder (1585–1625) xxvii, 258
Meyer, Lodewijk (1629–81), intellectual ally and collaborator of Spinoza xl, xv, xvii, xxvi, xxxi, xxxvi, xxxvii, 271
Micah 26
Micaiah 29, 31, 41
Miracles ix, xix, 9, 44, 46, 48, 81–96, 99, 104, 171, 172, 205, 227
monarchy xxiv, xxix, 6, 73, 202, 212, 215, 216, 228–9, 232, 233, 235, 251, 263
Moses xi, xviii, 17, 18–19, 28, 31, 36–8, 39, 52, 63, 69, 70, 74, 90, 100, 101, 103, 105, 112, 120, 122, 123, 156, 157, 158, 163, 176, 179, 192, 213, 214, 215, 216, 217, 227, 228, 240, 244, 248, 273, 274

Nietzsche *Writings from the Late Notebooks* (edited by Rüdiger Bittner, translated by Kate Sturge)

Novalis *Fichte Studies* (edited by Jane Kneller)

Reinhold *Letters on the Kantian Philosophy* (edited by Karl Ameriks, translated by James Hebbeler)

Schleiermacher *Hermeneutics and Criticism* (edited by Andrew Bowie)

Schleiermacher *Lectures on Philosophical Ethics* (edited by Robert Louden, translated by Louise Adey Huish)

Schleiermacher *On Religion: Speeches to its Cultured Despisers* (edited by Richard Crouter)

Schopenhauer *Prize Essay on the Freedom of the Will* (edited by Günter Zöller)

Sextus Empiricus *Against the Logicians* (edited by Richard Bett)

Sextus Empiricus *Outlines of Scepticism* (edited by Julia Annas and Jonathan Barnes)

Shaftesbury *Characteristics of Men, Manners, Opinions, Times* (edited by Lawrence Klein)

Adam Smith *The Theory of Moral Sentiments* (edited by Knud Haakonssen)

Spinoza *Theological-Political Treatise* (edited by Jonathan Israel, translated by Michael Silverthorne and Jonathan Israel)

Voltaire *Treatise on Tolerance and Other Writings* (edited by Simon Harvey)

Printed in Great Britain
by Amazon.co.uk, Ltd.,
Marston Gate.